OneStream Planning: The Why, How and When

Cameron Lackpour & Celvin Kattookaran

⟁ OneStream™ Press

Disclaimer

About the Authors

Cameron Lackpour first worked with Corporate Performance Management technology in the dinosaur days of mainframe multidimensional databases and saw the OneStream light in 2017. He has been in the consulting business since 1996, creating solutions for customers using best of breed planning and analytic tools. Cameron blogs on www.thetruthaboutcpm.com and is a host on the podcast www.epmconversations.com. Despite painful experience, this is his third book, and (as always) Cameron thought it would be "fun". He hopes you enjoy it.

Celvin Kattookaran has more than 17 years of experience in Business Intelligence and Corporate Performance Management. He has developed creative and practical business solutions to address clients' planning and analytical challenges. He has extensively worked in gathering requirements, interacting with the client, managing the development team, design analysis, implementation, and support. Celvin has successfully implemented enterprise-wide performance management solutions across many industries with heavy experience in the OneStream Platform and various Specialty applications. Celvin is an avid blogger and shares his ideas and utilities on his blog cpminsights.com. He is also a host on the podcast epmconversations.com

Technical Reviewers

Mel Lenhardt is a Group Product Manager focusing on Planning. Mel has consulted on Planning CPM systems for over 20 years, and worked in corporate FP&A before that. When consulting, he was responsible for the delivery of solutions for numerous multi-national "Fortune 500" companies. Mel is an avid runner who resides in Grosse Pointe, Michigan.

Jon Golembiewski is a Distinguished Architect on the OneStream Services team. Jon joined OneStream in 2013 as one of the first members of the Services Team. Jon's experience stretches across both Consolidation and Planning projects. He has worked on projects in over 20 countries, including OneStream's first customers in South Africa, Australia, Finland, and Norway. Jon has also helped build and deliver training for both customers and consultants. He has lived in Amsterdam and currently resides in Pittsburgh, Pennsylvania.

25% OFF VOUCHER

Certification

Validate your technical competence and gain industry recognition with OneStream Software.

In purchasing this book, you are eligible to claim a 25% discount on any OneStream Certification Exam.

To request your voucher, open a case with Credentialing via the ServiceNow Support Portal (https://onestreamsoftware.service-now.com/). Include proof of purchase that contains your name and address, the book title, date of purchase, and proof of payment.

Terms & Conditions:
One (1) certification exam voucher per book. All vouchers per receipt must be claimed at one time; if a receipt is for the purchase of 10 books, all 10 vouchers must be claimed at the same time. Vouchers are valid for post-beta production exams only. This offer is only valid for one year from the purchase date on the invoice or receipt.

 onestream

Zip Download

There is a substantial archive of code material that accompanies this book, available as a free download. Download the file from: **www.OneStreamPress.com/planning**

Note: Any Files provided for Exercises in this OneStream Press Book are for the use of Customers and Partners in an On-Premise environment and are not supported by the OneStream Support Team.

Errata

Despite best efforts, mistakes can sometimes creep into books. If you spot a mistake, please feel free to email us at **errata@OneStreamPress.com** (with the book title in the subject line).

The errata page for this book is hosted at **www.OneStreamPress.com/OneStreamPE**

Table of Contents

Chapter 2: Core Planning I – Data and Calculations   45

Chapter 3: Core Planning II – Command and Control the Cube   85

Chapter 4: Planning Without Limits
141

Chapter 5: All Data Points Lead to Reporting and Analysis   185

Chapter 6: Specialty Planning Analysis   237

Foreword

I've worked in the Enterprise or Corporate Performance Management industry for over 23 years. In that time, I've worked on many projects for a variety of companies. While different verticals have different drivers, they all tend to have some commonalities. Being able to predict the future or, at the very least, being able to explain why you failed to predict the future is among the most common requests from my clients. Software has evolved over time to be the solution to help fill this pressing need, and the OneStream platform represents the newest evolution of what Corporate Performance Management (CPM) systems can do to help the office of the CFO. Very often, I speak with customers that believe that they have a "non-traditional" use case. The truth is that OneStream has evolved what the "traditional" use of a CPM tool is. OneStream's flexibility to utilize relational and Cube technology, as well as its Extensible dimensionality, allows it to do more than any tool before it, but that flexibility makes the tool harder to master. OneStream is difficult to master because it is substantially more advanced than older CPM software.

Throughout my career, when I have run into something that requires more knowledge, I try to turn to those whom I see as experts in that particular field for insight and understanding. When researching CPM questions, I have most often turned to the blogs of two people: Cameron Lackpour and Celvin Kattookaran. Both understand any question I have, and – as importantly – they find a way to explain the complicated so that even mere mortals like me can understand. Not only are their blogs considered to be the best source of technical knowledge in the industry, they are entertaining to read.

If you are lucky in your professional life, you get to work with people who excel at their profession and are willing to teach you. If you are really lucky, you get to work with more than one. If your luck runs to the "I just won PowerBall" level, you get to work with two absolute geniuses who, while far ahead of the rest of the field, graciously share what they know. I've evidently been PowerBall lucky since I have had the pleasure of working with Celvin and Cameron over the last few years. During that time, I've come to realize just how deep an understanding they each have of the technology and the ways to exploit that technology.

This book is yet another example of Celvin and Cameron's ability to distill very complex software into digestible examples/approaches to various problems. Their ability to write about technical content in a way that makes it both interesting and an enjoyable read is truly a unique skill. There are many reasons to read this book. If you want to understand how OneStream can help your organization with the Planning process, you should read this book. Or, if you want to learn how to operate, implement, maintain, or in any way harness the power of OneStream in a Planning process, you should read this book. I'm reminded of a time back, a few years ago, when I worked on my first OneStream implementation with Cameron. I learned many things during that project; however, one piece of advice Cameron gave me and others on the project was that you should never write a book. So, the final reason I'd give to read this book is that you should read it because they may not write another!

Alex Ladd, CEO MindStream Analytics

Introduction

Never Write a Book

When OneStream sent out their call for authors, my immediate thought was, "Thank goodness I'm never doing *that* again. That's someone else's path to pain. Sucker." This has nothing to do with OneStream; I have dissuaded others from writing books when I thought the concept flawed, and shut down nascent book projects when the logistics were impossibly complex and vendor support nonexistent. Many start to write a book, few finish. That is because writing a book is *hard*, in terms of time (your authors spent well over 500 hours combined on the one you are reading), effort (some of the use cases in this book are not simple, and the writing is never easy), and dedication (our full-time jobs of consulting and personal lives continue apace). Yet here I am, writing the introduction to book number three, and here is Celvin (I certainly warned him about the experience, hence "never write a book"), joining me in this endeavor. Why?

The Market

One of the indicators of an established software product is an independent book market. Celvin and I were certainly aided by OneStream (more on this in the acknowledgments) in the preparation and writing of this book, but our contract is with P8tech, publishing under the OneStream Press imprint. The topics, content, and writing are ours alone, the hallmarks of independent work; this is a book *about* OneStream, not a OneStream book. One of the measures of an established and successful software company is that it encourages an independent and outwards-facing publishing environment. *OneStream Planning, The Why, How and When* is that philosophy manifested in print.

Community

A software company's community might be broadly defined as an ecosystem of product evangelism peopled by customers and consultants, gently prodded and pushed by the vendor. Companies foster community only when they are confident that their tool – inevitably imperfect like everything else in this world – can withstand the scrutiny of those outside that company's walls. Those inside a community gain much from its existence: discussion and discovery by their peers is different from a vendor's outreach in its focus and depth. Once fostered, a community becomes the most credible advocates of a product, for they have no direct monetary link to its success. Instead, it is part of their professional development, interest, and passion.

While there must be some way to measure community size, growth, and participation and its relation to sales, it is surely an inexact one because the geeks that advocate a product are not the ones who sign contracts; they are the ones that influence the contract signers. OneStream Press is a key component of that community. Your authors have probed deeply into OneStream's functionalities, identified missing functionality, proposed solutions, and incidentally gored a few oxen here and there. *That* is independence, and *that* is what a confident software company fosters. If it needs saying at this point, OneStream is confident about its product, and rightly so. Our expectation is that – as OneStream grows – so too will its community in influence and importance. Celvin and I were enthusiastic evangelists in our Prior Product Lives and are just as much today.

Education

The ultimate purpose of a community is education: how do I best use this feature, what can I do with the product that I would never have dreamt of, why on earth would anyone want to do that? Documentation and training are key components of understanding and comprehension, but they are necessarily constrained by budget and resources as they try to serve customers of different skill levels (Excel-has-always-been-great-why-would-I-want-to-change to performance management veterans), product focus (planners are not overmuch interested in account reconciliations), and roles (administrators versus consultants). Members of OneStream's community, those who live in OneStream day in and day out, are the ones who best understand its potential and usage. A vendor's focus and direction, while ultimately important, are tangential to what that community values the most and expends its efforts on. OneStream's practitioners – your authors and you – are the ones who know where the gaps and opportunities are when it comes to expanding everyone's understanding and mastery of OneStream.

Ultimately, the desire to discover, understand, and evangelize the power and potential of OneStream is why Celvin and I spent so much time on this book. We are driven by the opportunity to help others better understand the product, help it grow in functionality and features, and ultimately evangelize OneStream.

You, Gentle Reader, would not be here if education was not your passion as it is ours. This book is for all of us.

The How Drives the Why; The Why Drives the How

Your authors have been driven bonkers by the "Just figure it out" attitude because that direction drives a practice of finding out *how* (often from other practitioners) to do something for a specific use case with little understanding as to *why* it is done. In the shortest of all possible terms, this approach works because, after all, if we do not know how to do something, there is little value in understanding why. But this approach is short-sighted, for once the immediate solution is at hand, applying it beyond that instance may not make sense or lead to degraded performance or even result in an incorrect answer. If we only understand *how* to do something, we cannot truly understand *what* it does, *when* it should be used, *where* it is best applied, *why* it should be done, and ultimately *how* best to do it. Once we understand *why* a component or feature or block of code does what it does, the *how* flows easily from that understanding.

Our philosophy, both within this book and without, has been to first understand that all-important why, and then attempt to tell you the how. We hope that you will come to share this belief, if you do not already do so, and use it in your approach to all OneStream questions both large and small.

Cameron & Celvin Coffee Company

Writing this book required a *simple* sample application. Yes, OneStream's sample application GolfStream can be downloaded from the OneStream Marketplace readily enough, but GolfStream is *big* and must serve many masters as it attempts to encompass almost every bit of a very broad product. Moreover, it is in the hands of OneStream. What would happen to our use cases and code if it substantially changed? Would we have to change our use cases if so? Could we modify them and meet our publisher's (self-imposed by *Yr. Obt. Svts.*) deadlines without losing what little left we have of our minds?

The answer then was to come up with a very basic sample application that was just complex enough to support our work and no more, hence the sobriquet – A Very Basic Sample, shortened to **AVBS**.

Celvin and I seem to be caffeine addicts. I, for one, have consumed a somewhat alarming quantity of coffee during the writing of this book and hope to return to a normal two or three cups per day afterwards. Given our love for coffee and the need to have some kind of business to underpin that simple application, having AVBS describe the Cameron & Celvin (or Celvin & Cameron if you prefer) Coffee Company was an easy decision. For any readers actually in the coffee business, try not to laugh too much as we, alas, have never had the opportunity to work for a coffee business and are only enthusiasts.

A Very Basic Sample

When the seed of writing this book was planted, we jointly agreed that the book had to center around use cases – the *why* that is embedded in this book's essence is almost impossible to convey and to understand without them.

C&CCC

Creating an application is easy enough, the process of what makes sense in that application, what you, Gentle Reader, can relate to was the challenge. Everyone (practically) loves coffee, your authors love coffee, so why not have the business that drives the book's use cases be a small yet sophisticated coffee company that has embraced OneStream for its financial planning? The resulting imaginary customer: Cameron & Celvin's Coffee Company.

Figure 0.1

Dimensions

To our international readers, sorry, but simplicity and Americans' well known and deserved provinciality resulted in an Entity Dimension that consists only of the states and geographical regions of the United States. Perhaps AVBS will grow in the future to encompass the rest of the world, but not in this book.

All of the required Dimensions are there – OneStream will not allow anything else – with UD1/Products being the only custom Dimension. While some of the product names are silly, they are used throughout the book. Extensibility was added halfway through the writing as we discovered we needed it for use cases. The below is the primary hierarchy.

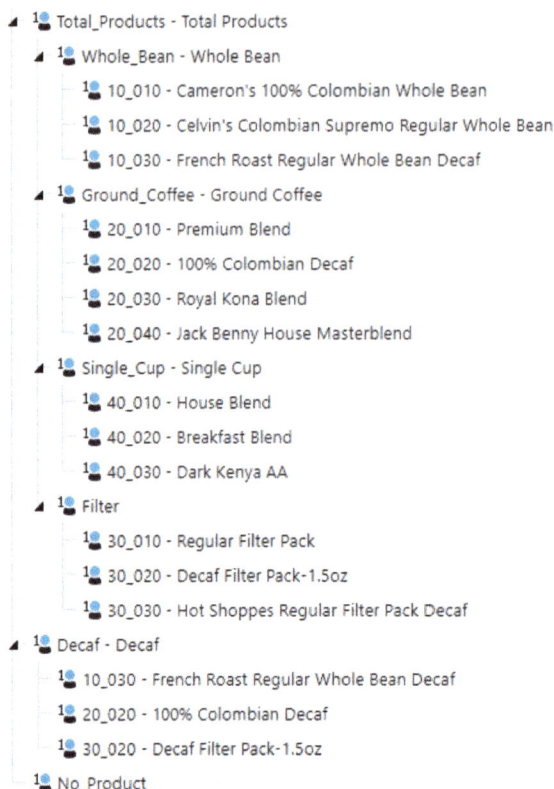

Figure 0.2

The customized required Dimensions, such as Flow and Accounts, are as complex (read simple) as the use cases required. Flow is stupendously simple in its single Member of `EndBal_Input`. Account comes from a database we both used and loved in another life.

Workflow

As with the rest of AVBS, it supports our book use cases and nothing more. Do not use them as a blueprint for a sophisticated real-world OneStream Planning application. Do use them as we did to explore OneStream's functionality.

The Data

Much of it is easy and is limited, sometimes tremendously so, in its size as our goal was not to create a data warehouse (or go through the effort of creating randomized data to support it) but instead to illustrate our use cases.

The Users

C&CCC's Finance, Planning, and Analysis team is populated by some of the smartest, nicest, and funniest people we know. Every one of them gave permission to use their first names. Natalie, Jessica, Sandra, Neviana, Amy, and Tiffany: thank you all. You are now for good, or for ill, immortalized in print.

Downloading AVBS For Fun and Profit

Download AVBS from: www.OneStreamPress.com/planning

Acknowledgments

Ours

Every quest or journey demands some sacrifices. At the end of it, some leave you in pain, some in sadness, some in profound happiness.

When Nicole Belanger and Peter Fugere reached out to us on August 25th 2020 about writing a book on OneStream, our reaction was excitement tempered with a fair measure of trepidation. With the resolve that can only come from an inability to learn from painful experience (Cameron) and naiveté (Celvin), we started the process of writing. Thank you for considering the two of us, and thank you for initiating the process. We are proud to be a part of the OneStream Press journey. Our competitive nature is well pleased by being the first two non-OneStream employees to write a book on OneStream.

To our OneStream technical editors, Jon Golembiewski and Mel Lenhardt, and key contacts, Tony Dimitrie and Peter Fugere, your patience, encouragement, and willingness to engage with two rather opinionated authors was inspirational and key to our completing this book. The care and time you took in your chapter reviews was evident and made the book better for it. The discussions we had were wide-ranging and exciting. We hope that we can continue the collaboration in the future.

Amanda Goralewski was our liaison with OneStream. With luck, our requests drove you only a tiny bit bonkers with their stupidity.

Our publisher, James Lumsden-Cook, took a chance on two complete unknowns. We pray that you find the gamble worthwhile. To our development team at OneStream Press, with luck, our grammar made you reconsider your cousins-across-the-sea's reputation for illiteracy.

To all of you: a book is a significant investment of blood, sweat, and tears, but we persevered and believe we have come up with a result worthy of that effort. This book could not exist without your encouragement and support.

Celvin's

To my family: the missed bedtime stories, the family dinners that I barely participated in because I was obsessing over my latest use case, I am sorry and profoundly grateful that you gave me the leeway and time to write this book with your sacrifice. I would like to thank my beautiful wife, three wonderful kids, and the two doggies for letting me pursue this journey. The unanswered questions, the blank stares, those cray crays are all going away (or at least I will no longer plead writing as an excuse). Thank you again.

However, my partner in crime, my best buddy, my older-smarter-shorter-not-so-handsome brother from a completely different set of parents – Cameron Lackpour warned me about the horror and pain involved in writing a book. I still signed up for it because he agreed to become a part of that journey. Thank you, Cameron, for the endless-yet-fruitful discussions, for the numerous edits to make my chapters better, and for not driving down here and strangling me.

Now that I am at the end of this journey, like Cameron, I will not allow painful experience to stop me from doing this again. The smell of freshly-printed paper has always filled me with joy, and this time it is personal.

Cameron's

My thankfully ever-patient and most certainly long-suffering family gave me all of the encouragement and succor any obsessed geek author could ever hope for and have, no matter how little deserved. I could not have written this book and would not have attempted to do so without you. Thank you all.

And – for those who know me, this will be of little surprise – I would like to express my thanks to Pickle and Peanut, the cats, who enjoyed my 12 immobile hours a day staring at a screen and thus provided a warm lap to sit in. I promise to feed you more stupendously unhealthy treats in the future, praying that they are not really the feline equivalents of potato chips.

Lastly, I want to thank my younger-brother-from-a-completely-different-father-and-mother, aka Celvin Kattookaran: working with you was a joy. Your patience as you explained difficult concepts to Someone Who Doesn't Quite Get It But Just Might If Given a Chance, your thoughtful critiques of my chapters, your infectious enthusiasm for so ambitious a project made this book possible. Thank you.

Errors and Omissions

Any and all mistakes are ours and ours alone.

Cameron Lackpour and Celvin Kattookaran, November 2021

1

Theory, Philosophy, and Practice

This chapter is Janus-like in that its first – Soft – section is the result of more than 40 years of combined consulting practice in planning and budgeting application implementations; its second – Hard – section advocates for specific technical practices. The Hard complements the Soft; the Soft directs the Hard.

Soft and Hard

In those 40 years, your authors have observed, taken part in, and designed planning applications that performed as promised (or even better), delivered accurate and actionable forecasts, and were a delight to develop, use, and administer. These applications were personally and professionally deeply satisfying efforts that were a credit to all involved: Clients, Planners, and Consultants alike.

We have also borne horrified witness to, and were unwilling participants, in complete and utter planning and budgeting stinkers: poorly designed, badly implemented, and practically useless systems that satisfied exactly no one because they were slow, inaccurate, cumbersome in use, painful to administer, and ultimately rejected by their intended audience. Planning applications like this besmirch reputations, can cause corporations to fail, get application owners fired, boot consultancies out the door, drive Users mad, and make everyone unfortunate enough to be associated with them extraordinarily sad. Sad sucks.

To avoid the suck, we shall list and explain what you – the client (aka normies) or the Consultant (often not terribly normal) – must adopt as your mindset and practice to produce planning applications that are fit for service.

Some of it may seem wise and profound, some of it obvious and trite, and some of it controversial and wrong-headed. Technical implementors naturally focus on the technical aspects of OneStream. However, a technical *tour de force* that ignores human, project, organizational, and political dynamics is not destined for success.

As noted, some of these dictums will ruffle some professional feathers because of their prescriptive nature. We have made practically every error we can make as Consultants. Experience is a cruel teacher but an effective one, so please think of these principles as the result of that experience, a moderate amount of pain, and much rumination. Ultimately, you as the reader will have to decide their merit; we think you will find them of some value.

The Soft

There are No Best Practices, only Good Ones, and even then Not Always

We hear the term "best practices" all the time in sales calls, design meetings, and technical discussions. It makes us, individually and collectively, go absolutely bonkers. Why? It has been our observation, as we flit from project to project, that while there are basic ground rules in OneStream, and practically every other planning technology (e.g., figure out the budgeting, reporting, and analytical needs *before* you design an application), there is no need to fit the entire world into a single Cube, no matter how well an application is tuned. Bigger Dimensions and more data means slower performance, etc.; *specific* requirements, not *general* ones, should drive what and how and why your shiny new OneStream application does what it does.

OneStream's Transformation Rules

An example is where data transformations within OneStream should take place. OneStream's Data Transformation Rules are used in conjunction with Data Sources to – as the name suggests – transform data so that it may be loaded into a OneStream application. That transformation might take the form of one-to-one mapping or composite mapping or list mapping or range mapping or wildcard mapping or Complex Expressions or Parser Rules. OneStream practitioners instinctively turn to this as the correct and proper (and only) place to perform transformations. It is, after all, right there in the Application pane as provided by the vendor itself. Performing data transformations with Transformation Rules is default practice; it is almost universally viewed as a Best Practice. But, is it?

Better at the Source in SQL

A common attribute of large corporations is centrally-defined mapping tables as part of data warehouses. These tables already contain – at a business and IT-defined and approved level – the standard mappings that will be used in all systems. When dimensional or system or business conditions change, the tables are modified to reflect those changes. If the OneStream application does not use those centrally-defined mappings, it will fall out of step with the rest of the business, impacting metadata and data quality. If complex mappings are required, the client will have a deep (and cheap, compared to OneStream resources) and business-aware bench of SQL developers that work with these mapping and transformation tables on a regular basis. If there are thousands of complex mappings across multiple Dimensions, is the transformation process best handled within a relational database via `INNER JOIN`s or in hundreds of pages within a Transformation Rule Editor on a Dimension-by-Dimension basis? Which will perform better and be more cost-effective when the dataset is large: OneStream or a large data warehouse?

Which?

Every one of the pro-SQL points can be refuted. OneStream serves a different purpose than a data warehouse and its data transformation needs – in definition and timing – are necessarily different. Internal IT SQL developers are almost certainly completely booked on other projects with a multi-month waitlist. Exporting the mappings to a `.trx` file and maintaining a large number of mappings in Excel ensures that the Administrator better understands the application's data. The criticality of performance is largely subjective.

Best is Situational. At Best

So, which is better practice: performing data transformations in OneStream or in a relational database?

As Consultants seem to constantly and consistently say, "It depends." This is because, within the context of the design, implementation, and maintenance of an application, one implementation task amongst many others must be to balance functionality and performance against cost in time and resources. Either is best, depending on the circumstances.

The knowledge that any design is necessarily a compromise between application desires and means is perhaps the *only* best practice; there are no other best practices, only the best that can be done within the circumstances.

A Product this Wide, this Deep, and this Flexible can Never be Fully Mastered – So Don't

How Big is Big?

For some of us, like your authors and quite possibly you, the notion that a product in its entirety – every bit and bob – cannot be understood and mastered through hard work and a will to learn is by turns both frustrating and dismaying. Other products, more limited in functionality, can often be understood in their entirety by one person. This is not the case with OneStream because it can do so much. How much?

Big, Really Big

Documentation page count is a handy, albeit rough, guide to product functionality. The *OneStream 6.5 Design and Reference Guide* alone is 1,104 pages. The *Studio Report Design Guide for WinForms* is 724 pages. There are 10 other design guides plus release notes and an upgrade guide as well as an exhaustive API documentation set. If installation instructions are included, the page count is 3,175 pages.

If we look outside of OneStream's product documentation, OneStream Press' *OneStream Foundation Handbook*, a companion book to this one, is 421 pages. You, Gentle Reader, are holding yet another book in your hand (or are viewing a PDF).

Is it Humanly Possible?

How can any one person understand and comprehend absolutely everything there is to know about *any* product when the available documentation exceeds 3,500 pages? No one can; not your authors, not you, not anyone. We put it to you that the act of reading this book is proof enough that you, too, need guidance and direction in your journey towards OneStream competence.

Yes, through Specialization

What you (and we) *can* do is narrow the focus of expertise: go pretty deep and only kind of wide and learn enough (more than enough as all of us, authors and readers alike, are obsessed with doing the very best we can) to do our jobs well. Part of that process is deciding if your area of expertise is Consolidations or Planning. This book is titled "OneStream Planning: The Why, How and When", so your task of specialization is well on its way.

This book, in spite of its six chapters – a Principles chapter (this one), Core Planning I and II, Planning Without Limits, All Data Points Lead to Reporting and Analysis, and the concluding Specialty Planning Analysis – covers only a portion of the product's capabilities, cf. the almost 3,600 pages of documentation, but it is the core of OneStream Planning practice.

View this specialization not as a limitation of the product, or one of professional curiosity and ability, but rather a guide to subject selection, study, and – yes – mastery. Your authors are not unique in their ability to learn, understand, and use OneStream to produce Planning and Budgeting systems that not only match but exceed others' work, whether within OneStream or without. If we can do it, so can you!

Over Time, Very Complex Applications Collapse under their Own Weight

Planning applications in OneStream can be complex from a business, functional, and technical perspective, any of which can be a fatal flaw. A complicated Planning application is hazardous to the survival of the organization because the plan it creates is the business' financial roadmap for the next year or more.

Robustness

Planning applications are used to create a Forecast of future business performance within unpredictable organizational (takeovers, acquisitions), political (contested elections, geopolitical tensions), regulatory (increased environmental statutes, financial standards), and social (widespread protest, cultural shifts) environments. These systems must be flexible and able to pivot from an established forecasting process to a new one when the world around it changes. If process resiliency is defined as an ability to react and adapt to change, the intrinsic inflexibility of complex and intricate systems forbids that ability to adapt, and are thus inherently fragile and not resilient. Fragile systems break.

Understanding

Moreover, overly complex Planning systems may result in poorly understood predictive outcomes. As an example, a centrally-defined complex multi-step waterfall allocation is well understood by the application's business owners who, after all, created the functional requirements. However, when such a system is rolled out to Planners at the affiliate level, the Users will either trust the code without understanding the result or – because they do not understand the logic – they mistrust the system. Poorly understood systems are abandoned.

The Human Factor

Availability and Retention

As an Implementer or Administrator or Owner of a OneStream Planning application, the danger of business and functional complexity is that it drives the technical complexity of the application and thus requires highly skilled individuals. This is not a question of OneStream's functionality but instead the distribution of practitioner technical skill within the Implementer ability distribution curve. Statistically, there are simply fewer of them than the rest of us, they will be in high demand, and their availability will be therefore limited. In addition, employees whose skill is in high demand are mobile. What happens when the Architect, Developer, or Administrator that is key to a complex project leaves for greener pastures? An Application design that relies on a limited and unstable resource pool cannot be implemented or maintained in the face of unavailability.

Ability

The last factor to appreciate in complex systems is unique to the implementation phase and is related to the above shortage of very advanced technical skill; if that gifted technical ability is unavailable, less talented practitioners may be unable to implement complex logic and product functionality. This can be partially ameliorated by training and education (hopefully, this book and the other titles published by OneStream Press contribute to those goals) and careful selection of consultancies and their personnel, but the fact remains that projects that cannot find and retain critical resources cannot be implemented.

Collapse

Complex systems are inherently fragile, difficult to understand, challenging to staff, and liable to lose key individuals. Any one of these failure points can be fatal.

Opportunity and Risk

OneStream Consultants often joke, "You can do anything in OneStream." It is, with very little exaggeration, astonishingly true. The rejoinder to that is, "Yeah, but should you?" Gallows humor aside, the question is an important one to ponder. The temptation to go outside the standard capabilities of the tool is strong because OneStream is an excellent platform for solving complex problems that other products struggle to address.

This extreme ability is where the danger lies. You – Business Owner, Administrator, Consultant alike – must think very carefully about the end state of a complex system. Can it be built on time and on budget? Can it adapt to changing circumstances? Who will maintain it? Does anyone understand it?

Simplicity and Success

A better approach is to consider what would have been lost if a given Planning application was simpler, or if the technical skills required were less extreme, more flexible but slightly more manual, less functional yet well understood, and had well suited and easily identified practitioners.

Resisting complexity and enforcing simplicity is not an easy task because what a system loses in sophistication is front-loaded, whereas the risk of failure from complexity is not.

Avoiding this risk requires constant questioning of process and technical design. Can it be done? Who can do it? Will Planners understand it? What happens when something breaks? Is it within the core functionality of OneStream? None of these are easy questions and the answers entail compromise with attendant project, system, and political risks. Nevertheless, an orientation towards the possible is the most likely to succeed because those systems simply work and keep working.

Ultimately, you will own the success or failure of the Planning application. Eschew complexity when simplicity suffices. Choose wisely.

Not OneStream, but an Example of What Celvin Should Not Do

Whenever I think of complex applications, I think of my home automation. I was without work for a few months because I was in Another Vendor's declining market and so, with free time staring me in the face, I started automating our new home with my wife's approval (she knows that I go crazy without a goal and hard work to reach it). I suppose she thought that if my ambition overtook my ability, the house could revert to its old manual – yet fully functional – self.

Little did she know that my cunning plan was to change every single switch in the house, automate the doors, garage openers, and anything else I could devise. Name it, and it was automated.

In the beginning, it was fun. Lights turned off; doors closed whenever we left the house. My favorite feature was lights automatically turning off when motion was not detected after a few minutes. We all got really used to it and liked the new automatic house.

I did put in a few failsafes to prevent Bad Stuff from happening. Then stuff *did* happen, albeit good at first. But after that, my wife got locked out of the house and our little one was inside. Whoopsie. However, I could remotely open the door for her from hundreds of miles/kilometers away. I guess that was the first time she appreciated my awesomeness at work.

After a while, more bad stuff started happening. We got to enjoy the mesh automation system's failures (I invite you to dive into the rabbit hole of home automation), the hassle of changing batteries, constant diagnosing of a broken mesh, healing the mesh, and on and on in a series of catastrophes. There were a few instances where I was locked out of my house, during work hours, when my wife left for work and I was outside in the yard. (There were *some* positive aspects to this. Kind of.) There were instances when the whole house lit up at midnight. You get the idea; there was constant attention needed, and only I could manage it.

Do not let your Planning system be like my automated home, where perpetual attention is needed to keep it running.

I do like the fun of metrics around how many times we opened the doors or how many times the garage door was open at night. It is "amusing" to be alerted when the kids leave the lights on for hours, racking up our electric bill.

Enjoyment aside, my home automation implementation was and is a complex work in progress, albeit a pretty cool one. Coolness, in this case, is fun – despite the added complexity. Coolness is not the goal of a good Planning system. An improved budgeting and forecast outcome should be the *only* goal of a good Planning system.

Everything you Know is (not) Wrong

It has been said by more than one OneStream practitioner, "You have to forget everything you've ever learned or done or thought of in that old product. It just holds you back." This sentiment is wrong because, for someone with knowledge in other tools, it ignores all of the functional Planning system knowledge we (likely) have, and most of the technical and design knowledge we (just as likely) have.

Functionally Right

Discounting functional knowledge is wrong: business needs are the same, how those issues are investigated are the same, the process of design is the same, understanding source data and its required transformations are the same, how an allocation works is the same, dimensional design is (largely, but with exceptions noted in this chapter) the same, *ad infinitum*. To think that your functional knowledge is useless (and that is the implication) smacks of hubris.

Technically Questionable

The technical argument is more on point because OneStream – like any performance management product – differs from other products, sometimes dramatically. You must change how you think of what sits in a Cube and what is relational, understand the value of Dimensional Extensibility, embrace VB.Net, delve deeply into OneStream's object model, use the mandatory Workflow, and comprehend the nuances of the Data Unit, amongst many other technical aspects of the tool. Notwithstanding these not insubstantial caveats, it has been our observation that understanding and implementing OneStream's features and functions is more an exercise in studying and experimentation than a complete rejection of prior knowledge.

Definitely Doable

As an example of the value of experience, consider an allocation that takes a base number – say distribution costs – that is then spread to products by using product sales as a percentage of the total as a driver.

To perform this allocation, there must be a non-aggregating Distribution Account to spread, there will be a series of non-consolidating Dimension Members that isolate the base amount to prevent double-counting (experience), the logic requires a ratio calculation at a base product against total sales at total product (experience), the products must be passed through or looped (experience), and the result must sit as a normal expense in the Account Dimension P&L(experience). The Finance Business Rule that performs this allocation with GetDataCell calls, DataBuffer loops, and Calculate methods are of course different (new) from the functions and methods in whatever your prior tool supported but are, at their core, the same. While not dismissing the technical effort, how this allocation will be performed is the same as any other tool.

Your experience and knowledge are of value, not of detriment. Your next step is understanding the unique technical nature of OneStream and incorporating its features into your Planning application, a far easier task than starting from Year Zero.

Everything you know *is* useful.

The Hard

The Soft is a prelude to specific Hard technical practice. How a OneStream practitioner implements a technical feature should be driven by philosophy and mindset as well as technical functionality. Does this system need a true Consolidation? How much detail is needed from a source file? What is the optimal mix of Excel and OneStream? Does Specialty Planning provide the right kind of analytical functionality?

These design choices do not exist in some sort of untethered-to-reality theoretical space. Instead, they influence and are influenced by those Soft principles such as solution complexity, resourcing, knowledge, and what ultimately are the best possible practices for a given implementation.

Given that this is a book about Planning in OneStream, this section's technical principles are necessarily viewed through the prism of that practice. Regardless, much of them are equally applicable to Consolidation and Reporting applications. Much of what is advocated reflects new (as of the writing of this book) Planning-specific functionality such as Aggregations and Direct Load that (with little exaggeration) are game-changing and will alter how we all implement Planning in OneStream. Large product improvements make for exciting times, but their novelty means that evaluating their impact within the Soft principles is all the more important.

Aggregated, Never (usually) Consolidated

The Need for Speed

The pattern of Planners' data interaction with OneStream is (roughly) as follows: retrieve, review, input, save, calculate, sum to totals, retrieve and then repeat, ending only when the Planning process is complete. The longest system step is typically around summing Entity Parents because the processing of tens of thousands (or hundreds of thousands or more) of Base Dimension data intersections to Parent hierarchy levels takes time to retrieve, compute in memory, and write to disk. Time-consuming or not, the ability to see the impact of inputs and calculations at summed hierarchy levels is key to understanding plan data.

Implementors try to alleviate the time impact by making the Entity Dimension Consolidation process optional at a Form level, or by running it on a scheduled basis. These approaches may improve the User Experience but will delay analysis and may lead to data quality issues when those totals become stale and do not foot to base data.

Adding It Up

Happily, the mitigation strategies of scheduled or explicitly delayed processing are required only for the Entity-type Dimension; all other Dimension totals in OneStream are dynamic Aggregations. Entity is a stored hierarchy (largely for the purposes of true accounting-focused Financial Consolidations), and its totals can only be viewed after a Consolidation materializes them. The overhead concomitant with accounting principles and statutory requirements are not typically needed in a Planning application.

The release of OneStream 6.5 removes the need to perform a Consolidation to see data at Entity Parents by providing the option of a simpler Aggregation. Aggregations are *fast*.

What'll It Do, Mister?

How fast? Using an example of a 17,000-Member Entity Dimension with two years' worth of data (UD1 through UD6 were also populated), aggregating was **seven** times faster than consolidating.

> **Note:** A 17,000-Member Entity Dimension is atypical in its size. A more reasonable Entity Dimension size of 700 saw an 83% improvement in speed. Fast, indeed. Of course, every Cube is different in size, density of data, and design of Dimensions, all of which impact Cube performance; therefore, actual performance in your Cube may vary.

Using It is Simplicity Itself

OneStream 6.5 introduced a new Consolidation Dimension Member: **Aggregated**.

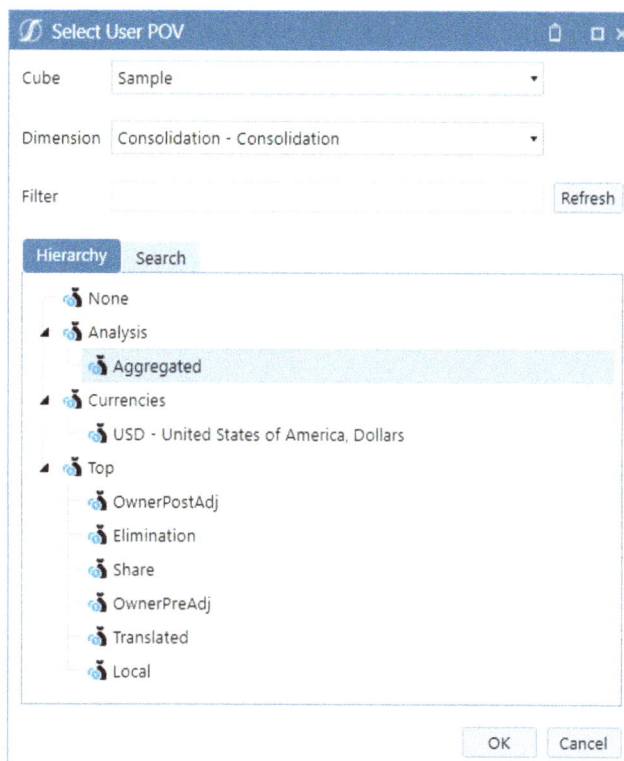

Figure 1.1

Chapter 1

C#Aggregated is – unsurprisingly – where aggregated data sits in the Consolidation Dimension.

Launching an Aggregation in a Data Management step is accomplished by using C#Aggregated in the Consolidation Filter instead of the more typical (and default) C#Local. This really and truly is *all there is* to aggregating instead of consolidating.

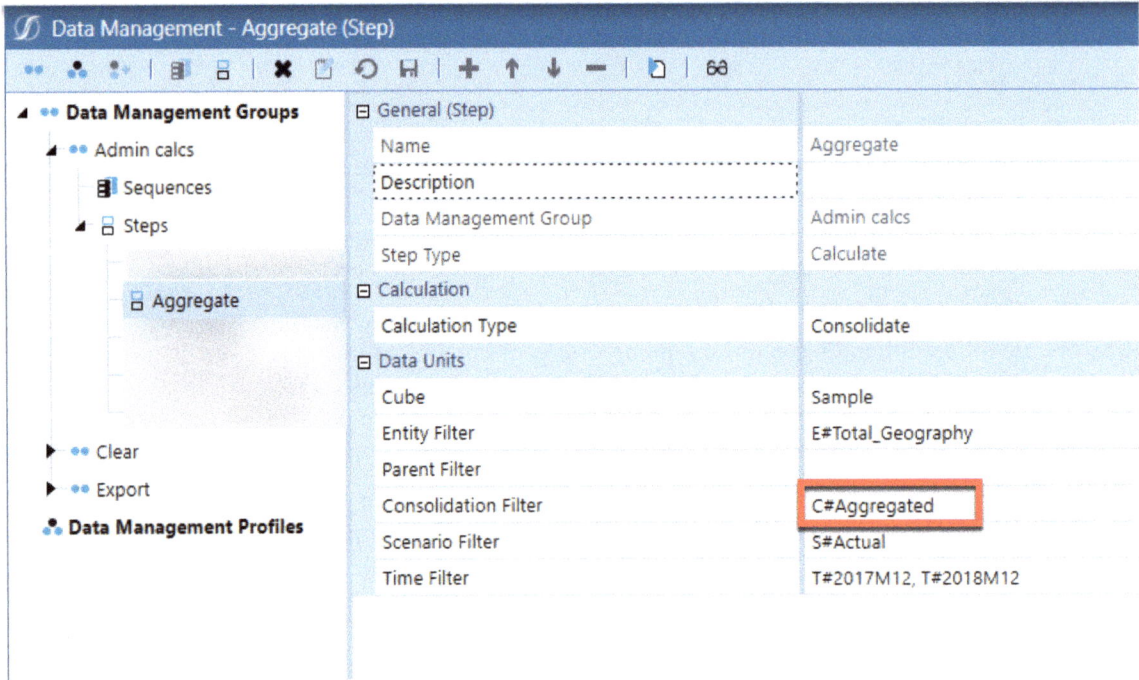

Figure 1.2

C#Aggregated Default Population

Even when an Aggregation is **not** executed, C#Aggregated is valued at Base Entities but not at Parent-level Members.

	A	B	C	D	E	F	G
1		2018M1	2018M1	2018M1	2018M1	2018M1	2018M1
2		East	East	Pennsylvania	Pennsylvania	New_York	New_York
3		10_010	10_030	10_010	10_030	10_010	10_030
4	None						
5	Analysis						
6	Aggregated			120	93	678	
7	Currencies						
8	CAD						
9	EUR						
10	GBP						
11	USD			120	93	678	
12	Top			120	93	678	
13	OwnerPostAdj						
14	Elimination						
15	Share			120	93	678	
16	OwnerPreAdj						
17	Translated			120	93	678	
18	Local			120	93	678	

Figure 1.3

An Aggregation returns data at `E#East:C#Aggregated` but *not* at `C#USD`, `C#Top`, `C#Share`, `C#Translated`, or `C#Local`, all Consolidation artifacts.

	A	B	C	D	E	F	G
		2018M1	2018M1	2018M1	2018M1	2018M1	2018M1
		East	East	Pennsylvania	Pennsylvania	New_York	New_York
		10_010	10_030	10_010	10_030	10_010	10_030
4	None						
5	Analysis						
6	Aggregated	1602	93	120	93	678	
7	Currencies						
8	CAD						
9	EUR						
10	GBP						
11	USD			120	93	678	
12	Top			120	93	678	
13	OwnerPostAdj						
14	Elimination						
15	Share			120	93	678	
16	OwnerPreAdj						
17	Translated			120	93	678	
18	Local			120	93	678	

Figure 1.4

A Consolidation will value the typical currency, `C#Share`, `C#Translated`, and `C#Local` data points and will not populate `C#Aggregated`.

	A	B	C	D	E	F	G
		2018M1	2018M1	2018M1	2018M1	2018M1	2018M1
		East	East	Pennsylvania	Pennsylvania	New_York	New_York
		10_010	10_030	10_010	10_030	10_010	10_030
4	None						
5	Analysis						
6	Aggregated			120	93	678	
7	Currencies						
8	CAD						
9	EUR						
10	GBP						
11	USD	1602	93	120	93	678	
12	Top	1602	93	120	93	678	
13	OwnerPostAdj						
14	Elimination						
15	Share	1602	93	120	93	678	
16	OwnerPreAdj						
17	Translated	1602	93	120	93	678	
18	Local	1602	93	120	93	678	

Figure 1.5

What's Kept

Beyond the Aggregation speed improvements, currency conversion, share percentage, and – most importantly – financial intelligence are all retained.

What's Lost

From a Consolidations Application perspective, the following Consolidations-only features are vital and thus preclude Aggregations: Business Rules on all Consolidation levels, recursive calculations on Entity and Consolidation to perform Eliminations, and accounting for Parent Journal Adjustments.

Three Notes

The Good

Aggregations consider already aggregated data values (e.g., if the Entity *Pennsylvania*'s data changes, impacting the ancestors *East* and *Total Geography*, the *South Carolina* and *South* hierarchy are not reaggregated).

The Bad

An Entity Dimension can be both aggregated *and* consolidated. Beyond the needless redundancy in having the same number stored twice in the Cube, the risk that a Consolidation and an Aggregation are not in step is high. Pick one, not the other, and in the case of Planning applications, pick Aggregations.

The Ugly

The `C#Aggregated` Member automatically reflects level zero Member data and will display Parent-level Member data on Aggregation. However, `C#Aggregated` is a read-only Member.

	A	B	C	D	E
1		Local	Local	Aggregated	Aggregated
2		2018M1	2018M1	2018M1	2018M1
3		10_010	10_030	10_010	10_030
4	Delaware				
5	New_Jersey	42		42	
6	Pennsylvania	120	93	120	93
7	New_York				
8	East			162	93

Figure 1.6

A single-month Quick View with nested Consolidation, Time, and UD1 Members poses no navigational issues but would quickly become untenable if expanded to a typical full year of 12 periods, resulting in 48 columns.

There are then two other approaches: separate input and reporting views, or a parameter-driven Consolidation toggle.

Separate Views

This approach creates two Cube Views that differ only in their Consolidation Member selection, i.e., `C#Local` versus `C#Aggregated`.

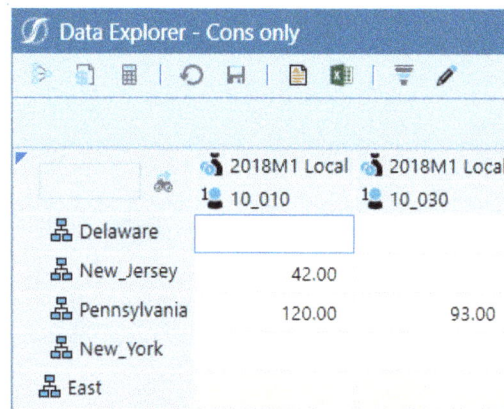

Figure 1.7

The above Cube View allows input but does not show a total at East.

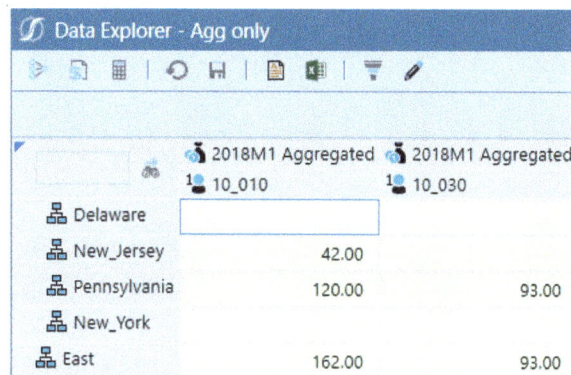

Figure 1.8

A C#Aggregated Cube View shows (after Aggregation) data at the individual state and region level. However, it is read-only.

A Planner could toggle between both Cube Views using Workflow or a custom Dashboard. Beyond the cumbersome nature of changing Cube Views, this approach requires two Cube Views with their follow-on maintenance.

Single Parametrized Consolidation View

A simpler approach is to use a **Delimited List parameter** to drive the C#Local/C#Aggregated selection and use it in the Column Member definition.

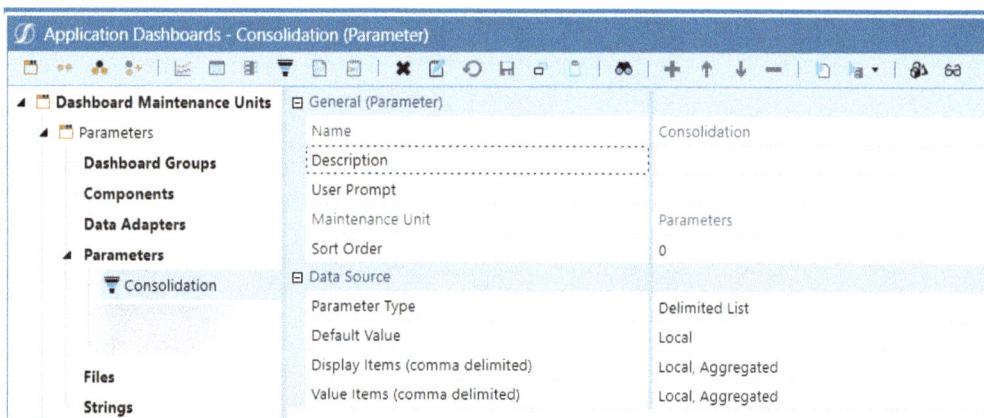

Figure 1.9

Modifying the columns to use the `||Consolidation!|` parameter will drive a popup Member selector on Cube View refresh…

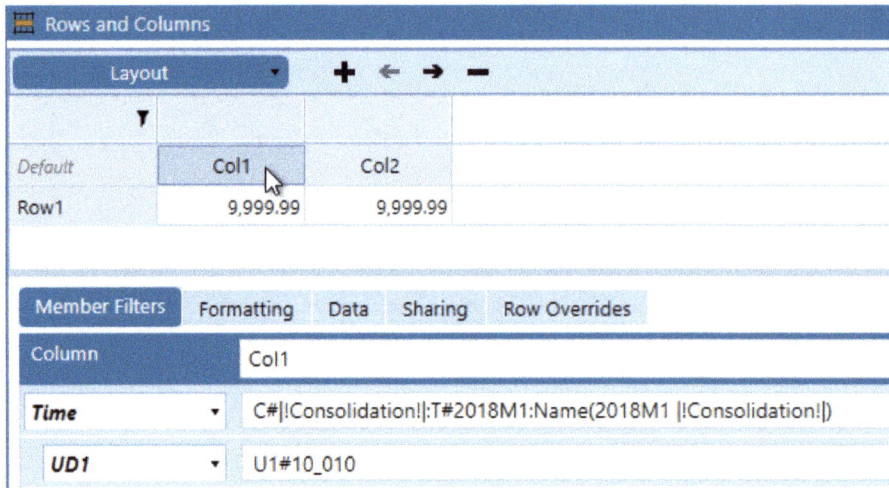

Figure 1.10

…which then allows the User to select `C#Aggregated` or `C#Local`.

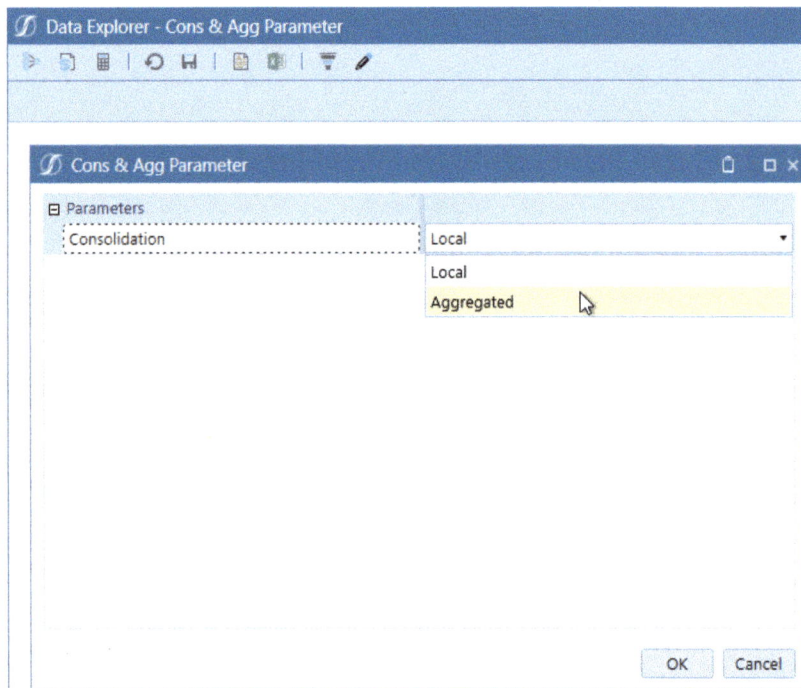

Figure 1.11

This results in a single Cube View that can display either Member.

Choosing Aggregated in the Member dropdown results in a `C#Aggregated`-valued Cube View that, when aggregated, can be used to view data totaled at `East`.

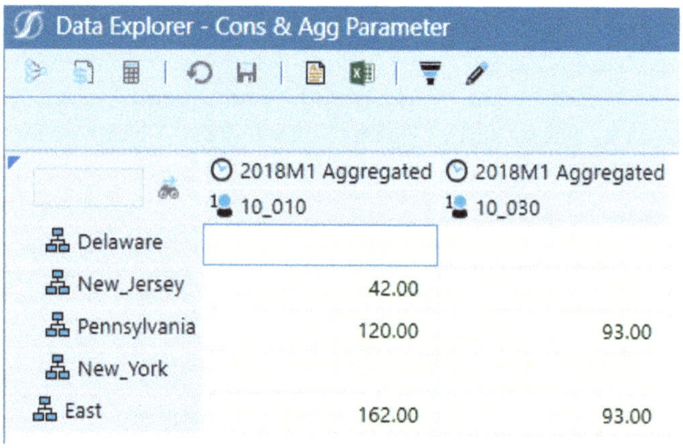

Figure 1.12

Selecting Local in the Member dropdown results in a C#Local-valued Cube View, allowing input at the East's constituent states.

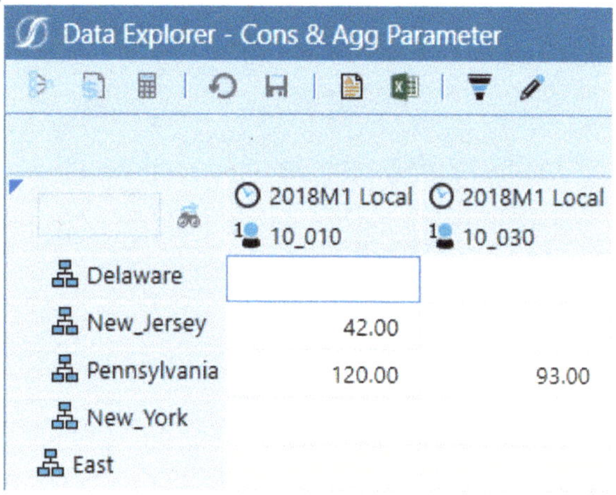

Figure 1.13

Reporting

This must surely be the shortest principle in this chapter: Aggregate the Cube and report on C#Aggregated.

Hobson's Choice

Unless true Consolidation requirements – like elimination – are required in the budgeting process, the performance boost so vital to User Experience means that Aggregation via the Consolidation Dimension's C#Aggregate should be the only choice for Planning applications.

Load Data, Don't Import It. Sometimes

Prior to OneStream 6.4, data loads for Planning and Consolidation applications used the same method: Import. Import incurs the cost of storing source and target data in Stage tables, a requirement relevant for Consolidations but largely not required for Planning applications.

OneStream 6.4 introduced the **Direct Load Workflow Type**. Direct Load does not store source and target in Stage but instead performs transformations in memory and writes the result to the target Cube, thus increasing performance. If there is a requirement to understand transformations or to drill back to source data, Direct Load should not be used.

Chapter 1

In decades of building planning and analytic applications, your authors have noticed that the actual usage, compared to the stated desirability for drill backs to source, is more honored in the breach than in the observance. Given that lack of use, and the performance increase that Direct Load promises, Planning applications should – with the caveat around losing auditability of transformations – use Direct Load.

Using It

OneStream have made this easy: create a new Workflow Profile using the Direct Default Workflow.

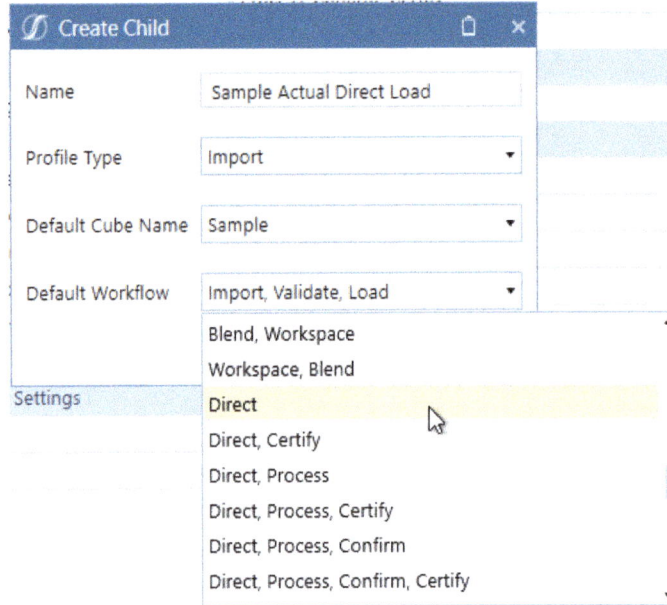

Figure 1.14

Select a Data Source.

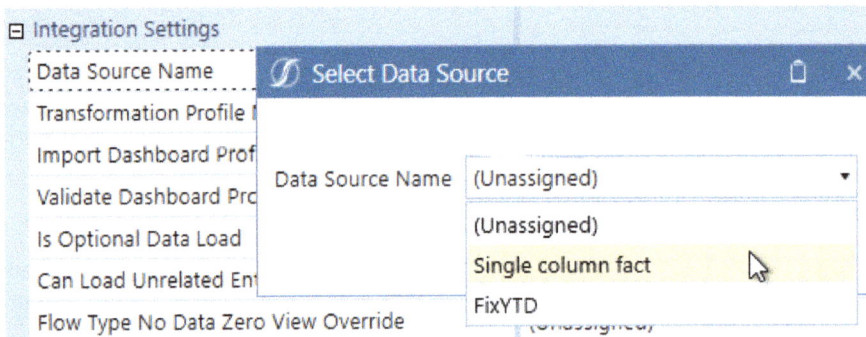

Figure 1.15

Select a Transformation Profile.

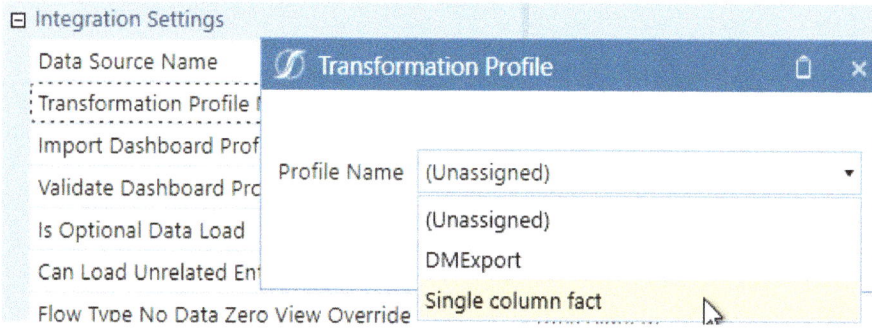

Figure 1.16

Set the Storage Type to Row.

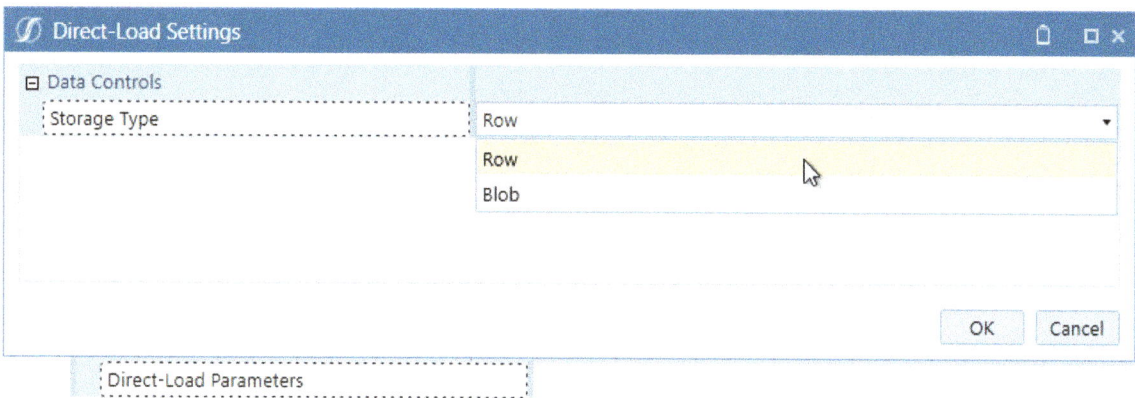

Figure 1.17

After confirming that the Profile Active property is set to True and optionally the Can Load Unrelated Entities property is also set to True, select the Workflow in OnePlace.

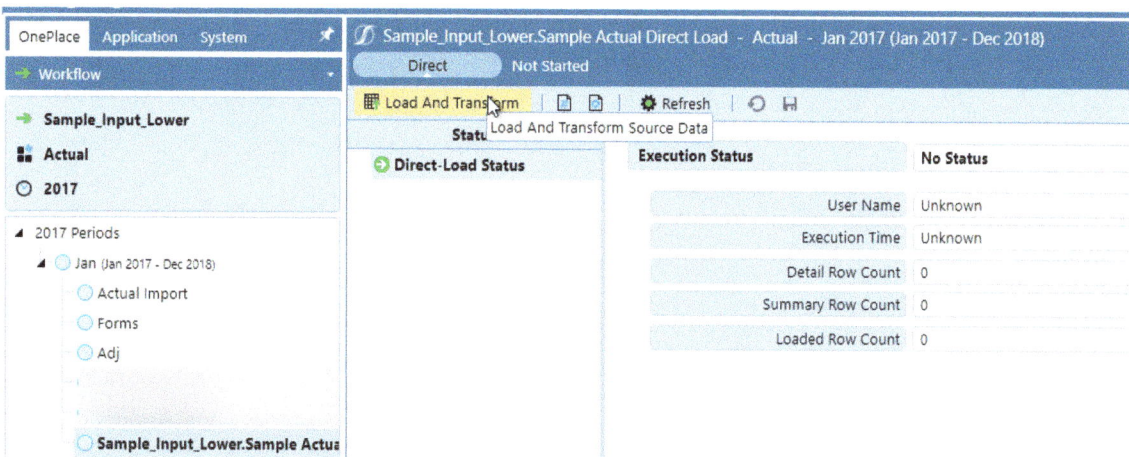

Figure 1.18

Chapter 1

As with Import, select the data file. Clicking on the OK button will start the Direct Load process.

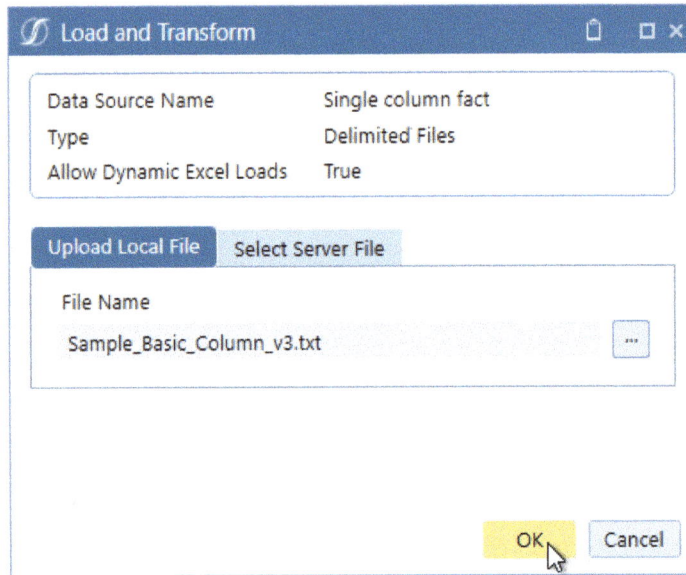

Figure 1.19

The Task Progress dialog box will indicate that Direct Load is being used.

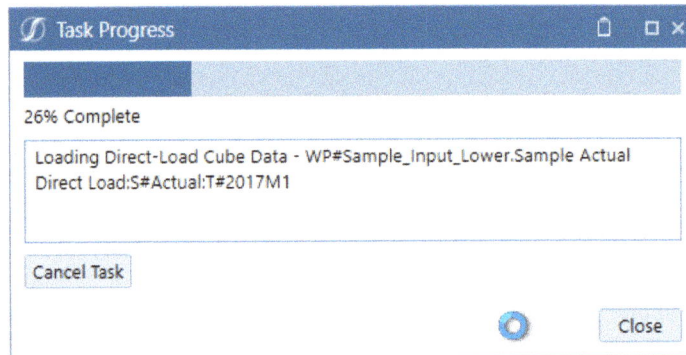

Figure 1.20

When successful, OneStream will show that the process has been completed. Note the Detail, Summary, and Loaded Row counts: Direct Load will aggregate identical file data intersections before loading to the target Cube.

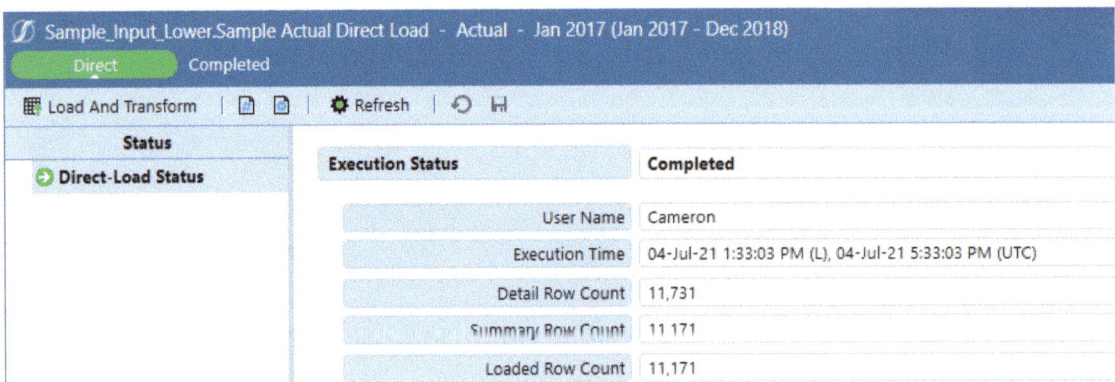

Figure 1.21

How Fast is Fast?

With the caveat that every data source is different, every Cube is different, and every server is different, performance increases up to 50% have been observed by your authors, although a 25% increase in speed seems more typical. That is *fast*.

Dealing with Errors

Error handling is the same as with Import, with the caveat that the displayed Validation error count cannot exceed 1,000 records. If there are more than 1,000 records, a reload is required to move to the next group of errors.

Figure 1.22

> **Note:** When dealing with *any* kind of error in data loads, whether Direct Load or Import, correct the data at the source, not during an interactive load process. Performance will be faster, the overall process (including human interaction) will be quicker, and data quality is ensured throughout. Remember, Direct Load does **not** store transformation history.

Row versus Binary Large Object (Blob)

Direct Load has two Storage Types: **Row** and **Blob**. Observed Blob performance shows little if any difference to Row although it is typically somewhat slower. There is an architectural storage difference (Row stores records in `StageSummaryTargetData`, Blob is in `StageDirectLoadInformation`), but this is not observable through Workflow. The typical use case for Blob is when there are rare SQL deadlock issues. Given the infrequency of these errors and the performance boost that Row provides, the latter should be the default choice.

What Happened to the Data?

The below behavior is valid for both Direct Load and Import. This issue occurs so frequently that your authors take this opportunity to illustrate a potentially fatal data quality event and its resolution.

A common data load error occurs when loading more than once to the same Data Unit (this example uses different UD1 Members) which will, by default, clear *all* other data loaded to that Data Unit whether the Direct Load Method property is set to Replace (the default) or Append.

A typical use case in Planning applications is different Planners loading to the same Data Unit (think of Planners who share responsibility for a single Entity state and UD1 product). If *Pennsylvania* data is loaded twice, once to `UD1 10_010` – Cameron's 100% Colombian Whole Bean, and then to `10_020` – Celvin's Colombian Supremo Regular Whole Bean, only the latter will have data. It is an understatement to state that this causes dismay on the part of implementors and Users alike.

Resolution, but a Clumsy One

One approach would be to combine data for both products into a single data source, but this forbids the business process of a Data Unit with multiple data sources.

A Much Better Way

The answer instead is twofold: create as many Direct Load Workflow Profiles as required and set their Direct Load Method to Append, ensuring that Planners use "their" Workflow Profile.

Chapter 1

Planner 1 loads a 120 to A#Sales:E#Pennsylvania:U1#10_010 using the Direct Row Pa 1st Profile.

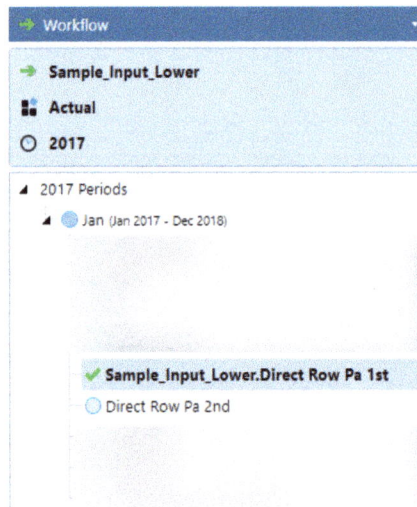

Figure 1.23

Planner 2 loads 93 to A#Sales:E#Pennsylvania:U1#10_020 using the Direct Row Pa 2nd Profile.

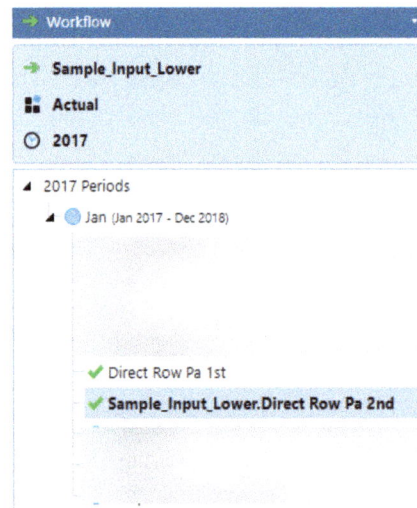

Figure 1.24

The result is that data in both products are successfully loaded to the Cube.

	A	B	C
1		Local	Local
2		2018M1 - Jan 2018	2018M1 - Jan 2018
3		10_010 - Cameron's 100% Colombian Whole Bean	10_020 - Celvin's Colombian Supremo Regular Who
4	Delaware		
5	New_Jersey		
6	Pennsylvania	120	93
7	New_York		
8	East		

Figure 1.25

26

Important Workflow Considerations

Import-only Data Loads

There is a danger to data quality when an Entity (or Entities) are present under multiple Workflow Profiles.

If a data load occurs within the same Entity from more than one Workflow Profile, the last data load wins and is loaded to the Cube. The danger (beyond the danger of miscommunication within a Planning process) is that drilldowns to Stage data will show two sets of source data, only one of which (the last one) was loaded to the Cube.

This is confusing.

Use multiple Import Load Child Workflow Profiles in a single Workflow Profile to ensure that the last loaded data goes to the Cube and is the only data visible in Stage.

Direct Load-Only

Performing Direct Loads in different Workflow Profiles *erases* the Cube completely and loads to the Cube only what was loaded in the last Workflow Profile used.

This is heart-rending.

Use multiple Direct Load Child Workflow Profiles in a single Workflow Profile to ensure that all other Direct Loads are retained in the Cube. Note, there is no drill through to Stage in Direct Load.

Direct Load Unless You Must Import

Direct Load's performance impact is significant. Use it in Planning applications unless the unlikely requirement of auditing data loads (this is drilling back to source data before transformations – not needed if the better practice of source transformations is followed) is required. The need for speed is as true for Direct Load as it is for Aggregations.

Never use Formulas unless they are Dynamic; use Custom Calculate Wherever and Whenever Possible

Dynamic Tension

Dynamic Member Formulas are typically lightweight calculations, valid at every (or almost every) Dimension intersection and are, as the name suggests, dynamically calculated on retrieve. They are suitable for reporting and should be used to provide instant feedback. Dynamic formulas are valid in Account, Flow, and all UD Dimensions.

A typical use case is Scenario variances. Within them, instead of simple subtraction, use the BWDiff Method, which flips the variance direction based on financial intelligence. In that context of Actual and Plan, Sales is Actual – Plan, while Distribution is Plan – Actual, reflecting the Account Type.

In this example, the variance is in Member UD8#Act_v_Plan with U8#None as part of the left and right Member tuple. This explicit Member reference prevents recursive calculation in the Member Formula.

```
Return api.Data.GetDataCell("BWDiff(S#Actual:U8#None,
S#Plan:U8#None)")
```

The result is as expected, with the direction of the variances flipped on Sales (Revenue) and Distribution (Expense): Actual sales is $3,175 lower than Plan – a bad thing – and Actual Distribution costs were less than Plan – a good thing. BWDiff intelligently calculates the variance without complex Account Type tests to flip the variance direction. Use BWDiff and BWPercent to correct directional variances and percent variances.

	A	B	D	E
1		Jan 2018	Jan 2018	Jan 2018
2		Actual	Plan	Plan
3		None	None	Act v Plan
4	Sales	8398	11573	-3175
5	Distribution	223	347.19	124.19

Figure 1.26

Use Dynamic Formulas whenever KPIs, variances, and other immediate calculations are needed.

Formula

OneStream's genesis was as a Consolidations tool. True financial reporting requires a full calculation of all possible data points, every time data is changed, performed through Member Formulas and Finance Business Rules attached to the Cube. OneStream calculates these stored calculations through the **Data Unit Calculation Sequence** (DUCS). See the *Design and Reference Guide* for more information but you can – largely – ignore attached rules and stored formulas because Planning applications do not require global recalculation.

Splendid Isolation

The concept is simple: within a Planning application, calculations in one Entity do not require the same calculation in other Entities.

An example with a US state Entity Dimension. Celvin is responsible for the *Palmetto State, South Carolina*; Cameron is the Planner for the *Keystone State, Pennsylvania*. Cameron's loads, inputs, and calculations in Pennsylvania do not affect South Carolina; the obverse is true for South Carolina. The two states' data only intersect at *Total US*, assuming *Pennsylvania* is a Child of *East* and *South Carolina* is a Child of *South*.

If calculation scope is limited by Entity, then there is no need to calculate anything other than the Entity in question. Formulas (or Business Rules) that are tied to the Consolidation process will run for all Entities. This redundancy will not result in incorrect results but does incur a needless performance penalty.

Less is More

Planning application design must always consider the Planner User Experience, which should be as performant as possible because of its repetitive and highly interactive nature. Scope reduction, along with code efficiency, is the surest path to faster performance. A parameter-driven Custom Calculate Finance Business Rule is the path to fast calculations.

Use Case

The Distribution expense is a fixed percent by month for all states and all products. The functional calculation is sales for all products * a distribution rate at a no geography, no product intersection.

More specifically, within the Finance Business Rule, `A#Distribution` is calculated by multiplying `A#Sales` at a given Entity/state and UD1/Product by `A#Distribution_Rate` at `E#No_Geography:UD1#No_Product`. Note that Sales for both `E#Pennsylvania` and `E#South_Carolina` are valued in the below Quick View.

	A	B	C	D	E
1			Sales	Sales	Sales
2			Jan 2018	Feb 2018	Mar 2018
3	Pennsylvania	Cameron's 100% Colombian Whole Bean	11,573.00	6,958.00	6,499.00
4	Pennsylvania	Celvin's Colombian Supremo Regular Whole Bean	13,670.00	6,205.00	6,637.00
5	South Carolina	Cameron's 100% Colombian Whole Bean	14,917.00	12,122.00	13,185.00
6	South Carolina	Celvin's Colombian Supremo Regular Whole Bean	9,607.00	10,978.00	6,615.00
7					
8					
9					
10			Distribution_Rate	Distribution_Rate	Distribution_Rate
11			Jan 2018	Feb 2018	Mar 2018
12	No_Geography	No_Product	0.03	0.06	0.07

Figure 1.27

Code

All `api.Data.Calculate` Methods that use a Durable setting of `True` should have an `api.data.ClearCalculatedData` statement to ensure that Null intersections from prior calculation runs are fully cleared.

```
api.data.ClearCalculatedData("A#Distribution:O#Forms", True, True,
True, True)
```

> **Note:** Member formulas can use a Durable flag of `True` and when that is used, the data in fact is durable on Consolidation, and thus requires explicit clearing. If the Scenario setting of `Clear Calculated Data During Calc` is set to `False`, the calculated result behaves as if it is Durable, even when that property is not used in `api.Data.Calculate`.

`A#Distribution` is calculated using the `MultiplyUnbalanced` Method to accommodate the unbalanced `E#No_Geography:U1#No_Product` rate tuple. `U1#Total_Products.Base` sets the scope of the `UD1#Product` Dimension to all Members.

```
api.Data.Calculate("A#Distribution:O#Forms:V#Periodic =
MultiplyUnbalanced(A#Sales:O#BeforeAdj:V#Periodic,
A#Distribution_Rate:O#BeforeAdj:V#Periodic:E#No_Geography:U1#No_Produc
t,
E#No_Geography:U1#No_Product)",,"F#EndBal_Input",,"I#None","U1#Total_P
roducts.Base",,,,,,,,,True)
```

There must be some excessive level of comments to code when it comes to understanding Business Rules, but your authors have yet to see it. Comment your code to help yourself and others.

```
1  ⊞Imports ...
18
19 ⊟''' Name:       DistributionExpense
20  ''' Purpose:    Calculate Distribution expense
21  ''' Modified:   3 July 2021, initial write
22  ''' Written by: Cameron Lcakpour
23  ''' Notes:      - Calculate Distribution expense via a global rate by period
24  '''             - Note that MultiplyUnbalanced allows multidimensional tuples in the "balance" parameter
25  '''
26 ⊟Namespace OneStream.BusinessRule.Finance.DistributionExpense
27 ⊟    Public Class MainClass
28 ⊟        Public Function Main(ByVal si As SessionInfo, ByVal globals As BRGlobals,
29 ⊟                    ByVal api As FinanceRulesApi, ByVal args As FinanceRulesArgs) As Object
30             Try
31
32                 ''' Clear target Distribution account just in case
33                 api.data.ClearCalculatedData("A#Distribution:O#Forms", True, True, True, True)
34
35                 ''' Calculate Distribution using unbalanced math
36                 ''' IsDurableCalculatedData is set to True
37                 api.Data.Calculate("A#Distribution:O#Forms:V#Periodic = MultiplyUnbalanced(A#Sales:O#BeforeAdj:V#Periodic, " & _
38                     "A#Distribution_Rate:O#BeforeAdj:V#Periodic:E#No_Geography:U1#No_Product, " & _
39                     "E#No_Geography:U1#No_Product)",,"F#EndBal_Input",,"I#None","U1#Total_Products.Base",,,,,,,,,True)
40
41                 Return Nothing
42             Catch ex As Exception
43                 Throw ErrorHandler.LogWrite(si, New XFException(si, ex))
44             End Try
45         End Function
46     End Class
47 End Namespace
```

Running the Script

A simple Member Dialog parameter driving Entity to a single, Planner-selected state, as part of a Custom Calculate Data Management step, is the foundation of calculation scope limitation. The below Member Dialog states parameter will be referenced in the Data Management step's Entity filter as `|!E#States!|`.

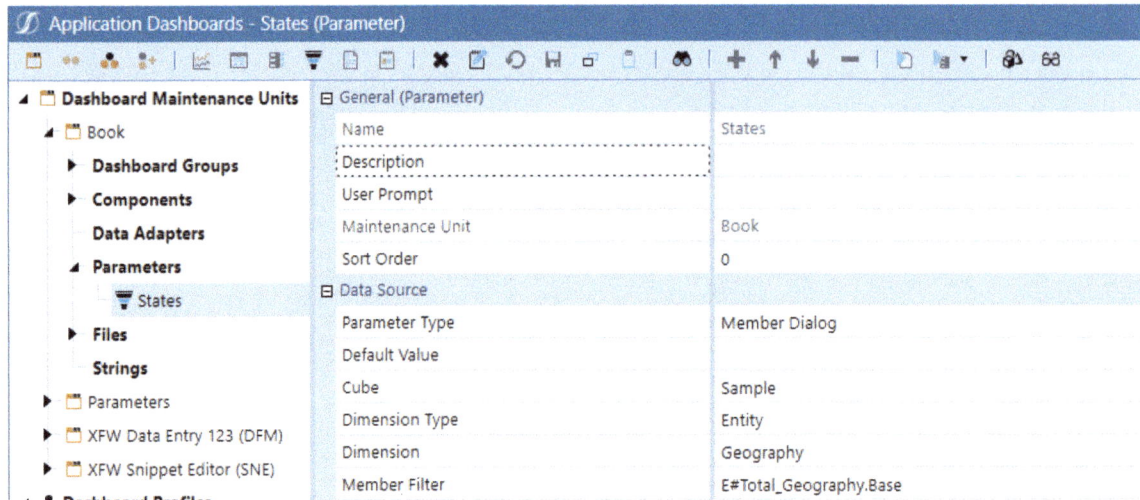

Figure 1.28

When the Data Management Step is executed, a Member dialog box appears, requiring the Planner to select a state.

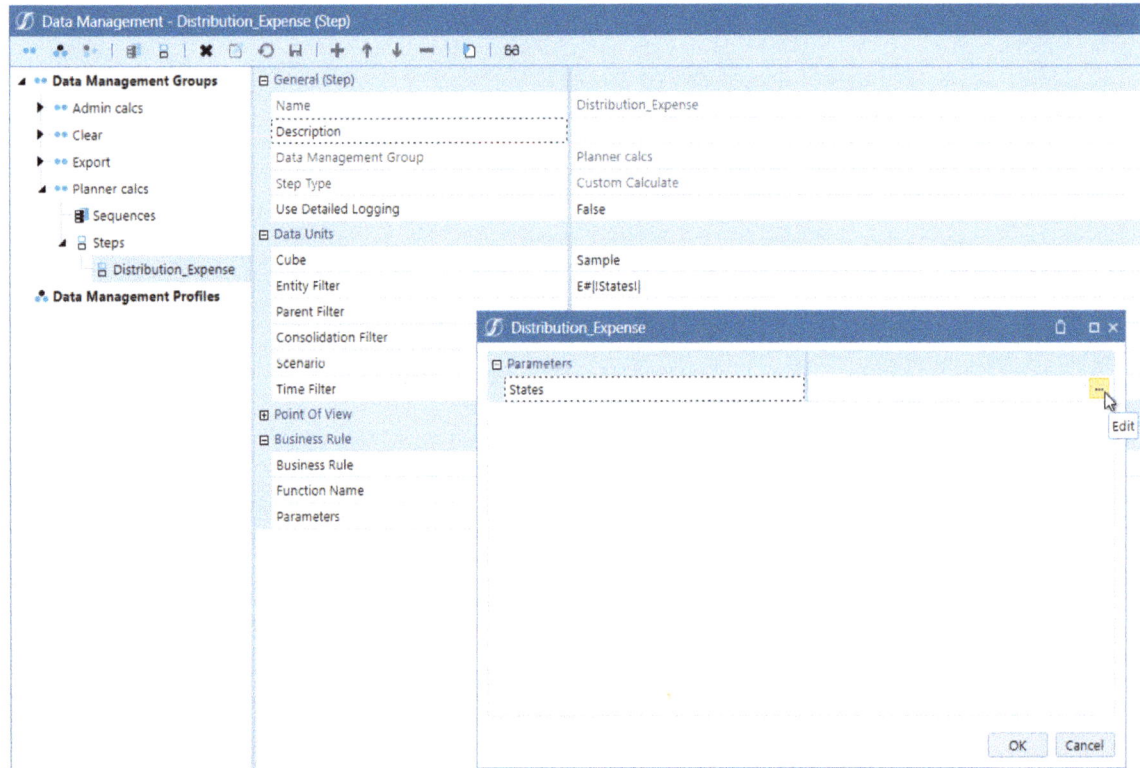

Figure 1.29

By clicking on the ellipsis, the Select Member dialog box appears. When the Planner selects Pennsylvania and then confirms by clicking OK to select the Entity and then OK again to confirm the Entity Member selection, the Data Management step runs the `DistributionExpense` Finance Business Rule. The scope of that calculation will be Pennsylvania-only.

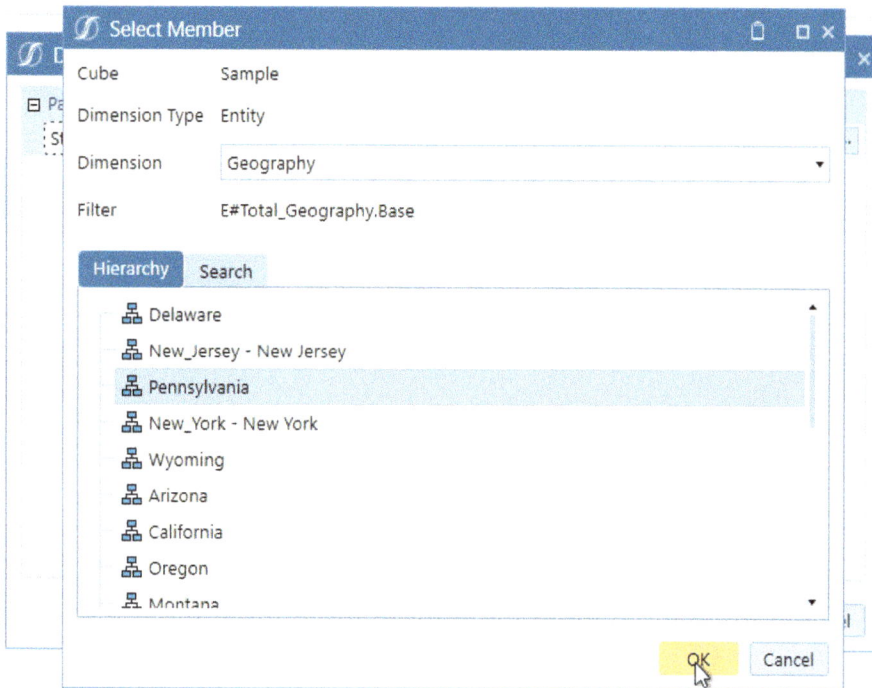

Figure 1.30

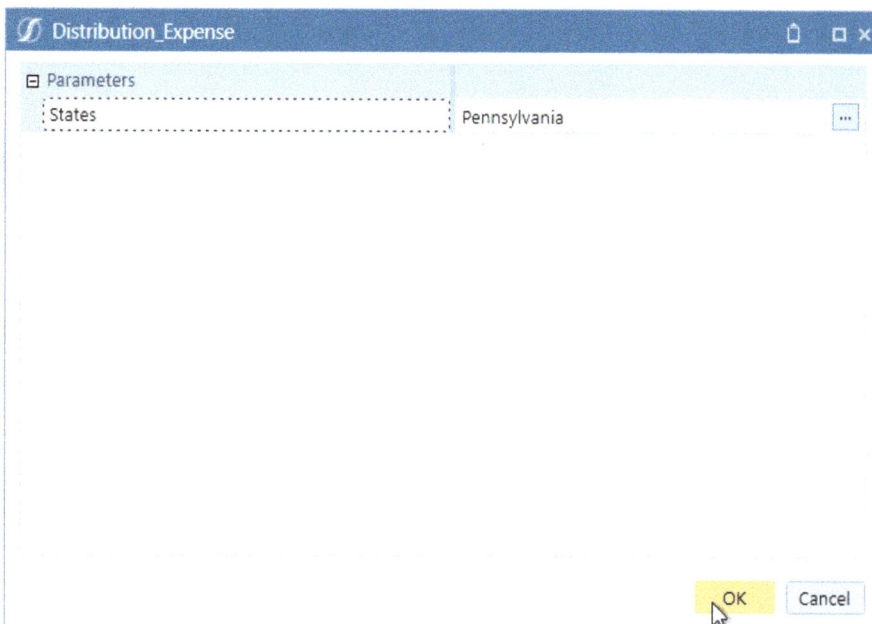

Figure 1.31

Only Pennsylvania is valued.

	A	B	C	D	E
1			Sales	Sales	Sales
2			Jan 2018	Feb 2018	Mar 2018
3	Pennsylvania	Cameron's 100% Colombian Whole Bean	11,573.00	6,958.00	6,499.00
4	Pennsylvania	Celvin's Colombian Supremo Regular Whole Bean	13,670.00	6,205.00	6,637.00
5	South Carolina	Cameron's 100% Colombian Whole Bean	14,917.00	12,122.00	13,185.00
6	South Carolina	Celvin's Colombian Supremo Regular Whole Bean	9,607.00	10,978.00	6,615.00
7					
8					
9					
10			Distribution_Rate	Distribution_Rate	Distribution_Rate
11			Jan 2018	Feb 2018	Mar 2018
12	No_Geography	No_Product	0.03	0.06	0.07
13					
14					
15					
16			Distribution	Distribution	Distribution
17			Jan 2018	Feb 2018	Mar 2018
18	Pennsylvania	Cameron's 100% Colombian Whole Bean	347.19	417.48	454.93
19	Pennsylvania	Celvin's Colombian Supremo Regular Whole Bean	410.10	372.30	464.59
20	South Carolina	Cameron's 100% Colombian Whole Bean			
21	South Carolina	Celvin's Colombian Supremo Regular Whole Bean			
22					
23			347.19	417.48	454.93
24			410.1	372.3	=E4*E$12

Figure 1.32

Custom Calculate is the Way

Limiting scope prevents unneeded calculations from occurring, returns results faster to Planners, and can be expanded or restricted to a desired dimensional range as required. The combination of Parameters, Custom Calculate Data Management steps, and Finance Business Rules limits that scope. Use this approach to speed Planning calculations.

Extend those Dimensions

When **Extensibility** was first mentioned in the initial Administrator Level 1 OneStream training, the comic book superhero character "Mr. Fantastic" came immediately to mind. The image of engineer Reed Richards stretching his arms and body to save people in danger works as a metaphor for Extensible dimensionality as that is what "Extensibility" is (the ability to stretch Dimensions and use cases, not the ability to save lives). Extensibility can extend OneStream Planning applications in ways legacy software cannot.

Dimensional Extensibility

A typical candidate for dimensional Extensibility is regional Planning that requires a lower level of Product detail in the Plan Scenario versus the Actual Scenario with the idea being that – in the case of the C&C Coffee Company – processing byproducts are sold onto other manufacturers, thus driving the production plan.

OneStream's Extensibility seamlessly supports this requirement of differing levels of dimensional detail.

UD1 Product

In this example, the `UD1` Products Dimension is extended to `ByProducts`.

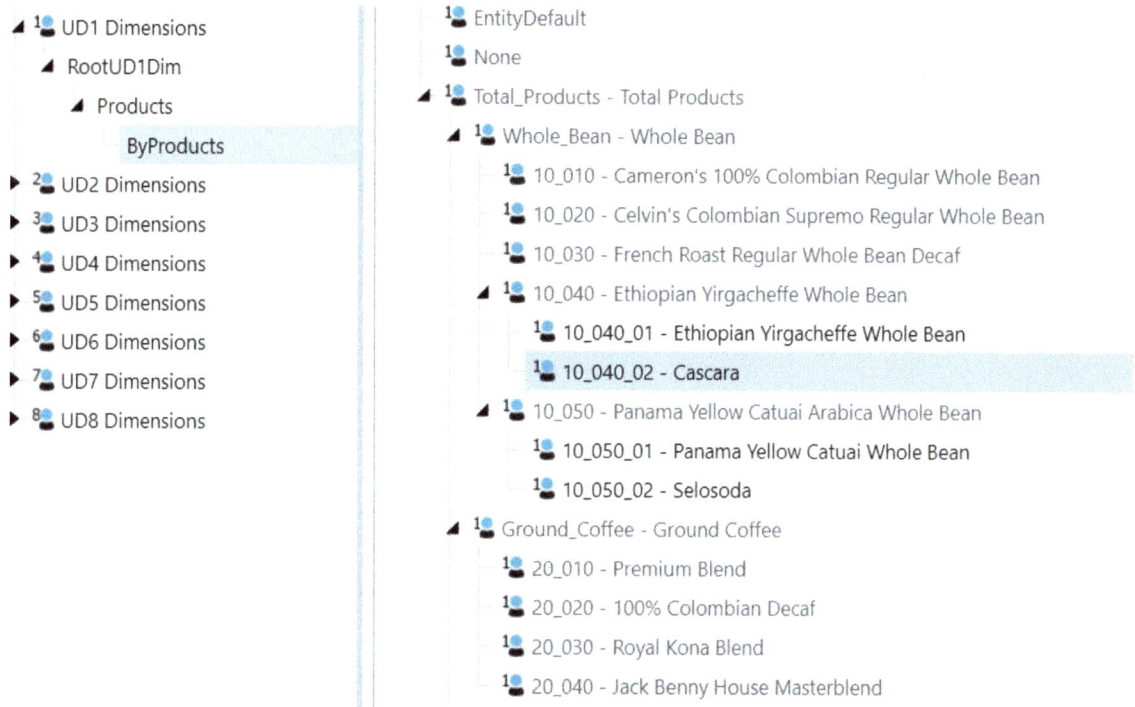

Figure 1.33

Extending the Cube

The Actual Scenario is not extended on the `UD1` Products Dimension.

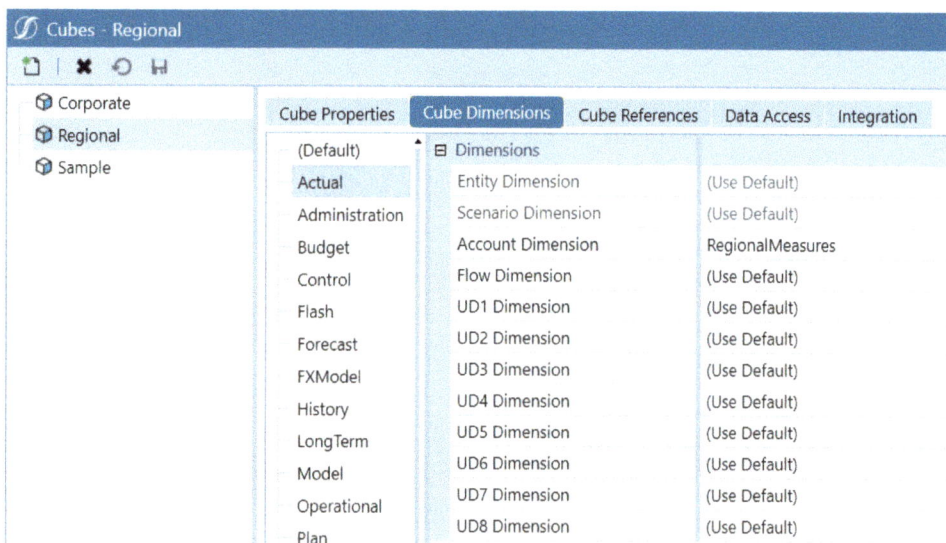

Figure 1.34

The Plan Scenario's `UD1` Dimension is extended to the lower detail level `Byproducts` Dimension.

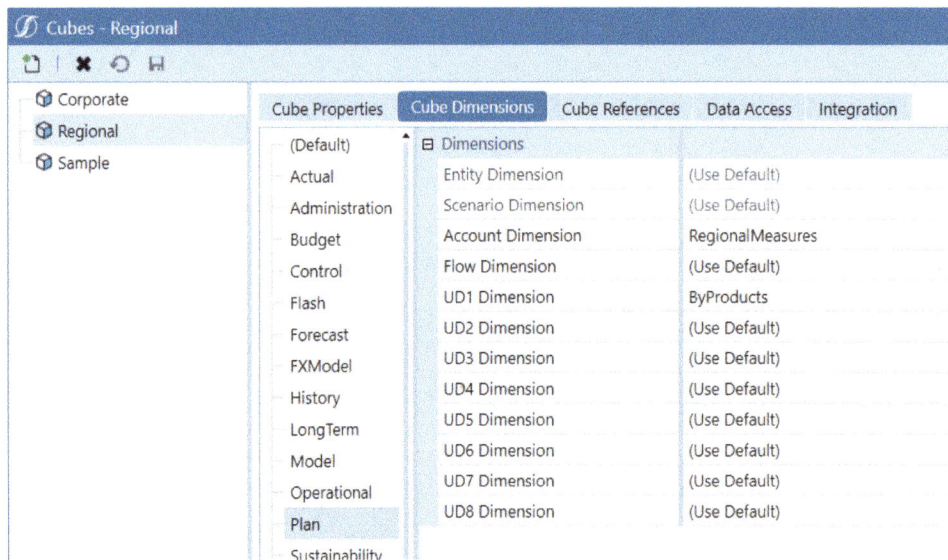

Figure 1.35

Extensibility in Practice

The Actual Scenario allows input at the Product level.

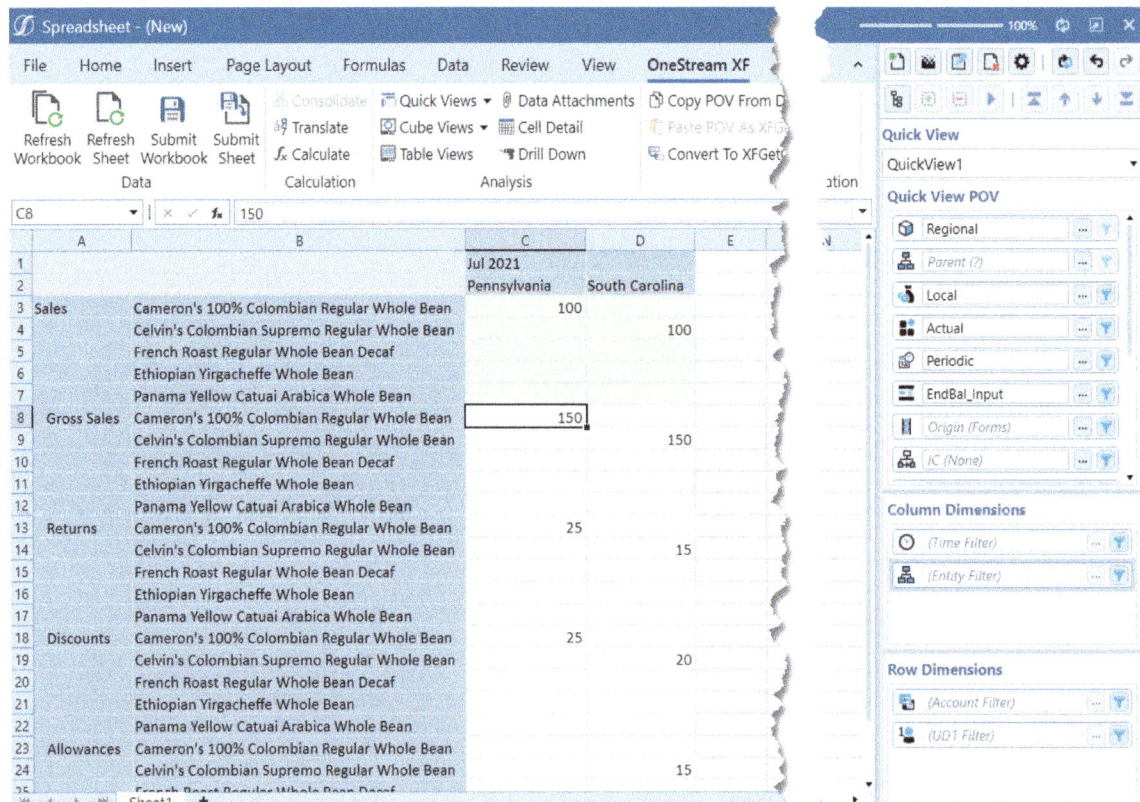

Figure 1.36

The Plan Scenario allows input at the Byproduct level for *Ethiopian Whole Bean* and *Panama Yellow Catuai*. The plan's byproduct detail has been extended below Actual's products while allowing Aggregation to Actual's product level.

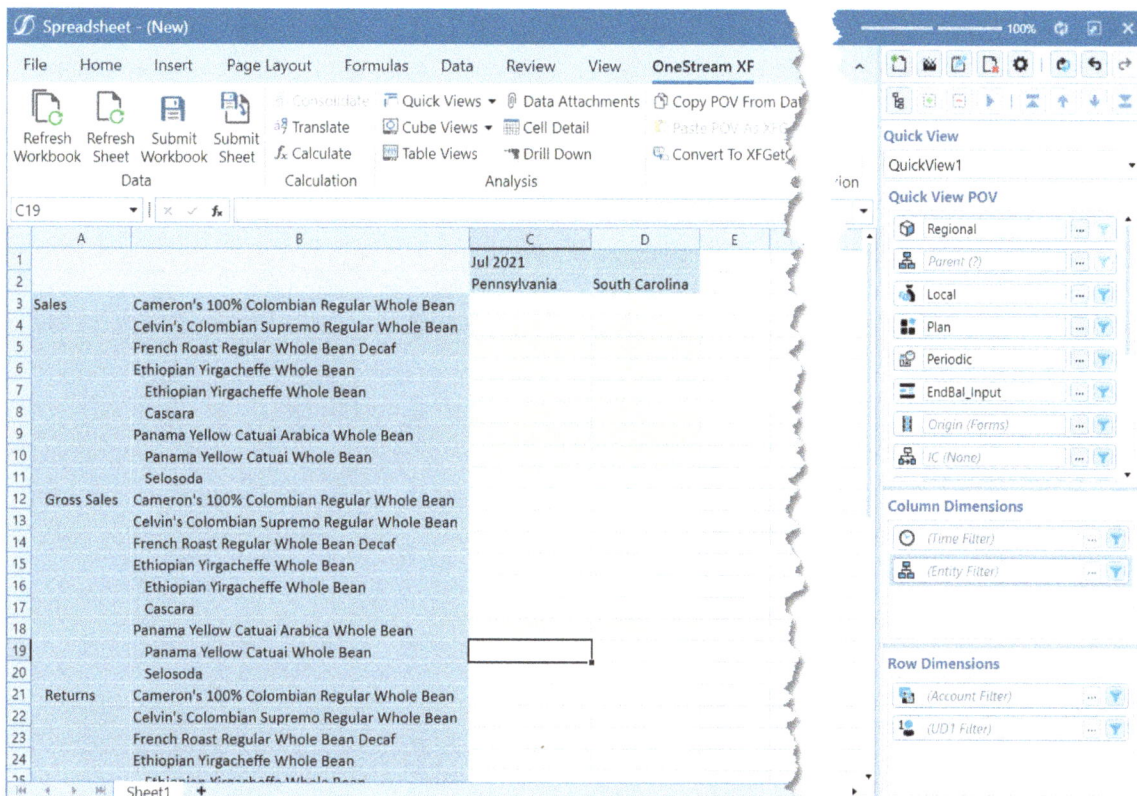

Figure 1.37

Extensibility Everywhere

Although this principle discusses Extensible Dimensions, one should not forget that Extensibility is part of the core product philosophy. There are Extensible documents, extended Cubes via Extensible Entity Dimensions, Member properties (aka varying Member properties), and Workflows. Planning applications that take advantage of Extensibility reduce application complexity while increasing flexibility. Its definition is simple, code-free, and powerful. Use it when you can.

FP&A Live in Excel. Deal with It

You, Gentle Reader, will and may have already built a wonderful, flexible, highly performant OneStream Planning application that brings together driver-based Planning, the flexibility of Specialty Planning, traffic-lighted Cube Views within Dashboards, and a sophisticated Workflow that drives data loads, input, calculation, and reporting. In short, this application will be, or is, OneStream Done Right, and yet the Planners submit data from Quick Views not Import, Direct Load Row, or Direct Load Blob, perform their reporting in Excel sheets linked to Quick View retrieves or via XFGetCell formulas instead of Reports, and in general spend as much time as possible outside of the OneStream client. What went wrong? Did anything go wrong?

Excel's Central Role

Simply put, FP&A's world revolves around Excel. Irrespective of OneStream's merits as a Planning and Budgeting tool, Excel is a source and transformer of data, a calculation engine, a database, a reporting tool, and the *lingua franca* of finance.

If the primacy of Excel is such – and it is – then we must accept that a OneStream application can support, supplement, and drive Excel usage for Planning and Budgeting but never replace it. A OneStream application and its implementation that ignores FP&A's desires and needs is a failed one.

Supported, but Arguably Tangential

Static exports of Cube Views to Excel and the incorporation of limited reporting datasets within Office via Extensible Documents are avenues of understanding and distributing OneStream data in Excel but are not the locus of OneStream and Excel – that role is served by the OneStream Excel add-in.

Missing in Action

The key, then, is to understand what is lost when a Planner goes outside of OneStream, what attracts usage within the OneStream client, and when they must use it because that functionality cannot be replicated within Excel proper.

At the time of writing this book (the fall of 2021), the following OneStream client functions are not supported in Excel:

1. Asymmetric retrieves

2. Workflow

3. Dashboards

4. Data Management sequences to launch Custom Calculate Business Rules

5. Table Views

Mitigating the Missing

Asymmetric Retrieves

Asymmetric retrieves are the ability to restrict nested Dimensions to irregular rows and columns. An example is a Q1 Report with Actual months January and February in columns B and C and Plan month March in column D.

Ad Hoc

Neither the Excel add-in nor the OneStream Spreadsheet tool support this in ad-hoc mode. A simple solution to this approach is to use Excel's hide column functionality. OneStream respects the hide function when drilling down/up. In the example below, column D's Actual March is hidden as are Plan January and February in columns E and F.

	A	B	C	G	H
1		Actual	Actual	Plan	
2		Jan 2018	Feb 2018	Mar 2018	Q1
3	Profit	140	139	145	424
4	Margin	185	185	182	552
5	Sales	130	130	122	382
6	COGS	55	55	60	170
7	Total Expenses	45	46	37	128
8	Marketing	18	18	10	46
9	Payroll	27	27	27	81

Figure 1.38

Cube Views

Cube Views provide asymmetrical column and row functionality through nested Dimension selectors. Cube Views are generally not a User-created OneStream artifact.

Doing It in Quick Views

Member Filters in Quick Views (and Cube Views) can create unique Member tuples (data values' cross-dimensional intersections) using the colon cross-dimensional indicator. Delimited lists of these dimensional selections can be used in a Member Filter. The Time and Scenario Member list…

```
T#2018M1:S#Actual, T#2018M2:S#Actual, T#2018M3:S#Plan
```

…in the column Member Filter Builder…

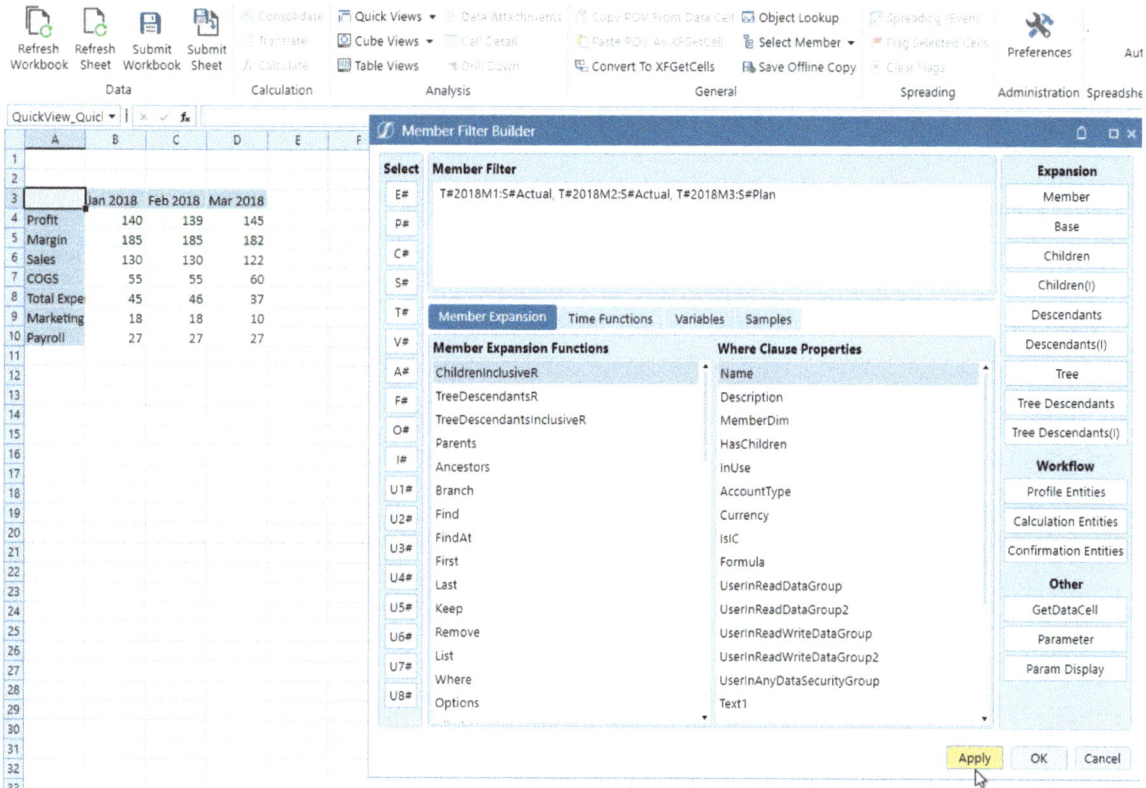

Figure 1.39

…results in an asymmetric retrieve without hidden columns.

	A	B	C	D	E
1					
2		Actual	Actual	Plan	Total
3		Jan 2018	Feb 2018	Mar 2018	Q1
4	Profit	140	139	145	424
5	Margin	185	185	182	552
6	Sales	130	130	122	382
7	COGS	55	55	60	170
8	Total Expenses	45	46	37	128
9	Marketing	18	18	10	46
10	Payroll	27	27	27	81

Figure 1.40

Custom Excel-only labels in the second row provide reporting context. Column E is an illustration of the flexibility Excel offers as it is a quarter total of different Scenarios, an analysis not natively available in OneStream.

Workflow

Excel ignores Form-level Workflow completion or Workflow locking for both Users and Administrators; only full Workflow Certification will lock data in QuickViews and XFSetCell formulas. One of OneStream's advantages is its control over data; if a Planner or Administrator can go outside of Workflow's restrictions that data quality may be lost.

Here is a Cube View with Complete Form Workflow selected. Within Workflow, all periods are read-only:

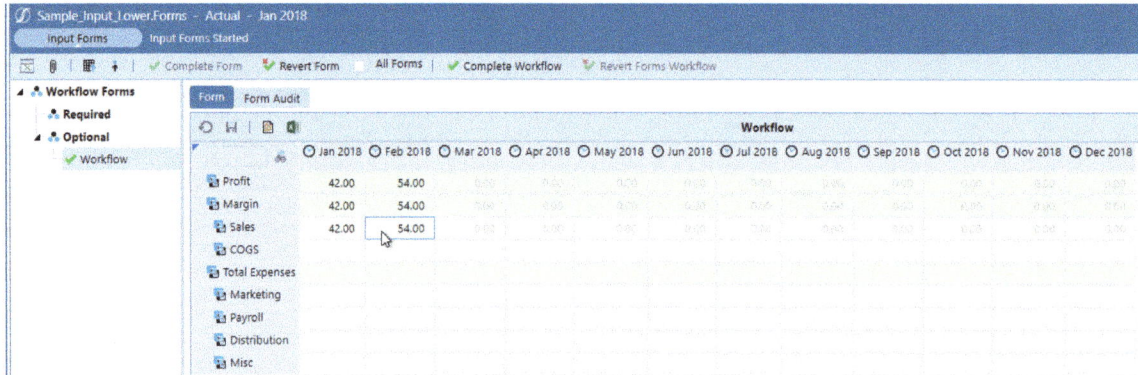

Figure 1.41

All periods are read/write in a Quick View.

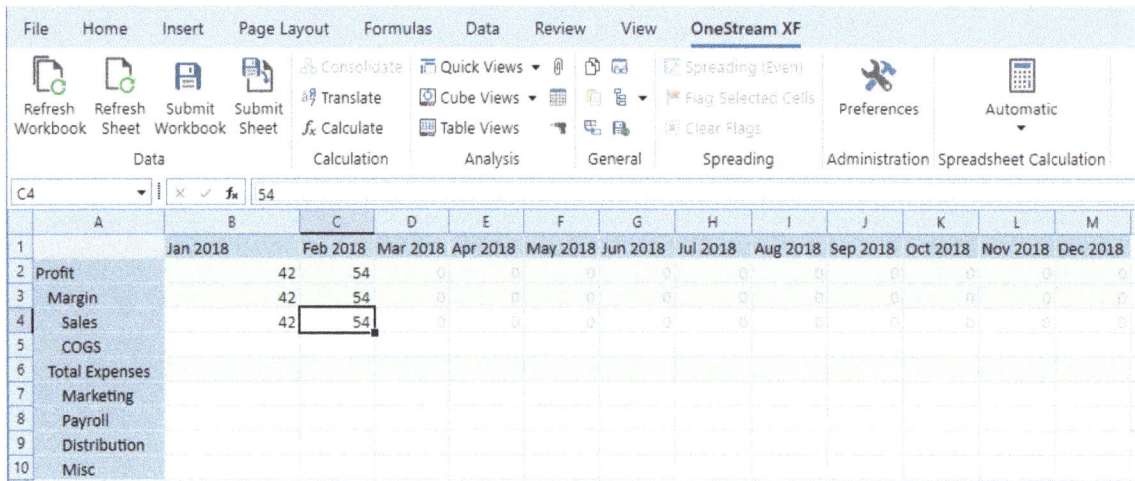

Figure 1.42

What to Do?
Without full Workflow Certification, Excel (and the OneStream Spreadsheet) ignores Form-level Workflow completion and locking. Given this, the only practical recourse is to design so that Form-based Workflow is irrelevant. Happily, within the context of a Planning application that addresses multiple Time periods (e.g., months within a year, year over year, etc.), closing down input for all Forecast Time periods is not required and, in fact, does not make sense.

However, what is required is preventing access to closed Actual periods. **Conditional Input** or the **No Input Periods Per Workflow Unit** property will stop the load, calculation, and input of data in any closed data intersection. In the case of closed periods within a Workflow, these typically take the form of Actual months within a Range Workflow as the sole Method to close periods. Conditional Input also works within the framework of a monthly Actual Workflow.

See the *Strives For Greatness, but Never Quite Makes It* and *On No Condition* sections of the *Core Planning II* chapter for more information on the pros and cons of Conditional Input and No Input Periods.

Going Around Excel. Maybe

Excel does not in any way support Data Management sequences, Table Views, Pivot Grids, or Dashboards. If you want to run context-aware (or not) Custom Calculate Business Rules, view or analyze relational data, or surround Forms and Reports with a rich User Interface, the Excel add-in simply does not and cannot support your needs.

The Spreadsheet

However, every one of these functions *are* supported in, or are used by, the Spreadsheet within the OneStream client. While the Spreadsheet is not Excel, it does largely support Excel functionality and reads and writes Excel Workbooks. Form and Report Spreadsheets must reside in a Dashboard no matter how simple, and once a Dashboard is used, Combo boxes, Buttons, and Data Management sequences are available, as are Table Views and Pivot Grids.

The option to bring Excel functionality into a OneStream application provides three potential Excel use cases: exclusion, co-option, and support.

Forbidden

A slice of a Consultant's life. I (Cameron) once had a somewhat surprising conversation with a fellow OneStreamer in a client conference room (to non-Consultants who believe we live and work in the very lap of luxury, this was a conference room turned storage closet for old IT equipment turned, partially, back into a very crowded and uncomfortable conference room) who strenuously said, "Nooooo, we never give Users the OneStream add-in." He was wrong – the client demanded and got it. Denying FP&A their number one tool is a non-starter.

Supplanted

The Spreadsheet's functionality fully supports a rich OneStream User Experience within a structured framework of providing high data quality (access via Workflow, the correct Members are selected every time, and an automatic refresh of data on opening) input and reporting. Given the oft-times superior performance and customization possible in the Spreadsheet, when compared to traditional Cube Views, one could argue that the Spreadsheet should be *the* only (or close to the only) User Interface within OneStream.

Benefits aside, the fact remains that the Spreadsheet is not Excel in its flexibility or ability to link to outside data sources. Although we have no insight into OneStream's product management group, we believe that its use case is as an alternative for structured interaction with OneStream data, but not as a replacement for Excel.

Accommodated

If denying the add-in's existence and replacing Excel entirely via the Spreadsheet are not acceptable approaches in FP&A's eyes, then the only possible approach is blending the core OneStream client and Excel.

Administrative Dashboards

Perhaps the most keenly felt Excel add-in feature gap is the inability to run Data Management sequences that execute Custom Calculate Finance Business Rules. A failure to run the required rules will inevitably result in incorrect data. As highlighted in the Custom Calculate section of this chapter, the ability to run focused calculations that impact only relevant slices of a OneStream Cube is key to performance.

The answer to calculated data quality issues is to instead create simple administrative Dashboards that allow Planners to quickly select relevant parameterized (the Planner can select Dimension Members as driven by parameters, XFBR Business Rules, or security) Finance Business Rules through simple Dashboard buttons. Once the model of enter and analyze in Excel, and calculate via Dashboards is adopted, Planners enjoy both the flexibility of Excel and the power of OneStream.

Input

If Planners have access to the Excel add-in, they can submit data to a OneStream Cube. There may be edge use cases where perhaps Excel is the only suitable vehicle for input in OneStream, (e.g., Workbooks that contain extensive links to external Workbooks or the incorporation of non-OneStream external data), but as noted these are unusual data requirements, not common.

OneStream Cube Views are robust, dynamic, centrally managed, and tightly controlled data input schedules. They can be directly imported into Excel as live data artifacts. Use them whenever a standard view of data is required.

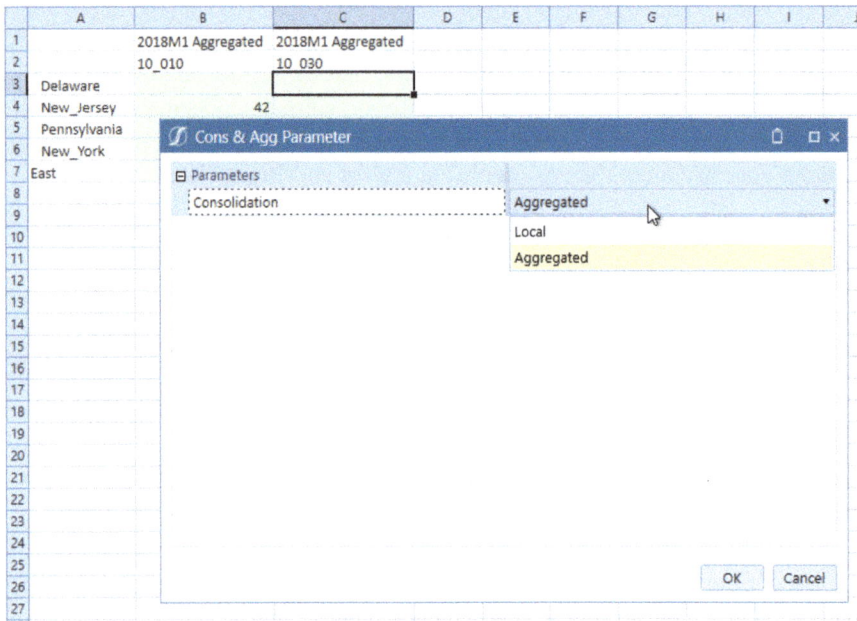

Figure 1.43

An even better practice is incorporating Cube Views into the OneStream Spreadsheet because it melds Excel flexibility, Cube View structure, and Dashboard controls.

This example Dashboard hides the Spreadsheet ribbons, has a Save button, an Aggregate button, and Consolidation dropdown that toggles between Local and Aggregated.

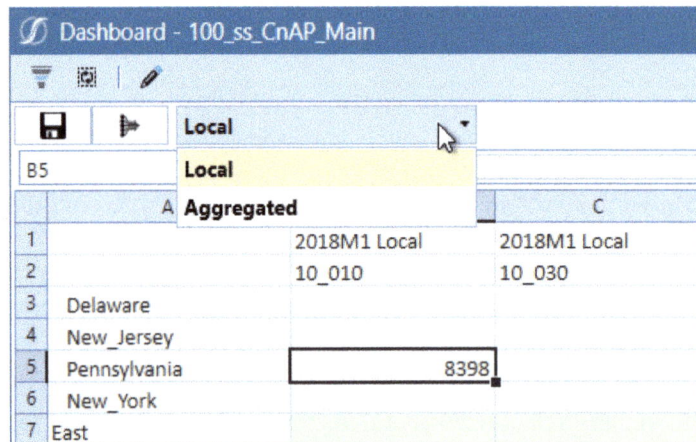

Figure 1.44

While this Dashboard may not be enough to wean Planners wholly away from Excel, it provides an avenue to a more structured data entry path.

Reporting is not an either/or situation. OneStream is the source for standard, highly formatted standard Reports; Excel is the home of ad-hoc querying and custom reports. A good practice is to survey Planners on an occasional basis to understand their custom reporting requirements as there may be an opportunity to incorporate those Excel Workbooks as a standard Report for all.

Having Dealt with It, Move On

Excel must surely be FP&A's most used software. It will not be abandoned in the face of even the best OneStream implementation there ever was or will be. OneStream is an amazing platform that extends and transforms the forecasting power of FP&A. Neither is in opposition; both are complementary. Incorporating Excel's flexibility with OneStream's power is key to Planner adoption and advocacy, as well as the fullest and best use of your OneStream application. Find that balance by supporting your Planners in Excel and in OneStream. FP&A will love you for it.

Blend is Not a Cube. Choose Wisely

Analyzing large datasets becomes challenging within a Cube because multidimensional Cube architecture and navigation fails when data and Dimension size becomes very large. Vendors have identified that functionality gap, and – in response – there are many products (open source ones as well) that can consume "Big Data" and produce pretty Dashboards in a matter of seconds. Your authors were fortunate enough to work with an innovative small start-up company whose product's flexibility, scalability, and User-friendliness just blew our collective geek minds with its awesomeness. The race was on, and as an answer to this, OneStream's BI Blend was born.

If It's Not a Cube, Just What is It?

BI Blend is not a Cube. It uses a robust columnar database as its back end, and analysis is performed using Pivot Grids – not OneStream's Cube interface in the form of Cube Views, Quick Views, XFBooks, and XFGetCell formulas.

BI Blend is not a Cube replacement. It is, instead, a tool to analyze larger volumes of data that cannot be contained within a traditional OneStream Cube. BI Blend supports more dimensionality – 32 in total – to a Cube's 17.

Pivot Grids are not Meant for Cubes

If your application's Users expect BI Blend to mimic a traditional Cube User Interface, you must disabuse them of that notion because, while they appear to be the same on the surface, their functionality is different and will be perceived that way by Users.

As a real-world example of failing to educate, we used BI Blend to satisfy a daily Cube snapshot requirement, confident that the flexibility and performance of BI Blend would overcome any differences in functionality. We were overconfident.

Failure, but Whose?

Instead of our prediction of User adoption, the Planners found BI Blend's Pivot Grids hard to use in the absence of the financial intelligence and the Cube/Quick View User Interface. This was **not** a product failure but more a compound failure of functional requirements analysis, client expectation setting, and technical implementation. BI Blend was (and is) likely the only reasonable way to get to this scope of data. However, once the introduction was botched, User acceptance was lost.

Ours

At the beginning of this chapter, we noted that we have made every possible mistake a Consultant can make which, alas, is demonstrably not true; this is just the latest. The lesson, then, is to be sure to educate the application owner, Administrators, and Users of BI Blend's purpose and usage before implementing.

The Choice is Yours

With that caveat, if your Planners want to analyze very large datasets and are comfortable with pivot tables, then BI Blend is your answer.

If you want to perform data slicing and dicing, and have financial intelligence, and in general have something that is not a Cube behave just like a Cube, then it is not.

Choose wisely.

Specialty Planning

Relational Artefacts

Specialty Planning is all about SQL tables and views. Whether these tables are in a cloud instance, or on-premise, there are a few naming conventions your application should use.

OneStream's current naming standard recommendation is to use `XFC_` as a table prefix when you create custom Specialty solutions. The prior practice was to use `XFW_` as a table prefix for all custom tables, but this leads to confusion with OneStream's Specialty solutions that are prefixed with `XFW_`.

OneStream Objects

When creating a custom solution (think of Celvin's MindStream Metadata Manager), it is good practice to use a consistently applied solution name (a three-letter or four-letter word) when naming Dashboard objects, Business Rules, and all other OneStream Components linked to the solution.

If you are terrible at creative naming, then there is a high probability that you will attempt to name (and be prevented from doing) objects with the same nomenclature in many Dashboard units. If the solution name is used as prefix or suffix, you will never run out of names because they help define name uniqueness.

As an example, TDM is a MarketPlace solution that stands for "Table Data Manager" that (unsurprisingly) manages custom tables through a User Interface to create, alter, import, and export data and schemas. Within OneStream, TDM's objects end with `_TDM`. TDM's role will be expanded further in the *Specialty Planning Solution vs. a Custom Solution* section in *Planning Without Limits*. If the vendor uses this naming convention to organize OneStream objects, we should as well.

Bringing It All Together

Despite the very first principle's admonition that there are no *best* practices, we can at least be sure that there are *good* practices; this chapter contains many but not all of them.

Despite that incompleteness, the ones listed here – both Soft and Hard – are vital to a OneStream Planning application's success.

When approaching a Planning application, we practitioners must appreciate that we cannot know everything there is to know about this sophisticated product, that overly complex applications fail (either in their implementation or their maintenance), and that our historical practice knowledge is valuable.

Technical design principles are just as important to application success:

- Aggregations and Direct Loads are faster than traditional Consolidations and Imports.

- Finance Business Rules executed via Custom Calculate Data Management steps perform quickly, touch less data, and are more flexible than Cube-attached rules or stored formulas.

- Dimensional Extensibility should be exploited where possible.

- FP&A's love and use of Excel will never go away.

- BI Blend differs from the traditional Cube.

The 10 principles in this chapter are not exhaustive and instead are limited by space and time – your experience will evince other ones as your experience grows. Learn from your mistakes and observations – as your authors have from theirs – and your OneStream Planning applications will thrive. Ignore them at your own peril. Choose wisely. Have fun.

2

Core Planning I – Data and Calculations

The Very Heart of OneStream Planning

The foundation of Planning in OneStream is the Cube. The power of Cube Planning is in its calculations. Writing effective code requires a deep understanding of the OneStream data architecture and Finance Business Rule Engine. Code must be written in a clear, concise, comprehensible, and reusable manner.

This Core I chapter covers these fundamental concepts through concrete examples that provide solutions to common Planning needs and the reasons behind the solutions to those use cases. As always, your authors attempt to explain the *why* in addition to the *how*. If you, Gentle Reader, understand the reasons behind OneStream's functionality, you will be able to expand upon this chapter's scope in your real-world applications.

The primary topics of Data and Calculations are intertwined in this chapter, as both necessarily depend on each other.

Data covers how OneStream really stores data and the impact on application performance, how to remove unnecessary data from both the data fact tables and within Finance Business Rules, and lastly, the surprising behavior of the Level 2 Data Unit.

Calculations describes the scope of data buffers, reviews different approaches to calculating data within data buffers, reveals how to smash through the calculation limitations of the Level 1 Data Unit, defines the importance of code style and commenting, and lastly, reviews how to significantly reduce coding effort and enhance reusability.

Any one of the sections can be read separately; all are important and deserve your attention.

The Riddle of the Data

How OneStream stores data is key to understanding how Finance Business Rules work, what makes them slow or fast, and how we must write them in a performant manner. The foundation of efficient code – the very foundation of OneStream itself – is its storage architecture. A OneStream SQL Server database without MarketPlace solutions or custom tables has (as of version 6.5) over 400 tables and 12 views. To the User, and even the developer, these database objects are, for the most part, irrelevant as they are abstracted by the OneStream Engine and User Interface. Regardless, they exist, and close examination of their storage schemas informs good code practice.

How Does OneStream Store Numeric Data?

Numeric Cube data is stored by year in 105 fully normalized fact tables from `DataRecord1996` to `DataRecord2100`. Each record contains the metadata and data for all stored data, including upper-level Entity Dimension Members. Dynamic Dimensions such as User-Defined, Account, and Flow are not stored above the Base level.

Just One Number

Real

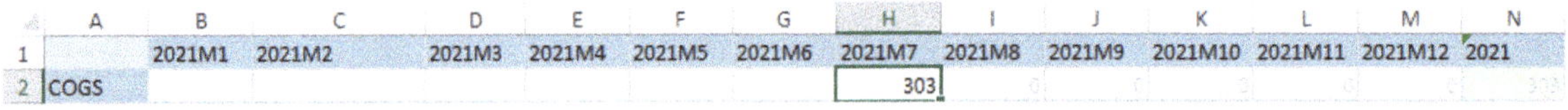

	A	B	C	D	E	F	G	H	I	J	K	L	M	N
1		2021M1	2021M2		2021M3	2021M4	2021M5	2021M6	2021M7	2021M8	2021M9	2021M10	2021M11	2021M12	2021
2	COGS								303	0					

Figure 2.1

This Quick View has just one number within an otherwise completely empty Plan Scenario. Note that the cells before 2021M7 are blank and the ones after show grayed out 0s. By right-clicking on cell H2, and selecting the OneStream pop-up Cell Status, we can see that the Cell Status has a Cell Amount of 303.00, Is Real Data, is not Derived Data, and its Storage Type is Input (Forms).

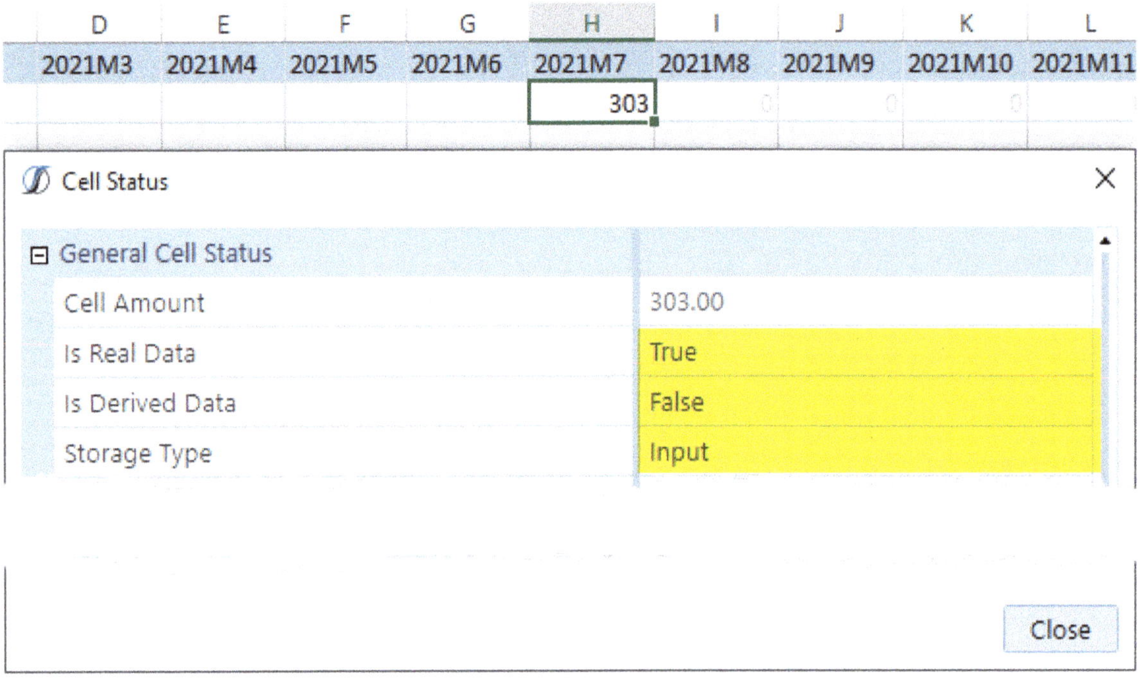

D	E	F	G	H	I	J	K	L
2021M3	2021M4	2021M5	2021M6	2021M7	2021M8	2021M9	2021M10	2021M11
				303	0	0	0	

Cell Status ✕

General Cell Status

Cell Amount	303.00
Is Real Data	True
Is Derived Data	False
Storage Type	Input

Close

Figure 2.2

This seems reasonable: there is a number there (your author typed it in himself) which makes it as real as a number in OneStream can be.

NoData

The same exercise in cell G2, shows that the Amount NoData cell is not Real Data, is not Derived Data, and its Storage Type is NotStored. As with the 303 data value in cell H2, this seems reasonable because no data has been entered in 2021M6.

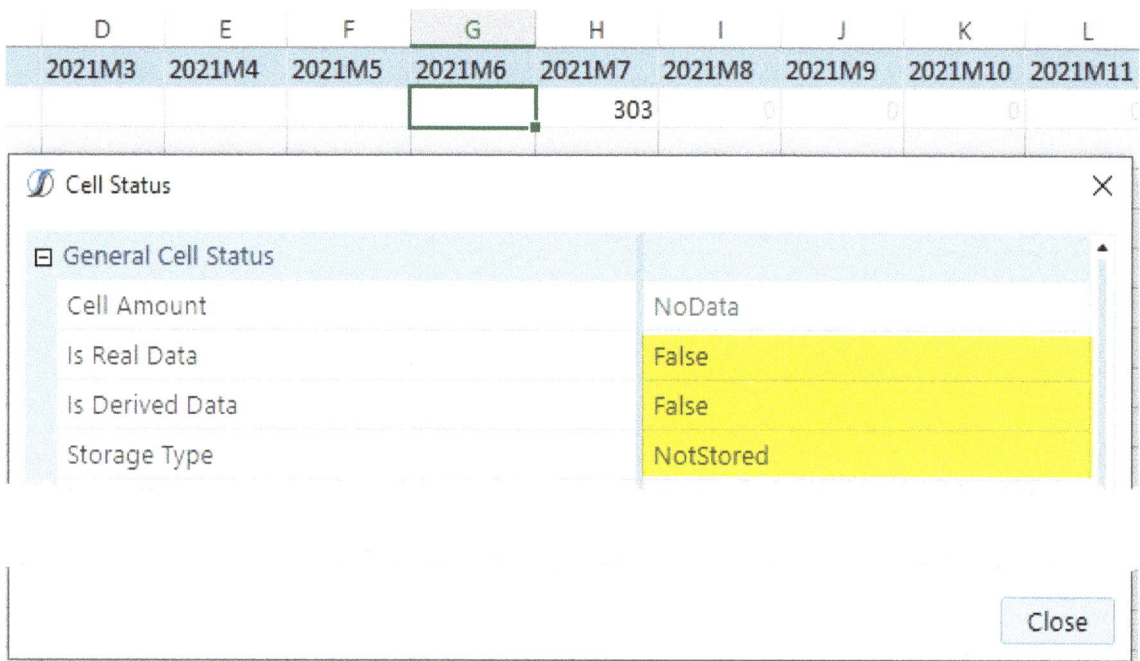

D	E	F	G	H	I	J	K	L
2021M3	2021M4	2021M5	2021M6	2021M7	2021M8	2021M9	2021M10	2021M11
				303	0	0	0	0

Cell Status ✕

⊟ General Cell Status

Cell Amount	NoData
Is Real Data	False
Is Derived Data	False
Storage Type	NotStored

Close

Figure 2.3

Derived

NoData and Real are self-explanatory; the data is not stored at all, or it is stored. Derived is not quite as straightforward because it is data that is *and* is not there.

Is it?

The zeros in cells I2 through M2 indicate that *something* is there, but what? If the View Dimension POV Member is changed from Periodic to YTD, the suggestion that data values *are* stored for Derived Data is clearer.

	A	B	C	D	E	F	G	H	I	J	K	L	M	N
1		2021M1	2021M2	2021M3	2021M4	2021M5	2021M6	2021M7	2021M8	2021M9	2021M10	2021M11	2021M12	2021
2	COGS							303						303
3														
4		2021M1	2021M2	2021M3	2021M4	2021M5	2021M6	2021M7	2021M8	2021M9	2021M10	2021M11	2021M12	2021
5	COGS							303	303	303	303	303	303	303

Figure 2.4

Cells I5 through M5 now show a grayed-out 303. Again, this seems logical; a real value of 303 exists in 2021M7, so YTD 2021M8 through 2021M12 should also show the same if they contain no additional data.

Checking cell I5's Cell Status shows that 2021M8 is not Real Data, Is Derived Data, and its Storage Type is NotStored; the same is true for M5.

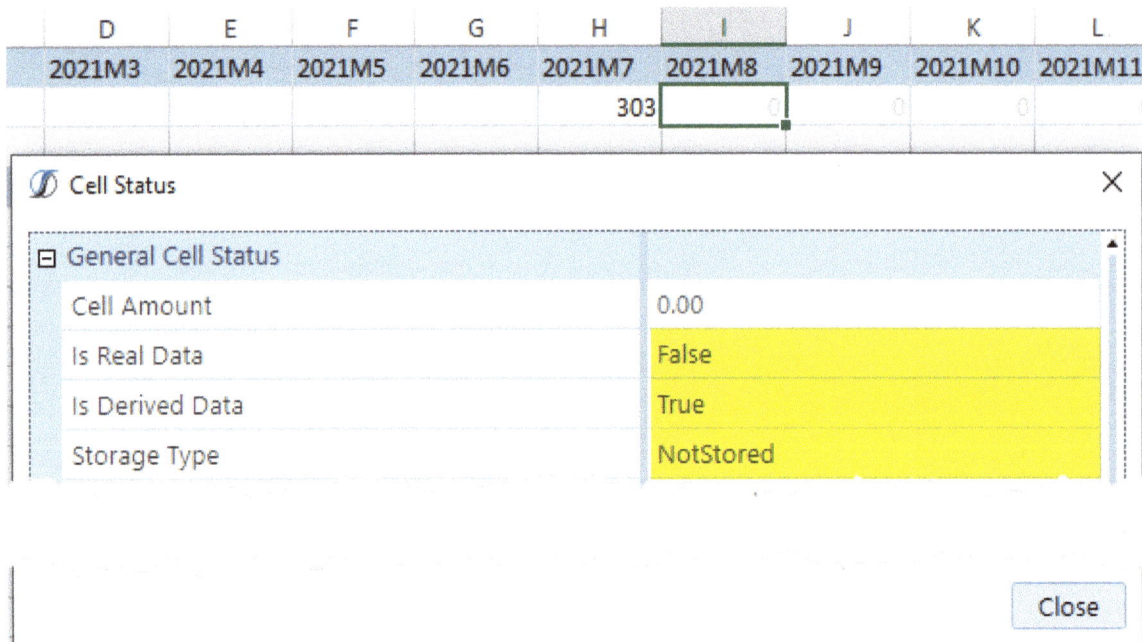

	D	E	F	G	H	I	J	K	L
	2021M3	2021M4	2021M5	2021M6	2021M7	2021M8	2021M9	2021M10	2021M11
					303		0	0	0

Cell Status ✕

General Cell Status	
Cell Amount	0.00
Is Real Data	False
Is Derived Data	True
Storage Type	NotStored

Close

Figure 2.5

It is

Examining the application's raw fact table `DataRecord2021` shows that a 0 is stored in the M6Value field and prior months, 303 is stored in the M7Value field, and 303 is stored in M8Value and beyond. *All* of the months are valued with either 0 (NoData) or 303 for both (Real Data) and (Derived Data). A *single* data value has triggered the storage of 11 additional fields.

Note the M6Status, M7Status, and M8Status field values: 16, 33, and 18; they mirror the Cell Status shown above and can be used to quickly look at the status of all period data.

PartitionId	CubeId	EntityId	Pa		M6Value	M6Status	M7Value	M7Status	M8Value	M8Status	N
27	0	4194331		5	0	16	303	33	303	18	

Figure 2.6

From Normalized to Denormalized

OneStream's normalized fact tables are difficult to read. A simple query that joins to the Member data table makes the data tables easier to understand.

Denormalized DataRecords2021

```
-- Not all MnStatus fields are resolved
SELECT
    C.Name AS Cube
    , M.Name AS Entity
    --, D.ConsId
    , CASE
        WHEN D.ConsId = 176 THEN 'USD'
        WHEN D.ConsId = -18 THEN 'Cons/Agg'
        ELSE CAST(D.Consid AS CHAR)
    END AS Consolidation
    , M1.Name AS Scenario
    , D.YearId AS Year
    , M2.Name AS Account
    --, D.OriginId
    , CASE
```

```sql
      WHEN D.OriginId = -30 THEN 'Forms'
      WHEN D.OriginId = -999 THEN 'Import'
      ELSE CAST(D.OriginId AS CHAR)
    END AS Origin
  --, D.ICId
  , CASE
      WHEN D.ICid = -999 THEN 'None'
      ELSE CAST(D.ICId AS CHAR)
    END AS Intercompany
  , M3.Name AS Flow
  , M4.Name AS UD1
  , M1Status
  , M1Value
  , M2Status
  , M2Value
  , M3Status
  , M3Value
  , M4Status
  , M4Value
  , M5Status
  , M5Value
  --, M6Status
  , CASE
      WHEN D.M6Status = 16 THEN 'No Data'
      WHEN D.M6Status = 17 THEN 'Aggregated'
      WHEN D.M6Status = 18 THEN 'Derived'
      WHEN D.M6Status = 33 THEN 'Real'
      WHEN D.M6Status = 97 THEN 'Consolidated'
      WHEN D.M6Status = 145 THEN 'Calculated'
      ELSE CAST(D.M6Status AS CHAR)
    END AS M6Status
  , M6Value
  --, M7Status
  , CASE
      WHEN D.M7Status = 16 THEN 'No Data'
      WHEN D.M7Status = 17 THEN 'Aggregated'
      WHEN D.M7Status = 18 THEN 'Derived'
      WHEN D.M7Status = 33 THEN 'Real'
      WHEN D.M7Status = 97 THEN 'Consolidated'
      WHEN D.M7Status = 145 THEN 'Calculated'
      ELSE CAST(D.M7Status AS CHAR)
    END AS M7Status
  , M7Value
  --, M8Status
  , CASE
      WHEN D.M8Status = 16 THEN 'No Data'
      WHEN D.M8Status = 17 THEN 'Aggregated'
      WHEN D.M8Status = 18 THEN 'Derived'
      WHEN D.M8Status = 33 THEN 'Real'
      WHEN D.M8Status = 97 THEN 'Consolidated'
      WHEN D.M8Status = 145 THEN 'Calculated'
      ELSE CAST(D.M8Status AS CHAR)
    END AS M8Status
  , M8Value
  , M9Status
  , M9Value
  , M10Status
  , M10Value
  , M11Status
  , M11Value
  , M12Status
  , M12Value
FROM DataRecord2021 D
  INNER JOIN Cube C
  ON D.CubeId = C.CubeId
  INNER JOIN Member M
```

```
    ON D.EntityId = M.MemberId
    INNER JOIN Member M1
    ON D.ScenarioId = M1.MemberId
    INNER JOIN Member M2
    ON D.AccountId = M2.MemberId
    INNER JOIN Member M3
    ON D.FlowId = M3.MemberId
    INNER JOIN Member M4
    ON D.UD1Id = M4.MemberId
ORDER BY Entity, UD1, Account, Consolidation, Origin, Flow
```

> **Note:** Some fields, e.g., `ConsId`, `OriginId`, `ICid`, and `MnStatus`, are not found in the Member table and are empirically derived instead. Given the small data sample and limited data forms, there are undoubtedly other values, hence the `CASE ELSE` condition for those fields.

DataRecord2021 in Human Format

Cube	Entity	Consolidation	Scenario	Year	Account	Origin	Intercompany	Flow	UD1	M:	≛	M6Status	M6Value	M7Status	M7Value	M8Status	M8Value	I
Sample	South_Carolina	USD	Plan	2021	COGS	Forms	None	EndBal_Input	10_010		0	No Data	0	Real	303	Derived	303	

Figure 2.7

Beyond the Member names (Member contains descriptions as well), the record and the by-month data status are now clear, and the way that OneStream stores data is clear as well; if a single month of data exists, the prior NoData months are in fact *stored* with 0 values, and the future Derived months are *stored* with repeated YTD data values. One data value is actually twelve.

In the case of this example, the OneStream Quick View suppresses the display of those NoData months and, when the View Dimension is Periodic, backs out the stored YTD values for future months.

Beyond academic interest, why does any of this matter? The answer: **data buffer calculation efficiency**.

Doing the Mostest with the Leastest

If NoData and Derived Data exist, and if a data buffer is a selection of data that exists, and if that selection logically should not exist in those months, it follows that any code that addresses them is redundant at best and always exacts a concomitant performance cost. Simply put, data buffers that address NoData and Derived data are – within Planning applications and their Periodic data orientation – almost always irrelevant. Performant calculations avoid irrelevant data because they address less data.

Correct calculations avoid irrelevant data, particularly within the scope of a data buffer, because a data buffer defines where a calculation occurs. Consider a rate calculation that fires before and after July 2021. Should it fire if – functionally – there is no data in those periods? Calculations that fire in unexpected places negatively impact data quality, sometimes significantly, and are difficult to identify because they are errors that spring from data that should not exist.

RemoveNoData and RemoveZeros

The `RemoveNoData` and `RemoveZeros` formula functions are simple additions to data buffer definitions that remove NoData and Derived data from data buffers. Use them.

Assuming a Data Management step that processes a single Entity and all 12 months of 2021, the impact of the two functions becomes apparent.

> **Note:** `strFixed` is used to store the tuple, or the dimensionally fully-defined memberscript, of the static Dimensions, e.g., `V#Periodic`, `U2#None`, etc.

Without Either

```
Dim dbDataBuffer As DataBuffer = api.Data.GetDataBufferUsingFormula("FilterMembers(" & _
                        strFixed & ", O#BeforeAdj.Base, A#Root.Base, U1#Root.Base)")
```

A simple formula-based data buffer that does not exclude NoData and Derived fires 12 times.

RemoveNoData

```
Dim dbDataBuffer As DataBuffer = api.Data.GetDataBufferUsingFormula("RemoveNoData(FilterMembers(" & _
                        strFixed & ", O#BeforeAdj.Base, A#Root.Base, U1#Root.Base))")
```

Adding RemoveNoData to the filter definition fires six times because derived data actually exists in the record.

RemoveZeros

```
Dim dbDataBuffer As DataBuffer = api.Data.GetDataBufferUsingFormula("RemoveZeros(FilterMembers(" & _
                        strFixed & ", O#BeforeAdj.Base, A#Root.Base, U1#Root.Base))")
```

RemoveZeros fires once as there is only one cell with Real data.

Less is More

Irrespective of code elegance, Cube design, or server speed, processing less data will always be faster. Fast calculations result in a better User Experience and a quicker path to results. Use these functions – particularly RemoveZeros because of the irrelevancy of YTD data in a Planning application – to remove extraneous (and potentially incorrect) data and fast.

Really Removing Zeros

Removing irrelevant values from a data buffer is important for calculation speed. Removing *rows* of irrelevant data makes Calculations, Aggregations/Consolidations, and Reporting faster. A single data value will force the creation of an additional six NoData cells and five Derived cells. If that single data value is a zero and if zero data values are generally not needed in Planning applications (they almost never are), getting rid of that data record is warranted with the happy result of smaller and faster datasets. Faster is always better.

The Zero Use Case

For a given 12 months of data, there must be one real zero stored in any of the months.

	2021M1	2021M2		2021M3	2021M4	2021M5	2021M6	2021M7	2021M8	2021M9	2021M10	2021M11	2021M12	2021
COGS								0						

Figure 2.8

This condition will trigger prior NoData and subsequent Derived data values. As all of the data values in the fact fields are zero, the record is not needed and should be removed.

When that Data Unit is aggregated in AVBS, that single zero value becomes 36: 12 zeros in South_Carolina, 12 at the Parent East, and a further 12 at Total_Geography. None of the zeros are meaningful, and yet they occupy space in the fact table.

Cube	Entity	Consolidation	Scenario	Year	Account	Origin	Intercompany	Flow	UD1	M...	...ue	M6Status	M6Value	M7Status	M7Value	M8Status	M8...	M12Status	M12Value
Sample	South	Cons/Agg	Plan	2021	COGS	Forms	None	EndBal_Input	10_010		0	No Data	0	Aggregated	0	Aggregated		17	0
Sample	South_Carolina	USD	Plan	2021	COGS	Forms	None	EndBal_Input	10_010		0	No Data	0	Real	0	Derived		18	0
Sample	Total_Geography	Cons/Agg	Plan	2021	COGS	Forms	None	EndBal_Input	10_010		0	No Data	0	Aggregated	0	Aggregated		17	0

Figure 2.9

Removing Zeros

Removing those zero rows requires looping through all data within a Data Unit, interrogating every number's value, and if zero assigning it to NoData. Remember, because of the way NoData and

Derived data are stored, only Real data will be removed – these will be those fact rows that are zero-only. Regardless of the scope of data, removing all-zero rows, wherever possible, is good practice because of their potential performance impact.

> **Note:** The technique of using the `RemoveZeros` function should *not* be used in this use case because – after all – the goal is to find zeros and then remove them.

RemoveZeros

This Finance Business Rule has six parts:

1. Static and POV Member assignments.

2. Declaring a destination tuple – a fully qualified Member intersection for all Dimensions – to receive the cleared zeros.

3. Defining a source data buffer as defined by `GetDataBufferUsingFormula` and a target `DataBuffer`.

4. Looping the cells in that data buffer.

5. Testing if the cell amount is zero and, if so, setting the target cells to `IsNoData = True`.

6. Committing the target data buffer and destination expression.

Fixed Members

Dimensions that are not used, or whose Member names are fixed, are assigned to a string variable, in this case, `strFixed`.

```
Dim strFixed As String =
"V#Periodic:F#EndBal_Input:I#None:U2#None:U3#None:U4#None:U5#None:U6#N
one:U7#None:U8#None"
```

Destination

The Expression Destination is instantiated as blank and will be assigned in the source data buffer definition.

```
Dim diDestination As ExpressionDestinationInfo =
api.Data.GetExpressionDestinationInfo("")
```

Data Buffer

Instantiate and assign a data buffer using `GetDataBufferUsingFormula`. Note that the `RemoveZeros` function is not used as the very point of this code is to remove zeros. The Expression Destination is assigned in this statement.

```
Dim dbSourceBufferToClear As DataBuffer =
api.Data.GetDataBufferUsingFormula("FilterMembers(" & strFixed & ",
A#Root.Base, U1#Root.Base, O#Top.Base)",
DataApiScriptMethodType.Calculate, False, diDestination)

Dim dbResultBufferToClear As New DataBuffer()
```

Looping

Loop the cells in the data buffer that have values. All values, zero or otherwise, are in scope.

```
For Each cellSource As DataBufferCell In
dbSourceBufferToClear.DataBufferCells.Values
    .
    .
    .
Next
```

Test and Set to Null

There will be many more non-zero rows than zero rows; only the zeros should be cleared. The assignment of zero to the `cellSource.CellAmount` is arbitrary – there must be some value. It is the `CreateDataCellStatus`' `isNoData` property set to `True` that removes the zeros. This behavior is similar to `api.Data.SetDataCell`.

Assigning the `isNoData` or null cell amount to the target data buffer creates a zero-only data buffer. This target will be far smaller than the source data buffer because the incidence of zero-only rows, while important, will be smaller than the other data values and hence rows.

```
Dim cellResult As New DataBufferCell(cellSource)
If cellSource.CellAmount = 0 Then
    cellResult.CellAmount = 0
    Dim objCellStatus As DataCellStatus =
DataCellStatus.CreateDataCellStatus(True, False)
    objCellStatus.IsCalcStatus = True
    cellResult.CellStatus = objCellStatus
    dbResultBufferToClear.SetCell(si, cellResult)
End If
```

Commit Null

The last step is an `api.Data.SetDataBuffer` that writes the zero-only data buffer to disk.

```
api.Data.SetDataBuffer(dbResultBufferToClear, diDestination)
```

Where's the Zeros?

This data clear occurs at the Base `South Carolina` Entity. If aggregated, ancestor data at `South` and `Total_Geography` remain after the level zero clear.

	A	B	C	D	E	F	G	H	I	J	K	L	M	N	O
1			2021M1	2021M2	2021M3	2021M4	2021M5	2021M6	2021M7	2021M8	2021M9	2021M10	2021M11	2021M12	2021
2	Local	South_Carolina													
6	Aggregated	South							0	0	0	0	0	0	0
7	Aggregated	Total_Geography							0	0	0	0	0	0	0

Figure 2.10

This can be seen from the `DataRecords2021` table as well.

Cube	Entity	Consolidatioi	Scenario	Year	Account	Origin	Intercompan	Flow	UD1	M1Str		ıe	M7Status	M7Value	M8Status	M8Value	M9
Sample	South	Cons/Agg	Plan	2021	COGS	Forms	None	EndBal_Inpu	10_010			0	Aggregated		0	Aggregated	0
Sample	Total_Geogr	Cons/Agg	Plan	2021	COGS	Forms	None	EndBal_Inpu	10_010			0	Aggregated		0	Aggregated	0

Figure 2.11

A **Consolidation** (`C#Aggregated` or `C#Local`) will clear out the upper-level Members and remove them from the fact tables.

How Important is this?

All-zero data rows are – in almost every instance – superfluous to requirements. Less data means a faster application. Schedule a daily administrative **Data Management Sequence** to run a remove zero Finance Business Rule with a Force Consolidate to remove unneeded data.

Removing Data

The Data Management Reset and Clear Data Steps will remove data. They are typically significantly slower than a Finance Business Rule approach. The above Buffer Calculations code to remove zeros can be easily adapted by commenting out the `If cellSource.CellAmount =`

`0/End If` test for zero. All values in the data buffer will then be cleared; the scope of the data buffer will control the cleared data.

> **Note:** A Finance Business Rule *does not* clear Stage data as a Scenario Reset will. This is typically not an issue but is worth remembering if that level of data clearing is required.

Code

```
cellResult.CellAmount = 0
'''    Must be set to isNoData = True if removing data.
Dim objCellStatus As DataCellStatus =
DataCellStatus.CreateDataCellStatus(True, False)
objCellStatus.IsCalcStatus = True
cellResult.CellStatus = objCellStatus
dbResultBufferToClear.SetCell(si, cellResult)
```

The Calculated Data Vanishes

Short and Sweet

Do not calculate data in `O#Import` if you plan to load data within the same Level 2 or Level 3 Data Unit.

Why Not? Everyone Does it. They (and you) Shouldn't. Ever.

At first blush, `O#Import` is a logical place to write calculations: it is read-only to Planners so it can be retained for analysis and yet be adjusted in `O#Forms` either directly or through `O#BeforeAdj`. Other Performance Management products do not have this luxury of both retention of calculated results and virtual adjustment. Why not calculate in `O#Import`, as practically everyone does?

Calculated data should *never* reside in `O#Import` because it may *disappear* without notice, which engenders a state of data quality sure to foster confusion, sow dismay, and deliver pain because calculated data must persist unless it is explicitly cleared or recalculated.

The cause of the deletion is OneStream's data architecture itself.

The Level 2 Data Unit

Data Unit levels define how OneStream manages data. There are three levels to the Data Unit.

1. Level 1: Cube, Entity, Scenario, Time, Consolidation, and Parent

2. Level 2, also known as the Workflow Data Unit: as Level 1 plus Account

3. Level 3: as Level 2 plus Channel (a single User-Defined Dimension)

Level 1 Data Unit

When developing and executing calculations, the Level 1 Data Unit sufficiently describes how data works: a Data Unit is comprised of four (technically five, but Parent is ignored for Planning-style calculations) Dimensions, Calculations must take place within the Data Unit (there is an important exception to this rule, see *Breaking the Data Unit with MemberScriptAndValue* elsewhere in this chapter), and Data Management Custom Calculate Steps control the scope of the Data Unit through its POV selections.

Workflow Level 2 Data Unit

However, this calculation-centric perspective ignores the role of the Planner's Workflow, which operates under the Level 2 Data Unit. When multiple Workflow Profiles are used to load to a single Entity, the same Account, and different User-Defined Dimension Members (see the *Principles* chapter for background on this approach), the Level 2 Data Unit's segregation based on Cube, Entity (again, ignoring Parent for the purposes of loading data), Scenario, Time, Consolidation, and

Account but *not* UD*n* will cause OneStream to *reload* data from Stage for the other data in the same Level 2 Data Unit. This happens automatically and cannot be turned off.

Data that is input or calculated at O#Forms is not impacted. However, when data is calculated at O#Import, that automatically triggered reload process will *delete* any calculated results in that Level 2 Data Unit and replace them with the previously loaded data.

Within the context of Planning applications, this is not as esoteric as it seems: financial Consolidations' strictures and data loading patterns often do not apply. Planning applications that often ignore Entity are not uncommon and focus instead on User-Defined Dimensions to manage the data load process.

Given the risk to data quality that this behavior presents, it is best to *never* calculate in O#Import.

A Use Case

What data pattern causes the deletion of calculated data in O#Import?

Level 2 Initial Load

The first data load of 1066 occurs at the E#Pennsylvania:T#2021M2:S#Plan:A#Distribution Level 2 Data Unit. U1#10_010 is within the Level 2 Data Unit.

UD1	Entity	Time	Scenario	Flow	Measures	Data
10_010	Pennsylvania	2021M2	Plan	EndBal_input	Distribution	1066

Figure 2.12

The result is as expected:

			Import	Forms
Pennsylvania	10_010 - Cameron's 100% Colombian Whole Bean	Sales		
Pennsylvania	10_010 - Cameron's 100% Colombian Whole Bean	Distribution	1066	
Pennsylvania	10_020 - Celvin's Colombian Supremo Regular Whole Bean	Sales		
Pennsylvania	10_020 - Celvin's Colombian Supremo Regular Whole Bean	Distribution		

Figure 2.13

Code

After a data load occurs (this could be a seeding from Actual or a preliminary Plan data load), business conditions may require a calculation to revalue an existing data intersection. This calculation, on top of the data already loaded in the Level 2 Data Unit, is the tripwire for the data quality behavior.

For the purposes of this example, the calculation is simple and explicit: calculate data at E#Pennsylvania:S#Plan:T#2021M2:A#Distribution:U1#10_010:O#Import (and E#Pennsylvania:S#Plan:T#2021M2: A#Distribution:U1#10_010:O#Forms) to illustrate how this data location is not impacted by the Level 2 Data Unit. Note the full tuple description excludes C#Local as it cannot be part of calculations and is implicitly assigned, as is Cb#Sample.

```
Dim strFixed As String =
"V#Periodic:F#EndBal_Input:I#None:U2#None:U3#None:U4#None:U5#None:U6#N
one:U7#None:U8#None"

api.Data.Calculate("A#Distribution:E#Pennsylvania:S#Plan:T#2021M2:U1#1
0_010:O#Import:" & strFixed & " = 42", True)
```

```
api.Data.Calculate("A#Distribution:E#Pennsylvania:S#Plan:T#2021M2:U1#1
0_010:O#Forms:" & strFixed & " = 42", True)
```

Again, an expected result. Note that 42 is now in both O#Import and O#Forms:

			Import	Forms
Pennsylvania 10_010 - Cameron's 100% Colombian Whole Bean	Sales			
Pennsylvania 10_010 - Cameron's 100% Colombian Whole Bean	Distribution		42	42
Pennsylvania 10_020 - Celvin's Colombian Supremo Regular Whole Bean	Sales			
Pennsylvania 10_020 - Celvin's Colombian Supremo Regular Whole Bean	Distribution			

Figure 2.14

Different Account, Same UD1

If data is then loaded to E#Pennsylvania:S#Plan:T#2021M1:C#Local:
A#Sales:U1#10_010, the calculated E#Pennsylvania:A#Distribution data is not impacted because Account Sales acts as a unique identifier – the Level 2 Data Unit – within the Level 1 Data Unit.

From this data file:

UD1	Entity	Time	Scenario	Flow	Measures	Data
10_010	Pennsylvania	2021M2	Plan	EndBal_input	Sales	303

Figure 2.15

E#Pennsylvania:A#Sales is loaded, E#Pennsylvania:A#Distribution is retained:

			Import	Forms
Pennsylvania 10_010 - Cameron's 100% Colombian Whole Bean	Sales		303	
Pennsylvania 10_010 - Cameron's 100% Colombian Whole Bean	Distribution		42	42
Pennsylvania 10_020 - Celvin's Colombian Supremo Regular Whole Bean	Sales			
Pennsylvania 10_020 - Celvin's Colombian Supremo Regular Whole Bean	Distribution			

Figure 2.16

Same Account, Different UD1

However, if data is loaded to A#Distribution:E#Pennsylvania:S#PlanT#2021M1:
U1#10_020:O#Import, the calculated
A#Distribution:E#Pennsylvania:S#Plan:T#2021M1:C#Local:U1#10_010:O#Import
is *erased* because User-Defined Dimensions are not part of the Level 2 Data Unit and thus do not segregate the two data files from one another – both are now the same Level 2 Data Unit, thus setting off the data quality mine. KABOOM!

From this data file:

UD1	Entity	Time	Scenario	Flow	Measures	Data
10_020	Pennsylvania	2021M2	Plan	EndBal_input	Distribution	39

Figure 2.17

`E#Pennsylvania:A#Distribution:U1#10_020` is loaded,
`E#Pennsylvania:A#Distribution:O#Import`'s value of 42 is *replaced* with its initial value
of 1066, and `E#Pennsylvania:A#Distribition:O#Forms` is unchanged.

			Import	Forms
Pennsylvania	10_010 - Cameron's 100% Colombian Whole Bean	Sales	303	
Pennsylvania	10_010 - Cameron's 100% Colombian Whole Bean	Distribution	1066	42
Pennsylvania	10_020 - Celvin's Colombian Supremo Regular Whole Bean	Sales		
Pennsylvania	10_020 - Celvin's Colombian Supremo Regular Whole Bean	Distribution	39	

Figure 2.18

What Happened?

The Task Activity log shows the last data load. Note the Task Type: Load Cube Batch. The normal
Task Type for an Import data load is Load Cube.

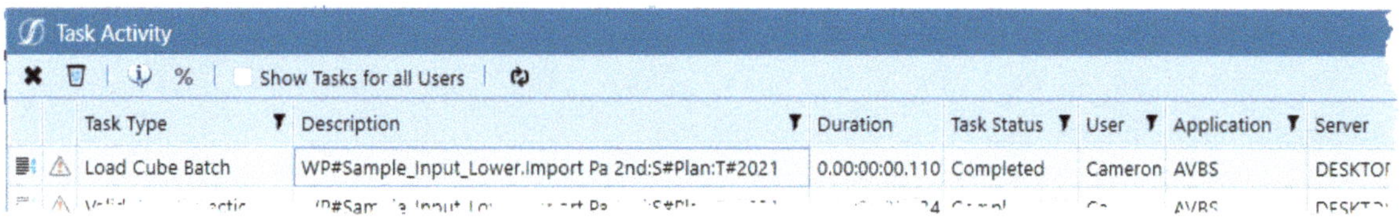

Figure 2.19

Unpossible!

Drilling into the task reveals OneStream's true behavior:

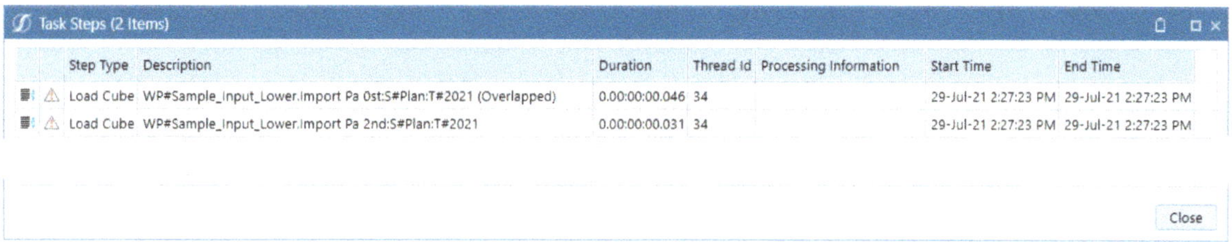

Figure 2.20

Both data files were loaded. The *entire* Level 2 Data Unit is *loaded from Stage every time* any data
is loaded into that Data Unit. The calculated value of 42 in `O#Import` is not in Stage and hence
cannot be reloaded.

If you plan to load data within the same Level 2 or Level 3 Data Unit, do not calculate data in
`O#Import`.

What About Level 3?

The Level 3 Data Unit, more commonly referred to as **Workflow Channels**, *can* further isolate the
Data Unit to a *single* User-Defined Dimension, thus solving the above data clear and reload use
case. However, it applies to just one User-Defined Dimension and does not resolve this issue when
more than one User-Defined Dimension is in play; the replacement of data calculated in `O#Import`
remains. Calculate data in `O#Forms`.

Learn to Code

Data Buffers

Just What Exactly is a Data Buffer?

A data buffer is nothing more than a slice of data within a Data Unit. For those practitioners familiar with multidimensional databases in general, a data buffer is a block of data.

That subset of data can be every single bit of data in a Data Unit (which is a data buffer itself) or a single number. Calculations occur at the dimensional intersections a data buffer defines.

Definitions

A data value's fully-defined cross-dimensional intersection is – in common practice – called a **tuple**. In OneStream, tuples and sets are defined by **Member Scripts**.

Data buffers are comprised of the individual existing data points within the buffer; these data points are **cells**.

Cells can be traversed by **loops** within data buffers.

The cells are addressable via what is commonly termed a **Name Value Pair**; within OneStream, these are typically referred to as **Key Value Pair**. The *Primary Key* of that Key Value Pair can be used to identify the cell's location within the data buffer's collection of cells.

Cells contain data in the form of a numeric value as well as metadata such as the Dimension Members that define the data value's Member Script.

A Very Simple Data Buffer

The Distribution expense calculation requirement is direct: Distribution = Sales * 0.042.

Finance Business Rule

How is that calculated in OneStream? By creating a Finance Business Rule and running it via a Data Management Custom Calculate Step.

The Business Rule is as straightforward as its requirement.

First, a clear to ensure that whatever data value existed before is now removed (this should be overwritten by the calculation itself, so is largely a just-in-case measure). Although `A#Distribution:O#Forms` is not a complete tuple, it is a data buffer because the undefined Dimensions such as UD1, Flow, etc., are implicit.

```
api.data.ClearCalculatedData("A#Distribution:O#Forms", True, True,
True, True)
```

The second step is the actual calculation which uses overloaded properties to explicitly assign Members or Member Functions to Dimensions, i.e., `F#EndBal_Input` and `U1#Total_Products.Base`.

```
api.Data.Calculate("A#Distribution:O#Forms = A#Sales:O#BeforeAdj *
0.042)",,"F#EndBal_Input",,"I#None","U1#Total_Products.Base",,,,,,,,,T
rue)
```

There are two explicitly defined data buffers in this calculation: the Distribution target and the Sales source with its factor rate of 0.042. There are filter definitions that define the data buffer scope: Flow's `EndBal_Input`, Intercompany's `None`, and all Base level Products.

To calculate Distribution in South Carolina, the Data Management Step must specify the Data Unit's Cube, Entity, Consolidation, Scenario, Time, and Business Rule, which – in this example – is Sample, South_Carolina, Local, Plan, and 2021M8. Accounts, Flow, Intercompany, UD*n*s, and all other dynamic Dimensions are encompassed by the Data Unit itself and are thus not required parameters. These parameters can be queried within a Finance Business Rule, although this functionality is not germane to the following examples.

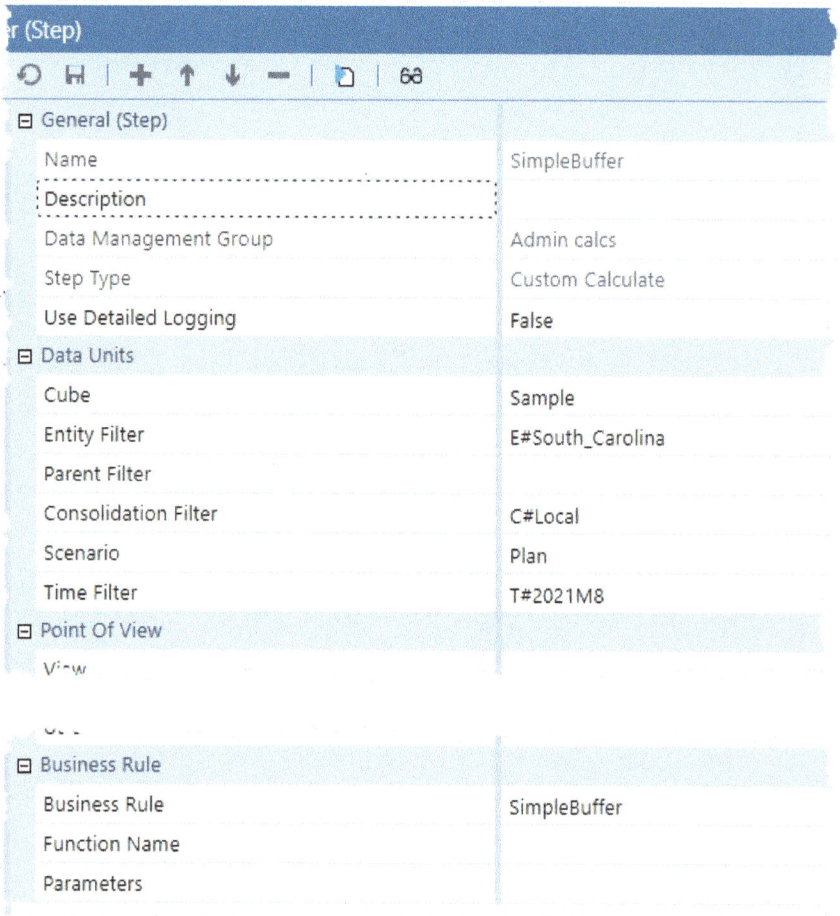

Figure 2.21

When executed, the Sales of 220 and 204 in products 10_010 and 10_020 respectively are multiplied by the constant 0.042.

	A	B	C
1			2021M8
2	10_010 - Cameron's 100% Colombian Whole Bean	Sales	220
3	10_010 - Cameron's 100% Colombian Whole Bean	Distribution	
4	10_020 - Celvin's Colombian Supremo Regular Whole Bean	Sales	204
5	10_020 - Celvin's Colombian Supremo Regular Whole Bean	Distribution	
6	10_030 - French Roast Regular Whole Bean Decaf	Sales	
7	10_030 - French Roast Regular Whole Bean Decaf	Distribution	
8	Whole_Bean - Whole Bean	Sales	424
9	Whole_Bean - Whole Bean	Distribution	

Figure 2.22

Which produces the following result:

	A	B	C
1			2021M8
2	10_010 - Cameron's 100% Colombian Whole Bean	Sales	220
3	10_010 - Cameron's 100% Colombian Whole Bean	Distribution	9.24
4	10_020 - Celvin's Colombian Supremo Regular Whole Bean	Sales	204
5	10_020 - Celvin's Colombian Supremo Regular Whole Bean	Distribution	8.568
6	10_030 - French Roast Regular Whole Bean Decaf	Sales	
7	10_030 - French Roast Regular Whole Bean Decaf	Distribution	
8	Whole_Bean - Whole Bean	Sales	424
9	Whole_Bean - Whole Bean	Distribution	17.808

Figure 2.23

But what happens when the contents of a data buffer need to be interrogated? A simple `api.Data.Calculate` does not allow the testing of data or metadata properties of cells within a data buffer.

Testing must take place at an individual cell level. Short of explicitly defining every tuple within a data buffer, a loop of all the existing data cells in the data buffer must be performed to allow the evaluation and calculation of data within and without that data buffer.

> **Note:** A data buffer is a Method of addressing *existing* cells but does not exclude reaching outside the data buffer. Once the data buffer cells are in play, other Member intersections can be read from and written to. The data buffer examples, below, show creating a Sales-only data buffer, reading from a Distribution Rate outside the data buffer, and writing to an Account – Distribution – that is outside the data buffer.

Defining the Data Buffer

See the Rules and Calculations chapter in OneStream Press' *OneStream Foundation Handbook* and OneStream Software's *Design and Reference Guide* for an overview of the multiple data buffer definition Methods. This book will use the `api.Data.GetDataBufferUsingFormula` Method as it uses familiar and easily understood dimensional functions.

Three Approaches

There are three general approaches to working with data buffers beyond a simple `api.Data.Calculate`: **Calculate Within**, **Calculate With Eval**, and **Buffer Calculations**.

All three approaches create data buffers, loop their data, and perform calculations within that loop. They differ, significantly so, in how those operations are performed.

Their order is one of performance or at least a theoretical one. Efficiency or lack thereof will be most observable when range restricted Custom Calculate Data Management Steps are not used, i.e., Finance Business Rules attached to a Cube or Data Management Custom Calculate Steps that apply to a wide Data Unit scope, not Finance Business Rules attached to a Form that execute for one Data Unit. If code is not efficient but its data scope is small, the perceived performance penalty is unlikely to be noticed.

A note about performance for these data buffer techniques and indeed any other Component of a OneStream application: it is difficult, almost impossible except in the most obvious of contexts, to definitively state that a given approach is faster or slower than another without benchmarking on a realistic set of data. Theory is one thing, how a process performs when fully implemented is another. Test your solutions because common practice can be wrong.

Regardless of theoretical performance considerations, all three Methods work. As always with real world applications, test, test, test to ensure that the calculation is executing within its required performance specifications and not incidentally deliver the correct results.

Calculate Within

The Calculate Within technique uses `api.Data.Calculate` and `api.Data.SetDataCell` Methods to calculate data on a cell-by-cell basis. It is metadata-centric because it needs the Member tuple as target.

Calculate With Eval

Calculate With Eval also uses `api.Data.Calculate` but instead of executing the Method within a surrounding data buffer loop, it uses that Method's `AddressOf` property to call a private subroutine that performs the loop, testing, and valuation of `A#Distribution` within a single data buffer read and write.

Buffer Calculations

The Buffer Calculations process addresses the cells within the source data buffer, directly performs calculations on those cells' data and properties, and writes the results back to the database through a target data buffer in an all-at-once operation.

Performance Implications

Theoretically, the Calculate Within approach should be the slowest of the three because, although it loops a focused data buffer, the `api.Data.Calculate` within the loop brings the Data Unit's entire data buffer into memory for each pass when writing to the target tuple, thus causing many unnecessary memory operations.

Calculate With Eval should be faster than Calculate Within logic because it brings the Data Unit's data buffer into memory once before it performs `api.Data.Calculate.`

The Buffer Calculations' block operations that read, evaluate, and commit in-memory data buffers without the overhead of `api.Data.Calculate` should be the fastest of the three approaches.

Looping the Data Buffer

The Distribution expense calculation use case is now complex: if Sales is between 200 and 300, multiply Sales by 0.042; if Sales is over 300, multiply Sales by a Product-specific/No_Geography distribution rate; and if neither condition is true, clear out the Account.

By looping the data buffer's contents, the Sales' Member data value can be tested for the first two conditions and could, if a valuation of Sales were assured, handle all three Scenarios.

However, if Sales is *not* valued then it cannot be looped because there is no data buffer to traverse, and hence the clear of Distribution cannot occur. The approach must then be to unilaterally clear it in a Destination-only data buffer, and then calculate it based on Sales.

Less Than Zero

An extremely important note: a loop that traverses the individual data points within the data buffer **must** have data to traverse. That means that a data buffer definition must encompass at least one data cell. No data means no buffer and hence no loop. If your code runs suspiciously fast and fails to produce a result, the culprit is a data buffer definition that points to a null data slice.

Use `databuffername.DataBufferCells.Count` to log the cell count.

Be aware of the performance cost of this approach and comment it out or completely remove it when code development is complete.

```
api.LogMessage("Cells: " & dbDataBuffer.DataBufferCells.Count)
```

Calculate Within

The Calculate Within technique differs from the other Methods in this section in its use of `api.Data.SetDataCell` and `api.Data.Calculate` – operating on a cell instead of data buffer basis – with a potential knock-on performance impact.

With that important consideration in mind, the Calculate Within approach is easy to understand and, within the right use case, a valid approach.

There are five components to the `LoopingBuffer` Finance Business Rule:

1. Declare and assign the fixed and POV Dimension Members.

2. Create a Distribution data buffer.

3. Loop and clear the Distribution data buffer.

4. Create a Sales data buffer.

5. Loop the `A#Sales` data buffer, evaluate `A#Sales`' data, and perform a rate calculation to value `A#Distribution`.

Fixed and POV Members

Dimensions that are not used, or whose Member names are fixed, are assigned to a string variable, in this case, `strFixed`.

The Data Management Custom Calculate Step provides Data Unit POV values.

```
Dim strFixed As String =
"V#Periodic:F#EndBal_Input:I#None:U2#None:U3#None:U4#None:U5#None:U6#N
one:U7#None:U8#None"
Dim strGeography As String = api.Pov.Entity.Name
Dim strTime As String = api.Pov.Time.Name
Dim strScenario As String = api.Pov.Scenario.Name
```

Defining the Distribution Data Buffer

The `RemoveZeros` function is used with `api.Data.GetDataBufferUsingFormula` to delineate the scope of the Distribution data buffer.

```
Dim dbSourceDistBuffer As DataBuffer =
api.Data.GetDataBufferUsingFormula("RemoveZeros(FilterMembers(" &
strFixed & ":O#Forms:A#Distribution, U1#Total_Products.Base))")
```

Loop and Remove

With the data buffer declared, loop its contents, setting A#Distribution to zero using `api.Data.SetDataCell`. Note that the `isNoData` and `isDurableCalculatedData` properties must be set to `True` to perform the clear and make the cell status persist. The `CalculateWithEval` and `BufferCalculations` code perform the same logic through the data cell's `IsCalcStatus` Method.

```
For Each cell As DataBufferCell In
dbSourceDistBuffer.DataBufferCells.Values
    Dim cellPKFordbDataBuffer As New
DataBufferCellPk(cell.DataBufferCellPk)
    Dim strProduct As String = cellPKFordbDataBuffer.GetUD1Name(api)

    Dim strClearDistribution As String = "A#Distribution:U1#" &
strProduct & ":O#Forms" & ":E#" & strGeography & ":T#" & strTime &
":S#" & strScenario & ":" & strFixed
    api.Data.SetDataCell(strClearDistribution, 0.00, True, True)

Next
```

Defining the Sales Data Buffer

With Distribution cleared, a separate buffer for Sales must be created and looped.

```
Dim dbDataBuffer As DataBuffer =
api.Data.GetDataBufferUsingFormula("RemoveZeros(FilterMembers(E#" &
strGeography & ":T#" & strTime & ":S#" & strScenario & ":" & strFixed
& ":O#Forms:A#Sales, U1#Total_Products.Base))")
```

Looping, Testing, and Calculating

A For Each…Next loop of the data buffer cell value provides the pointers to the cells and their data and metadata.

The steps are as follows:

1. Loop the data buffer object's cells in dbDataBuffer.DataBufferCells.Values.

2. Create a cell reference in cellPKFordbDataBuffer.

3. Get the UD1/Product Dimension Member name using cellPKFordbDataBuffer.GetUD1Name(api).

4. As the data buffer has been created using Sales, cell.CellAmount will assign Sales to decSales.

5. Evaluate A#Sales:

    a. If A#Sales is between 200 and 300, use api.Data.Calculate to multiply A#Sales by 0.042.

    b. If A#Sales is greater than 300, create a Member Script that defines the Distribution Rate at the Product, retrieve the rate value into a decimal variable, and then use api.Data.Calculate to multiply that rate by A#Sales.

```
For Each cell As DataBufferCell In dbDataBuffer.DataBufferCells.Values
   Dim cellPKFordbDataBuffer As New
DataBufferCellPk(cell.DataBufferCellPk)
   Dim strProduct As String = cellPKFordbDataBuffer.GetUD1Name(api)
   Dim decSales As Decimal = cell.CellAmount
   If decSales >= 200 And decSales <= 300 Then
      api.Data.Calculate("A#Distribution:V#Periodic:U1#" & strProduct
& " = A#Sales:V#Periodic:U1#" & strProduct & " * 0.042)", True)
   ElseIf decSales > 300 Then
      Dim strRate As String = "A#Distribution_Rate:U1#" & strProduct &
":O#Forms" & ":E#No_Geography:T#" & strTime & ":S#" & strScenario &
":" & strFixed
      Dim decRate As Decimal =
api.Data.GetDataCell(strRate).CellAmount
      api.Data.Calculate("A#Distribution:V#Periodic:U1#" & strProduct
& " = A#Sales:V#Periodic:U1#" & strProduct & " * " & decRate, True)
   End If
Next
```

CalculateWithin

Below is the code in full.

```
Namespace OneStream.BusinessRule.Finance.CalculateWithin
    Public Class MainClass
        Public Function Main(ByVal si As SessionInfo, ByVal globals As BRGlobals,
        ByVal api As FinanceRulesApi, ByVal args As FinanceRulesArgs) As Object
            Try
                Dim strFixed As String = "V#Periodic:F#EndBal_Input:I#None:U2#None:U3#None:U4#None:U5#None:U6#None:U7#None:U8#None"
                ''' Get the POV Data Unit members for the SetDataCell method
                Dim strGeography As String = api.Pov.Entity.Name
                Dim strTime As String = api.Pov.Time.Name
                Dim strScenario As String = api.Pov.Scenario.Name
                Dim dbSourceDistBuffer As DataBuffer = api.Data.GetDataBufferUsingFormula("RemoveZeros(FilterMembers(" & _
                    strFixed & ":O#Forms:A#Distribution, U1#Total_Products.Base))")

                For Each cell As DataBufferCell In dbSourceDistBuffer.DataBufferCells.Values
                    ''' Create a cell reference
                    Dim cellPKFordbDataBuffer As New DataBufferCellPk(cell.DataBufferCellPk)
                    ''' Get Product member
                    Dim strProduct As String = cellPKFordbDataBuffer.GetUD1Name(api)
                    ''' Define the Distribution tuple to be cleared
                    Dim strClearDistribution As String = "A#Distribution:U1#" & strProduct & ":O#Forms" & _
                        ":E#" & strGeography & ":T#" & strTime & ":S#" & strScenario & ":" & strFixed
                    ''' Clear Distribution; the numeric value is irrelevant as the IsNoData propety overrides it.
                    api.Data.SetDataCell(strClearDistribution, 0.00, True, True)
                Next

                Dim dbDataBuffer As DataBuffer = api.Data.GetDataBufferUsingFormula("RemoveZeros(FilterMembers(E#" & _
                    strGeography & ":T#" & strTime & ":S#" & strScenario & ":" & strFixed & _
                    ":O#Forms:A#Sales, U1#Total_Products.Base))")

                For Each cell As DataBufferCell In dbDataBuffer.DataBufferCells.Values
                    Dim cellPKFordbDataBuffer As New DataBufferCellPk(cell.DataBufferCellPk)
                    Dim strProduct As String = cellPKFordbDataBuffer.GetUD1Name(api)
                    Dim decSales As Decimal = cell.CellAmount
                    api.LogMessage("cell.CellAmount " & cell.CellAmount)
                    If decSales >= 200 And decSales <= 300 Then
                        api.Data.Calculate("A#Distribution:V#Periodic:U1#" & strProduct & _
                            " = A#Sales:V#Periodic:U1#" & strProduct & " * 0.042)", True)
                    ElseIf decSales > 300 Then
                        Dim strRate As String = "A#Distribution_Rate:U1#" & strProduct & _
                            ":O#Forms" & ":E#No_Geography:T#" & strTime & ":S#" & strScenario & ":" & strFixed
                        Dim decRate As Decimal = api.Data.GetDataCell(strRate).CellAmount
                        api.Data.Calculate("A#Distribution:V#Periodic:U1#" & strProduct & _
                            " = A#Sales:V#Periodic:U1#" & strProduct & " * " & decRate, True)
                    End If
                Next
                Return Nothing
            Catch ex As Exception
                Throw ErrorHandler.LogWrite(si, New XFException(si, ex))
            End Try
        End Function
    End Class
End Namespace
```

Calculate With Eval

The Calculate With Eval approach uses `api.Data.Calculate` to instantiate data buffer processing. The key advantage to this approach is that, unlike Calculate Within, the data buffer is considered just once, thus improving performance.

The Calculate With Eval Method has eight parts:

1. Declare the fixed Dimension constants.
2. Perform an `api.Data.Calculate` Method using the Eval's `AddressOf` Method to call the private `OnEvalDataBuffer` subroutine to perform buffer math. `Eval(A#Sales..)` is used to kick off the buffer math – traditional right of the equals sign logic does not occur.
3. Within `OnEvalDataBuffer`:
    a. The EvalDataBufferEventArgs eventArgs object's cells are cleared.
    b. `eventArgs`'s DataBuffer1 is looped.
    c. Declare and assign the fixed and POV Dimension Members.
    d. Evaluate `A#Sales`' data, and perform a rate calculation to value `A#Distribution`.
    e. Write the results of the data buffer evaluation to disk.

Defining Fixed Dimensions

Dimensions that are not used, or whose Member names are fixed, are assigned to a string variable, in this case, strFixed.

```
Dim strFixed As String =
"O#Forms:V#Periodic:F#EndBal_Input:I#None:U2#None:U3#None:U4#None:U5#N
one:U6#None:U7#None:U8#None"
```

Evaluating Sales

While the left hand side of api.Data.Calculate is used to ultimately assign the results of the Eval Method, the actual looping and logic tests within the data buffer occurs within the OnEvalDataBuffer subroutine.

```
api.Data.Calculate("A#Distribution:" & strFixed & " = Eval(A#Sales:" &
strFixed & ")", AddressOf OnEvalDataBuffer)
```

By passing just the Member A#Sales into Eval, Sales' data buffer is then passed to the OnEvalDataBuffer subroutine. There is no need to use api.Data.GetDataBufferUsingFormula to create a data buffer as there was in the Calculate Within Method.

The name OnEvalDataBuffer is a convention, not a required name; use whatever subroutine name makes most sense.

Clearing eventArgs

Eval's AddressOf operator performs a by value pass of EvalDataBufferEventArgs which contains Sales' data buffer as can be seen in the Private Sub declaration.

Once in the subroutine, before any processing occurs in DataBufferResult, clear any potential cells.

```
Private Sub OnEvalDataBuffer(ByVal api As FinanceRulesApi, ByVal
evalName As String, ByVal eventArgs As EvalDataBufferEventArgs)
    Try
        eventargs.DataBufferResult.DataBufferCells.Clear()
        .
        .
        .
    Catch ex As Exception
        Throw errorhandler.logwrite(api.SI, New XFException(api.SI,ex))
    End Try
End Sub
```

Looping DataBuffer1

EvalDataBufferEventArgs supports up to three data buffers. This use case requires just DataBuffer1.

RemoveNoData and RemoveZeros are not valid once within the data buffer, so the test for a cell's isNoData status and a <> 0 amount perform the same function of removing data that does not need to be considered.

```
For Each cellSource As DataBufferCell In
eventArgs.DataBuffer1.DataBufferCells.Values
    If (Not cellSource.CellStatus.IsNoData) And (cellSource.CellAmount
<> 0.0) Then
    .
    .
    .
    End If
Next
```

Fixed and POV Members and a Result Cell

Fixed and POV-driven Members must be queried for use in the Buffer Math.

cellSource is instantiated in the For Each…Next DataBuffer1 loop and is the source Sales value. cellResult will be Sales' target cell.

```
Dim cellResult As New DataBufferCell(cellSource)
Dim strFixed As String =
"V#Periodic:F#EndBal_Input:I#None:U2#None:U3#None:U4#None:U5#None:U6#N
one:U7#None:U8#None"
Dim strTime As String = api.Pov.Time.Name
Dim strScenario As String = api.Pov.Scenario.Name
Dim strProduct As String = cellSource.DataBufferCellPk.GetUD1Name(api)
```

Testing and Calculating

The same logic branching based on Sales' value occurs as it did in Calculate Within but with data buffer math instead of api.Data.Calculate Methods within a data buffer.

The clear of Distribution occurs in the last Else condition by setting the cellResult object's cell isNoData and isInvalid properties to True and False.

```
If (cellSource.CellAmount >= 200 And cellSource.CellAmount <= 300)
Then
    cellResult.CellAmount = cellSource.CellAmount * .042
ElseIf cellSource.CellAmount > 300
    Dim strRate As String = "A#Distribution_Rate:U1#" & strProduct &
":O#Forms:E#No_Geography:T#" & strTime & ":S#" & strScenario & ":" &
strFixed
    Dim decRate As Decimal = api.Data.GetDataCell(strRate).CellAmount
    cellResult.CellAmount = cellSource.CellAmount * decRate
Else
    Dim objCellStatus As DataCellStatus =
DataCellStatus.CreateDataCellStatus(True, False)
    objCellStatus.IsCalcStatus = True
    cellResult.CellStatus = objCellStatus
End If
```

Writing the Results

With each pass through the loop, the eventargs.DataBufferResult.SetCell Method receives the calculated result and then passes it back to the originating api.Data.Calculate Method once all the cells are evaluated.

```
eventargs.DataBufferResult.SetCell(api.Si, cellResult, False)
```

CalculateWithEval

Below is the code in full.

```
Namespace OneStream.BusinessRule.Finance.CalculateWithEval
    Public Class MainClass
        Public Function Main(ByVal si As SessionInfo, ByVal globals As BRGlobals,
            ByVal api As FinanceRulesApi, ByVal args As FinanceRulesArgs) As Object
            Try
                Dim strFixed As String = "O#Forms:V#Periodic:F#EndBal_Input:I#None:U2#None:" & _
                    "U3#None:U4#None:U5#None:U6#None:U7#None:U8#None"
                api.Data.Calculate("A#Distribution:" & strFixed & " = Eval(A#Sales:" & _
                    strFixed & ")", AddressOf OnEvalDataBuffer)
                Return Nothing
            Catch ex As Exception
                Throw ErrorHandler.LogWrite(si, New XFException(si, ex))
            End Try
        End Function

        Private Sub OnEvalDataBuffer(ByVal api As FinanceRulesApi, ByVal evalName As String,
            ByVal eventArgs As EvalDataBufferEventArgs)
            Try
                eventargs.DataBufferResult.DataBufferCells.Clear()
                For Each cellSource As DataBufferCell In eventArgs.DataBuffer1.DataBufferCells.Values
                    If (Not cellSource.CellStatus.IsNoData) And (cellSource.CellAmount > 0.0) Then
                        Dim cellResult As New DataBufferCell(cellSource)
                        Dim strFixed As String = "V#Periodic:F#EndBal_Input:I#None:U2#None:" & _
                            "U3#None:U4#None:U5#None:U6#None:U7#None:U8#None"
                        Dim strTime As String = api.Pov.Time.Name
                        Dim strScenario As String = api.Pov.Scenario.Name
                        Dim strProduct As String = cellSource.DataBufferCellPk.GetUD1Name(api)
                        If (cellSource.CellAmount >= 200 And cellSource.CellAmount <= 300) Then
                            cellResult.CellAmount = cellSource.CellAmount * .042
                        ElseIf cellSource.CellAmount > 300
                            Dim strRate As String = "A#Distribution_Rate:U1#" & strProduct & _
                                ":O#Forms:E#No_Geography:T#" & strTime & ":S#" & strScenario & ":" & strFixed
                            Dim decRate As Decimal = api.Data.GetDataCell(strRate).CellAmount
                            cellResult.CellAmount = cellSource.CellAmount * decRate
                        Else
                            Dim objCellStatus As DataCellStatus = DataCellStatus.CreateDataCellStatus(True, False)
                            objCellStatus.IsCalcStatus = True
                            cellResult.CellStatus = objCellStatus
                        End If
                        eventargs.DataBufferResult.SetCell(api.SI, cellResult, False)
                    End If
                Next
            Catch ex As Exception
                Throw errorhandler.logwrite(api.SI, New XFException(api.SI,ex))
            End Try
        End Sub
    End Class
End Namespace
```

Buffer Calculations

The calculation requirements are the same but are approached from a data buffer math methodology. `api.Data.Calculate` is not used in any form.

There are eight sections in the `BufferCalculations` Business Rule:

1. Declare and assign the fixed and POV Dimension Members as well as a data buffer Destination Info variable.

2. Create a `A#Distribution` data buffer.

3. Loop and clear the `A#Distribution` data buffer.

4. Commit the cleared `A#Distribution` data buffer to disk.

5. Create a `A#Sales` data buffer.

6. Get the `A#Distribution` Member's `MemberId` to use in assigning the target data buffer cell.

7. Loop the `A#Sales` data buffer, evaluate `A#Sales`' data, and perform a rate calculation to value `A#Distribution`.

8. Commit the calculated `A#Distribution` data buffer to disk.

Fixed and POV Members and Destination Info

Dimensions that are not used, or whose Member names are fixed, are assigned to a string variable, in this case, strFixed.

The Data Management Custom Calculate Step provides Data Unit POV values.

```
Dim strFixed As String =
"V#Periodic:F#EndBal_Input:I#None:U2#None:U3#None:U4#None:U5#None:U6#N
one:U7#None:U8#None"
Dim strGeography As String = api.Pov.Entity.Name
Dim strTime As String = api.Pov.Time.Name
Dim strScenario As String = api.Pov.Scenario.Name
```

api.Data.SetDataBuffer Methods require an ExpressionDestinationInfo object to define target Dimension intersections. In the case of this use case, this is not necessary.

```
Dim diDestination As ExpressionDestinationInfo =
api.Data.GetExpressionDestinationInfo("")
```

Defining the Distribution Data Buffer

There are multiple data buffer definition Methods. This chapter uses: api.Data.GetDataBufferUsingFormula.

```
Dim dbSourceDistBuffer As DataBuffer =
api.Data.GetDataBufferUsingFormula("RemoveZeros(FilterMembers(" &
strFixed & ", O#Forms, A#Distribution, U1#Total_Products.Base))",
DataApiScriptMethodType.Calculate, False)
```

Note that the Buffer Calculations approach requires the optional scriptMethodType and changeIdsToCommonIfNotUsingAll properties to be valued.

Looping and Clearing A#Distribution

The dbBufferToClear data buffer object is created, and then the source dbSourceDistBuffer is looped.

Within the loop, the cell amount is set to zero and then defined as NoData. The numeric value is meaningless because the CreateDataCellStatus Method will remove it; zero is used as a convention.

As the cells are set to NoData, the target data buffer receives the cell's address and its NoData status.

```
Dim dbBufferToClear As New DataBuffer()
For Each cellSource As DataBufferCell In
dbSourceDistBuffer.DataBufferCells.Values
   Dim cellResult As New DataBufferCell(cellSource)
   cellResult.CellAmount = 0
   Dim objCellStatus As DataCellStatus =
DataCellStatus.CreateDataCellStatus(True, False)
   objCellStatus.IsCalcStatus = True
   cellResult.CellStatus = objCellStatus
   dbBufferToClear.SetCell(si, cellResult)
Next
```

Commit The Cleared A#Distribution Data Buffer

A single line commits the in-memory data buffer dbBufferToClear to disk.

```
api.Data.SetDataBuffer(dbBufferToClear, diDestination)
```

All A#Distribution data in the overall Data Unit has now been cleared.

Defining the Sales and Result Data Buffers

Defining a data buffer to address A#Sales mirrors A#Distribution's.

```
Dim dbSourceBuffer As DataBuffer =
api.Data.GetDataBufferUsingFormula("RemoveZeros(FilterMembers(" &
strFixed & ":O#Forms:A#Sales,,, U1#Total_Products.Base))",
DataApiScriptMethodType.Calculate, False)
Dim dbResultBuffer As New DataBuffer()
```

A#Distribution's Member ID

A#Sales data buffer cells do not address A#Distribution. To convert A#Sales to A#Distribution, the latter's internal MemberId must be queried, stored as an Integer variable, and then used to assign the A#Sales' cell value to A#Distribution.

```
Dim intDistribution As Integer =
api.Members.GetMemberId(DimTypeId.Account, "Distribution")
```

Looping, Testing, and Calculating

A For Each…Next loop of the data buffer cell value provides the pointers to the cells and their data and metadata.

As the loop traverses dbSourceBuffer's Sales data cells, a new target cell is instantiated and the cell's A#Sales value is evaluated:

1. If it is between 200 and 300, the source cell Sales amount is assigned to the target cell and then multiplied by the constant 0.042. A#Distribution's previously queried MemberId is assigned to that target cell for addition to the target data buffer dbResultBuffer.

2. If it is greater than 300, after the assignment of the source cell to the target, the source cell's UD1 Product Dimension Member is queried and then used with api.Data.GetDataCell to retrieve A#Distribution_Rate's data value. As with the first branch, the rate calculation is assigned to A#Distribution via its MemberId.

At the end of the loop, the target cell is added to the dbResultBuffer.

```
For Each cellSource As DataBufferCell In
dbSourceBuffer.DataBufferCells.Values
    Dim cellResult As New DataBufferCell()
    If cellSource.CellAmount >= 200 And cellSource.CellAmount <= 300
Then
        cellResult = cellSource
        cellResult.CellAmount = cellSource.CellAmount * 0.042
        cellResult.DataBufferCellPk.AccountId = intDistribution
    ElseIf cellSource.CellAmount > 300 Then
        cellResult = cellSource
        Dim strProduct = cellSource.DataBufferCellPk.GetUD1Name(api)
        Dim decDistRate As Decimal =
api.Data.GetDataCell("E#No_Geography:A#Distribution_Rate:C#Local:O#For
ms:" & strFixed & ":U1#" & strProduct & ":S#" & strScenario & ":T#" &
strTime).CellAmount
        cellResult.CellAmount = cellSource.CellAmount * decDistRate
        cellResult.DataBufferCellPk.AccountId = intDistribution
    End If
    dbResultBuffer.SetCell(si, cellResult)
Next
```

Commit to Disk

The target data buffer is in memory and must now be written to the year's fact table. This is done outside of the loop of the source buffer for better performance.

```
api.Data.SetDataBuffer(dbResultBuffer, diDestination)
```

BufferCalculations

Below is the code in full.

```
Namespace OneStream.BusinessRule.Finance.BufferCalculations
    Public Class MainClass
        Public Function Main(ByVal si As SessionInfo, ByVal globals As BRGlobals,
            ByVal api As FinanceRulesApi, ByVal args As FinanceRulesArgs) As Object
            Try
            Dim strFixed As String = "V#Periodic:F#EndBal_Input:I#None:U2#None:" & _
                "U3#None:U4#None:U5#None:U6#None:U7#None:U8#None"
            Dim strScenario = api.Pov.Scenario.Name
            Dim strTime = api.Pov.Time.Name
            Dim diDestination As ExpressionDestinationInfo = api.Data.GetExpressionDestinationInfo("")
            Dim dbSourceDistBuffer As DataBuffer = api.Data.GetDataBufferUsingFormula("RemoveZeros(FilterMembers(" & _
                strFixed & ", O#Forms, A#Distribution, U1#Total_Products.Base))", DataApiScriptMethodType.Calculate, False)

            Dim dbBufferToClear As New DataBuffer()
            For Each cellSource As DataBufferCell In dbSourceDistBuffer.DataBufferCells.Values
                Dim cellResult As New DataBufferCell(cellSource)
                cellResult.CellAmount = 0
                Dim objCellStatus As DataCellStatus = DataCellStatus.CreateDataCellStatus(True, False)
                objCellStatus.IsCalcStatus = True
                cellResult.CellStatus = objCellStatus
                dbBufferToClear.SetCell(si, cellResult)
            Next

            api.Data.SetDataBuffer(dbBufferToClear, diDestination)

            Dim dbSourceBuffer As DataBuffer = api.Data.GetDataBufferUsingFormula("RemoveZeros(FilterMembers(" & _
                strFixed & ", O#Forms, A#Sales, U1#Total_Products.Base))", DataApiScriptMethodType.Calculate, False)
            Dim dbResultBuffer As New DataBuffer()
            Dim intDistribution As Integer = api.Members.GetMemberId(DimTypeId.Account, "Distribution")
            For Each cellSource As DataBufferCell In dbSourceBuffer.DataBufferCells.Values
                Dim cellResult As New DataBufferCell()
                If cellSource.CellAmount >= 200 And cellSource.CellAmount <= 300 Then
                    cellResult = cellSource
                    cellResult.CellAmount = cellSource.CellAmount * 0.042
                    cellResult.DataBufferCellPk.AccountId = intDistribution
                ElseIf cellSource.CellAmount > 300 Then
                    cellResult = cellSource
                    Dim strProduct = cellSource.DataBufferCellPk.GetUD1Name(api)
                    Dim decDistRate As Decimal = api.Data.GetDataCell("E#No_Geography:A#Distribution_Rate:C#Local:O#Forms:" & _
                        strFixed & ":U1#" & strProduct & ":S#" & strScenario & ":T#" & strTime).CellAmount
                    cellResult.CellAmount = cellSource.CellAmount * decDistRate
                    cellResult.DataBufferCellPk.AccountId = intDistribution
                End If
                dbResultBuffer.SetCell(si, cellResult)
            Next
            api.Data.SetDataBuffer(dbResultBuffer, diDestination)
            Return Nothing
            Catch ex As Exception
                Throw ErrorHandler.LogWrite(si, New XFException(si, ex))
            End Try
        End Function
    End Class
End Namespace
```

Data Before and After Calculation

All three Methods have identical functional requirements and broadly similar code patterns which are: clear A#Distribution, loop A#Sales' data buffer to test A#Sales, and then either multiply it by a constant or a U1#productname:E#No_Geograpy rate depending on A#Sales' value.

Calculate Within loops data buffers as Buffer Calculations and writes data on a cell-by-cell value either to clear or calculate Distribution. It reads and writes the Data Unit's entire data buffer many times.

Calculate With Eval uses one data buffer to test, calculate, and clear Distribution in an Eval subroutine. It performs one pass through the Data Unit's data buffer.

Buffer Calculations, as the name implies, performs its clear and calculations in two data buffers.

Regardless of how the logic is performed, the result is the same.

Before

The three conditions of Sales between 200 and 300, greater than 300, and less than 200 (or nothing at all) are evaluated and calculated.

	A	B	C	D
1				2021M8
2	South Carolina	Cameron's 100% Colombian Whole Bean	Sales	303
3	South Carolina	Cameron's 100% Colombian Whole Bean	Distribution	20
5	South Carolina	Celvin's Colombian Supremo Regular Whole Bean	Sales	204
6	South Carolina	Celvin's Colombian Supremo Regular Whole Bean	Distribution	15
8	South Carolina	French Roast Regular Whole Bean Decaf	Sales	54
9	South Carolina	French Roast Regular Whole Bean Decaf	Distribution	7.75
11	South Carolina	Whole Bean	Sales	561
12	South Carolina	Whole Bean	Distribution	42.75
16	No_Geography	Cameron's 100% Colombian Whole Bean	Distribution_Rate	0.0455
19	No_Geography	Celvin's Colombian Supremo Regular Whole Bean	Distribution_Rate	0.045
22	No_Geography	French Roast Regular Whole Bean Decaf	Distribution_Rate	0.044

Figure 2.24

After

Data buffers have been looped, Sales' value has been tested, and appropriate logic and calculations were applied to Distribution. The calculated results match the stated requirements.

	A	B	C	D
1				2021M8
2	South Carolina	Cameron's 100% Colombian Whole Bean	Sales	303
3	South Carolina	Cameron's 100% Colombian Whole Bean	Distribution	13.7865
5	South Carolina	Celvin's Colombian Supremo Regular Whole Bean	Sales	204
6	South Carolina	Celvin's Colombian Supremo Regular Whole Bean	Distribution	8.568
8	South Carolina	French Roast Regular Whole Bean Decaf	Sales	54
9	South Carolina	French Roast Regular Whole Bean Decaf	Distribution	
11	South Carolina	Whole Bean	Sales	561
12	South Carolina	Whole Bean	Distribution	22.3545
16	No_Geography	Cameron's 100% Colombian Whole Bean	Distribution_Rate	0.0455
19	No_Geography	Celvin's Colombian Supremo Regular Whole Bean	Distribution_Rate	0.045
22	No_Geography	French Roast Regular Whole Bean Decaf	Distribution_Rate	0.044

Figure 2.25

Breaking the Data Unit with MemberScriptAndValue

Common knowledge holds that calculations cannot take place outside the current Data Unit.

This belief is wrong.

Calculations Bound by the Data Unit

Finance Business Rules commonly retrieve data from other Data Units for use in calculations, e.g., a calculation in `Cb#Sample:E#South_Carolina:T#2018M1:S#Plan:C#Local` can retrieve data from `E#Pennsylvania`, but cannot write to `E#Pennsylvania`. OneStream will throw an Invalid destination data unit in script message when this is attempted through an `api.Data.Calculate` or an `api.Data.SetDataCell`.

MemberScriptAndValue Calculations Outside the Data Unit

However, the need to write outside a Data Unit exists. This is accomplished through the `MemberScriptAndValue` object, the `List(Of MemberScriptAndValue)` collection, and the `BRApi.Finance.Data.SetDataCellsUsingMemberScript` Method.

Using a Member Script string, the MemberScriptAndValue is assigned a tuple and data value, the MemberScriptAndValue is added to the List(Of MemberScriptAndValue) list collection (collections can have many Key Value Pairs or just one), and the BRApi.Finance.Data.SetDataCellsUsingMemberScript Method writes the list collection to the database.

This technique ignores Data Unit boundaries; values can be written to any Data Unit in the Cube or even outside the Cube.

The MemberScriptAndValue approach cannot write to O#Import; it is O#Forms only. As discussed in the Level 2 Data Unit section, this is a net positive as O#Import data can be overwritten given the right data circumstances.

> **Note:** Although the primary use case for this technique is for writing outside the Data Unit, it can be used within as well.

Outside the Data Unit Use Case

The use case for this Business Rule is running within the Entity *South Carolina*'s Data Unit and writing outside to the Entity *Pennsylvania*.

There are four components to the BreakTheDataUnit Finance Business Rule:

1. Declaring the MemberScriptAndValue object, List(Of MemberScriptAndValue) collection, and Member Script tuple string.

2. Assignment of a numeric value, isNoData as False, and the Member Script tuple properties to the MemberScriptAndValue object.

3. Add the MemberScriptAndValue object to the List(Of MemberScriptAndValue) collection.

4. A commit of the collection to the Cube via the BRApi.Finance.Data.SetDataCellsUsingMemberScript Method within an XFResult object with an error check.

Declarations

Three variables must be defined: the MemberScriptAndValue object, a collection of those objects (this example uses just one – collections can be *n* objects long), and a tuple definition. No values have been assigned to these variables.

```
Dim objMemberScriptValue As New MemberScriptAndValue
Dim objMemberScriptValues As New List(Of MemberScriptAndValue)
Dim strMemberScript As String
```

MemberScriptAndValue Assignments

With the variables declared, the tuple's Member intersection, data value, and a isNoData status as False (which means that it is Real data) must be assigned. To aid code comprehension, the fixed Dimension's Members are assigned to a string variable and then appended to the tuple string.

```
Dim strFixed As String =
"V#Periodic:F#EndBal_Input:I#None:U2#None:U3#None:U4#None:U5#None:U6#N
one:U7#None:U8#None"
strMemberScript =
"Cb#Sample:A#Sales:E#Pennsylvania:O#Forms:U1#10_010:S#Plan:T#2021M1:I#
None:" & strFixed
objMemberScriptValue.Amount = 303
objMemberScriptValue.IsNoData = False
objMemberScriptValue.Script= strMemberScript
```

MemberScriptAndValue Collection Assignment

The MemberScriptAndValue object is now ready for assignment to the objMemberScriptValues collection.

```
objMemberScriptValues.Add(objMemberScriptValue)
```

Write to Cube with SetDataCellsUsingMemberScript

The collection has been valued and is now ready to write to disk via SetDataCellsUsingMemberScript within an XFResult object.

> **Note:** The XFResult object's BoolValue = True property *must* be tested to trap errors; this Method will *not* log errors otherwise.

```
If objMemberScriptValues.Count > 0 Then
    Dim objXFResult As XFResult =
BRApi.Finance.Data.SetDataCellsUsingMemberScript(si,
objMemberScriptValues)
    If Not objXFResult.BoolValue Then
        Throw ErrorHandler.LogWrite(si, New XFException(si,
objXFResult.Message, String.Empty))
    End If
End If
```

Data Management Step

Note that the Data Unit definition is for South_Carolina, not Pennsylvania.

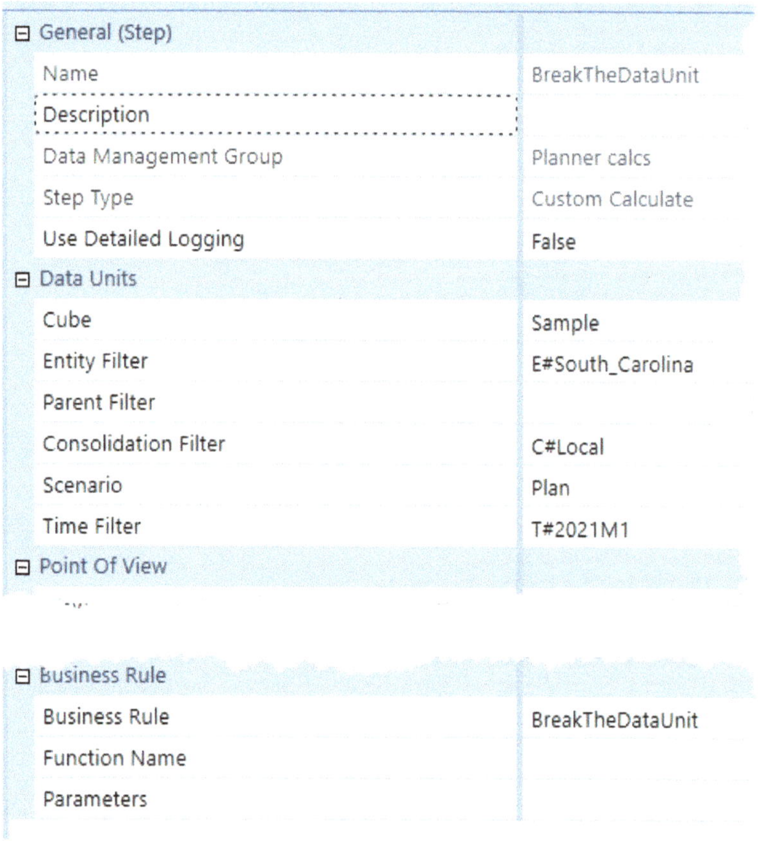

General (Step)	
Name	BreakTheDataUnit
Description	
Data Management Group	Planner calcs
Step Type	Custom Calculate
Use Detailed Logging	False
Data Units	
Cube	Sample
Entity Filter	E#South_Carolina
Parent Filter	
Consolidation Filter	C#Local
Scenario	Plan
Time Filter	T#2021M1
Point Of View	
Business Rule	
Business Rule	BreakTheDataUnit
Function Name	
Parameters	

Figure 2.26

Executing the Step results in values of 42 in the inside-the-Data-Unit E#South_Carolina and 303 in the outside-the-Data-Unit E#Pennsylvania.

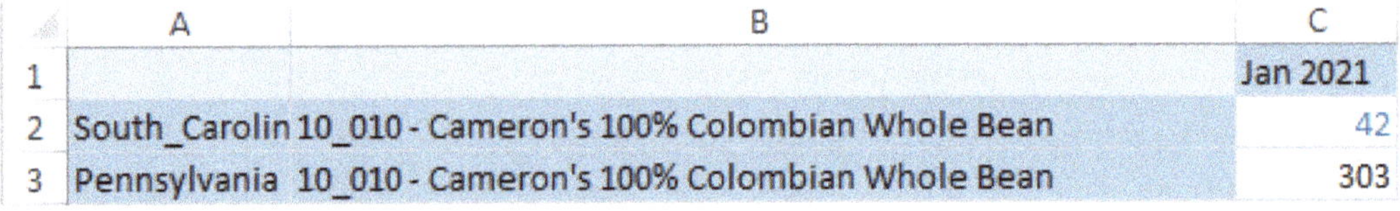

	A	B	C
1			Jan 2021
2	South_Carolin	10_010 - Cameron's 100% Colombian Whole Bean	42
3	Pennsylvania	10_010 - Cameron's 100% Colombian Whole Bean	303

Figure 2.27

Note C2's and C3's different text colors.

DurableCalculation versus Input

When examining a data value in a Quick View or Cube View, `MemberScriptAndValue` does not (as far as OneStream's Data Type tracking is concerned) calculate data. Instead, the technique results in Input data.

There is no functional difference between the two storage Types, but instead evidence of how different `MemberScriptAndValue` is from traditional calculations.

42 Inside the Data Unit

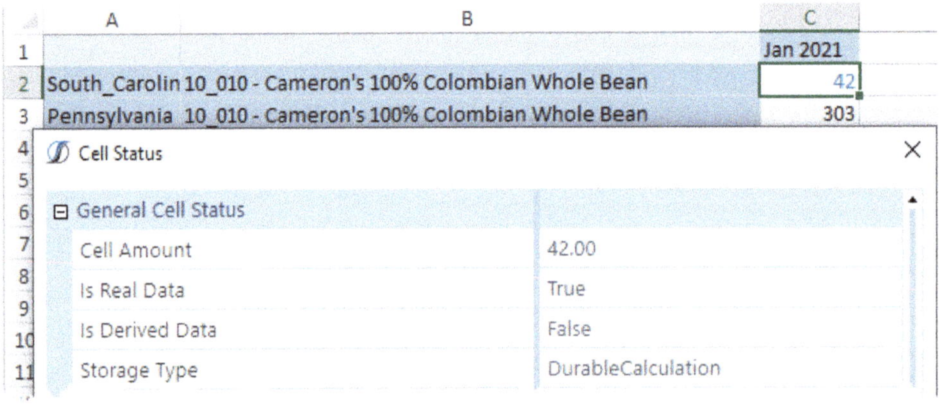

Figure 2.28

303 Outside the Data Unit

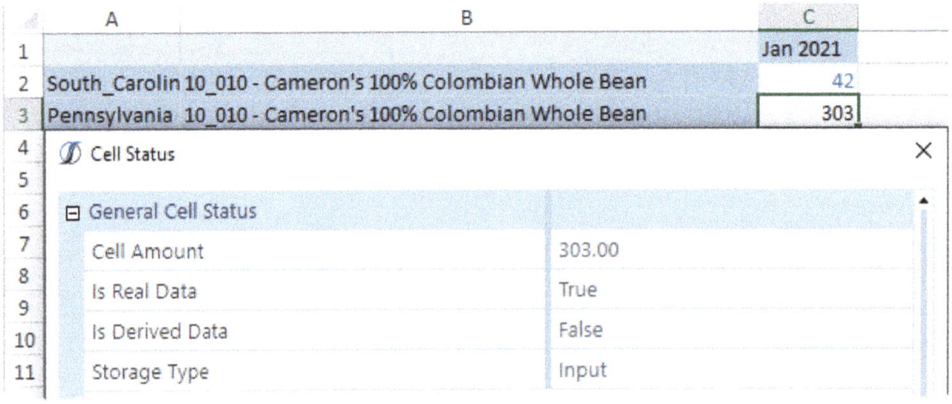

Figure 2.29

Pros and Cons around MemberScriptAndValue

The ability to write outside the Data Unit is useful because it allows a source location to define calculated data targets within the Cube.

Its non-calculated status means that `api.Data.ClearCalculatedData` cannot be used to clear it.

That caution aside, `MemberScriptAndValue` is a powerful and flexible tool for writing to places where code should not – and in theory cannot – go. It can with `MemberScriptAndValue`.

You've Either Got or You Haven't Got Style

Comments and Why We ~~Should~~ Must Use Them

Your authors have produced elegant, highly performant, and sometimes almost witty code – or so they like to think – across the decades. They have written in languages obscure (APL) and common (VBA), obsolete (JCL) and as modern as today (Groovy). Every one of their roles – hobbyist, student, employee, consultant – has revolved around code and its application. It is intrinsic to what they do, the bedrock of their professional reputation, and not incidentally how they earn their daily crust.

And, yet, they cannot remember how or why they wrote a given bit of code if it was written over a week ago and sometimes even less than that. Why?

A OneStream practitioner must play many roles: designer, documenter, tester, trainer, evangelist, and developer. Where one starts and the other ends can be difficult. The pace is frenetic and does not decrease with time.

We are busy, too busy. You are too. We forget many details, as do you, because of our job's other pressures and demands. When we forget, we suffer errors in the form of rework, unpleasant error messages, and worst of all – data errors.

And, yet, all of this can be avoided if we adhere to the discipline of consistently writing concise and meaningful code comments. Good comments – sometimes just *any* kind of comments – can make the difference between OMG-what-did-I-do, and yeah-it's-awesome-the-way-it-works.

You must – we all must – write comments in a form such that we, and those who inherit our code, can understand, maintain, and extend our hard work.

> **Note:** This discussion around comments does not include the larger subject of formal documentation, although your authors have noted that when they fail to write good comments, the formal documentation process is even more excruciating than usual.

The Philosophy of Commenting

Coders seem to either dismiss or embrace the practice of comments. Here are two true, personally-witnessed-by-Cameron stories. In both cases, I was in the very beginning of my career and so even more wide-eyed in wonder than I usually am.

Why Bother?

In what was surely a wildly misplaced although much-appreciated opportunity, I was thrust into an expat opening in A Country That Makes Awfully Good Beer and swapped jobs with a programmer Over There; he took my job, and I took his. He was – and I presume still is – an incredibly gifted programmer and a good 10 years ahead of me in experience. There I was, all of 23, a stranger in a strange land, and I was handed a not-inconsiderable list of systems he owned and that I was slated to maintain. The language (spoken and written, although I was familiar with the programming language) was different, the systems were completely different, even the AZERTY keyboards were different. I was all at sea and desperate for some direction. Like the naïve fool that I was (and still am), I asked if there was commented source code so I could try to make sense out of what appeared to me to be chaos.

The response? "Good programmers can read code." Ouch.

For the record, figuring out his admittedly brilliant work was torture. Whatever I wrote in the course of maintenance was profusely commented. I probably kept the comments' sarcasm level down to barely-acceptable-by-corporate-standards, but likely only just. That was a Not Fun Experience.

Because You Must

Years later, older and only somewhat wiser, I was having a philosophical discussion around comments (yes, I really did and still do, cf. this section) with a usually calmer fellow consultant who – when challenged on the importance and style of commenting – excitedly told me, "For the love of all that is good, don't waste time commenting how you wrote something because I can read code. Tell me *why* you wrote it. Tell me the why, and the rest is easy."

Those are real words of wisdom, ones that even the densest of programmers like *Yr Obt. Svt* can appreciate. Why are they wise? They are wise because the act of writing comments as code is developed like creating a map in a deep and wooded forest for yourself and for everyone else who touches your work. Comments keep us all from getting lost. Getting lost is by turns frustrating and even frightening. Write comments.

Competent Comments

There are two main components to comments: a header block and inline explanations.

Header

Header comments are at the beginning of each code function or subroutine.

1. Identify the code name.

2. Describe the purpose of the code section.

3. Document who wrote the code originally (and when) as well as any modifications. Modified dates must include what was changed and who changed it.

4. Note any special considerations.

5. Indicate what modules or objects call the code in question.

Inline

There must be some ratio of comment-to-code where the value of concise comments decreases… but your authors have yet to experience that.

Inline comments can be as short as a few words or as long as several sentences. Length is not important; conveying why a given block of code does what it does is.

An Example

Header

Reading a Business Rule header comment block should tell the reader the above required header components and impart the code's *raison d'être*.

All five of the header code components are present: name, purpose, modified, author, special considerations, and calling processes.

```
''' Name:        PassingParameters
''' Purpose:     Illustrate how to get/set literal parameters and read parameters from a Data Management step
''' Modified:    18 July 2021, initial write
''' Written by: Cameron Lackpour
''' Notes:       - Data Management parameters CANNOT accept comma-delimited lists.
'''                  * The parameter names themselves are comma-delimited
'''                  * The parameter values for the names CANNOT be comma-delimted but
'''                    _can_ use other delimter characters, e.g. | or ;
'''              - Literal parameters as defined in dashboards are easier but have a completely different syntax.  They too
'''                  * CANNOT receive comma-delimted members
'''              - Parameters example: DimName=Products,Ground_Coffee=20_020|20_030|20_040
```

Inline

Every block of code within the Business Rule is called out and explained.

```
''' Get the name of the UD1 dimension
Dim strUD1 = args.CustomCalculateArgs.NameValuePairs.xfgetvalue("DimName")
''' Log the dimension name
api.LogMessage("DimName: " & strUD1)

''' Get a list of delimted parameters -- this is a two parameter list
''' Note the "U1#" prefix because the first member in the list doesn't have a delimiter
Dim strGroundCoffee As String = "U1#" & args.CustomCalculateArgs.NameValuePairs.XFGetValue("Ground_Coffee").Replace("|", ", U1#")
''' Log the products
api.LogMessage("Ground_Coffee (partial): " & strGroundCoffee)

''' Convert parameter strings into MemberInfo lists
Dim lstGroundCoffee As List(Of MemberInfo) = BRApi.Finance.Metadata.GetMembersUsingFilter(si, strUD1, strGroundCoffee, True, Nothing, Nothing)

''' NB -- Looping and writing members can be necssary but expensive.  Be careful.
For Each mbrProduct As MemberInfo In lstGroundCoffee
    ''' Write out the member name to the error log
    api.LogMessage("mbrProduct: " & mbrProduct.Member.Name)
Next
```

Easy Peasy

There are more than twice as many comments as actual code lines in the function. The effort behind that level of commenting was low (and certainly lower than the code itself). The end result is that the *what* and the *how* of the code is easily understandable because the *why* is fully explained.

Always perform this easy practice and your code will shine. Fail to do so and expose your hard work to error.

Comments In This Chapter

You will note that comments are *not* generally used in code to maximize code clarity. The textual descriptions around code blocks serve the same purpose as comments. Review of the sample application – as available on OneStream Press's site – contains fully-commented code.

Variable Naming

In VB.Net, variables can be named any combination of alphanumeric characters. Special characters such as ! or @ are not valid and will fail on syntax check.

Variable names should be meaningful. Dim X As *Variabletype* is obvious when inline with an assignment, e.g., `Dim X As Decimal = 42.75` and is incomprehensible when viewed 120 or even 12 code lines later.

When naming variables, use the Hungarian notation mnemonic identifier naming convention to help identify the variable Type and purpose. Use lower CamelCase to delineate the variable Type, e.g., `Dim strSales As String` and `Dim decSales As Decimal`. That a string value of some kind should be assigned to `strSales` and a numeric value should be assigned to `decSales` is easy to understand when first read and later through the code.

Variable names can be as long as 255 characters. A variable name that is 255 characters is considered bad form if for no other reason that it makes code line length either unnecessarily break to the next line or scroll off the screen to the right. Make the variable name long enough to be understandable and no more.

Be consistent in your naming convention for your sake and for others who may take ownership of your code.

For more information on programming style, see: https://docs.microsoft.com/en-us/dotnet/visual-basic/programming-guide/program-structure/naming-conventions

Doing It With Class

Common data, metadata, security, and other core operations are used repeatedly within an application, e.g., getting the ancestors of a Base level Member or its siblings returned as a list of Members. Practitioners can (and do) write these on an as-needed basis or create their own code snippets that are copy-pasted into rules or applications.

This ad hoc and informal Method of sharing code would be easier if a central repository of these functions could be created and then be made addressable within other Business Rules. If those functions' complexity could be abstracted so that the Methods could be more easily used, so much the better. Ideally, this collection of functionalities would be importable into an application as a standard OneStream Business Rule.

All of this can be done with a custom OneStream class, an object that defines properties, Methods, and events.

Every (or practically so) operation in a Business Rule calls a class, e.g., `api.Data.Calculate` calls the DataApi class' Calculate Method and passes properties such as a formula and a Boolean for `isDurableCalculatedData`. Navigating through the OneStream API documentation shows this directly.

Via the API Documentation

The DataApi class is referenced in Business Rules through the `Imports OneStream.Finance.Engine` statement at the top of every Business Rule.

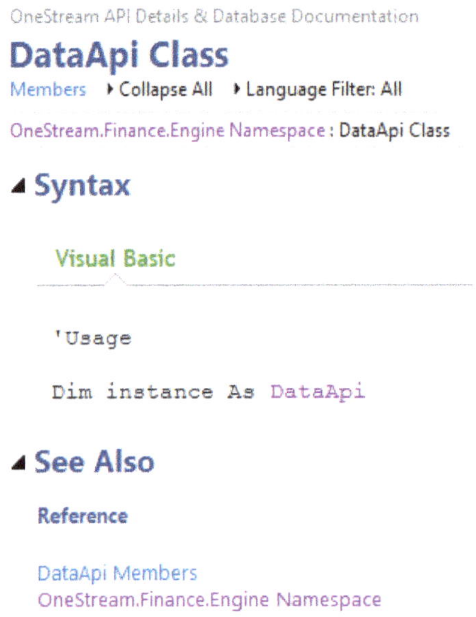

OneStream API Details & Database Documentation

DataApi Class

Members ▸ Collapse All ▸ Language Filter: All

OneStream.Finance.Engine Namespace : DataApi Class

◢ Syntax

Visual Basic

```
'Usage

Dim instance As DataApi
```

◢ See Also

Reference

DataApi Members
OneStream.Finance.Engine Namespace

Figure 2.30

Clicking on DataApi Members links to DataApi Class Members, which (amongst many other public Methods) contains Calculate:

OneStream API Details & Database Documentation

DataApi Class Members

Properties   Methods   ▸ Collapse All   ▸ Members Options: Show All

OneStream.Finance.Engine Namespace : DataApi Class

The following tables list the members exposed by DataApi.

◢ Public Properties

	Name	Description
▦	FormulaVariables	
▦	WritableDataCache	

Top

◢ Public Methods

	Name	Description
≡◈	Calculate	Overloaded.

Figure 2.31

The overloaded `Calculate` Method supports three different parameter sets:

OneStream API Details & Database Documentation

Calculate Method

▸ Collapse All   ▸ Language Filter: All

OneStream.Finance.Engine Namespace > DataApi Class : Calculate Method

◢ Overload List

Overload
Calculate(String,Boolean)
Calculate(String,EvalDataBufferDelegate,Object)
Calculate(String,String,String,String,String,String,String,String,String,String,String,String,String,EvalDataBufferDelegate,Object,Boolean)

◢ See Also

Reference

DataApi Class
DataApi Members

Figure 2.32

The first of which is the overloaded parameter `String,Boolean`:

OneStream API Details & Database Documentation

Calculate(String,Boolean) Method

▸ Collapse All   ▸ Language Filter: All

OneStream.Finance.Engine Namespace > DataApi Class > Calculate Method : Calculate(String,Boolean) Method

▴ **Syntax**

Visual Basic

```
'Usage

Dim instance As DataApi
Dim formula As String
Dim isDurableCalculatedData As Boolean

instance.Calculate(formula, isDurableCalculatedData)
```

Parameters

formula
isDurableCalculatedData

Figure 2.33

As noted, *every* Method in a Business Rule comes from a class of some kind because OneStream is a modern object-oriented, class-based development language.

The Importance of Classes

Why does this matter? It matters because Business Rules themselves are functions (Methods) that run within the Business Rule's class. This can be deduced by examining the start and end of every Business Rule in OneStream, no matter the type.

Business Rules start with a Function declaration within an overall MainClass and when complete return Nothing, thus acting akin to a subroutine.

Header

Here it is:

```
Namespace OneStream.BusinessRule.Finance.RemoveZeros
    Public Class MainClass
        Public Function Main(ByVal si As SessionInfo, ByVal globals As BRGlobals,
            ByVal api As FinanceRulesApi, ByVal args As FinanceRulesArgs) As Object
            Try
```

Footer

```
            Return Nothing
        Catch ex As Exception
            Throw ErrorHandler.LogWrite(si, New XFException(si, ex))
        End Try
    End Function
    End Class
End Namespace
```

Custom Classes

If classes are objects that have properties and Methods that can be instantiated and used within a Business Rule, and Business Rules themselves are classes, then writing custom classes is a matter of creating a Business Rule with functions (Methods), referring to it in a separate Business Rule, and executing the Methods.

Classless

Here is some code to return a comma-delimited list of Base-level Members of Parent:

```
Dim strDimensionName As String = "Products"
Dim strMemberName As String = "Total_Products"

Dim objDimPk As DimPk =
BRApi.Finance.Dim.GetDimPk(si,strDimensionName)
'''    Get the member id from supplied dimension name
```

```
Dim mbrID As Integer = BRApi.Finance.Members.GetMemberId(si,
objDimPk.DimTypeId, strMemberName)

Dim allBaseMembers As List(Of Member) =
BRApi.Finance.Members.GetBaseMembers(si, objDimPk, mbrID, Nothing)

Dim strAllBaseMembers As New List(Of String)

For Each baseMember As Member In allBaseMembers
    strAllBaseMembers.Add(baseMember.Name)
Next
```

Which produces this:

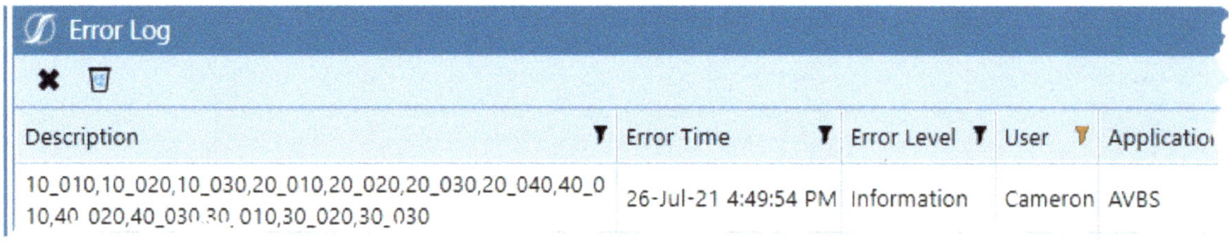

Figure 2.34

Code as a Class

Creating the above code as a function within a custom class removes the explicit Dimension and Member name assignment – the rest of the code is the same with the addition of a Namespace, Class name, and public GetRelative0Members Function:

```
Namespace OneStream.BusinessRule.Finance.MemberFunctions
    Public Class MainClass
        Public Function GetRelative0Members(ByVal si As SessionInfo,
ByVal mbrName As String, ByVal dimName As String) As List (Of String)

        Try
            ''' Get the dimpk from supplied dimension name
            Dim objDimPk As DimPk =
BRApi.Finance.Dim.GetDimPk(si,dimName)
            '''    Get the member id from supplied dimension name
            Dim mbrID As Integer =
BRApi.Finance.Members.GetMemberId(si, objDimPk.DimTypeId, mbrName)

            '''    Get all base members of a given member
            Dim allBaseMembers As List(Of Member) =
BRApi.Finance.Members.GetBaseMembers(si, objDimPk, mbrID, Nothing)

            ''' Add base members to a string list
            Dim strAllBaseMembers As New List(Of String)

            '''    Loop the base members and add them to a string as a
comma-delimted list
            For Each baseMember As Member In allBaseMembers
                strAllBaseMembers.Add(baseMember.Name)
            Next

            '''    Return the list
            Return strAllBaseMembers

        Catch ex As Exception
            Throw ErrorHandler.LogWrite(si, New XFException(si, ex))
        End Try
```

```
        End Function

    End Class
End Namespace
```

Referring to a Business Rule

The TestClassInExtender Extender (This could easily be of Type Finance) Business Rule is calling the Finance MemberFunctions Business Rule.

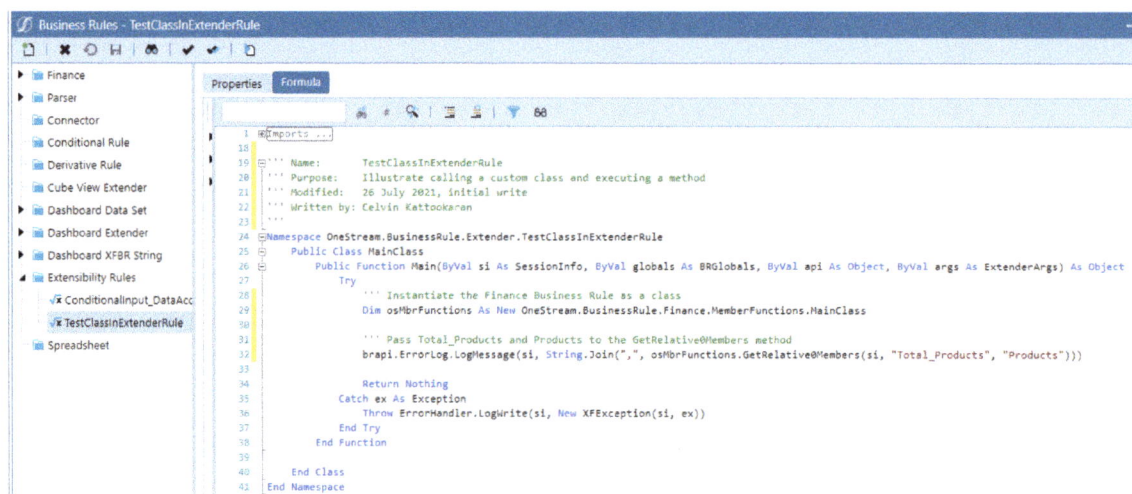

Figure 2.35

Referenced Assemblies

To make the external Business Rule available to the calling Rule, select that Rule's Properties tab and set the Referenced Assemblies property to BR\rulename.

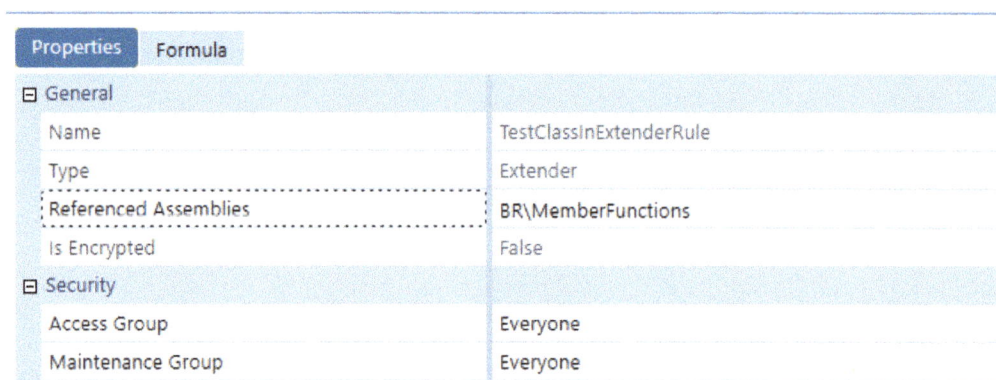

Figure 2.36

Instantiating and Executing GetRelative0Members

In the calling Rule, instantiate the external Business Rule and its core class:

```
Dim osMbrFunctions As New
OneStream.BusinessRule.Finance.MemberFunctions.MainClass
```

Writing the level zero descendants of U1#Total_Products to the log is now one line of code in the calling Business Rule:

```
brapi.ErrorLog.LogMessage(si, String.Join(",",
osMbrFunctions.GetRelative0Members(si, "Total_Products", "Products")))
```

82

The output is the same:

Description	Error Time	Error Level	User	Application
10_010,10_020,10_030,20_010,20_020,20_030,20_040,40_0 10,40_020,40_030,30_010,30_020,30_030	26-Jul-21 5:24:57 PM	Information	Cameron	AVBS

Figure 2.37

Consistent and Portable

A class that contains multiple functions is valuable because it can be written once, used many times, always works the same way, and is easily moved across applications.

> **Note:** Consulting companies that create code libraries could (and should if they have not already done so) compile similar functions into classes and then use them in *all* of their implementations. Customers and clients should create their own custom classes and use them as well, for the same reasons. The effort is low; the reward is high. Use custom classes wherever you can.

The End of Core I

This chapter has covered important good practices in subjects both common and unusual. Even the commonplace (data buffers, code style) topics have nuances; the uncommon are the product of your authors encountering unexplained behavior (Level 2 Data Units) or realizing an opportunity to explore how OneStream really works (data storage).

The next chapter, Core II – Commanding and Controlling OneStream Planning, is the companion to the Cube-oriented subject matter in this chapter. The marriage of Slice Security and Conditional Input, SQL as a Cube data source and driver of Finance Business Rules, dynamic Excel retrieves via XFBR Business Rules, Extended Dimensionality, the role of Stage reporting in a Cube-centric system, and a new way of thinking about Planning Scenarios are all covered in detail.

These subjects can be consumed in isolation but are best studied holistically in conjunction with this chapter. Understanding the Core(s) of OneStream is vital to our understanding of how to use OneStream to its fullest potential.

3

Core Planning II – Command and Control the Cube

Directing OneStream Planning

The Core Planning I chapter examined the Cube core of Planning in OneStream. This chapter continues in that vein of detailed exploration of Cube functionality and how you, Gentle Reader, can best expand its potential through XFBR Business Rules, understand ostensibly simple Scenario Workflow, and define vital data security through Conditional Input, Entity read-write, and Data Cell Access Security.

As before, this chapter is thematically organized but can be read individually by subject.

Are you sitting comfortably? Then let us begin.

I've Got the World on a String

The ability to drive behavior in OneStream through programmatically-driven strings seems (on its surface) to be a minor capability – but just what value are short text strings to a numerically-oriented database? In fact, the ability to create string values on the fly is an incredible boon – not for directly displaying text in a Cube View or Dashboard – but instead for dynamically driving practically everything OneStream.

If a property in OneStream is a string (practically everything is) and if those properties are ubiquitous throughout the product (they are), the ability to intelligently drive them to reflect business and system conditions without Planner or Administrator intervention is a huge advantage that few if any of OneStream's competitors can match. Understanding and exploiting this opportunity wherever possible is a perspective and practice that *all* OneStream developers must adopt if they wish to fully benefit from OneStream's power. How is it done? In a word: XFBRs.

What's In a Name?

A note about OneStream's Business Rules taxonomy: XFBRs are Dashboard String Function Business Rules that return strings. What "XFBR" *stands* for, beyond the now-deprecated "XF" part of the product name, is a mystery to all and sundry. Was it the first kind of Business Rule (the last two BR characters in XFBR)? That seems unlikely given the central role of Finance Business Rules. A lack of imagination on the part of OneStream's architects and developers? Given OneStream's depth and breadth and the 11 different kinds of Business Rules and the eight different Event Handlers, the notion that a Rule Type name that consumes the product and feature names seems just as unlikely.

Whatever the name's genesis, do not be confused: XFBR Business Rules replace manually entered hard-coded text with code-driven output. Given that Member names and filters, Business Rule names, parameters, and practically every other property in OneStream are textual, the opportunities for dynamic string substitution through XFBR code are abundant. It is a powerful feature and one that any well-formed OneStream application will use to the utmost because XFBRs will make that application robust, dynamic, and low maintenance.

Piece by Piece

To call an XFBR, use this format: `BRString(rulename, functionname, param1=param1value, param2=param2value, paramn=paramnvalue)`. The XFBR name is required, as is the function name (more anon). Optional parameters are defined in a comma-delimited list. Parameters can be used in lieu of `param<n>value`, using `|!` and `!|` symbols to delineate a parameter name. Substitution Variables can also be used using `|` and `|` symbols as identifiers. Functions are required even if an XFBR has only one function.

An XFBR is a BRString is an XFBR

XFBR Business Rules can be called using either `XFBR` or `BRString`. This chapter will use `BRString` to differentiate between a command and the Rule Type.

Multiple Function XFBR Unit Versus Regression Testing

A Business Rule (XFBRs included) that contains more than one function should – were OneStream developers to adhere to professional software development practice – be fully regression-tested whenever a single function is changed. That means, in practical terms, changing or adding a single function to a multi-function Business Rule should trigger testing for *all* of the functions that are in the XFBR.

Gentle Reader, before you scoff (or despair at the workload) at this approach, inadvertently changing a line of code in *any* of the functions (including the one that you, pinky-promise, was untouched by human hands) in an XFBR – even by a single character – is enough to break that code and, if it compile checks successfully, will not reveal itself until it is called because VB.Net treats everything inside double quotes as a String, and a String cannot be checked for validity.

Given the common practice of multiple functions per Business Rule – your author has observed this code style in every Business Rule that supports function branching – you *must* test *all* of the functions in your code when you make a code change in any function in the Business Rule. Really. You Have Been Warned.

Driving Excel

The Principles Chapter covered the OneStream Excel add-in and its (generally) powerful functionality as well as its (minor but still annoying) missing features, particularly the one around the inability to support asymmetrical columns. Asymmetric row and column retrieves *are* possible if a multidimensional Member script is employed in a Member Filter.

The Excel add-in supports asymmetrical row and column selection through concatenated multidimensional Member Filters,

e.g., a Time Member Filter of: `T#2021M1:S#Actual:Name(2021M1 Actual), T#2021M2:S#Actual:Name(2021M2 Actual), T#2021M3:S#Plan:Name(2021M3 Plan)` returns an asymmetrical column retrieve that retrieves both Actual and Plan where the Quick View POV is Actual-only.

	2021M1 Actual	2021M2 Actual	2021M3 Plan
Profit	25	30	25
Margin	180	185	180
Sales	200	210	190
COGS	20	25	10
Total Expenses	155	155	155
Marketing	5	5	5
Payroll	150	150	150
Distribution			
Misc			

Figure 3.1

This approach, however, requires the Planner to understand how to create cross-dimensional partial tuples, how the `Name()` function works, and the importance of matching a replacement description with the Member tuple. Moreover, if this was a quarterly Report, the cross-dimensional tuple and alias must follow the march of Actuals across the year. While this is certainly possible for a single analyst within a single Quick View, a correct Member Filter across multiple Quick Views and for more than one analyst is unlikely given the complexity and maintenance requirements.

From a Quarter Whisper to a Year Scream

This issue around Planner comprehension, maintenance effort, and error potential becomes more problematic when the common use case of a 12-month mixed Actual and Plan Quick View is examined.

Following the same multidimensional tuple approach, this Member Filter –
`T#2021M1:S#Actual:Name(2021M1 Actual), T#2021M2:S#Actual:Name(2021M2 Actual), T#2021M3:S#Plan:Name(2021M3 Plan), T#2021M4:S#Plan:Name(2021M4 Plan), T#2021M5:S#Plan:Name(2021M5 Plan), T#2021M6:S#Plan:Name(2021M6 Plan), T#2021M7:S#Plan:Name(2021M7 Plan), T#2021M8:S#Plan:Name(2021M8 Plan), T#2021M9:S#Plan:Name(2021M9 Plan), T#2021M10:S#Plan:Name(2021M10 Plan),T#2021M11:S#Plan:Name(2021M11 Plan), T#2021M12:S#Plan:Name(2021M12 Plan)` – produces a 12-month column set that shows a 2021M3 Plan start:

	2021M1 Actual	2021M2 Actual	2021M3 Plan	2021M4 Plan	2021M5 Plan	2021M6 Plan	2021M7 Plan	2021M8 Plan	2021M9 Plan	2021M10 Plan	2021M11 Plan	2021M12 Plan
Profit	25	30	25	25	25	25	25	25	25	25	25	25
Margin	180	185	180	183	183	183	183	183	183	183	183	183
Sales	200	210	190	200	200	200	200	200	200	200	200	200
COGS	20	25	10	17	17	17	17	17	17	17	17	17
Total Expenses	155	155	155	158	158	158	158	158	158	158	158	158
Marketing	5	5	5	5	5	5	5	5	5	5	5	5
Payroll	150	150	150	145	145	145	145	145	145	145	145	145
Distribution				7	7	7	7	7	7	7	7	7
Misc				1	1	1	1	1	1	1	1	1

Figure 3.2

As time passes in the year, and Plan months are replaced by Actuals, the Planner will have to edit the Time and Scenario Dimensions as well as the Name property.

A Better Way

What this hypothetical Planner needs is a dynamic, parameterized, and system-driven approach. An XFBR can do exactly this while making the Time Dimension Member Filter simple and, once used, maintenance-free.

This XFBR Business Rule must create a 12-column Member Filter that mixes Actual and Plan using the `T#time:S#scenario:Name(alias)` Member definition.

To do this, the XFBR Business Rule must:

1. Accept a four-digit year parameter.

2. Accept a Scenario name parameter.

3. Read a Dashboard Literal Parameter value that defines the current Forecast Time in YYYYMm(m) format.

4. Compare the XFBR year parameter with the Literal Parameter Forecast Time's year.

5. If the XFBR year parameter is not equal to the Literal Parameter Forecast Time's year, return the 12 months of the parameter year.

6. If the XFBR year parameter is equal to the Literal Parameter Forecast Time's year, create a 12-month Member list that:

   a. Concatenates `S#Actual` for all Time periods before the Literal Parameter value.

   b. Concatenates `S#scenarioname` to all Time periods equal to or greater than the Literal Parameter value.

The XFBR Member Filter

This is it: `BRString(Book_ParamHelper, MixedYear, Year = 2021, Scenario = Plan)`.

Book_Parameter Code

There are two sections to the XFBR Business Rule `Book_Parameter`: `Public Function Main` and `Private Function functionname`.

Public Function Main

This fires when the XFBR is called, and branches based on the passed function name to the private function that performs the logic.

```
Namespace OneStream.BusinessRule.DashboardStringFunction.Book_ParamHelper
    Public Class MainClass
        Public Function Main(ByVal si As SessionInfo, ByVal globals As BRGlobals,
            ByVal api As Object, ByVal args As DashboardStringFunctionArgs) As Object
            Try

                If args.FunctionName.XFEqualsIgnoreCase("MixedYear")
                    Return Me.MixedYear(si, globals, args)
                End If

                Return Nothing
            Catch ex As Exception
                Throw ErrorHandler.LogWrite(si, New XFException(si, ex))
            End Try
        End Function
    End Function
```

Calling MixedYear

The `If` test for `args.FunctionName.XFEqualsIgnoreCase("MixedYear")` tests for the function name and then calls the function by `Me.MixedYear`.

The `Return Me.functionname(si, globals, args)` directs the class to branch to the function and then passes the result of that function back to the calling Component, which – for this use case – is the Excel add-in Member Filter. Unlike Finance Business Rules, the `Return` statement here is significant because it passes the string result to the calling Component, which could be a Dashboard button, a Cube View column, or anywhere a String is supported.

```
If args.FunctionName.XFEqualsIgnoreCase("MixedYear") Then
            Return Me.MixedYear(si, globals, args)
```

The `SessionInfo`, `BRGlobals`, and `DashboardStringFunctionArgs` arguments are required for this Rule to work. Depending on the function's requirements, only `SessionInfo` is required; the commonly used `API` is absent from this example.

Variables and Parameters

The Year and Scenario passed as parameters are assigned to string variables using the `args.NameValuePairs.XFGetValue("parametername")` Method.

The Dashboard Literal Parameter `ForecastMonth` is queried via `BRApi.Dashboards.Parameters.GetLiteralParameterValue(si, False, "literalparametervalue")`.

OneStream supports many kinds of parameters, of which a Literal Value Type is the simplest, being a parameter name and a text value.

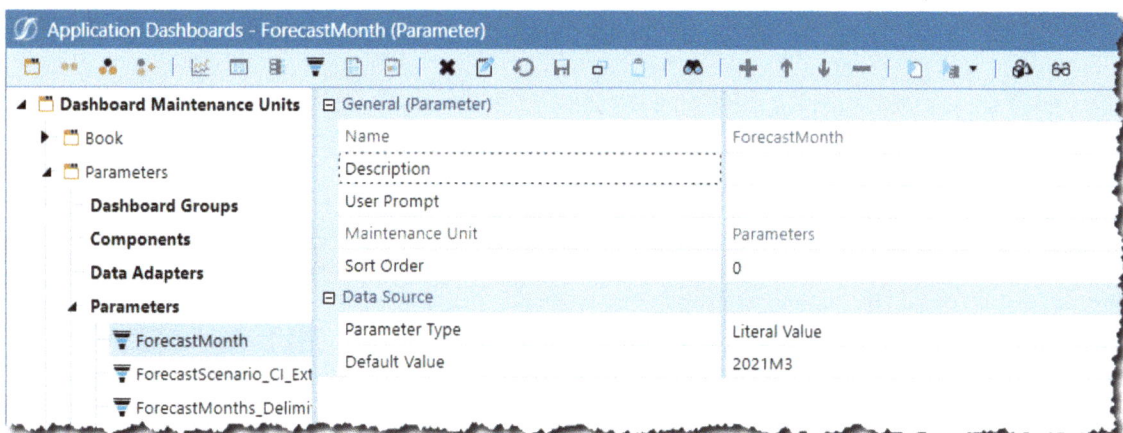

Figure 3.3

Consider organizing parameters that are used across multiple functions in a OneStream application within a separate **Dashboard Maintenance Unit**.

```
Dim strYear As String = args.NameValuePairs.XFGetValue("Year")
Dim intYear As Integer = CInt(strYear)
Dim strScenario As String = args.NameValuePairs.XFGetValue("Scenario")
Dim strForecastMonth As String =
BRApi.Dashboards.Parameters.GetLiteralParameterValue(si, False,
"ForecastMonth")
Dim intForecastYear As Integer = CInt(Left(strForecastMonth, 4))
```

Declare and value Time variables for comparison and looping. While value tests of numbers as strings are possible (the string "1967" is less than the string "1980"), your author is driven bonkers by strings-as-numbers for value testing, and so converts string numbers like calendar years to integers.

```
Dim strTime As New List(Of String)
Dim intMonth As Integer = Right(strForecastMonth,2).Replace("M","")
```

Forecast Year Less Than Parameter Year

If the ForecastMonth Literal Parameter's year is less than the XFBR Year parameter, year is pure (in this example, as that is the XFBR Scenario value) Plan. Return the months of the XFBR Year cross-dimensioned to the XFBR Scenario; use the XFBR Scenario in the Name property.

A simple loop is used to concatenate the 1-based counter to the year.

```
If intForecastYear < intYear Then
    For intKount As Integer = 1 To 12
        strTime.Add("T#" & strYear & "M" & intKount.ToString & ":S#" &
strScenario & ":Name(" & strYear & "M" & intKount.ToString & "-" &
strScenario & ")")
    Next intKount
```

Forecast Year Greater Than Parameter Year

If the ForecastMonth Literal Parameter's year is greater than the XFBR Year, the year is pure Actual. Return the months of the XFBR Year cross-dimensioned to Actual; use Actual in the Name property.

```
Else If intForecastYear > intYear Then
    For intKount As Integer = 1 To 12
        strTime.Add("T#" & strYear & "M" & intKount.ToString &
":S#Actual:Name(" & strYear & "M" & intKount.ToString & "-" &
"Actual)")
    Next intKount
```

Forecast Year is the Same as the Parameter Year

If the ForecastMonth Literal Parameter's year is the same as the XFBR Year, the year is a mix of Actual and (again, this example's passed Scenario) Plan.

Within the loop of the months, if the counter value is greater than or equal to the ForecastMonth Literal Parameter's month, the period is Plan, the XFBR Year is cross-dimensioned to the XFBR Scenario; use the XFBR Scenario in the Name property. If the counter value is less than the ForecastMonth Literal Parameter's month, the period is Actual, the XFBR Year is cross-dimensioned to Actual; use Actual in the Name property.

```
ElseIf intForecastYear = intYear Then
    For intKount = 1 To 12
        If intKount >= intMonth Then
            strTime.Add("T#" & strYear & "M" & intKount.ToString & ":S#"
& strScenario & ":Name(" & strYear & "M" & intKount.ToString & "-" &
strScenario & ")")
        Else
```

```
        strTime.Add("T#" & strYear & "M" & intKount.ToString &
":S#Actual:Name(" & strYear & "M" & intKount.ToString & "-" & "Actual"
& ")")
      End If
   Next intKount
End If
```

Returning the Result

A 12-element `List(Of String)` has been created, whatever the condition branching. The OneStream add-in requires a string. Use `String.Join` to return a comma-delimited list to the calling Quick View Member Filter via the Main function.

```
Return String.Join(",", strTime)
```

When writing XFBRs, an easy check to see if the desired string has been generated is a write to the Error Log. Be sure to remove or comment out any writes after testing.

```
brapi.ErrorLog.LogMessage(si, string.Join(",", strTime))
```

Description	Error Time	Error Level	User	Application
T#2022M1:S#Plan:Name(2022M1-Plan),T#2022M2:S#Plan:Name(2022M2-Plan),T#2022M3:S#Plan:Name(2022M3-Plan),T#2022M4:S#Plan:Name(2022M4-Plan),T#2022M5:S#Plan:Name(2022M5-Plan),T#2022M6:S#Plan:Name(2022M6-Plan),T#2022M7:S#Plan:Name(2022M7-Plan),T#2022M8:S#Plan:Name(2022M8-Plan),T#2022M9:S#Plan:Name(2022M9-Plan),T#2022M10:S#Plan:Name(2022M10-Plan),T#2022M11:S#Plan:Name(2022M11-Plan),T#2022M12:S#Plan:Name(2022M12-Plan)	12-Sep-21 3:07:29 PM	Information	Cameron	AVBS
T#2021M1:S#Actual:Name(2021M1-Actual),T#2021M2:S#Actual:Name(2021M2-Actual),T#2021M3:S#Plan:Name(2021M3-Plan),T#2021M4:S#Plan:Name(2021M4-Plan),T#2021M5:S#Plan:Name(2021M5-Plan),T#2021M6:S#Plan:Name(2021M6-Plan),T#2021M7:S#Plan:Name(2021M7-Plan),T#2021M8:S#Plan:Name(2021M8-Plan),T#2021M9:S#Plan:Name(2021M9-Plan),T#2021M10:S#Plan:Name(2021M10-Plan),T#2021M11:S#Plan:Name(2021M11-Plan),T#2021M12:S#Plan:Name(2021M12-Plan)	12-Sep-21 3:07:29 PM	Information	Cameron	AVBS
T#2020M1:S#Actual:Name(2020M1-Actual),T#2020M2:S#Actual:Name(2020M2-Actual),T#2020M3:S#Actual:Name(2020M3-Actual),T#2020M4:S#Actual:Name(2020M4-Actual),T#2020M5:S#Actual:Name(2020M5-Actual),T#2020M6:S#Actual:Name(2020M6-Actual),T#2020M7:S#Actual:Name(2020M7-Actual),T#2020M8:S#Actual:Name(2020M8-Actual),T#2020M9:S#Actual:Name(2020M9-Actual),T#2020M10:S#Actual:Name(2020M10-Actual),T#2020M11:S#Actual:Name(2020M11-Actual),T#2020M12:S#Actual:Name(2020M12-Actual)	12-Sep-21 3:07:29 PM	Information	Cameron	AVBS

Figure 3.4

Note that XFBRs must use the `brapi.ErrorLog.LogMessage` Method.

ParamHelper

```
Namespace OneStream.BusinessRule.DashboardStringFunction.Book_ParamHelper
    Public Class MainClass
        Public Function Main(ByVal si As SessionInfo, ByVal globals As BRGlobals,
            ByVal api As Object, ByVal args As DashboardStringFunctionArgs) As Object
            Try
                If args.FunctionName.XFEqualsIgnoreCase("MixedYear")
                    Return Me.MixedYear(si, globals, args)
                End If
                Return Nothing
            Catch ex As Exception
                Throw ErrorHandler.LogWrite(si, New XFException(si, ex))
            End Try
        End Function
        Private Function MixedYear(ByVal si As SessionInfo, ByVal globals As BRGlobals,
        ByVal args As DashboardStringFunctionArgs) As String
            Try
                Dim strYear As String = args.NameValuePairs.XFGetValue("Year")
                Dim intYear As Integer = CInt(strYear)
                Dim strScenario As String = args.NameValuePairs.XFGetValue("Scenario")
                Dim strForecastMonth As String = BRApi.Dashboards.Parameters.GetLiteralParameterValue(si, False, "ForecastMonth")
                Dim intForecastYear As Integer = CInt(Left(strForecastMonth, 4))
                Dim strTime As New List(Of String)
                Dim intMonth As Integer = Right(strForecastMonth,2).Replace("M","")
                If intForecastYear < intYear Then
                    For intKount As Integer = 1 To 12
                        strTime.Add("T#" & strYear & "M" & intKount.ToString & ":S#" & strScenario & _
                            ":Name(" & strYear & "M" & intKount.ToString & "-" & strScenario & ")")
                    Next intKount
                Else If intForecastYear > intYear Then
                    For intKount As Integer = 1 To 12
                        strTime.Add("T#" & strYear & "M" & intKount.ToString & ":S#Actual:Name(" & _
                            strYear & "M" & intKount.ToString & "-" & "Actual)")
                    Next intKount
                ElseIf intForecastYear = intYear Then
                    For intKount = 1 To 12
                        If intKount >= intMonth Then
                            strTime.Add("T#" & strYear & "M" & intKount.ToString & ":S#" & strScenario & _
                                ":Name(" & strYear & "M" & intKount.ToString & "-" & strScenario & ")")
                        Else
                            strTime.Add("T#" & strYear & "M" & intKount.ToString & ":S#Actual:Name(" & strYear & _
                                "M" & intKount.ToString & "-" & "Actual" & ")")
                        End If
                    Next intKount
                End If
                Return String.Join(",", strTime)
            Catch ex As Exception
                Throw ErrorHandler.LogWrite(si, New XFException(si, ex))
            End Try
        End Function
    End Class
End Namespace
```

So, What Do We Have?

A combination of the Dashboard Literal Parameter ForecastMonth with the XFBR function MixedYear results in a dynamic, maintenance-free (except for the setting of ForecastMonth) and simple way of creating an asymmetric Time/Scenario column set.

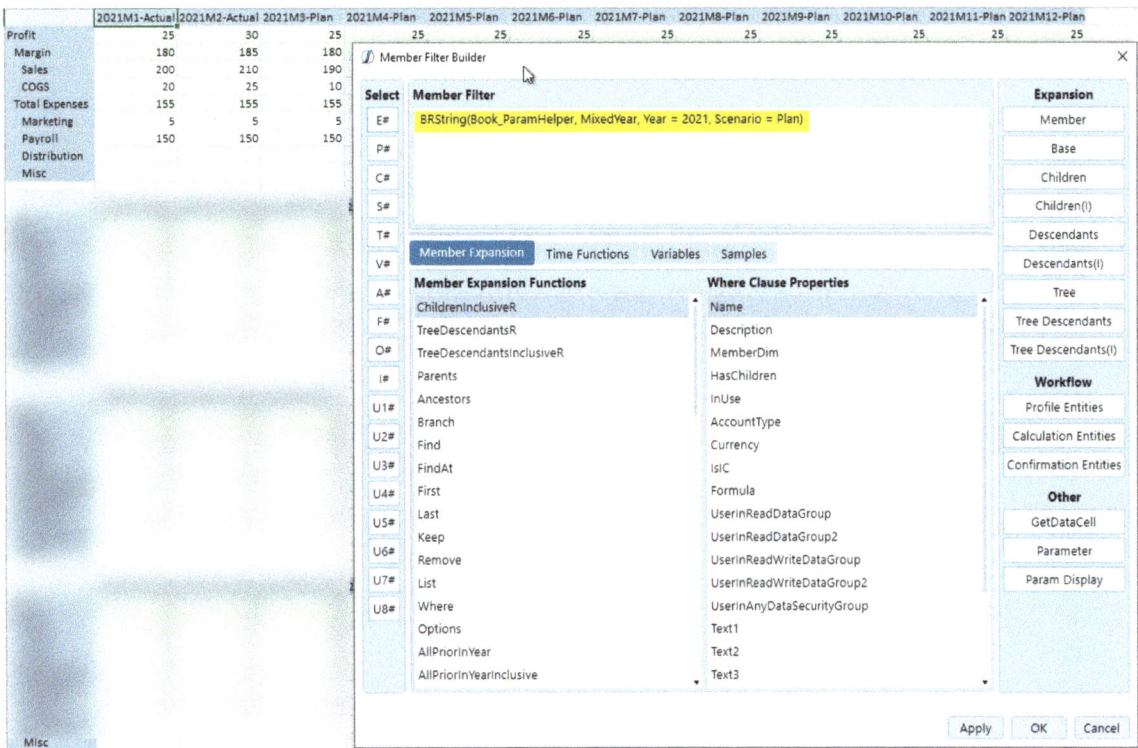

Figure 3.5

Simpler and Simpler

An XFBR returns a string. The definition of an XFBR within a calling object is a string. A **Literal Parameter** is a variable that substitutes a string. A Literal Parameter that is the string that calls the XFBR Rule can be used in a Member Filter (as well as everywhere an XFBR is valid).

The Literal Parameter `PlanMonths` has a Default Value of `BRString(Book_ParamHelper, MixedYear, Year = 2021, Scenario = Plan)`.

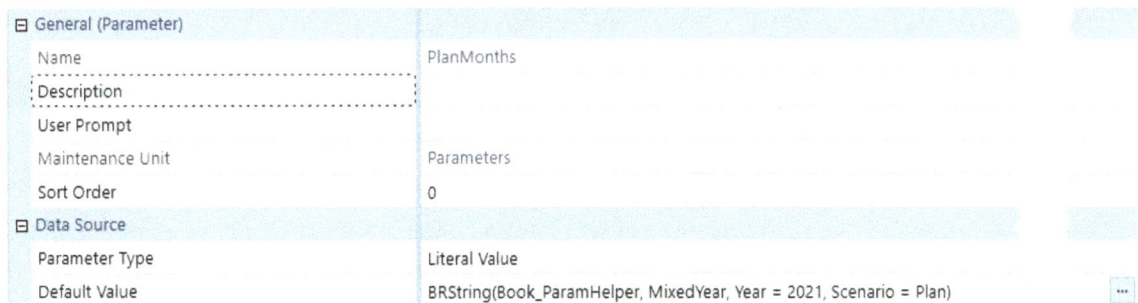

Figure 3.6

It can be called within the Excel add-in Member Filter as `|!PlanMonths!|`:

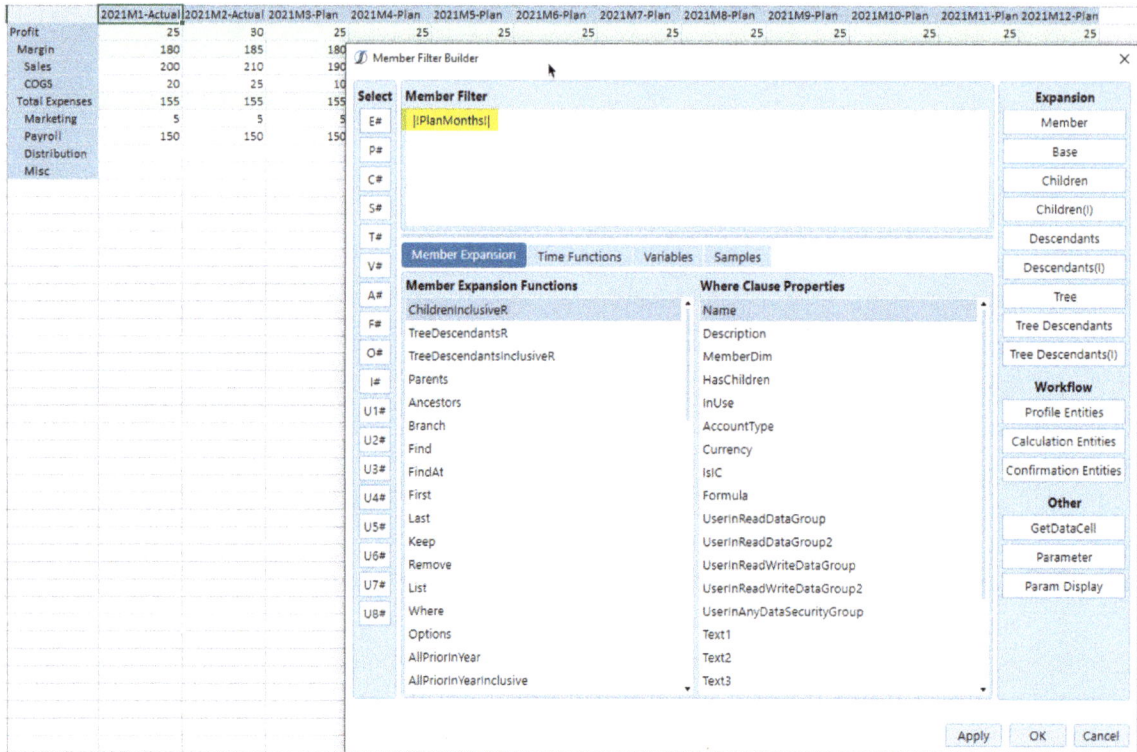

	2021M1-Actual	2021M2-Actual	2021M3-Plan	2021M4-Plan	2021M5-Plan	2021M6-Plan	2021M7-Plan	2021M8-Plan	2021M9-Plan	2021M10-Plan	2021M11-Plan	2021M12-Plan
Profit	25	30	25	25	25	25	25	25	25	25	25	25
Margin	180	185	180									
Sales	200	210	190									
COGS	20	25	10									
Total Expenses	155	155	155									
Marketing	5	5	5									
Payroll	150	150	150									
Distribution												
Misc												

Figure 3.7

A 14-character parameter is significantly more dynamic, maintenance-free, and simple than a 432-character Time/Scenario/Name Member list.

Using XFBRs in Excel

XFBRs within Excel are but one use case for this powerful and flexible Business Rule Type. A small amount of code can drive a large amount of functionality. The application of XFBRs within OneStream applications is almost boundless and is limited only by our collective imagination.

Consolidating in a Multi-Year Workflow

Month by Month by Month

Actual-Type Scenarios typically have a Workflow Tracking Frequency of All Time Periods. This results in a month-by-month Workflow:

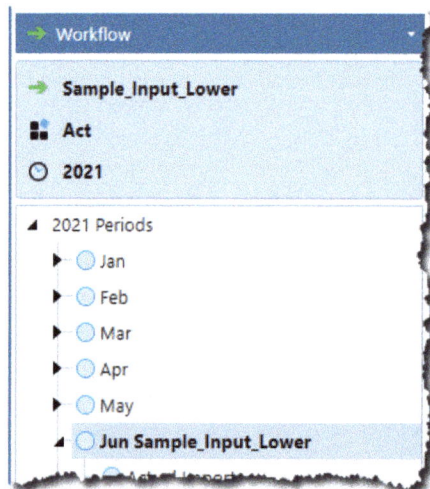

Figure 3.8

Consolidating the current Workflow month is both logical in that Actual data is by month, and easy because the `|WFTime|` system Substitution Variable drives the Time Member.

Running this Data Management Step when 2021M6 is selected in Workflow…

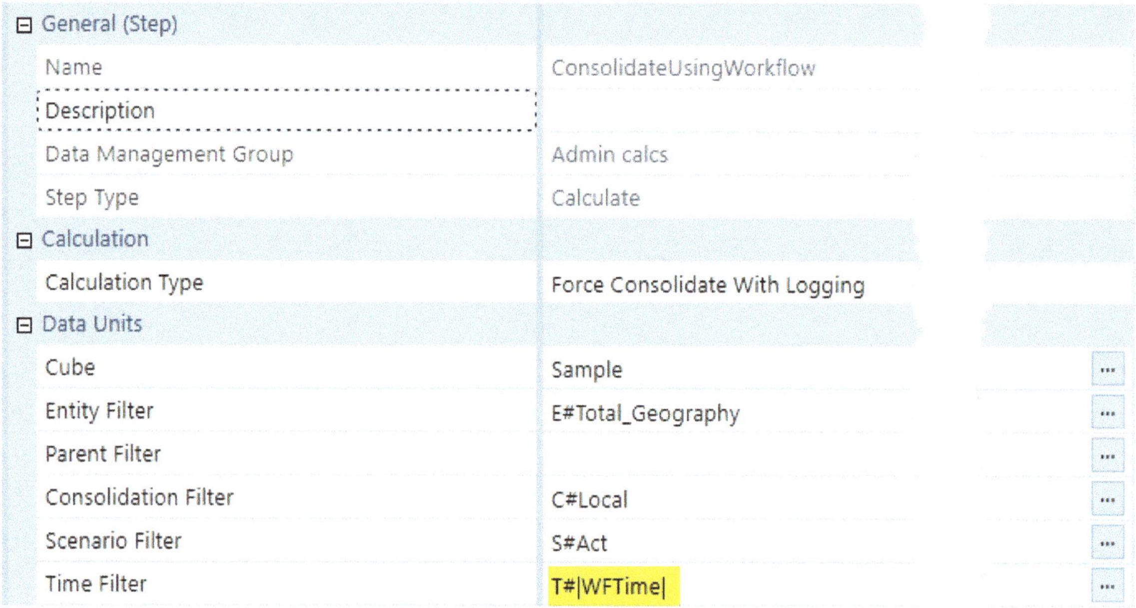

General (Step)	
Name	ConsolidateUsingWorkflow
Description	
Data Management Group	Admin calcs
Step Type	Calculate
Calculation	
Calculation Type	Force Consolidate With Logging
Data Units	
Cube	Sample …
Entity Filter	E#Total_Geography …
Parent Filter	…
Consolidation Filter	C#Local …
Scenario Filter	S#Act …
Time Filter	T#|WFTime| …

Figure 3.9

…results in `T#2021M6`'s Consolidation.

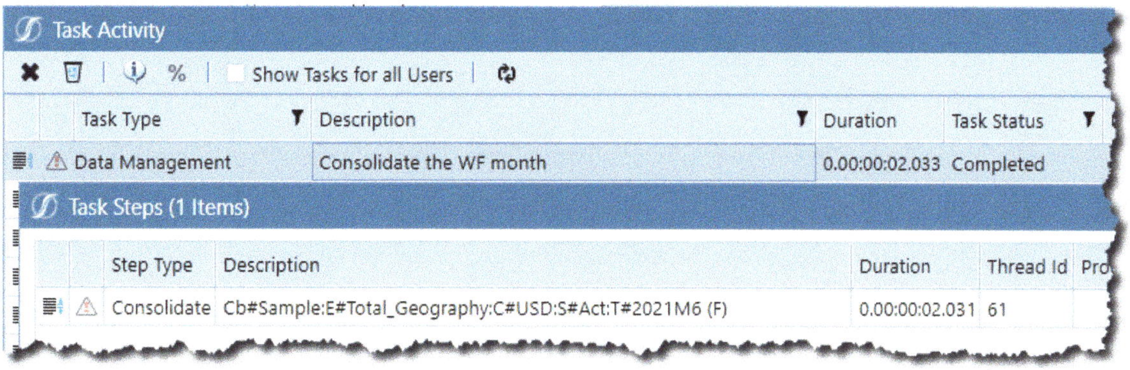

Task Activity				
✖ 🗑 ⬇ % ☐ Show Tasks for all Users ↻				
Task Type ▼	Description ▼		Duration	Task Status ▼
⚠ Data Management	Consolidate the WF month		0.00:00:02.033	Completed
Task Steps (1 Items)				
Step Type	Description		Duration	Thread Id Pro
⚠ Consolidate	Cb#Sample:E#Total_Geography:C#USD:S#Act:T#2021M6 (F)		0.00:00:02.031	61

Figure 3.10

This native approach fulfills the monthly Consolidation requirement because `|WFTime|` returns both the year and the month, cf. the example above, which returns `2021M6`.

Range and Yearly

A single-year Forecast and Budget spans all 12 months; multi-year Planning goes to 24 and beyond. These Plan Scenarios will have a Workflow Tracking Frequency of Range or Yearly.

A single-year Plan range *can* use `T#|WFYear|M12` to drive that year's Time Consolidation range.

Once more than one year is used in the Workflow, `T#|WFYear|` cannot return the correct Time Dimension Member range because the Substitution Variable returns only the first year of the Workflow.

Member Properties	Relationship Properties	
⊟ General		
Dimension Type	Scenario Dimension Type	
Dimension	Scenarios Dimension	
Member Dimension	Scenarios Dimension	
Id	11	
Name	Plan	

Use In Workflow	True	
Workflow Tracking Frequency	Range	
Workflow Time	2021	...
Workflow Start Time	2021M1	...
Workflow End Time	2050M12	...
Number Of No Input Periods Per Workflow Unit	0	

Figure 3.11

When the Plan Scenario is selected in OnePlace:

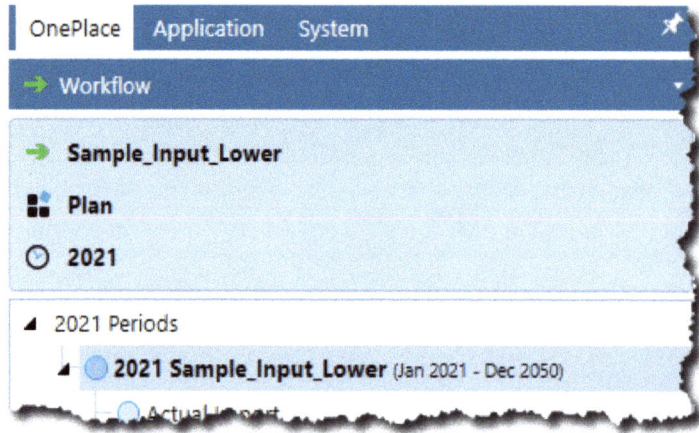

Figure 3.12

A Force Consolidate With Logging step using |WFYear| to drive the M12 Time period…

General (Step)	
Name	ConsolidateUsingWorkflow
Description	
Data Management Group	Admin calcs
Step Type	Calculate
Calculation	
Calculation Type	Force Consolidate With Logging
Data Units	
Cube	Sample
Entity Filter	E#Total_Geography
Parent Filter	
Consolidation Filter	C#Local
Scenario Filter	S#Plan
Time Filter	T#|WFYear|M12

Figure 3.13

…will result in 2021-only as the Consolidation timespan:

		Step Type	Description	Duration
	⚠	Consolidate Children	Cb#Sample:E#Total_Geography:S#Plan_Yearly:T#2021M12	0.00:00
	⚠	Consolidate Entity	Cb#Sample:E#Total_Geography:S#Plan_Yearly:T#2021M1	0.00:00
	⚠	Consolidate Entity	Cb#Sample:E#Total_Geography:S#Plan_Yearly:T#2021M2	0.00:00
	⚠	Consolidate Entity	Cb#Sample:E#Total_Geography:S#Plan_Yearly:T#2021M3	0.00:00
	⚠	Consolidate Entity	Cb#Sample:E#Total_Geography:S#Plan_Yearly:T#2021M4	0.00:00
	⚠	Consolidate Entity	Cb#Sample:E#Total_Geography:S#Plan_Yearly:T#2021M5	0.00:00
	⚠	Consolidate Entity	Cb#Sample:E#Total_Geography:S#Plan_Yearly:T#2021M6	0.00:00
	⚠	Consolidate Entity	Cb#Sample:E#Total_Geography:S#Plan_Yearly:T#2021M7	0.00:00
	⚠	Consolidate Entity	Cb#Sample:E#Total_Geography:S#Plan_Yearly:T#2021M8	0.00:00
	⚠	Consolidate Entity	Cb#Sample:E#Total_Geography:S#Plan_Yearly:T#2021M9	0.00:00
	⚠	Consolidate Entity	Cb#Sample:E#Total_Geography:S#Plan_Yearly:T#2021M10	0.00:00
	⚠	Consolidate Entity	Cb#Sample:E#Total_Geography:S#Plan_Yearly:T#2021M11	0.00:00
	⚠	Consolidate Entity	Cb#Sample:E#Total_Geography:S#Plan_Yearly:T#2021M12	0.00:00

Task Steps (13 Items)

Figure 3.14

What is needed is a way to address two or more years. The solution is an XFBR Rule.

1 + 1 = 2

Workflow drives the first year of the Plan Consolidation range. To derive this second year, the XFBR Rule must:

1. Read the current year from the Workflow as called by a Data Management Step.

2. Convert the Workflow year into an integer.

3. Add *n* years to the start year.

4. Concatenate "M12" to the years.

5. Return the years in a comma-delimited list with a leading "T#" and a trailing "M12".

XFBR Calling

Call the XFBR within a Data Management Step with:

```
BRString(Book_ParamHelper, M12sForAgg, Year = |WFYear|, NumberOfYears
= 2)
```

General (Step)	
Name	M12sForAggs
Description	
Data Management Group	Admin calcs
Step Type	Calculate
Calculation	
Calculation Type	Force Consolidate
Data Units	
Cube	Sample
Entity Filter	E#Total_Geography
Parent Filter	
Consolidation Filter	C#Aggregated
Scenario Filter	S#Plan
Time Filter	BRString(Book_ParamHelper, M12sForAgg, Year = |WFYear|, NumberOfYears = 2)

Figure 3.15

The XFBR Business Rule `Book_ParamHelper` is the first parameter, the second is the `M12sForAgg` function name, the third is the start year (in this case `|WFYear|` but it could be any four-digit year, and the last is the number of years to consider.

In Book_ParamHelper

Calling M12sForAgg in Public Function Main

The `If…Then...Else` test is expanded to handle the new `M12sForAgg` function:

```
If args.FunctionName.XFEqualsIgnoreCase("MixedYear") Then
    Return Me.MixedYear(si, globals, api, args)
ElseIf args.FunctionName.XFEqualsIgnoreCase("M12sForAgg") Then
    Return Me.M12sForAgg(si, globals, args)
End If
```

Private Function M12sForAgg

The function must be declared within the overall XFBR Business Rule. XFBRs return strings to their calling object, so the function is typed as String.

```
Private Function M12sForAgg(ByVal si As SessionInfo, ByVal globals As
BRGlobals, ByVal args As DashboardStringFunctionArgs) As String
```

Variables and Parameters

The Year and NumberOfYears string parameters (all parameters are strings) must be queried and then converted to integers, as they will be used as start year and an outer bound of a For...Next loop.

```
Dim intYear As Integer = CInt(args.NameValuePairs.XFGetValue("Year"))
Dim intYearCount As Integer =
CInt(args.NameValuePairs.XFGetValue("NumberOfYears"))
Dim strTimeFilter As New List(Of String)
```

Just The One

If the range is only one year, then the Year parameter has no further string manipulation other than a prefixed "T#" and a trailing "M12". The Time Filter single year string is now ready to be added to the return list.

```
If intYearCount = 1 Then
    strTimeFilter.Add("T#" & intYear & "M12")
Else
```

Greater Than One

If the NumberOfYears parameter is more than one, loop from the Year parameter's value for the number of years specified. This must be a zero-based loop to include the start year, so the end loop limit must be the NumberOfYears less one.

```
    Dim intKounter As Integer
    For intKounter = 0 To intYearCount - 1
    strTimeFilter.Add("T#" & intYear + intKounter & "M12")
    Next intKounter
End If
Return String.Join(",", strTimeFilter)
```

A List(Of String) reflecting the NumberOfYears has been created, whatever the condition branching. The Data Management Time Filter requires a string. Use String.Join to return a comma-delimited list to the calling Data Management Step via the Main function.

ParamHelper

```
Private Function M12sForAgg(ByVal si As SessionInfo, ByVal globals As BRGlobals,
    ByVal api As Object, ByVal args As DashboardStringFunctionArgs) As String
    Try
        Dim intYear As Integer = CInt(args.NameValuePairs.XFGetValue("Year"))
        Dim intYearCount As Integer = CInt(args.NameValuePairs.XFGetValue("NumberOfYears"))
        Dim strTimeFilter As New List(Of String)
        If intYearCount = 1 Then
            strTimeFilter.Add("T#" & intYear & "M12")
        Else
            Dim intKounter As Integer
            For intKounter = 0 To intYearCount - 1
                strTimeFilter.Add("T#" & intYear & "M12")
            Next intKounter
        End If

        Return String.Join(",", strTimeFilter)

    Catch ex As Exception
        Throw ErrorHandler.LogWrite(si, New XFException(si, ex))
    End Try
End Function
```

So, What Do We Have?

The XFBR function M12sForAgg aggregates 2021 and 2022, given the start year of 2021 and the number of years count of two.

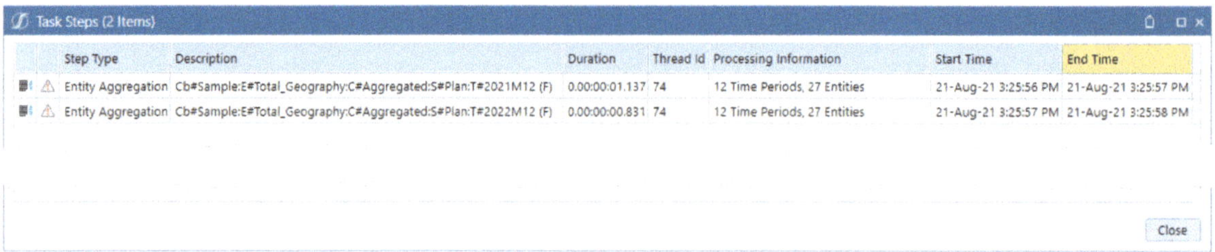

Figure 3.16

What Do We *Really* Have?

In XFBR Business Rules, we have a tool that can programmatically drive practically every text property in OneStream (and even the Excel add-in). This dynamic code-driven nature means that systems are more flexible, powerful, and maintenance-free. XFBR Business Rules are powerful, flexible, and robust Methods that transform applications. Use them wherever you can.

Shattering Scenario Workflow Shibboleths

> **Note:** This section concerns itself with monthly Forecasts; however, the recommendations hold true for all Plan Scenarios. Also, the below use cases run within the context of application Allow Loads Before/After Workflow View Year properties set to True.

The use case for loaded Plan data is invariably more than one month because Plans have a perspective of all of the months in a year or across multiple years. This multi-month and multi-year orientation has a significant impact on how Workflow must be configured.

A Word to The Wise

This section will – hopefully – encourage you to play with Scenario Workflow properties. Know that if any sort of Workflow processing has occurred in a Scenario, changes to Workflow properties will produce an error message like the one below (this is on a change from a Workflow End Time from 2050M12 to 2100M12).

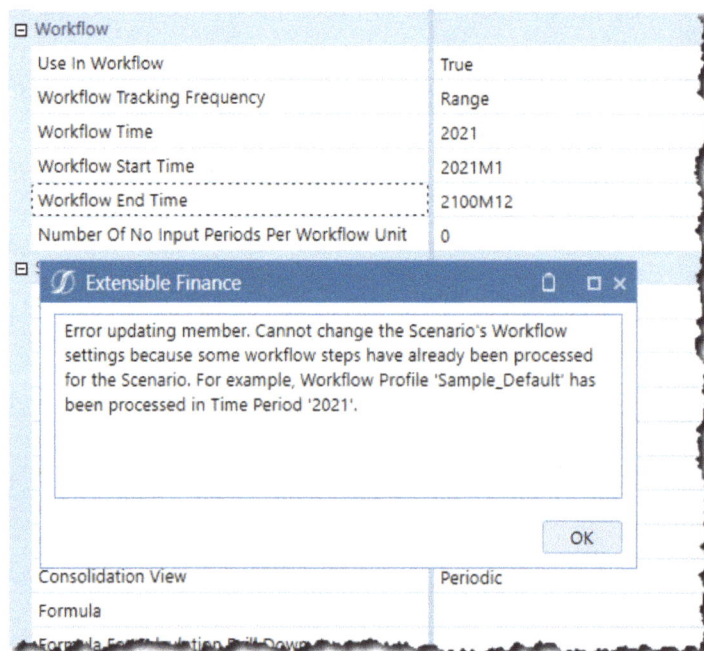

Figure 3.17

To successfully change this value, the Scenario must be Reset via a Data Management Step, which will *completely* erase all of the loaded, inputted, and calculated data in the Scenario. Data Management's Copy Data function can copy both Stage and Cube data to a backup Scenario; a custom Finance Business Rule can do the same but only for Cube data.

> **Note:** Other Scenario properties within an already processed Workflow may allow a change and save within the Dimension editor but not actually take effect.

Be sure to reset the Scenario before making any changes.

Just The One

The common Workflow Tracking Frequency for Actual data is All Time Periods; it is the default for any new Scenario. What is ideal for Actual data – data that is loaded one month at a time as business transactions occur – fails for Plan data that spans more than a month.

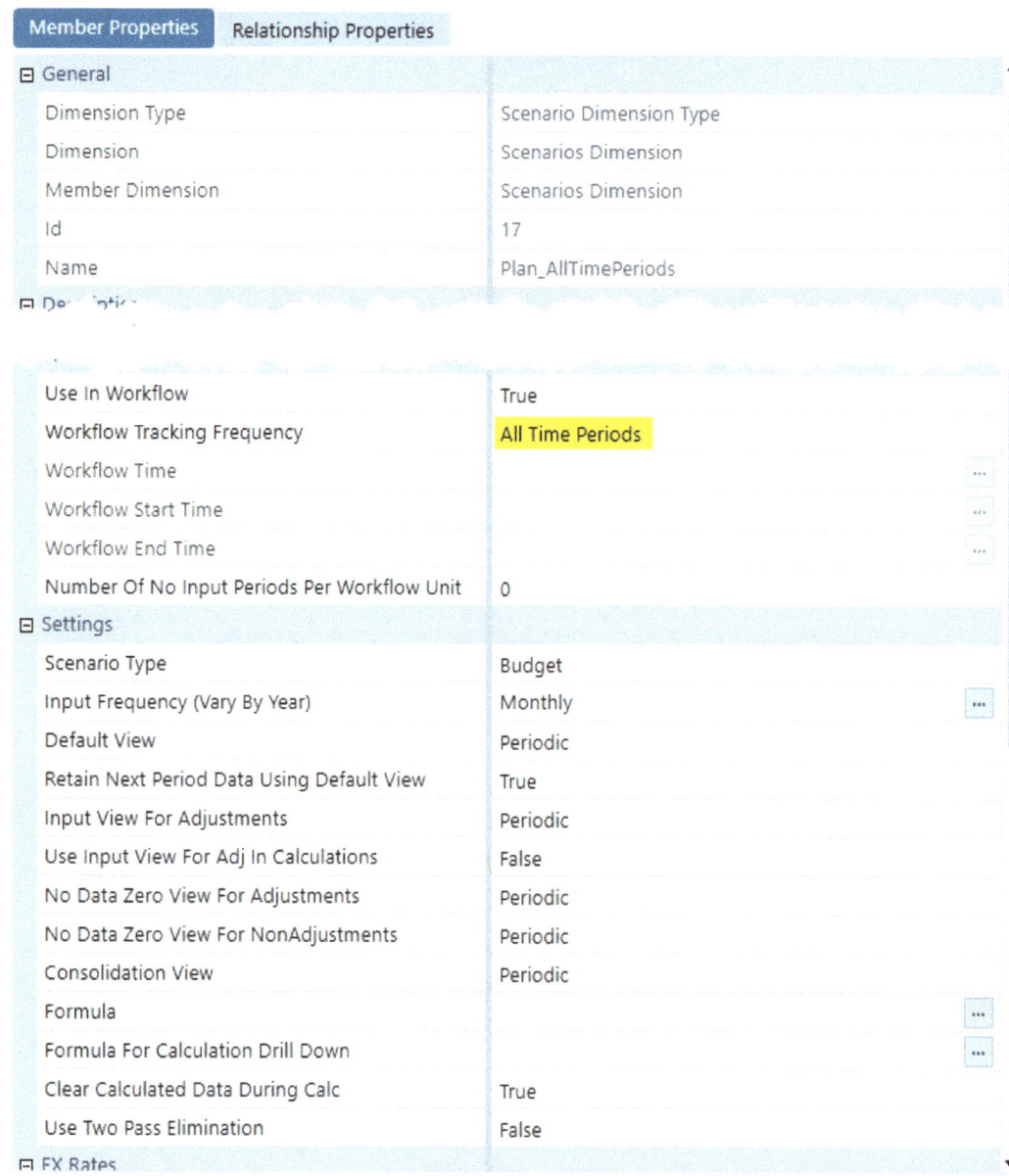

Member Properties	Relationship Properties
General	
Dimension Type	Scenario Dimension Type
Dimension	Scenarios Dimension
Member Dimension	Scenarios Dimension
Id	17
Name	Plan_AllTimePeriods
Use In Workflow	True
Workflow Tracking Frequency	All Time Periods
Workflow Time	
Workflow Start Time	
Workflow End Time	
Number Of No Input Periods Per Workflow Unit	0
Settings	
Scenario Type	Budget
Input Frequency (Vary By Year)	Monthly
Default View	Periodic
Retain Next Period Data Using Default View	True
Input View For Adjustments	Periodic
Use Input View For Adj In Calculations	False
No Data Zero View For Adjustments	Periodic
No Data Zero View For NonAdjustments	Periodic
Consolidation View	Periodic
Formula	
Formula For Calculation Drill Down	
Clear Calculated Data During Calc	True
Use Two Pass Elimination	False
FX Rates	

Figure 3.18

Note how the Default View, Input View For Adjustments, No Data Zero View For Adjustments, and No Data View for NonAdjustments are all set to Periodic; these all default to YTD on Scenario creation. As Planning data is at a monthly level, set these properties to their correct Periodic value.

If the Scenario has been processed in Workflow, the Scenario must be Reset via a Data Management Step to allow property changes to "stick", e.g., properties like Default View can be changed, but they will not take effect if that is not done.

Month by Month

All Time Periods results in a monthly view of Workflow:

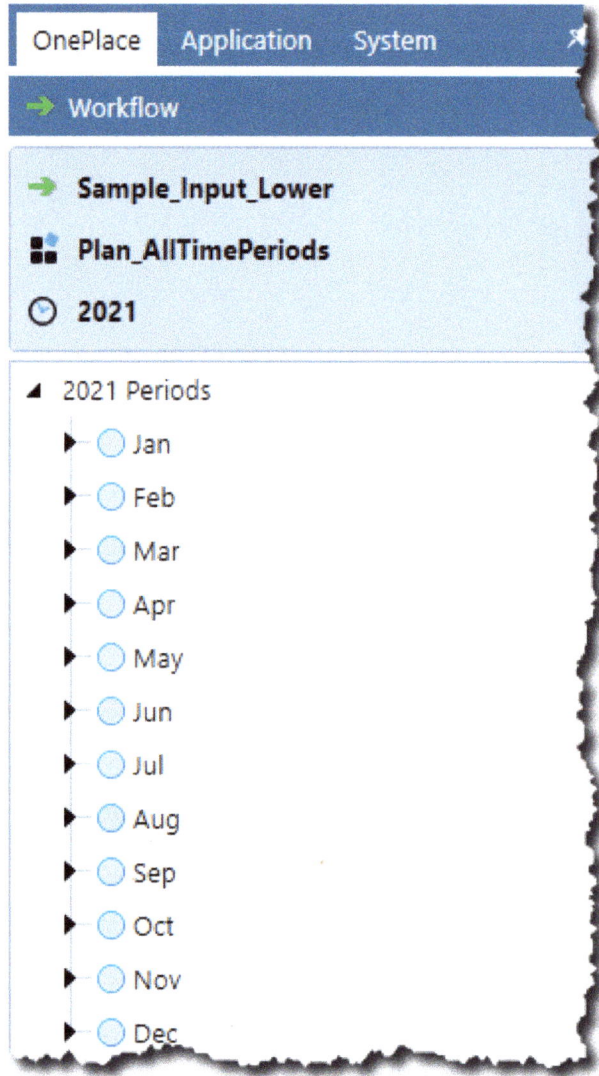

Figure 3.19

A single-month data file, as shown below, will load just that month.

UD1	Entity	Time	Scenario	Flow	Measures	Data
10_010	Pennsylvania	2021M1	Plan_AllTimePeriods	EndBal_input	Sales	303
10_020	Pennsylvania	2021M1	Plan_AllTimePeriods	EndBal_input	Distribution	39

Figure 3.20

OnePlace shows a successful data load:

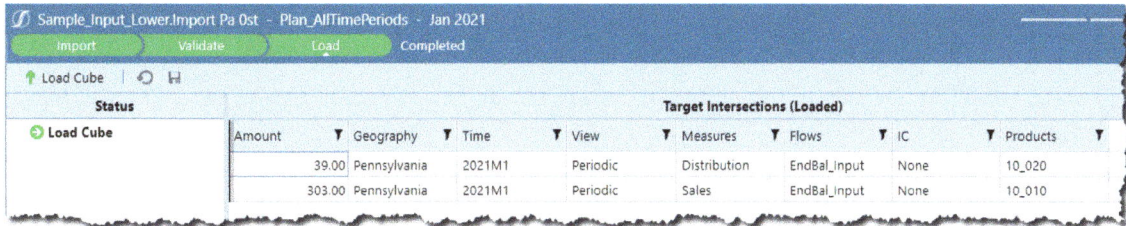

Figure 3.21

As does a Quick View retrieve:

Figure 3.22

In The Wrong Place, At The Wrong Time

After running a Reset Scenario, what happens if that January data is inadvertently loaded through February?

The answer, in February at least, is nothing or at least apparently so:

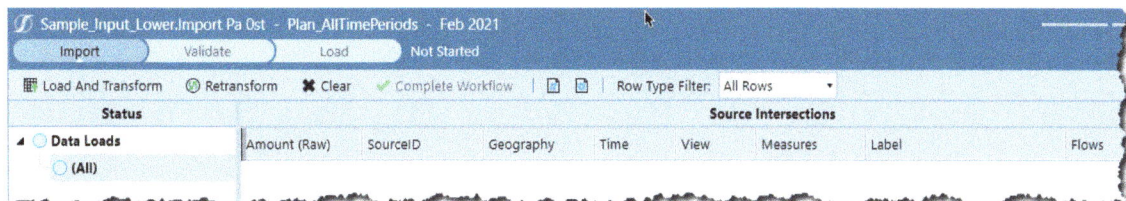

Figure 3.23

When January is opened in OnePlace, it shows that data *was*, in fact, imported but is not visible in February.

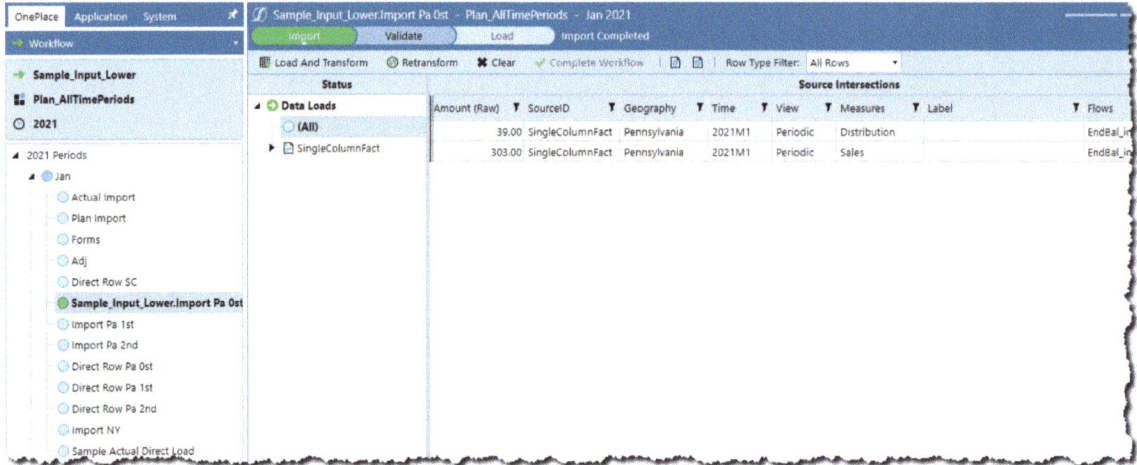

Figure 3.24

Logically enough, data cannot be loaded to the Cube in February because the data is, in fact, January's and the import process took place in February's Workflow.

Wrong Again, This Time More Than Once

A multiperiod data file – one that is far more likely to be used in a Planning Scenario – evinces a similar mismatch between the selected Workflow month and where data can be loaded to the Cube.

UD1	Entity	Time	Scenario	Flow	Measures	Data
10_010	Pennsylvania	2021M1	Plan_AllTimePeriods	EndBal_input	Sales	303
10_020	Pennsylvania	2021M1	Plan_AllTimePeriods	EndBal_input	Distribution	39
10_010	South_Carolina	2021M2	Plan_AllTimePeriods	EndBal_input	Distribution	54
10_010	Pennsylvania	2021M2	Plan_AllTimePeriods	EndBal_input	Distribution	1066

Figure 3.25

On load, the 2021M1's and 2021M2's data is imported to the right months but must be validated and loaded from the right Workflow time. In the above example, the validation and load process must be performed *twice*. This behavior extends to multi-year data loads.

When Direct Load Fails

The above examples use the traditional Import Method. What happens when more than one month is loaded using the new (and recommended) Direct Load Method?

When loaded from January, that four record 2021M1 and 2021M2 data file does *not* throw an error message and does *not* load more than January's data.

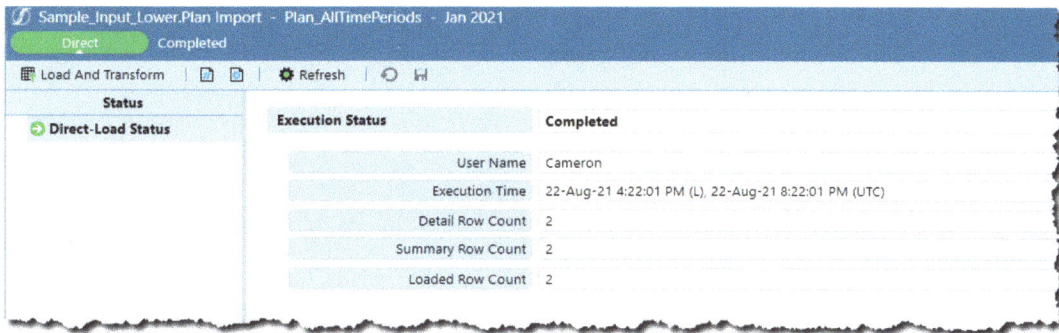

Figure 3.26

There is no option in February's Workflow to load data to the Cube, which is not surprising given that Direct Load's behavior is to load data directly to the Cube.

			Jan 2021	Feb 2021	Mar 2021
Pennsylvania	10_010 - Cameron's 100% Colombian Whole Bean	Sales	303	0	0
Pennsylvania	10_010 - Cameron's 100% Colombian Whole Bean	Distribution			
Pennsylvania	10_020 - Celvin's Colombian Supremo Regular Whole Bean	Sales			
Pennsylvania	10_020 - Celvin's Colombian Supremo Regular Whole Bean	Distribution	39	0	0
South_Carolina - South Carolina	10_010 - Cameron's 100% Colombian Whole Bean	Sales			
South_Carolina - South Carolina	10_010 - Cameron's 100% Colombian Whole Bean	Distribution			
South_Carolina - South Carolina	10_020 - Celvin's Colombian Supremo Regular Whole Bean	Sales			
South_Carolina - South Carolina	10_020 - Celvin's Colombian Supremo Regular Whole Bean	Distribution			

Figure 3.27

Just Don't

It would be a very unusual Planning data load pattern that purposely loaded data a month at a time. This approach also has a high potential for error in that a Planner or Administrator may mistake where data is loaded.

Do not use a Workflow Tracking Frequency of All Time Periods when loading Plan data.

The Yearling

Multiple month data loads make more sense with a Workflow Tracking Frequency of Yearly. The below use cases have `Plan_Yearly` as their Scenario.

The `Plan_Yearly` data file now has two months of 2021 data.

UD1	Entity	Time	Scenario	Flow	Measures	Data
10_010	Pennsylvania	2021M1	Plan_Yearly	EndBal_input	Sales	303
10_020	Pennsylvania	2021M1	Plan_Yearly	EndBal_input	Distribution	39
10_010	South_Carolina	2021M2	Plan_Yearly	EndBal_input	Distribution	54
10_010	Pennsylvania	2021M2	Plan_Yearly	EndBal_input	Distribution	1066

Figure 3.28

Now It's Working

An Import in 2021 results in 2021M1 and 2021M2's data load in OnePlace.

Chapter 3

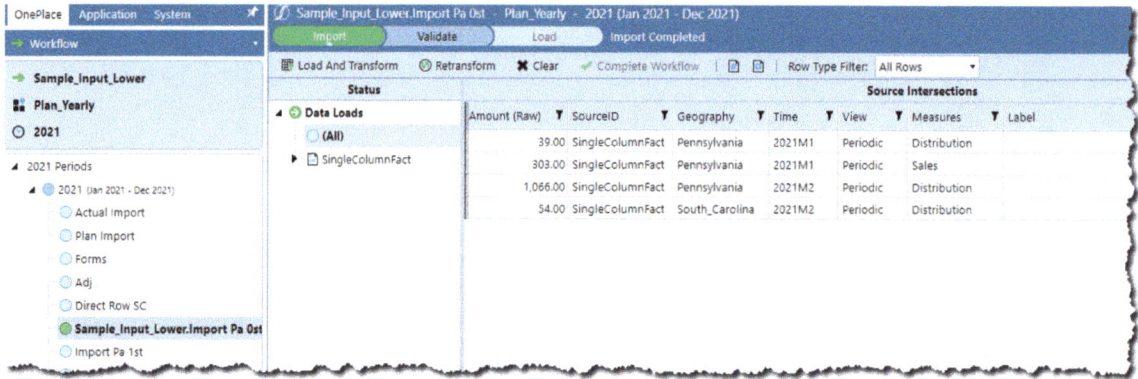

Figure 3.29

The data appears in a Quick View as well.

			Jan 2021	Feb 2021	Mar 2021
Pennsylvania	10_010 - Cameron's 100% Colombian Whole Bean	Sales	303	0	0
Pennsylvania	10_010 - Cameron's 100% Colombian Whole Bean	Distribution		1066	
Pennsylvania	10_020 - Celvin's Colombian Supremo Regular Whole Bean	Sales			
Pennsylvania	10_020 - Celvin's Colombian Supremo Regular Whole Bean	Distribution	39	0	0
South_Carolina - South Carolina	10_010 - Cameron's 100% Colombian Whole Bean	Sales			
South_Carolina - South Carolina	10_010 - Cameron's 100% Colombian Whole Bean	Distribution		54	0
South_Carolina - South Carolina	10_020 - Celvin's Colombian Supremo Regular Whole Bean	Sales			
South_Carolina - South Carolina	10_020 - Celvin's Colombian Supremo Regular Whole Bean	Distribution			

Figure 3.30

The same holds true for Direct Import.

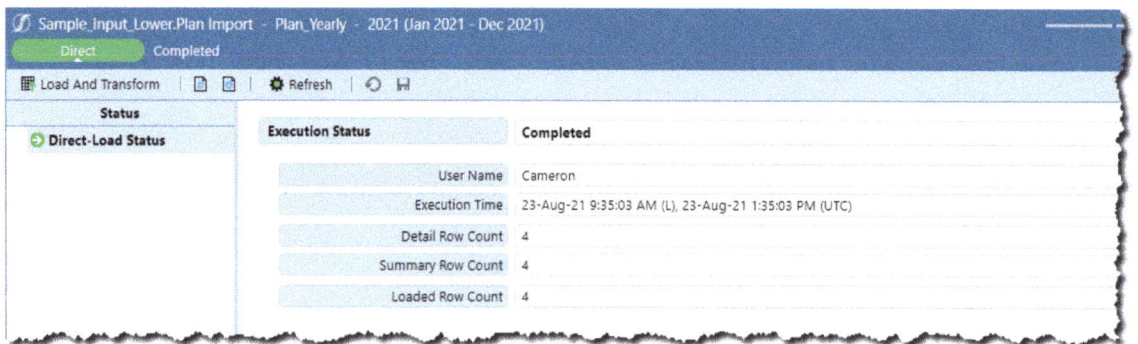

Figure 3.31

Unlike the All Time Periods Workflow Tracking Frequency, a Yearly one loads across months within a single year. If an application's Budget is only a single year, a Yearly frequency is appropriate.

However, many Plans are either rolling or simple multi-year Forecasts. Does Yearly correctly span years on a multi-year data load?

New Import, Same Old Import

It does not. It behaves just like All Time Periods, except across years instead of months.

Given the two-year data file, Import allows a data load in 2021 and 2022, displays only the current year's data, imports the data to the other year, and requires two validate and load steps to the Cube.

Import in 2021 shows only 2021M2.

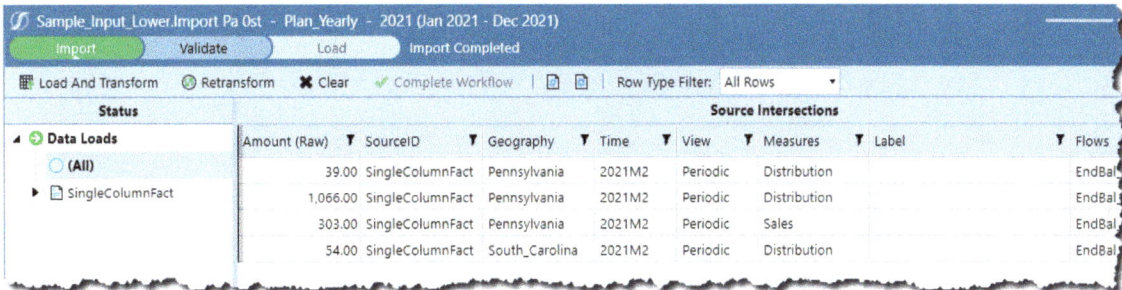

Figure 3.32

A load to the Cube in 2021 does not load 2022 data.

Figure 3.33

2022's data records show in 2022's OnePlace.

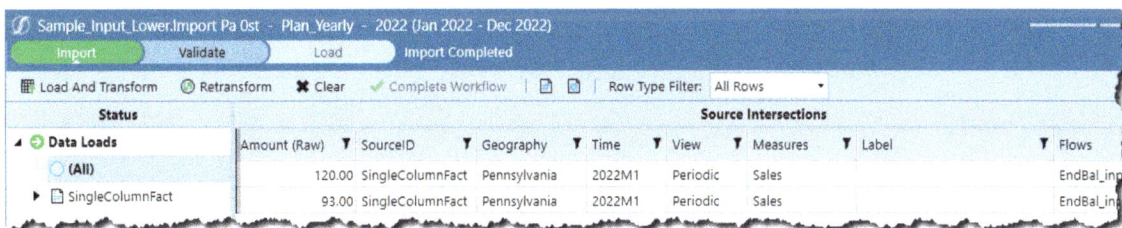

Figure 3.34

A second load to the Cube populates 2022.

Figure 3.35

Data Load Across Years

Direct Load behavior is the same across years in a Yearly Workflow Tracking Frequency as in across months in All Time Periods. As with Import, no error is thrown when 2022's data is not loaded.

Figure 3.36

2022's Data Load appears to not be processed.

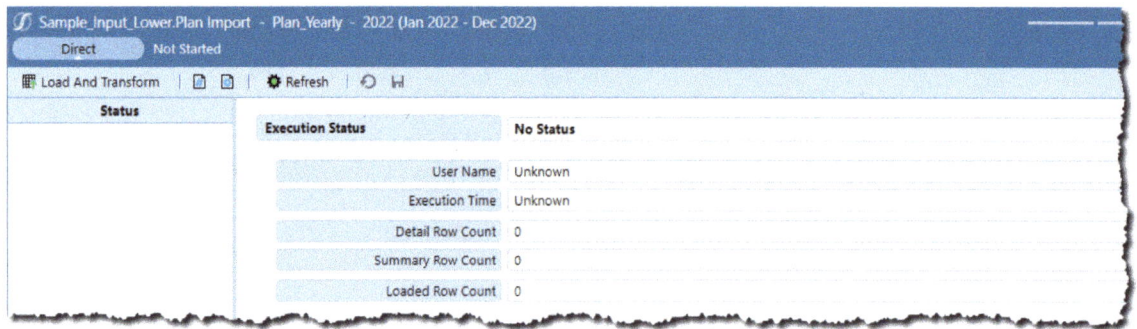

Figure 3.37

This is confirmed in Excel.

Figure 3.38

What to do?

The Multi-Year Home On The Range

The way – the only way – to handle multi-year data loads in Planning applications is through the **Range Workflow Tracking Frequency**.

This Is The Way

Workflow	
Use In Workflow	True
Workflow Tracking Frequency	Range
Workflow Time	2021
Workflow Start Time	2021M1
Workflow End Time	2022M12
Number Of No Input Periods Per Workflow Unit	0

Figure 3.39

Simply set the Workflow Time, Start Time, and End Time to the very limits of a possible Plan, in this case 2021 through 2022.

It Just Works

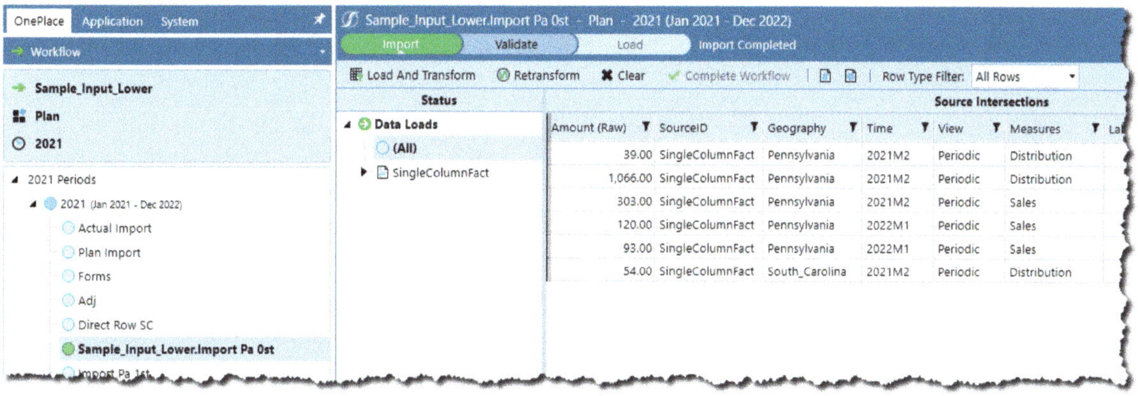

Figure 3.40

2021M2 and 2022M1 were both loaded in a single process.

			Jan 2021	Feb 2021	Mar 2021	Jan 2022	Feb 202;	Mar 202;
Pennsylvania	10_010 - Cameron's 100% Colombian Whole Bean	Sales		303		120		
Pennsylvania	10_010 - Cameron's 100% Colombian Whole Bean	Distribution		1066				
Pennsylvania	10_020 - Celvin's Colombian Supremo Regular Whole Bean	Sales				93		
Pennsylvania	10_020 - Celvin's Colombian Supremo Regular Whole Bean	Distribution		39				
South_Carolina - South Carolina	10_010 - Cameron's 100% Colombian Whole Bean	Sales						
South_Carolina - South Carolina	10_010 - Cameron's 100% Colombian Whole Bean	Distribution		54				
South_Carolina - South Carolina	10_020 - Celvin's Colombian Supremo Regular Whole Bean	Sales						
South_Carolina - South Carolina	10_020 - Celvin's Colombian Supremo Regular Whole Bean	Distribution						

Figure 3.41

Direct Load works as well – note the six rows loaded.

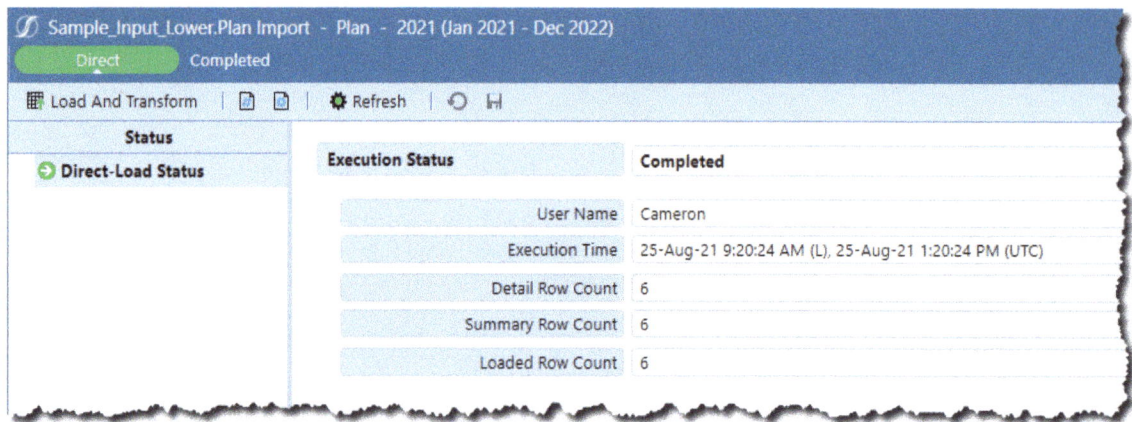

Figure 3.42

What To Do and Where

Of the three most commonly used Workflow Tracking Frequencies – All Time Periods, Yearly, and Range – multi-month Plans must use Yearly or Range. The other Workflow frequencies: Monthly, Quarterly, and Half Yearly behave similarly to All Time Periods and Yearly when it comes to data loads outside their time range, and are thus unsuitable except within very specialized circumstances.

Yearly

A Yearly frequency is a good fit for 12-month Plans for two reasons: all 12 or fewer months can be loaded within the Workflow, and on year change, no modification to the Scenario properties are required.

Range

A Range frequency must be the *only* option for 12 or more period Plans because it can load beyond the current Workflow year. What it *cannot* do is modify Workflow Time, Workflow Start Time, or Workflow End Time once any sort of Workflow has been processed.

On calendar year change, this becomes problematic because code and processes that rely on Workflow settings cannot function properly. Even if the Application properties Allow Loads Before Workflow View Year and Allow Loads After Workflow View Year are both set to True – thus allowing data loads outside of the defined Workflow Time range – Workflow Time itself becomes out of date. If the working Plan Scenario cannot be incremented on calendar year change, the only approach then is to have a monthly archive and yearly reset process.

Controlling Scenarios

Apart from pure-Plan Budget Scenarios, Planning Scenarios are a mix of already-occurred (Actual) and predicted (Plan or Forecast) business activity. As the year advances, the Plan data must be cleared, replaced with Actual numbers, and then locked so that the Planner cannot change closed months.

No matter the mix of Actual and Plan data, most organizations keep archival copies of Planning data.

To support these requirements of data loading, locking, inputting, and archiving, there are two common Scenario management patterns:

Working Forecast

A working Forecast Scenario, (e.g., Plan) is used consistently in Reports, data loads, Quick Views, Cube Views, and Data Management Steps; wherever a Scenario must be used, that single Scenario is employed.

Archive Scenarios are set to read-only by having the Read and Write Data Group, Calculate From Grids Group, and Manage Data Group set to Administrators. As the whole purpose of the archive Scenario is to allow Planners to review prior Forecasts, the Read Data Group should be set to Everyone.

Assuming new July Actuals are available and loaded into the Actual Scenario, and the working Forecast Scenario is called "Plan", this Method requires the following steps:

1. Use a Data Management Data Copy or Custom Calculate step and subsequent Consolidate/Aggregate step to archive the working Forecast Plan to a selected historical Scenario.

2. Clear out July in the Plan Scenario via a Custom Calculate Finance Business Rule or Data Management's Clear Data function.

3. Load the new July Actual data into Plan, either through a Custom Calculate Finance Business Rule or Data Management's Copy Data function.

4. Consolidate/Aggregate Plan.

5. Increment the Plan's No Input Periods number to seven to prevent Planner input/data loads to the new Actual month and its predecessors.

The data movement can be stitched together in a Data Management Sequence, although the Scenario No Input Periods property update must be performed manually.

This approach brings a key advantage of stability, clarity, and comprehension. OneStream objects and Planners work with the Plan Scenario, and no other, regardless of its time span of one year or many.

Rolling Forecasts

> **Note:** This section does not address the notion of a perpetual Forecast that moves in time across months and years, but instead an outline of versioning single year Forecast Scenarios through a controlled change of the Forecast Scenario.

This approach uses a series of predetermined Forecast Scenarios that are archives in themselves, e.g., 1+11 Forecast is the working Forecast Scenario in the month of February, representing January Actual data and 11 months of Plan.

As the calendar year progresses, the Scenario changes with it, i.e., if February's Plan is the 1+11 Forecast Scenario, so then March's will be 2+10 Forecast, and April's 3+9 Forecast. By April, the 1+11 Forecast and 2+10 Forecast Scenarios are locked via Scenario Security Group assignments.

Removing the need to copy a standard Working Forecast to an archive Scenario comes at the cost of User comprehension and flexibility. What is the current Forecast if the Forecast name changes every month? What happens to Quick Views that are hard-coded to 6+6 Forecast as the working Forecast when that Scenario is now 8+4 Forecast?

Confusion aside, processing Actual data has fewer steps and gets triggered (as with the Working Forecast approach) by the availability of Actual data. Assuming that the No Input Periods have been defined in the Forecast periods and using 6+6 Forecast as the starting Scenario, the process is as follows:

1. Use a Data Management Copy Data or Custom Calculate step to copy old Actual and current Plan from the current to the new Forecast Scenario 7+5 Forecast.

2. Set 6+6 Forecast's Read and Write Data Group, Calculate From Grids Group, and Manage Data Group properties to Administrators or Nobody. This Scenario is now an archived Forecast Scenario.

3. Clear out July in the 7+5 Forecast Scenario.

4. Copy July's Actuals into the now-current working Forecast (No Input Periods do not constrain Copy Data or Finance Business Rules).

5. Aggregate the working Forecast Scenario 7+5 Forecast.

As with the Working Forecast approach, data movement can be automated through Data Management Sequences. Scenario Security Group settings must be performed manually or via custom code.

The potential for confusion around just what the current Forecast Scenario is, within the range of possible Scenarios is high, particularly when Excel and its Quick Views are heavily used.

You Pays Your Money, and You Takes Your Chances

Although either approach to Scenario data movement is valid, the advantage of having a constant working Forecast Scenario makes it – in the eyes of your author at least – the optimal approach.

However, there is a problem with both approaches that Workflow and No Input Periods cannot resolve.

Strives For Greatness, but Never Quite Makes It

In the Principles Chapter, the *FP&A Live In Excel. Deal With It.* section briefly mentions how Quick Views do **not** respect Workflow Time restrictions. This functionality (or lack of it) is important both within the scope of Workflow and *outside* of it.

To review, for example, completing Workflow on a Cube View locks data.

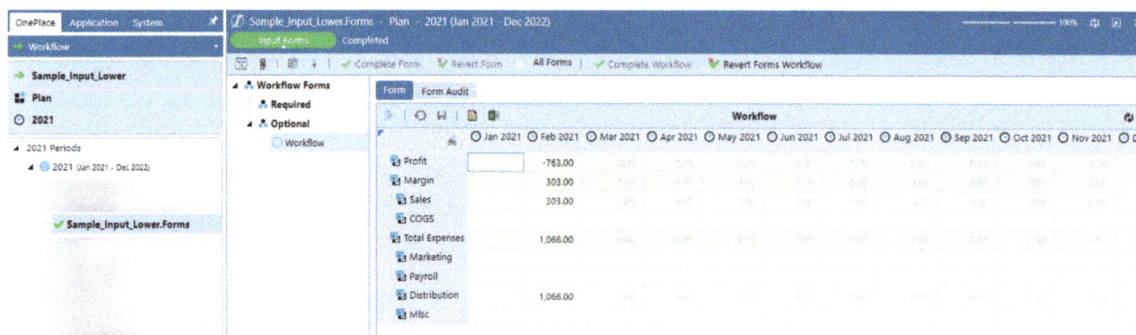

Figure 3.43

It does not in Excel or the OneStream Spreadsheet.

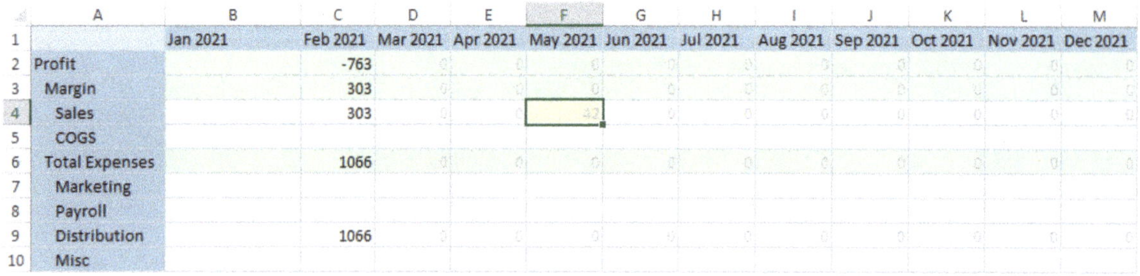

Figure 3.44

A send of data in the Quick View results in new data in the Cube View, despite its completed Workflow status.

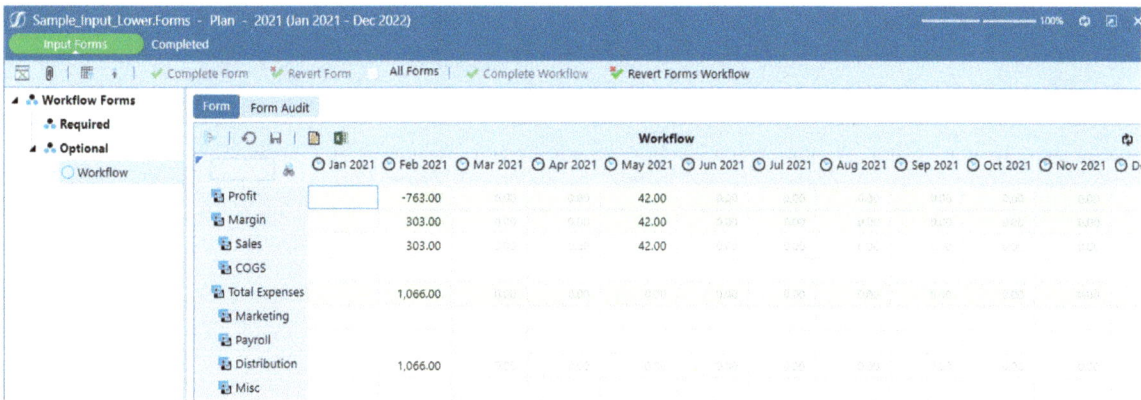

Figure 3.45

Given the need for ad hoc analysis and adjustment, we must accept that in Planning (and indeed all OneStream) applications, Workflow does not completely control the open and closed status of data, including periods in a working Forecast model with what should be closed Actual periods.

Number of No Input Periods per Workflow Unit

Actual periods within a working Forecast Scenario can be closed to input and data loads through the No Input Periods setting.

Setting No Input Periods to 5 closes 2022M1 through 2022M12 in both Cube Views and Quick Views.

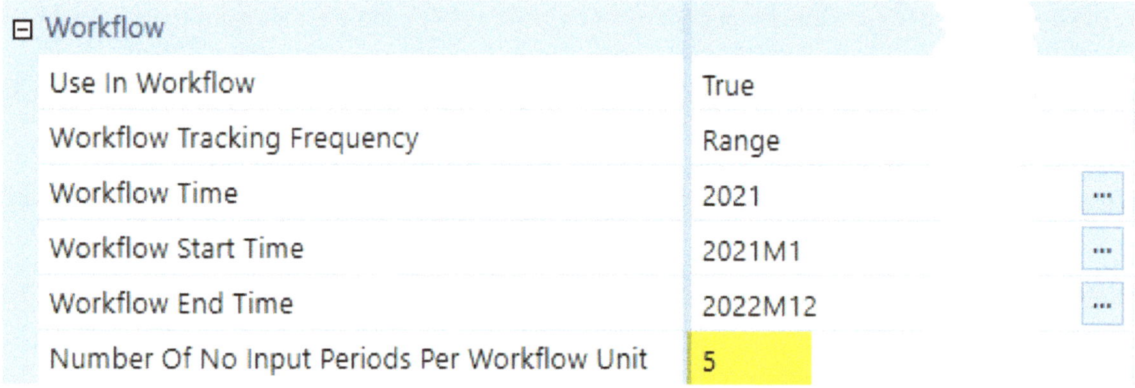

Figure 3.46

This is manifested in Cube Views:

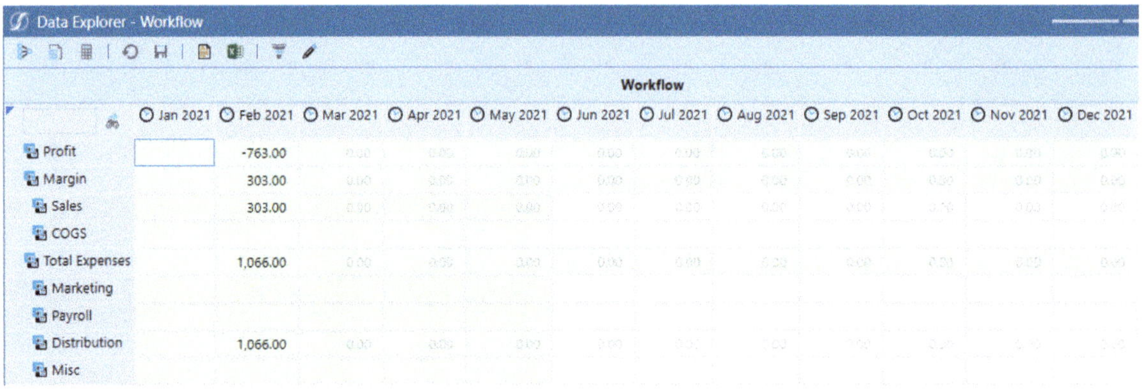

Data Explorer - Workflow

	Workflow											
	Jan 2021	Feb 2021	Mar 2021	Apr 2021	May 2021	Jun 2021	Jul 2021	Aug 2021	Sep 2021	Oct 2021	Nov 2021	Dec 2021
Profit		-763.00	0.00	0.00	0.00	0.00	0.00	0.00	0.00	0.00	0.00	0.00
Margin		303.00	0.00	0.00	0.00	0.00	0.00	0.00	0.00	0.00	0.00	0.00
Sales		303.00	0.00	0.00	0.00	0.00	0.00	0.00	0.00	0.00	0.00	0.00
COGS												
Total Expenses		1,066.00	0.00	0.00	0.00	0.00	0.00	0.00	0.00	0.00	0.00	0.00
Marketing												
Payroll												
Distribution		1,066.00	0.00	0.00	0.00	0.00	0.00	0.00	0.00	0.00	0.00	0.00
Misc												

Figure 3.47

As well as Quick Views:

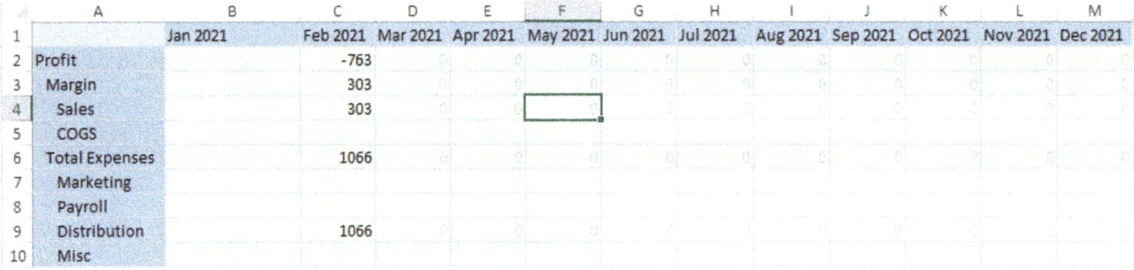

	A	B	C	D	E	F	G	H	I	J	K	L	M
1		Jan 2021	Feb 2021	Mar 2021	Apr 2021	May 2021	Jun 2021	Jul 2021	Aug 2021	Sep 2021	Oct 2021	Nov 2021	Dec 2021
2	Profit		-763	0	0	0	0	0	0	0	0	0	0
3	Margin		303	0	0	0	0	0	0	0	0	0	0
4	Sales		303	0	0	0	0	0	0	0	0	0	0
5	COGS												
6	Total Expenses		1066	0	0	0	0	0	0	0	0	0	0
7	Marketing												
8	Payroll												
9	Distribution		1066	0	0	0	0	0	0	0	0	0	0
10	Misc												

Figure 3.48

Outside Workflow

Data that is outside Workflow is not controlled by No Input Periods. Periods prior to the current Workflow scope should be – whether they represent Actual data or some version of Forecast – closed as they have already occurred. Periods that are after the Workflow Time should also not be open for input to prevent Planner error.

The below Quick View illustrates open periods in 2020 and 2023 despite a Scenario that has a Range Workflow Start and End Time of 2021M1 to 2022M12.

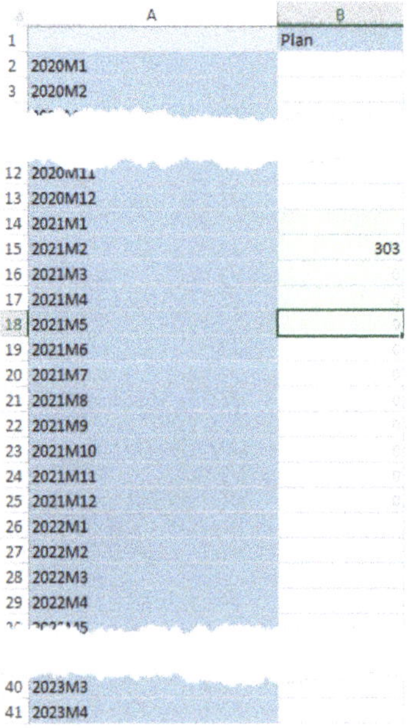

	A	B
1		Plan
2	2020M1	
3	2020M2	
12	2020M11	
13	2020M12	
14	2021M1	
15	2021M2	303
16	2021M3	
17	2021M4	
18	2021M5	
19	2021M6	
20	2021M7	
21	2021M8	
22	2021M9	
23	2021M10	
24	2021M11	
25	2021M12	
26	2022M1	
27	2022M2	
28	2022M3	
29	2022M4	
40	2023M3	
41	2023M4	

Figure 3.49

Taking a Slice Out of Periods

Slice Security, also known as **Data Cell Access Security**, can – for Planners only, not Administrators – lock periods outside of Workflow.

By setting the Access Level to Read Only in an initial Category and then defining a Time Member Filter of `T#2020.Base` and `T#2023.Base` in the Category before and after, those periods are closed.

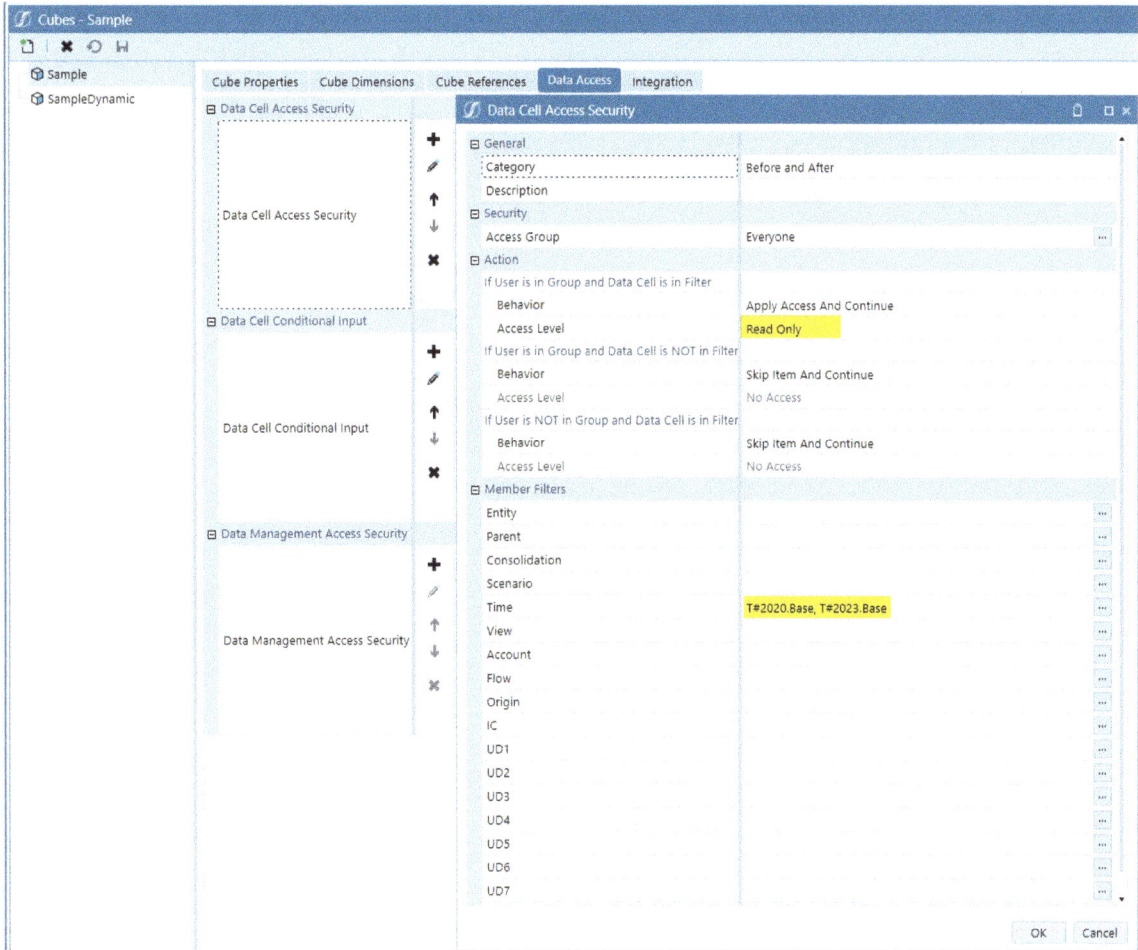

Figure 3.50

Neviana, a Planner in C&CCC's FP&A group, cannot edit 2020 or 2023; 2021M6 through 2022M12 remain open.

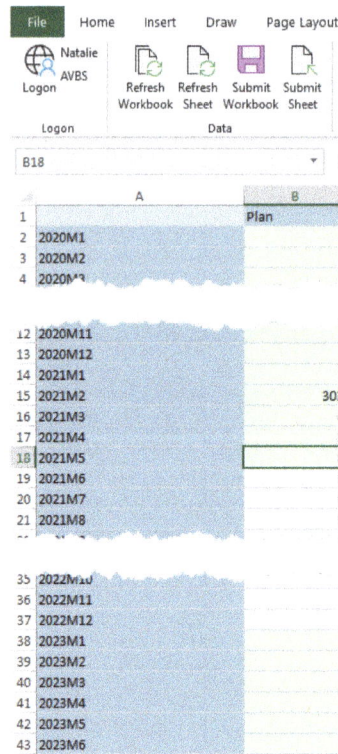

Figure 3.51

Does Not Compute

Slice Security does *not* apply to Members of the Administrators security group, of which Cameron is a Member.

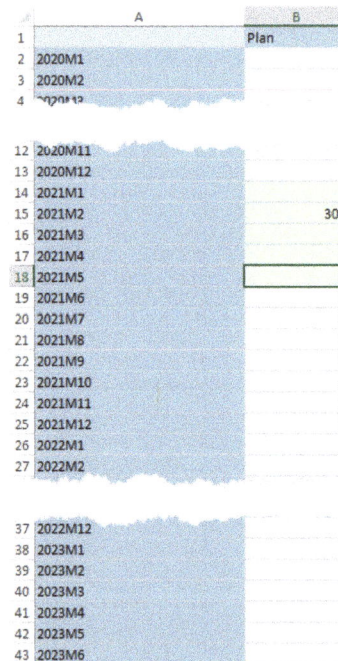

Figure 3.52

Given that Administrators are in the class of User most likely to go outside of the Workflow in the course of application maintenance, good data quality demands that it be locked. If Workflow does not lock the periods, and Slice Security fails as well, how can this be done?

On No Condition

The answer is **Conditional Input** as it will lock data for *all* Users, Planners, and Administrators alike, and affects human input through Cube Views and Quick Views as well as data loads.

Conditional Input Rules can be applied in two ways: via a Finance Business Rule attached to the Cube, or Cube Data Cell Conditional Input filters; both result in the same data security.

Given the same functionality, generally identical performance, and very different technical approach, determining which approach is best is rooted in philosophy: is it better to drive security through a code-dependent model or via a sequence of Member Filter definitions? OneStream often provides many ways to achieve the same thing with varying levels of effort and opportunities for customization – Conditional Input is one of those. The exercise of understanding the advantages and tradeoffs of the two techniques is an exemplar of the practice OneStream practitioners must exercise if we are to develop superior OneStream applications in security and all other product aspects.

Following the theme of more than one way to perform an action in OneStream, the following Conditional Input examples can also be used in lieu of the No Input Periods Scenario property. If Conditional Input is employed, it is likely that the *Number of No Input Periods Per Workflow Unit* Scenario property is redundant.

The use case is simple: a Literal Parameter defines the beginning of read-write periods within a Range Workflow Tracking Frequency. If the period accessed is between the start of the read-write periods and the end of the Workflow range, the data is read-write; otherwise, it is read-only.

Finance Business Rule

A note about the Finance Business Rule approach: execution speed relies on data scope and code quality. Unlike the code-free approach of Cube Data Access, performance is in the hands of the developer.

ConditionalInput

`ConditionalInput` is a Finance Business Rule that is attached to the Cube. It runs for *every* cell that is displayed on a Cube View or Quick View as well as every record in a data load, hence the comment about the importance of efficient code.

The Business Rule must:

1. Run on Cube access, cf. the above.

2. Interrogate `api.FunctionType` and then check to see if the `FinanceFunctionType.ConditionalInput` is `True`.

3. Conditional Input should fire only if the Scenario name is `ForecastScenario_CI_Fin_BR`.

4. Read the first read-write period from a Literal Parameter.

5. Grab the Workflow Tracking Frequency start and stop periods.

6. Interrogate the current POV Time period.

7. Compare the parameter and the POV Time periods.

8. If the POV Time period is between the start and stop periods and less than the start period, return `ConditionalInputResultType.NoInput`.

9. If the POV Time period is between the start and stop periods and greater than the start period, return `ConditionalInputResultType.Default`. As the Scenario's Read and Write Data Group is set to Everyone, the valid Time periods will be read-write.

Firing ConditionalInput

For `CondtionalInput` to run, it must be attached to the Cube to execute on retrieval. This book recommends running Finance Business Rules through Custom Calculate Data Management Steps precisely because they are focused in their scope and rely on Planner-driven timing. However, in the case of Conditional Input, the opposite must happen – the Rule must fire constantly.

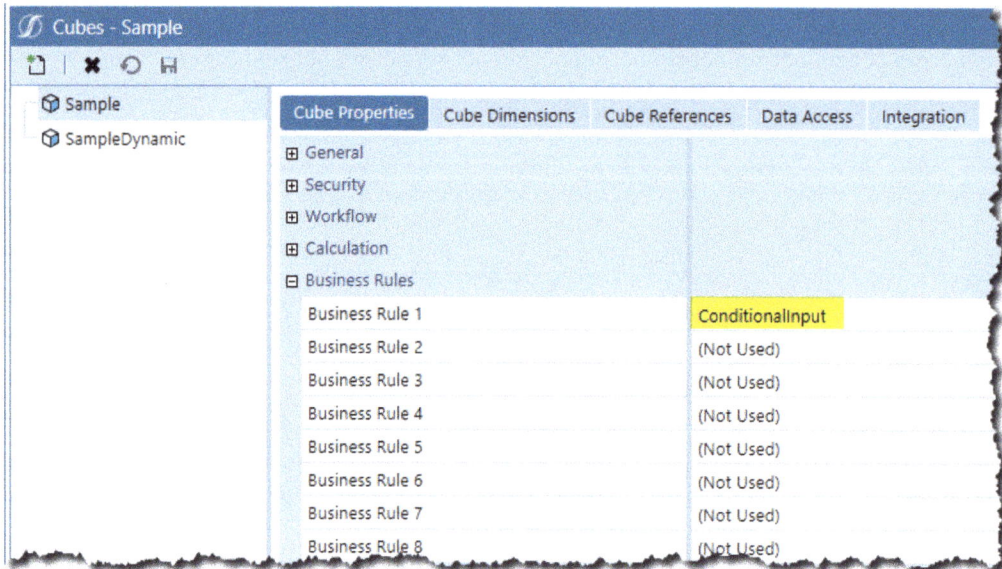

Figure 3.53

Code

Test for ConditionalInput

By default. Finance Business Rules test for seven different kinds of `FinanceFunctionType`. This Business Rule fires for every data cell and should not calculate anything other than that cell's Conditional Input status, hence the test for the Function Type.

```
Select Case api.FunctionType
    Case Is = FinanceFunctionType.ConditionalInput
```

Test For Scenario

The `ConditionalInput` Business Rule then tests for a Scenario called `"Plan_CI_Fin_BR"` but could easily read the current Workflow's Scenario or read a Literal Parameter. Within the context of Planning applications, Conditional Input makes the most sense when applied to the working Forecast Scenario. Keep in mind that archived Scenarios will be set to read-only for everyone.

```
Dim strPOVScenario As String = api.Pov.Scenario.Name
Dim strForecast As String = "Plan_CI_Fin_BR"
If strPOVScenario.XFEqualsIgnoreCase(strForecast) Then
```

Determining The Current Time POV And Start/Stop Periods

The Literal Parameter `ForecastMonth` holds the current Forecast month: 2021M6.

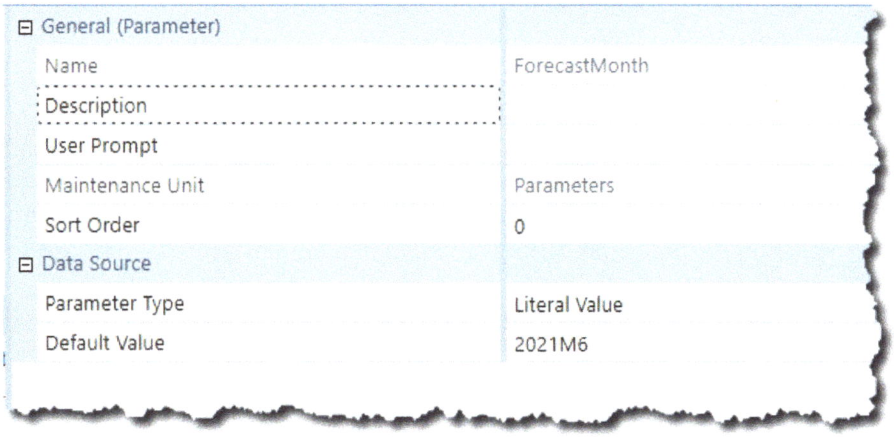

Figure 3.54

That month period is stored as an integer value along with the Start and End Time of the Range Workflow.

OneStream stores Time in a YYYYMm/YYYYMmm format, (e.g., 2021M1 through 2021M12). That difference in month number length makes string ordinal testing impossible (2021M10 is greater than 2021M1 but less than 2021M2). The function funcIntegerTime enables precedence testing by converting string period names to integers. Private functions reside outside the Public Function Main but in the same Business Rule.

```
Dim intForecastTime As Integer =
funcIntegerTime(BRApi.Dashboards.Parameters.GetLiteralParameterValue(s
i, False, "ForecastMonth"))
Dim intPOVTime As Integer = funcIntegerTime(api.Pov.Time.Name)
Dim intStartTime As Integer =
funcIntegerTime(TimeDimHelper.GetNameFromId(api.Scenario.GetWorkflowSt
artTime(ScenarioDimHelper.GetIdFromName(si, strForecast))))
Dim intEndTime As Integer =
funcIntegerTime(TimeDimHelper.GetNameFromId(api.Scenario.GetWorkflowEn
dTime(ScenarioDimHelper.GetIdFromName(si, strForecast))))
```

funcIntegerTime

The private function funcIntegerTime converts the string Literal Parameter and Workflow Scenario times into integers using a YYYYMM format, (e.g., 2021M1 becomes 202101 and 2021M10 becomes 202110).

```
Private Function funcIntegerTime(ByVal strTime As String) As Integer
    Return TimeDimHelper.GetSubComponentsFromName(strTime).Year * 100 +
TimeDimHelper.GetSubComponentsFromName(strTime).Month
End Function
```

Checking POV Time And Returning ConditionalInputResultType

The POV period of every cell can now be tested against the Start and End Workflow Time and the Start of Forecast Literal Parameter value.

ConditionalInputResultType.NoInput sets the cell to read-only. The default read-write Scenario property enables input and loading to open months.

Note the third Return – this is used to close down periods outside the Workflow range.

```
If intPOVTime >= intStartTime And intPOVTime <= intEndTime Then
    If intPOVTime < intForecastTime Then
        Return ConditionalInputResultType.NoInput
    Else
        Return ConditionalInputResultType.Default
    End If
```

```
Else
    Return ConditionalInputResultType.NoInput
End If
```

Return Nothing

The above `If…Then…Else` test should catch all possible outcomes, but the OneStream compiler does not check those conditions. If the last `Return Nothing` does not exist, OneStream throws this warning:

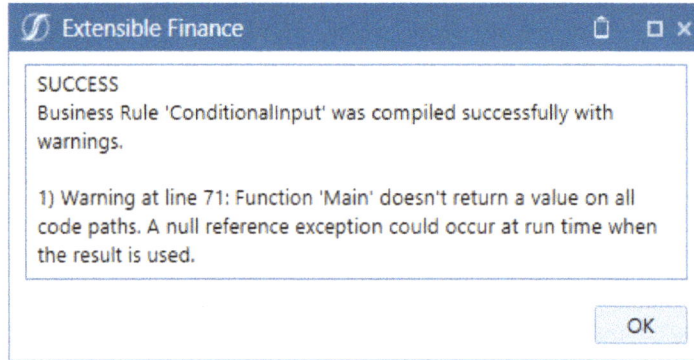

Figure 3.55

A `Return Nothing` before the error trap satisfies the compiler's code path value return requirement.

```
            End If

    End Select

    Return Nothing
  Catch ex As Exception
    Throw ErrorHandler.LogWrite(si, New XFException(si, ex))
  End Try
End Function
```

The Code in Total

```
Namespace OneStream.BusinessRule.Finance.ConditionalInput
    Public Class MainClass
        Public Function Main(ByVal si As SessionInfo, ByVal globals As BRGlobals,
            ByVal api As FinanceRulesApi, ByVal args As FinanceRulesArgs) As Object
            Try
            Select Case api.FunctionType
                Case Is = FinanceFunctionType.ConditionalInput

                    Dim strPOVScenario As String = api.Pov.Scenario.Name
                    Dim strForecast As String = BRApi.Dashboards.Parameters.GetLiteralParameterValue(si,
                        False, "ForecastScenario_CI_Fin_BR")

                    If strPOVScenario.XFEqualsIgnoreCase(strForecast) Then

                        Dim intForecastTime As Integer =
                            funcIntegerTime(BRApi.Dashboards.Parameters.GetLiteralParameterValue(si, False, "ForecastMonth"))
                        Dim intPOVTIme As Integer = funcIntegerTime(api.Pov.Time.Name)

                        Dim intStartTime As Integer =
                            funcIntegerTime(TimeDimHelper.GetNameFromId(api.Scenario.GetWorkflowStartTime(ScenarioDimHelper.GetIdFromName(si,
                            strForecast))))
                        Dim intEndTime As Integer =
                            funcIntegerTime(TimeDimHelper.GetNameFromId(api.Scenario.GetWorkflowEndTime(ScenarioDimHelper.GetIdFromName(si,
                            strForecast))))

                        If intPOVTIme >= intStartTime And intPOVTIme <= intEndTime Then
                            If intPOVTIme < intForecastTime Then
                                Return ConditionalInputResultType.NoInput
                            Else
                                Return ConditionalInputResultType.Default
                            End If
                        Else
                            Return ConditionalInputResultType.NoInput
                        End If
                    End If

            End Select

            Return Nothing
            Catch ex As Exception
                Throw ErrorHandler.LogWrite(si, New XFException(si, ex))
            End Try
        End Function

        Private Function funcIntegerTime(ByVal strTime As String) As Integer
            Return TimeDimHelper.GetSubComponentsFromName(strTime).Year * 100 + TimeDimHelper.GetSubComponentsFromName(strTime).Month
        End Function

    End Class
End Namespace
```

Results

Cameron, the Administrator (and everyone else in the Cube), cannot input data before 2021M5 and after 2022M12 in the Scenario Plan_CI_Fin_BR.

	A	B
1		Plan_CI_Fin_BR
2	2020M1	
3	2020M2	
13	2020M12	
14	2021M1	
15	2021M2	303
16	2021M3	
17	2021M4	
18	2021M5	
19	2021M6	
20	2021M7	
21	2021M8	
22	2021M9	
23	2021M10	
24	2021M11	
25	2021M12	
26	2022M1	
27	2022M2	
37	2022M12	
38	2023M1	
39	2023M2	
40	2023M3	
41	2023M4	
42	2023M5	
43	2023M6	
44	2023M7	

Figure 3.56

Conditional Input: More Prevalent Because It's Better?

Per the beginning of this section, the performance of a Conditional Input Business Rule depends on code efficiency. Be careful when using the `api.LogMessage` Method as a moderately large Cube View or Quick View can result in hundreds if not thousands of Error Log messages with concomitant poor performance.

An admittedly unscientific survey of OneStream applications suggests that Finance Business Rules driving Conditional Input is common practice. Should it be… when there is another way to perform the same function?

Data Cell Conditional Input

Conditional Input can be set at the Cube using simple (or complicated) Member Filters. The requirement to open up the Plan Scenario's input after 2021M5 and not after 2022M12 requires just two steps.

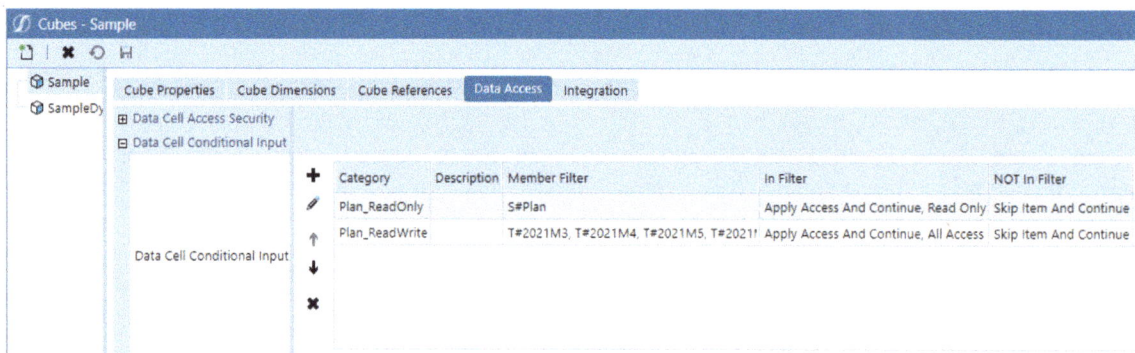

Figure 3.57

Member Filters fire in sequential order, with any latter steps modifying the behavior of the former, creating AND, OR, and NOT conditions. These interact with implicit logical conditions within individual Member Filters. As the potential for sophisticated and powerful Conditional Input Rules is manifest, so too is the chance of incorrect data access. Be sure to extensively test the outcome of Conditional Input Rules in isolation and in concert with any Data Cell Access Security filters.

Plan as Read-Only

The first Category step must make all of the Plan read-only; subsequent Category steps will open specific Time periods for input and loading within Plan.

Category filter scope drives Conditional Input behavior. Conditional Input filters test for data cells inside and out of the Member Filter, granting or restricting access as defined by behavior and access level.

If Data Cell Is In Filter

The settings here, in combination with the Actual Member selection, will determine what happens to data within the Plan Scenario.

Behavior

There are eight different behaviors. For this use case, only Apply Access and Continue are required. This property will allow filter processing after the Member Filter has fired.

Access Level

Read Only and All Access are the only options for Access Level: Read Only affects the desired read-only state of Plan.

If Data Cell Is NOT In Filter

Other Scenarios, at least in the case of this use case, will remain untouched.

The default behavior of Skip Item and Continue will exclude other Scenarios from the scope of this filter.

When Skip Item and Continue is specified, the only possible Access Level is Read Only. At first blush, this seems to suggest that data cells outside of this Member Filter will be read-only. However, the Skip Item behavior means that this access is not applied.

Member Filters

Unspecified Member Filters represent all data intersections in the Dimension. Member Filters with specific assignments define the scope of that Dimension's data cells. These definitions (or lack thereof), in combination, define Conditional Input scope across the Cube.

Specifying just a Member Filter of `S#Plan` and nothing else in the Member Filter means that *all* other Dimensions are included in the scope of the `Plan_ReadOnly` Conditional Input Category; the act of specifying a single Member in a Dimension (Scenario), and no other, excludes the balance of that Dimension's Members.

This Plan-only Data Cell Conditional Input filter…

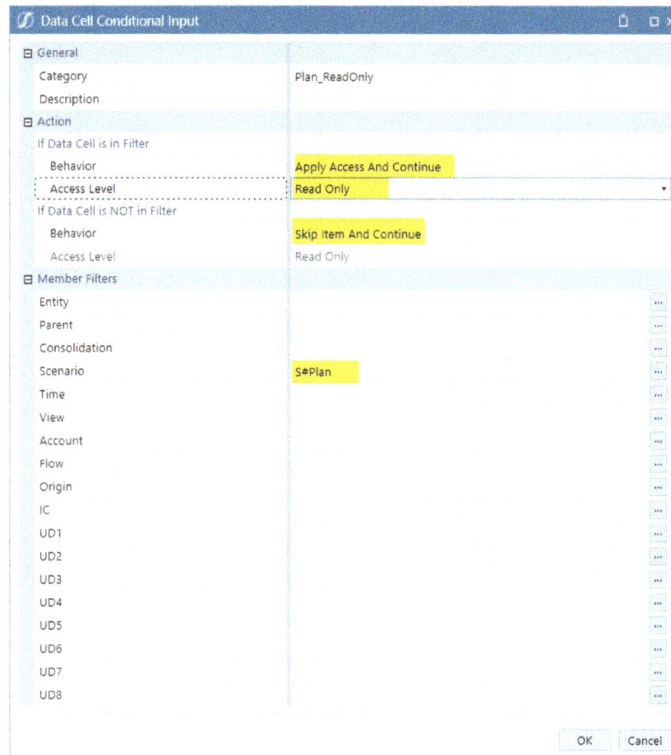

Figure 3.58

…results in just the Plan as read-only; other Scenarios are limited by their own Conditional Input properties or are driven by Scenario read-write settings.

	A	B	C	D
1		Plan_CI_Fin_BR Plan		Actual
2	2020M1			
3	2020M2			
12	2020M11			
13	2020M12			
14	2021M1			
15	2021M2	303		303
16	2021M3			
17	2021M4			
18	2021M5			
19	2021M6			
20	2021M7			
21	2021M8			
22	2021M9			
23	2021M10			
24	2021M11			
25	2021M12			
26	2022M1			
27	2022M2			
28	2022M3			
29	2022M4			
30	2022M5			
31	2022M6			
32	2022M7			
33	2022M8			
34	2022M9			
35	2022M10			
36	2022M11			
37	2022M12			
38	2023M1			
	2023M2			
44	2023M7			

Figure 3.59

Time as Read-Write

The Plan Scenario is now read-only. Opening 2021M6 to 2022M12 requires increasing the access to All Access and defining a Time Member Filter that includes those periods.

There is no need to define anything beyond Time as Data Cell Conditional Input filters are order-based: a Plan read-only filter followed by a Time read-write one is functionally an AND condition between the two Categories. No further filters are required.

> **Note:** This order-based functionality must be considered when the usage of Conditional Input is increased to other data cell definitions, (e.g., Conditional Input for Actual or Budget, etc.). Adding Plan to this filter would help restrict the access if there were other Conditional Input requirements.

If Data Cell Is In Filter

Behavior

The same behavior – Apply Access and Continue – is used in Time's filter as was used in Scenario's. Member definitions in this filter will apply to all defined Member combinations.

Access

All Access is equivalent to read-write.

If Data Cell Is NOT In Filter

Behavior

As with Plan's Conditional Input filter, data cells outside of this definition are skipped.

Access

The Skip Item and Continue property excludes other data cell combinations, keeping in mind that this Time filter is acting in conjunction with Plan's.

Member Filters

Time is specified from 2021M6 through 2021M12 and 2022.Base.

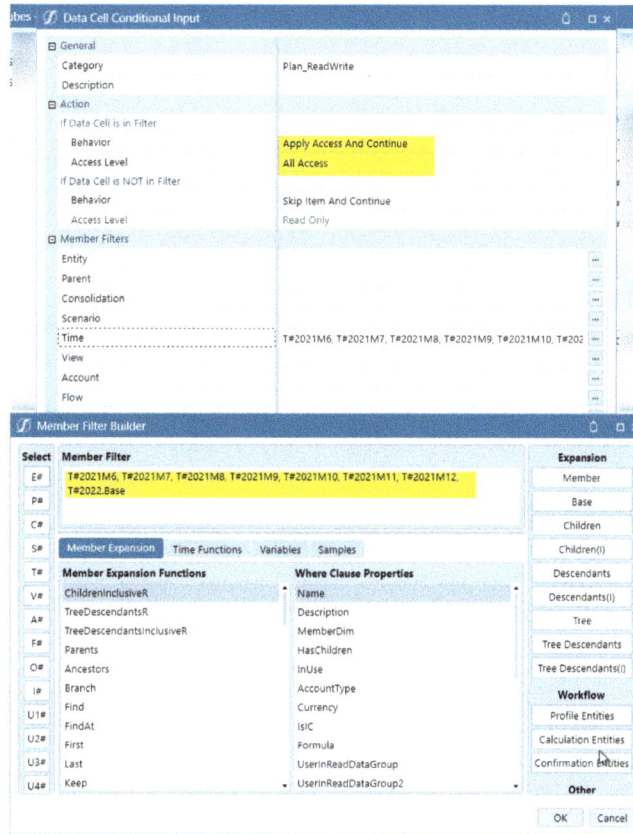

Figure 3.60

The result is a read-write 2021M6 through 2022M12 with all other Time periods in Plan as read-only.

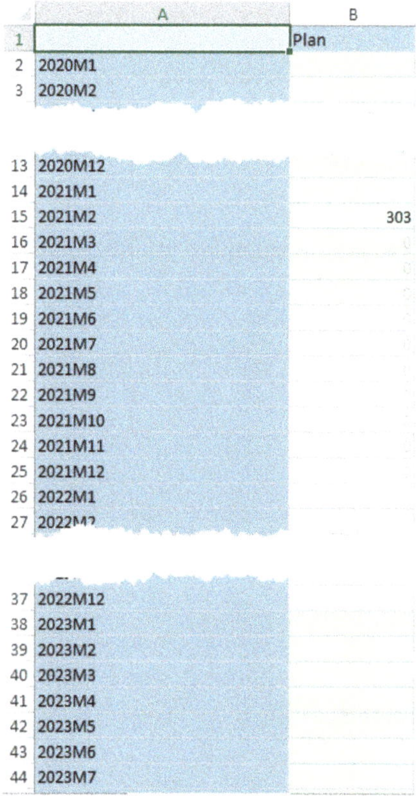

Figure 3.61

Administering Data Cell Conditional Input

The Time Member Filter can be manually changed as needed. However, a more realistic use case is an administrative process that programmatically updates the Conditional Input filter.

This example shows a Dashboard with a period Combo box and Save button that updates a Literal Parameter that in turn drives the filter – items outside the scope of Conditional Input itself – and thus will not be covered.

Dashboard

Again, noting that only the Dashboard element that drives the actual update of the Conditional Input filter will be covered here, an administrative Dashboard to perform this function might look like this:

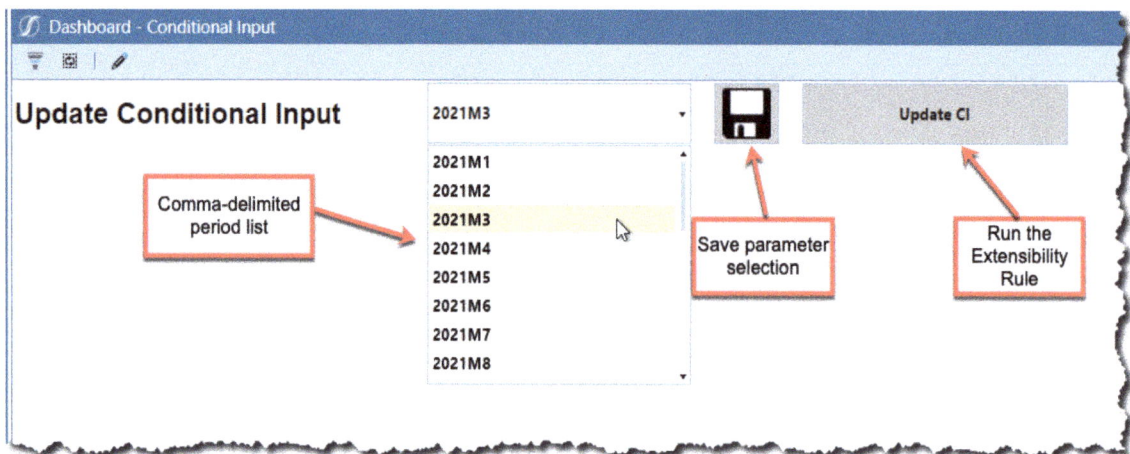

Figure 3.62

Your author is aware that he will likely never win awards for Dashboard design or aesthetics. Regardless of his artistic illiteracy, the above is sufficient.

Parameters

Two Literal Parameters drive the process: `ForecastMonth` and `ForecastScenario_CI_Ext_BR` with the respective values of 2021M5 and Plan.

Button

`btn_200_UpdateCI` drives the Data Management Sequence `Update_Conditional_Input` through the Selection Changed Server Task and calls `{Update_Conditional_Input}{}` through the Selection Changed Server Task Arguments. The empty curly brace set at the end of the argument's property is used to drive Data Management parameters which are not used in this example, hence their blank nature.

This Data Management Sequence has one step also named `Update_Conditional_Input`. The Extensibility Rule `ConditionalInput_DataAccess` can be run through an Execute Business Rule step if the `ExtenderFunctionType.ExecuteDataMgmtBusinessRuleStep` is enabled in the Extender Rule and by launching it directly if the `ExtenderFunctionType.Unknown` is enabled.

Data Management Step

Extensibility Rules are not run through Custom Calculate Steps as Finance Business Rules are, but instead are run via an Execute Business Rule Step Type.

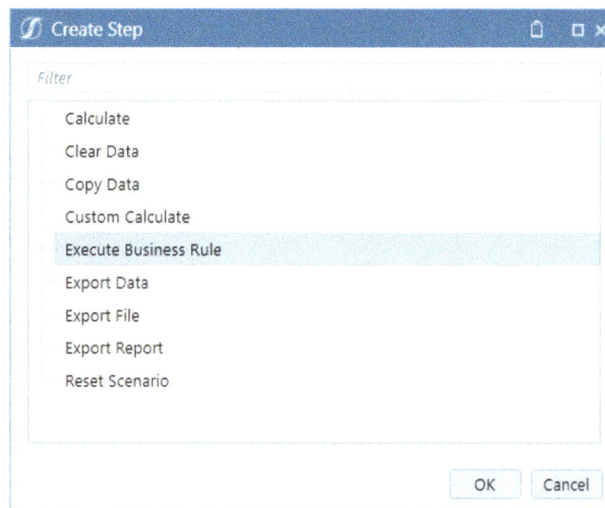

Figure 3.63

The Conditional Input use case shall use the ConditionalInput_DataAccess Rule.

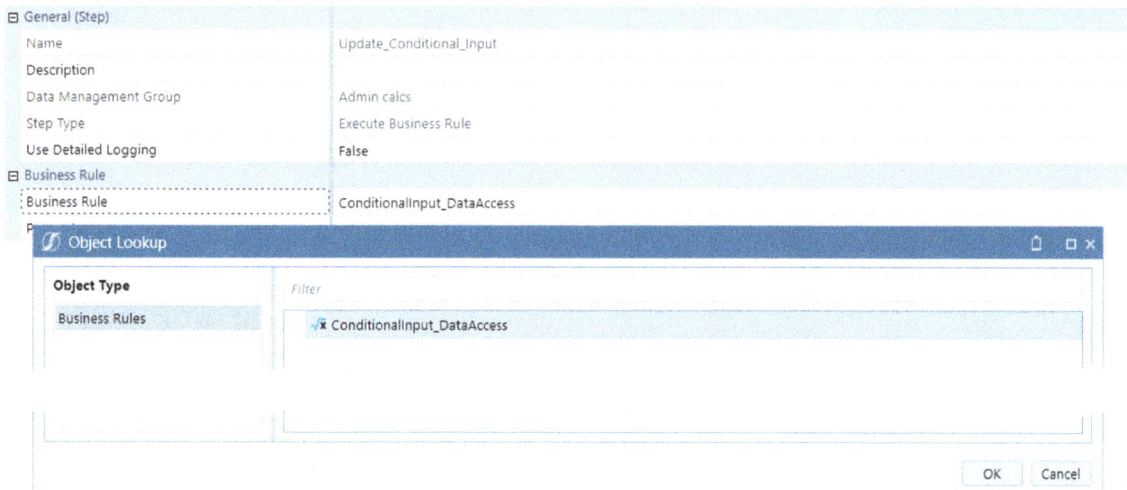

Figure 3.64

Business Rule

ConditionalInput_DataAccess must perform the following steps to change the Conditional Input filter:

1. Test to make sure the Rule is run from a Data Management Step.

2. Instantiate the Cube's ID and Conditional Input data access Type.

3. Get the Literal Parameters' values.

4. Define the Time periods to be updated.

   a. Grab the Scenario's Workflow Tracking Frequency end range; the Start Time is based on the Literal Parameter ForecastMonth.

   b. Define the Time periods by looping from the Forecast month to M12 to create a string list of the Forecast month's outstanding Time periods. Loop from the year after the Forecast month's year and append .Base to the year within the Time period string list.

5. Loop the Data Cell Conditional Input Categories for the `Plan_ReadWrite` filter. When the category name is `Plan_ReadWrite`, update the Time Member Filter with the Time period string list.

6. Update the `InsertOrUpdateCubeDataAccessTimestamp` and `InsertOrUpdateCubesCacheTimestamp` caches to persist the filter change.

Run From Data Management?

This `Case` statement ensures that the Rule is being run from a Data Management Step.

```
Select Case args.FunctionType
    Case Is = ExtenderFunctionType.ExecuteDataMgmtBusinessRuleStep
.
.
.
End Select
```

Instantiate

Get the Cube ID and the Conditional Input Access Type.

```
Dim intCubeID As Integer = BRApi.Finance.Cubes.GetCubeInfo(si,
"Sample").Cube.CubeId
Dim objConditionalInputAccessType As CubeDataAccessType =
CubeDataAccessType.DataCellConditionalInput
```

Parameters

Note that the `ForecastScenario_CI_Ext_BR` parameter could have been hard-coded as a string.

```
Dim strForecastTime As String =
BRApi.Dashboards.Parameters.GetLiteralParameterValue(si, False,
"ForecastMonth")
Dim strForecast As String =
BRApi.Dashboards.Parameters.GetLiteralParameterValue(si, False,
"ForecastScenario_CI_Ext_BR")
```

Time

The Rule needs to identify the Start and End Time of the Conditional Input range. `intStartYear` could have used the `BRApi.Finance.Scenario.GetWorkflowStartTime` Method to get the Start Time instead of reading the `ForecastMonth` Literal Parameter. Note that VB.Net will convert a number to an Integer even if it is typed as String.

```
Dim intStartYear As Integer = Left(strForecastTime, 4)
Dim intEndYear As Integer =
TimeDimHelper.GetYearFromId(BRApi.Finance.Scenario.GetWorkflowEndTime(
si, ScenarioDimHelper.GetIdFromName(si, strForecast)))
```

Two Time scope definitions are required: one to handle the future months in the current year based on the start month, and a second to contain all the periods in the second or greater years.

The first loop builds a Time Member string from YYYYM1 through YYYYM12 and assigns it to the string list `lstFutureMonths`.

```
Dim lstFutureMonths As New List(Of String)
For intCYMonths As Integer = Right(strForecastTime,2).Replace("M","")
To 12
    lstFutureMonths.Add(Left(strForecastTime,4) & "M" & intCYMonths)
Next
```

The second loops from the second year to the last one, adding YYYY.Base as required to `lstFutureMonths`.

```
For intFYMonths As Integer = intStartYear + 1 To intEndYear
    lstFutureMonths.Add(intFYMonths & ".Base")
Next
```

Update

The Categories in the Cube Data Cell Conditional Input properties are now looped and tested so that only the Category Plan_ReadWrite is updated. The Time Member Filter is updated with a comma-delimited string from the lstFutureMonths string list.

The FinanceTimeStamps.InsertOrUpdateCubeDataAccessTimestamp and FinanceTimeStamps.InsertOrUpdateCubesCacheTimestamp Methods force the Data Access caches to refresh.

```
Using dbConn As DbConnInfo =
BRApi.Database.CreateApplicationDbConnInfo(si)
    For Each objCubeDataAccessItem As CubeDataAccessItem In
CubeDataAccessDbAccess.ReadCubeDataAccessItems(dbConn, intCubeID,
objConditionalInputAccessType)
        If
objCubeDataAccessItem.Category.XFEqualsIgnoreCase("Plan_ReadWrite")
            Dim updatedAccessItem As New
CubeDataAccessItem(objCubeDataAccessItem)
            updatedAccessItem.MemberFilters.Time = "T#" & String.Join(",
T#", lstFutureMonths)

    CubeDataAccessDbAccess.InsertOrUpdateCubeDataAccessRow(dbConn,
updatedAccessItem)
        End If
    Next

    FinanceTimeStamps.InsertOrUpdateCubeDataAccessTimestamp(dbConn,
DateTime.UtcNow)
    FinanceTimeStamps.InsertOrUpdateCubesCacheTimestamp(dbConn,
DateTime.UtcNow)

End Using
```

> **Note:** CubeDataAccessDBAccess is not an exposed object and is liable to change by OneStream without warning.

Change to 2021M3

Executing the Extensibility Rule through the Dashboard results in the Time Member Filter updated to allow read-write access from 2011M3 through 2022M12.

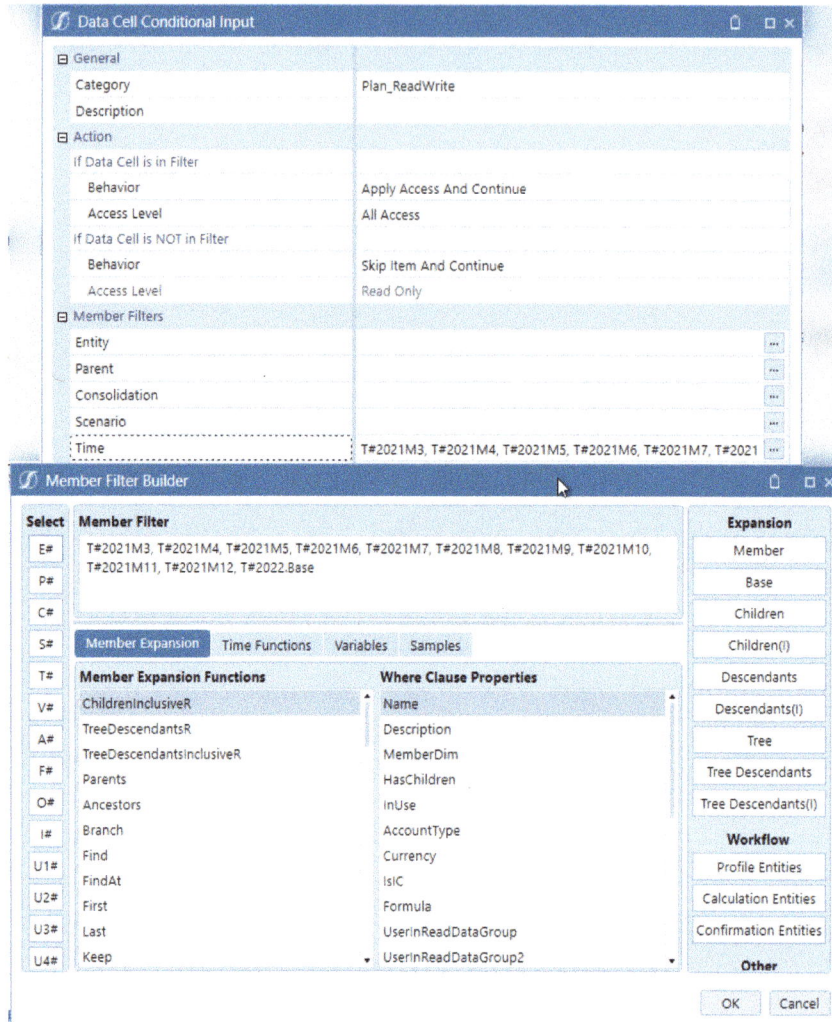

Figure 3.65

Conditional Input Materialized In Excel

The Time Member Filter has been updated to start at 2021M3, extends through 2021M12, and then adds 2022.Base. A Quick View query shows that the range of open periods has changed.

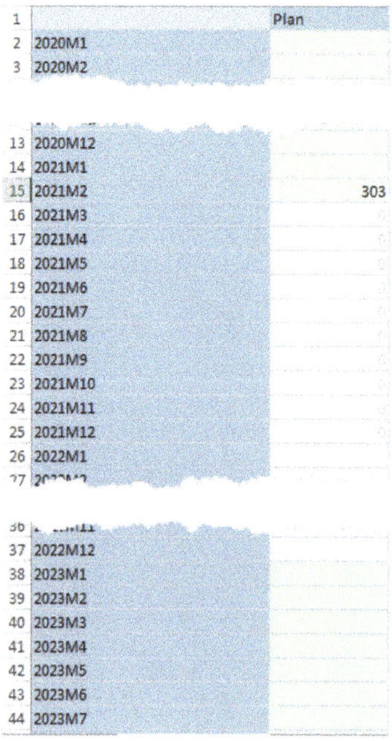

Figure 3.66

The Code In Total

```
Namespace OneStream.BusinessRule.Extender.ConditionalInput_DataAccess
    Public Class MainClass
        Public Function Main(ByVal si As SessionInfo, ByVal globals As BRGlobals,
            ByVal api As Object, ByVal args As ExtenderArgs) As Object
            Try
            Select Case args.FunctionType
            Case Is = ExtenderFunctionType.ExecuteDataMgmtBusinessRuleStep

                Dim intCubeID As Integer = BRApi.Finance.Cubes.GetCubeInfo(si, "Sample").Cube.CubeId
                Dim objConditionalInputAccessType As CubeDataAccessType = CubeDataAccessType.DataCellConditionalInput
                Dim strForecastTime As String = BRApi.Dashboards.Parameters.GetLiteralParameterValue(si, False, "ForecastMonth")
                Dim strForecast As String = BRApi.Dashboards.Parameters.GetLiteralParameterValue(si, False, "ForecastScenario_CI_Ext_BR")

                Dim intStartYear As Integer = Left(strForecastTime, 4)
                Dim intEndYear As Integer = TimeDimHelper.GetYearFromId(BRApi.Finance.Scenario.GetWorkflowEndTime(si,
                    ScenarioDimHelper.GetIdFromName(si, strForecast)))

                Dim lstFutureMonths As New List(Of String)
                For intCYMonths As Integer = (Right(strForecastTime,2).Replace("M","") - 1) + 1 To 12
                    lstFutureMonths.Add(Left(strForecastTime,4) & "M" & intCYMonths)
                Next

                For intFYMonths As Integer = intStartYear + 1 To intEndYear
                    lstFutureMonths.Add(intFYMonths & ".Base")
                Next

                Using dbConn As DbConnInfo = BRApi.Database.CreateApplicationDbConnInfo(si)
                    For Each objCubeDataAccessItem As CubeDataAccessItem In CubeDataAccessDbAccess.ReadCubeDataAccessItems(dbConn,
                        intCubeID, objConditionalInputAccessType)
                        If objCubeDataAccessItem.Category.XFEqualsIgnoreCase("Plan_ReadWrite")
                            Dim updatedAccessItem As New CubeDataAccessItem(objCubeDataAccessItem)
                            updatedAccessItem.MemberFilters.Time = "T#" & String.Join(", T#", lstFutureMonths)
                            CubeDataAccessDbAccess.InsertOrUpdateCubeDataAccessRow(dbConn, updatedAccessItem)
                        End If
                    Next

                    FinanceTimeStamps.InsertOrUpdateCubeDataAccessTimestamp(dbConn, DateTime.UtcNow)
                    FinanceTimeStamps.InsertOrUpdateCubesCacheTimestamp(dbConn, DateTime.UtcNow)

                End Using

            End Select

            Return Nothing
            Catch ex As Exception
                Throw ErrorHandler.LogWrite(si, New XFException(si, ex))
            End Try
        End Function

    End Class
End Namespace
```

Two Paths to the Same Place

The Conditional Input functional result from the Finance Business Rule and Data Cell Conditional Input Methods is the same; the approaches differ sharply in their implementation. The true difference is that the Finance Business Rule Conditional Input is code that a OneStream developer must write, and the Data Cell Conditional Input is free of code.

The above Extensibility Rule is not required to use Data Cell Conditional Input. It merely facilitates the pre-Plan cycle administrative tasks.

Is one better than the other? If beauty is said to be in the eye of the beholder, solution elegance is where the practitioner finds it. Your author prefers an easy and clear visual indication of how Conditional Input is defined as manifested with the Cube property Data Access Conditional Input. You must decide what is most appropriate for your application on the basis of clarity, performance, and flexibility.

Slice Data Access

Conditional Input controls data within and without Workflow. However, it is (at best) a very blunt ax because it does not assign security by group; read or write access is for *all* Users in a OneStream application. What is needed is security that works in concert with Conditional Input's absolute access to create a User-specific slice of security. As was hinted at, at the beginning of the Conditional Input section, Data Cell Access Security – aka Slice Security – can do just that.

It is important to note that OneStream Slice Security allows AND, NOT, and OR security conditions, both explicit and implicit. Its sequentially additive nature must be considered when determining security as it is easy to get lost in the filtering order of operations.

Security at AVBS

C&CCC's FP&A group divides its Planning responsibility by geography and product. Planners who do not have responsibility by product or geography cannot see the data. In the real world, security this granular is an exception, but the coffee business is cutthroat, and all financial information is on a need-to-know basis.

C&CCC's Planning Security Requirements

1. Natalie, the Vice President of Finance, monitors and plans for all regions and products.

2. Jessica, the analyst for the West, can plan for West and all products.

3. Amy, the analyst for the Midwest, can plan for Midwest and all products.

4. Neviana, the analyst for the East, can plan for East and all products.

5. Sandra, the analyst for the South, can plan for South and all products.

6. Tiffany, a core market and strategic product analyst, must be able to:

    a. Plan in East for Whole Bean and Ground Coffee but not their decaffeinated products nor see those product categories' totals.

    b. Plan in West for Decaf but no other, nor view decaffeinated products' Parent product totals.

The Role of Groups

A simple rule: never apply security directly to a Username because Planners change, whether that be a promotion, taking leave, or resigning their position. All security assignments should be by group, even if a group has a single Member. As Planners come and go, group membership is the only maintenance point instead of examining and modifying Dimensions, Conditional Input, Data Access, Workflow, and other artifacts.

Inherit Upwards

Just as children inherit from their ancestors, so too do OneStream security groups. If the group AVBS grants access to the application AVBS, the groups AVBS_West, AVBS_Mid_West, AVBS_East, and AVBS_South inherit application access by being Child groups. Neviana, a Child User of AVBS_East, gains access to the application because she inherits the access through AVBS_East, which is a Child of AVBS.

Parent Group	Child Group	Planners
AVBS	AVBS_Total_Geopgrahy	Natalie
	AVBS_East	Neviana, Tiffany, Natalie
	AVBS_West	Jessica, Tiffany, Natalie
	AVBS_Mid_West	Amy, Natalie
	AVBS_South	Sandra, Natalie

Figure 3.67

Application and Cube Access

The AVBS Parent group provides OpenApplication, ModifyData, and ManageData rights to the Application AVBS for non-Administrators.

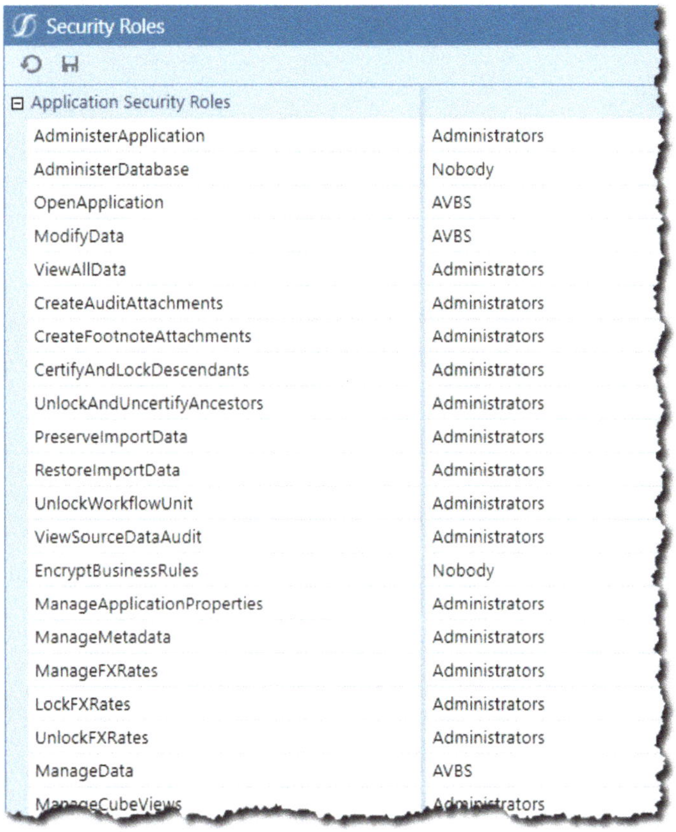

Figure 3.68

AVBS also provides access to the Cube Sample.

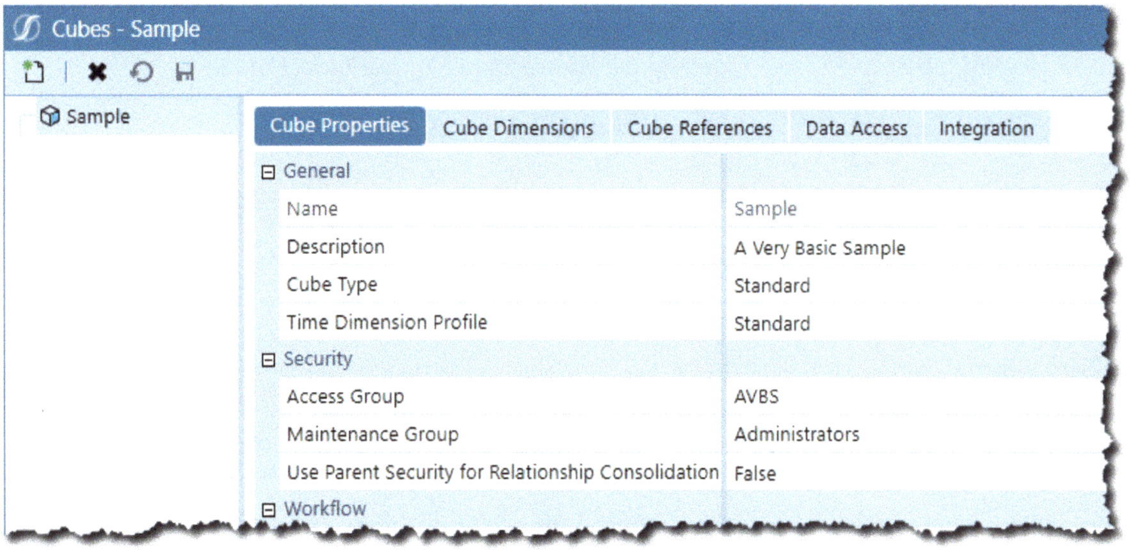

Figure 3.69

Real-world security group dependencies can be confusing. If possible, try to use naming conventions that indicate familial relationships. Map out an application's security design before creating groups and assigning Users.

Two Axes of Planning Security

Entity/Geography

Entity – Geography in the case of AVBS – security drives read/write access by individual Entity. There are no hierarchical functions that assign, (e.g., read-write security at East does not apply to Pennsylvania, New Jersey, New York, or Delaware).

Entities have three kinds of Member security:

- A single Display Member Group (metadata)

- Two Read Data Groups

- Two Read and Write Groups

- Use Cube Data Access Security (Boolean value for Data Access/Slice Security)

- Cube Data Cell Access Categories (Slice Security by category name)

- Cube Conditional Input Categories (Conditional Input by category name)

- Cube Data Management Access Categories (Data Management access by category name)

This use case will not incorporate Display Member Group or Entity-specific Category security but will instead focus on the mandatory display, read, and read/write security types in conjunction with Data Cell Access that applies to all Entities.

AVBS' security groups map to their similarly named Entity, e.g., AVBS_East applies to East and its descendants.

Group	Entity	Planners
AVBS_Total_Geopgrahy	All Entities	Natalie
AVBS_East	East and its descendants	Neviana, Tiffany, Natalie
AVBS_West	West and its descendants	Jessica, Tiffany, Natalie
AVBS_Mid_West	Mid_West and its descendants	Amy, Natalie
AVBS_South	South and its descendants	Sandra, Natalie

Figure 3.70

Natalie must be a Member of all of the security groups to get access to their Entities as well as AVBS_Total_Geography to give her full access to the Entity Dimension.

Data Access/Slice Security

Where Entity security exists in isolation, (i.e., security exists on a Member-by-Member basis), Slice Security is additive in that it applies in steps (or slices) of access, with latter steps building on the former ones. Access is also controlled within the Category's Member Filter by applying Member selections in dimensional Member Filters. Member Filters support hierarchical functions.

This combination of access, Category order, and Member Filter selections within Categories, combine to affect OneStream Slice Security's AND, OR, and NOT logical conditions. Care must be taken when designing Slice Security because of the interactions between Categories.

UD1/Product and Entity/Geography

Product groups in AVBS have a twofold purpose: access to Products, and where specified, logical AND combinations of Geography and Product.

Parent Group	Geography->Product	Planners
Total_Products	Total_Products	Natalie, Jessica, Amy, Neviana, Sandra
Ground_Coffee_East	West->Decaf	Tiffany
West_Decaf	East->Whole_Bean, East->Ground_Coffee	Tiffany
No_Product	No_Product	Natalie, Jessica, Amy, Neviana, Sandra

Figure 3.71

Use Cube Data Access Security

This property *must* be set to True if Slice Security is to be applied to the Entity in question. Unpredictable results will ensue if this is left at the default of False.

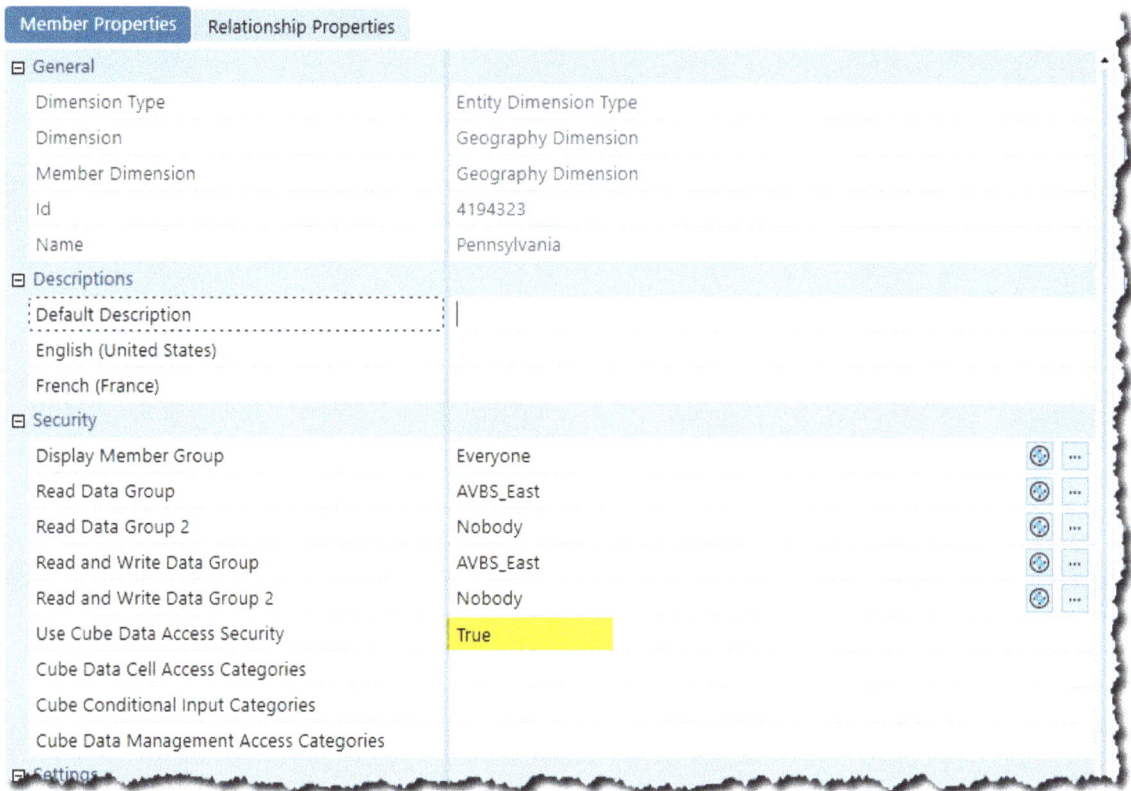

Figure 3.72

The Anatomy of Data Cell Access

Like Conditional Input, Data Cell Security is a Cube-level property.

Assigning Security

Order	Category	Group	Purpose	Entity/Geography	UD1/Products
1	Product_NoAccess	Everyone (in-built)	Deny access to all Products	N/A	U1#Total_Products.DescendantsInclusive
2	Product_Total	Total_Products	Allow access to all Products	N/A	U1#Total_Products.DescendantsInclusive
3	Ground_Coffee_East	Ground_Coffee_East	Read/write access for East and Ground Products (not Decaf)	E#East.DescendantsInclusive	U1#Ground_Coffee.Descendants.Remove (U1#20_020).Base
4	Whole_Bean_East	Whole_Bean_East	and Whole Bean Products (not Decaf)	E#East.DescendantsInclusive	U1#10_020, U1#10_010
5	West_Decaf	West_Decaf	Read/write access for West and Decaf products	E#West.DescendantsInclusive	U1#Decaf.DescendantsInclusive

Figure 3.73

Total_Products

For all Planners but Tiffany, the first two Categories of security are sufficient: Product_NoAccess denies access to all Planners through the in-built Everyone group, Product_Total opens up the Products Dimension for Planners in the Product_Total group. These two security definitions would not be necessary if her geographical and product restrictions did not exist because dimensional security is, by default, open to all for read/write access.

In the Product_Total Category, the Action property If User is NOT in Group and Data Cell is in Filter is set to Skip Item and Continue, thereby enabling subsequent security definitions to apply to Planners not in Product_Total. The UD1/Products Member Filter is set to U1#Total_Products.DescendantsInclusive, thus defining the scope of security to be all products except U1#No_Product and U1#Decaf, a Parent of an alternate hierarchy of decaffeinated coffee products. Tiffany's access must be supplied by Categories three through five.

Key Markets and Products

Categories three and four apply to East and the product categories Ground_Coffee and Whole_Bean. These two East Categories could have been combined into one via a common UD1/Products Member Filter but are separated for illustration.

Tiffany already has Entity access to East and its descendants through the AVBS_East group. Specifying E#East.DescendantsInclusive in these Categories executes an AND condition against the Ground_Coffee and Whole_Bean product families. If East was not specified, she would be able to access these products in West as she is also a Member of AVBS_West. Note also that Ground_Coffee_East uses a Member function to exclude the decaffeinated product U1#20_020 instead of an explicit list of products like Whole_Bean_East; both Methods are valid.

Data Cell Access Security uses the same dialog box as Data Cell Conditional Input Member Categories.

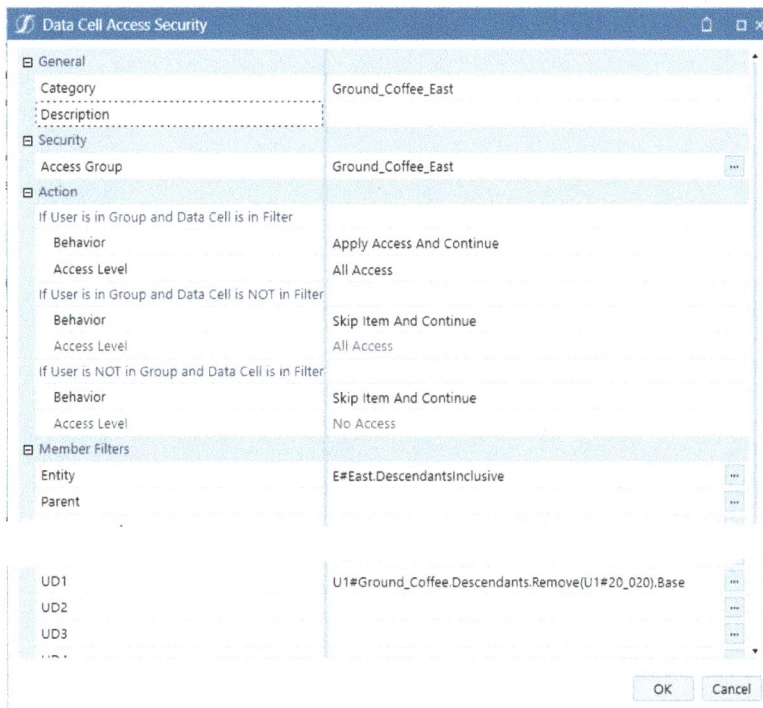

Figure 3.74

The West_Decaf Category provides read/write access to the region West and the shared Decaf product hierarchy. The Ground_Coffee_East and Whole_Bean_East Categories explicitly exclude their respective U1#20_020/100% Colombian Decaf and U1#10_030/ French Roast Regular Whole Bean Decaf decaffeinated products because Tiffany does not forecast those products in East. If West_Decaf was not in an AND condition between E#West and U1#Decaf, it would open up those decaffeinated products in East.

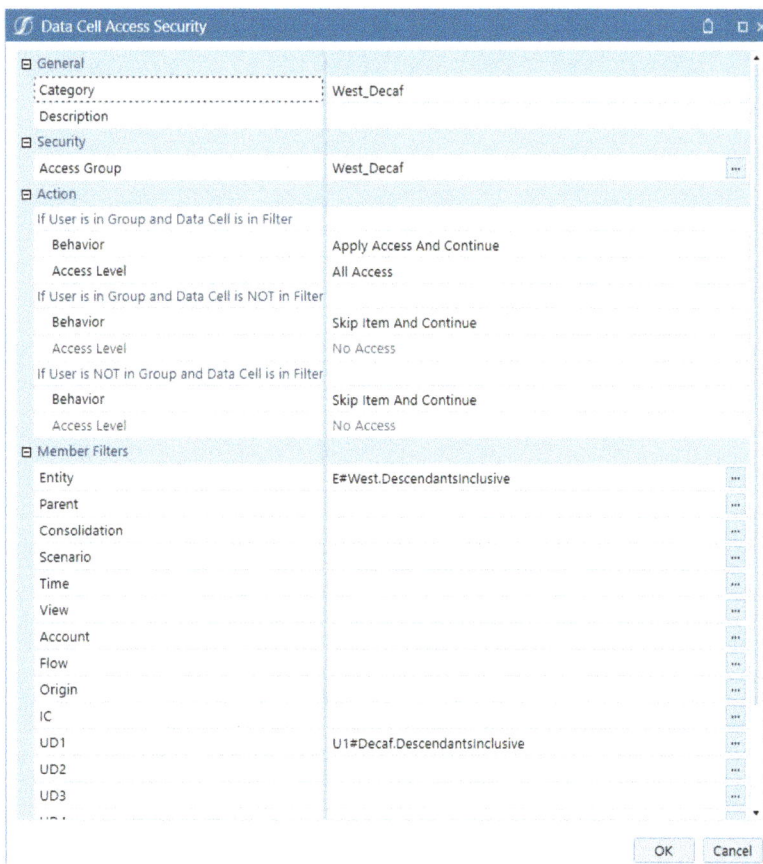

Figure 3.75

No_Product

Lastly, because U1#No_Product was not included in the initial denial of all access to U1#Total_Products.DescendantsInclusive (it is a sibling), it is read/write for all Planners.

The Complete Categories

When complete, the Categories appear as below.

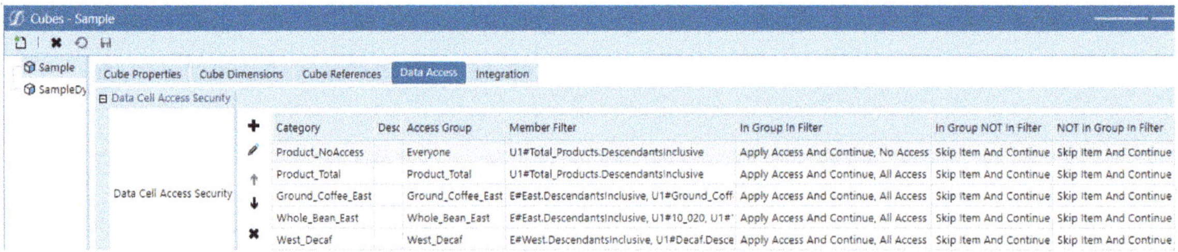

Figure 3.76

Three Views of Security

Natalie

As Vice President of Finance, Natalie has full access to all regions and products:

	A	B	C	D	E	F	G	H	I	J
1		Plan	Plan	Plan	Plan	Plan	Plan	Plan	Plan	Plan
2		2021M6	2021M6	2021M6	2021M6	2021M6	2021M6	2021M6	2021M6	2021M6
3		Total_Geography	East	Pennsylvania	West	California	Mid_West	Ohio	South	South_Carolina
4	10_010 - Cameron's 100% Colombian Whole Bean	3397	990	990	991	991	514	514	902	902
5	10_020 - Celvin's Colombian Supremo Regular Whole Bean	1237	524	524	251	251	22	22	440	440
6	10_030 - French Roast Regular Whole Bean Decaf	2513	69	69	732	732	816	816	896	896
7	Whole_Bean - Whole Bean	7147	1583	1583	1974	1974	1352	1352	2238	2238
8	20_010 - Premium Blend	1196	533	533	6	6	498	498	159	159
9	20_020 - 100% Colombian Decaf	1518	966	966	64	64	341	341	147	147
10	20_030 - Royal Kona Blend	1205	557	557	443	443	77	77	128	128
11	20_040 - Jack Benny House Masterblend	1832	874	874	545	545	105	105	308	308
12	Ground_Coffee - Ground Coffee	5751	2930	2930	1058	1058	1021	1021	742	742
13	40_010 - House Blend	2146	688	688	903	903	530	530	25	25
14	40_020 - Breakfast Blend	1434	100	100	589	589	295	295	450	450
15	40_030 - Dark Kenya AA	417	109	109	155	155	128	128	25	25
16	Single_Cup - Single Cup	3997	897	897	1647	1647	953	953	500	500
17	30_010 - Regular Filter Pack	1361	344	344	743	743	251	251	23	23
18	30_020 - Decaf Filter Pack-1.5oz	1845	67	67	805	805	293	293	680	680
19	30_030 - Hot Shoppes Regular Filter Pack Decaf	1953	146	146	163	163	967	967	677	677
20	Filter	5159	557	557	1711	1711	1511	1511	1380	1380
21	Total_Products - Total Products	22054	5967	5967	6390	6390	4837	4837	4860	4860
22	10_030 - French Roast Regular Whole Bean Decaf	2513	69	69	732	732	816	816	896	896
23	20_020 - 100% Colombian Decaf	1518	966	966	64	64	341	341	147	147
24	30_020 - Decaf Filter Pack-1.5oz	1845	67	67	805	805	293	293	680	680
25	Decaf	5876	1102	1102	1601	1601	1450	1450	1723	1723
26	No_Product									

Figure 3.77

Amy

As the Planner for the Midwest, she has a more circumscribed view of just `Mid_West` and its descendants and access to all products.

	A	B	C	D	E	F	G	H	I	J
1		Plan	Plan	Plan	Plan	Plan	Plan	Plan	Plan	Plan
2		2021M6	2021M6	2021M6	2021M6	2021M6	2021M6	2021M6	2021M6	2021M6
3		Total_Geography	East	Pennsylvania	West	California	Mid_West	Ohio	South	South_Carolina
4	10_010 - Cameron's 100% Colombian Whole Bean	No Access	No Access	No Access	No Access	No Access	514		514 No Access	No Access
5	10_020 - Celvin's Colombian Supremo Regular Whole Bean	No Access	No Access	No Access	No Access	No Access	22		22 No Access	No Access
6	10_030 - French Roast Regular Whole Bean Decaf	No Access	No Access	No Access	No Access	No Access	816		816 No Access	No Access
7	Whole_Bean - Whole Bean	No Access	No Access	No Access	No Access	No Access	1352		1352 No Access	No Access
8	20_010 - Premium Blend	No Access	No Access	No Access	No Access	No Access	498		498 No Access	No Access
9	20_020 - 100% Colombian Decaf	No Access	No Access	No Access	No Access	No Access	341		341 No Access	No Access
10	20_030 - Royal Kona Blend	No Access	No Access	No Access	No Access	No Access	77		77 No Access	No Access
11	20_040 - Jack Benny House Masterblend	No Access	No Access	No Access	No Access	No Access	105		105 No Access	No Access
12	Ground_Coffee - Ground Coffee	No Access	No Access	No Access	No Access	No Access	1021		1021 No Access	No Access
13	40_010 - House Blend	No Access	No Access	No Access	No Access	No Access	530		530 No Access	No Access
14	40_020 - Breakfast Blend	No Access	No Access	No Access	No Access	No Access	295		295 No Access	No Access
15	40_030 - Dark Kenya AA	No Access	No Access	No Access	No Access	No Access	128		128 No Access	No Access
16	Single_Cup - Single Cup	No Access	No Access	No Access	No Access	No Access	953		953 No Access	No Access
17	30_010 - Regular Filter Pack	No Access	No Access	No Access	No Access	No Access	251		251 No Access	No Access
18	30_020 - Decaf Filter Pack-1.5oz	No Access	No Access	No Access	No Access	No Access	293		293 No Access	No Access
19	30_030 - Hot Shoppes Regular Filter Pack Decaf	No Access	No Access	No Access	No Access	No Access	967		967 No Access	No Access
20	Filter	No Access	No Access	No Access	No Access	No Access	1511		1511 No Access	No Access
21	Total_Products - Total Products	No Access	No Access	No Access	No Access	No Access	4837		4837 No Access	No Access
22	10_030 - French Roast Regular Whole Bean Decaf	No Access	No Access	No Access	No Access	No Access	816		816 No Access	No Access
23	20_020 - 100% Colombian Decaf	No Access	No Access	No Access	No Access	No Access	341		341 No Access	No Access
24	30_020 - Decaf Filter Pack-1.5oz	No Access	No Access	No Access	No Access	No Access	293		293 No Access	No Access
25	Decaf	No Access	No Access	No Access	No Access	No Access	1450		1450 No Access	No Access
26	No_Product	No Access	No Access	No Access	No Access	No Access			No Access	No Access

Figure 3.78

Tiffany

Tiffany's complex security is now manifested as read/write access in `E#East` to `U1#Ground_Coffee` and `U1#Whole_Bean` but not to the decaffeinated `U1#20_020` and `U1#10_030`. In West, she has access to all descendants of `U1#Decaf` across `U1#Ground_Coffee`, `U1#Whole_Bean`, and `U1#Filter`.

	A	B	C	D	E	F	G	H	I	J
1		Plan	Plan	Plan	Plan	Plan	Plan	Plan	Plan	Plan
2		2021M6	2021M6	2021M6	2021M6	2021M6	2021M6	2021M6	2021M6	2021M6
3		Total_Geography	East	Pennsylvania	West	California	Mid_West	Ohio	South	South_Carolina
4	10_010 - Cameron's 100% Colombian Whole Bean	No Access	990		990 No Access	No Access	No Access	No Access	No Access	No Access
5	10_020 - Celvin's Colombian Supremo Regular Whole Bean	No Access	524		524 No Access	No Access	No Access	No Access	No Access	No Access
6	10_030 - French Roast Regular Whole Bean Decaf	No Access	No Access	No Access	732		732 No Access	No Access	No Access	No Access
7	Whole_Bean - Whole Bean	No Access	No Access	No Access	No Access	No Access	No Access	No Access	No Access	No Access
8	20_010 - Premium Blend	No Access	533		533 No Access	No Access	No Access	No Access	No Access	No Access
9	20_020 - 100% Colombian Decaf	No Access	No Access	No Access	64		64 No Access	No Access	No Access	No Access
10	20_030 - Royal Kona Blend	No Access	557		557 No Access	No Access	No Access	No Access	No Access	No Access
11	20_040 - Jack Benny House Masterblend	No Access	874		874 No Access	No Access	No Access	No Access	No Access	No Access
12	Ground_Coffee - Ground Coffee	No Access	No Access	No Access	No Access	No Access	No Access	No Access	No Access	No Access
13	40_010 - House Blend	No Access	No Access	No Access	No Access	No Access	No Access	No Access	No Access	No Access
14	40_020 - Breakfast Blend	No Access	No Access	No Access	No Access	No Access	No Access	No Access	No Access	No Access
15	40_030 - Dark Kenya AA	No Access	No Access	No Access	No Access	No Access	No Access	No Access	No Access	No Access
16	Single_Cup - Single Cup	No Access	No Access	No Access	No Access	No Access	No Access	No Access	No Access	No Access
17	30_010 - Regular Filter Pack	No Access	No Access	No Access	No Access	No Access	No Access	No Access	No Access	No Access
18	30_020 - Decaf Filter Pack-1.5oz	No Access	No Access	No Access	805		805 No Access	No Access	No Access	No Access
19	30_030 - Hot Shoppes Regular Filter Pack Decaf	No Access	No Access	No Access	No Access	No Access	No Access	No Access	No Access	No Access
20	Filter	No Access	No Access	No Access	No Access	No Access	No Access	No Access	No Access	No Access
21	Total_Products - Total Products	No Access	No Access	No Access	No Access	No Access	No Access	No Access	No Access	No Access
22	10_030 - French Roast Regular Whole Bean Decaf	No Access	No Access	No Access	732		732 No Access	No Access	No Access	No Access
23	20_020 - 100% Colombian Decaf	No Access	No Access	No Access	64		64 No Access	No Access	No Access	No Access
24	30_020 - Decaf Filter Pack-1.5oz	No Access	No Access	No Access	805		805 No Access	No Access	No Access	No Access
25	Decaf	No Access	1102	1102	1601		1601 No Access	No Access	No Access	No Access
26	No_Product	No Access					No Access	No Access	No Access	No Access

Figure 3.79

Security As You Like It

Access to data in OneStream can be as sophisticated or as simple as an application requires. It is multidimensional – both figuratively and literally – encompassing Entity and User-Defined Dimensions as well as being controlled by Conditional. An application's valid data combinations can be defined explicitly or implicitly inherited through security definition order. The only downside to OneStream's security model is its potential complexity, which is a function of requirements and design.

To confirm a security model's design, OneStream practitioners should *briefly* create temporary dummy Accounts that fit required security profiles for testing in data-free application copies. These temporary Usernames *must* be deleted as quickly as possible, as must the application copy. OneStream applications contain the key financial data of an organization. Not securing data externally (or indeed internally) is a professional, organizational, and possibly criminal failure of the highest order.

A last note about security during application implementations: the task of assigning security is often an afterthought, assigned to a junior practitioner because of its perceived non-technical nature. As this chapter's Data Cell Conditional Input and Access Security use cases show, this belief is not true. Security's importance is paramount, its design potentially complex, and the potential for error is high. Whoever is responsible for the security model must have it checked and double-checked.

Command and Control

The theme of this chapter has been one of expanding functionality through XFBR Business Rules and constraining data access through Conditional Input and Cell Access security. Your authors have never seen a OneStream application that did not utilize both concepts. Both concepts are powerful and need careful consideration to enable the greatest and most secure OneStream application possible.

The Core I and this Core II chapters have focused on what is – after all – the core of OneStream applications: the Cube. The following chapters on Specialty Planning and Analysis go beyond the Cube into some of the key differentiators of OneStream from its Performance Management competitors. Much of the content is advanced in nature and – seemingly – orthogonal to OneStream Cube-based Planning applications. A careful examination of the following chapters will disabuse the skeptical of that notion by exploring, illustrating, and explaining the almost unlimited potential of the OneStream platform.

Planning Without Limits

Gentle Reader, if you are from the school of thought "Was there ever a limit?", then you have come to the right place; this chapter is all about going beyond – far beyond – the normal scope of Planning solely in a Cube. If you are from the "What's the limit look like?" (like me) school of thought, read on.

Boxed In by The Cube

Multidimensional databases, typically called Cubes in OneStream parlance, are a powerful metaphor for describing, managing, and navigating hierarchical data structures. The concept is powerful, the tool is powerful, its uses are broad and deep.

However, by its very nature, in a multidimensional world *everything* is a Cube. The reason is simple: in this world view, data cannot be addressed without it being present in the Cube and to have it in the Cube, it must have all the metadata in the Cube to represent the data. The Cube is the beginning and ending of all.

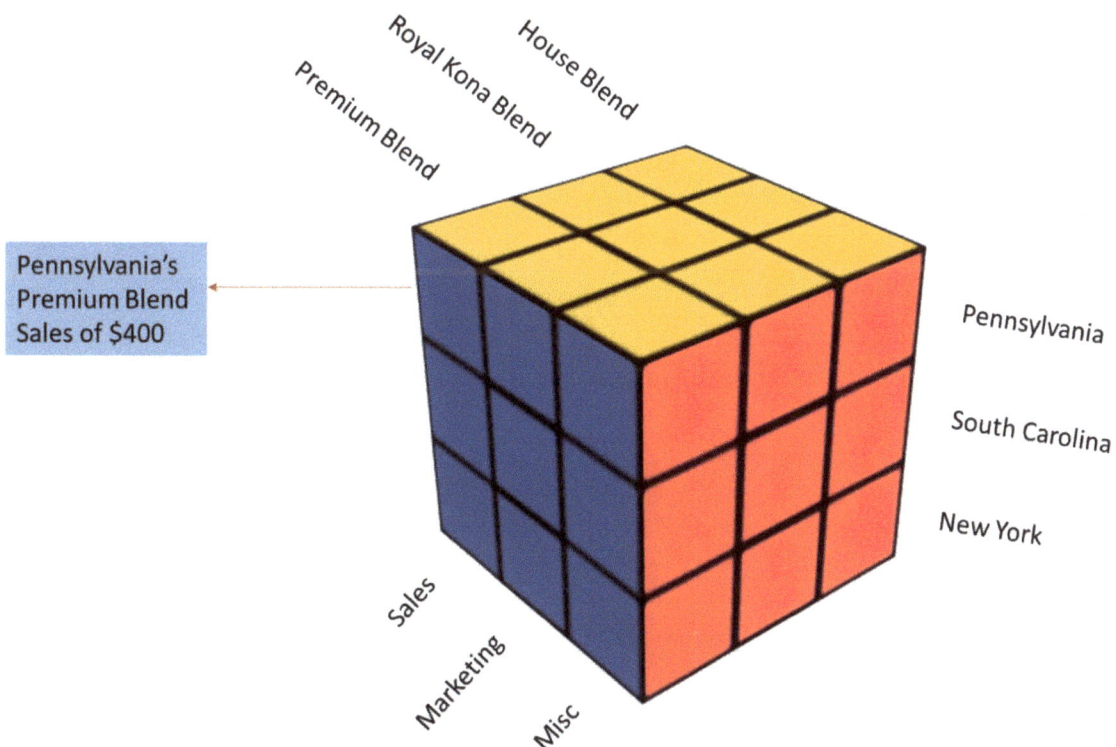

Figure 4.1

But a Cube is not always the answer. Planning does not always fit within a Cube. Sometimes Planners need to work with data that, because of its textual nature, data level, or rapidly-changing metadata, is a poor candidate for the dimensionality that a Cube requires.

Some legacy platforms attempted to overcome this through a limited merging of the relational with the multidimensional. Let us travel, Gentle Reader, down a memory lane of XOLAP and supporting details where the data store could be entirely relational (but still Cube-based) or supplemental to the Cube by supporting User-driven, non-Cube detail. In theory, those techniques helped achieve the commingling of two separate worlds. In practice, this approach proved to be cumbersome to implement, use, and report.

The Cube that provides so much power and flexibility boxes the Planning process in because its paradigm of multidimensionality is necessarily hierarchical, where hierarchy is not sufficient to describe and solve Planning and Budgeting requirements.

How does OneStream then break the limitations of the Cube?

Planning without Limits

Where other vendors remain wedded to the Cube for all data, whatever the appropriateness might be because they have no other option, OneStream rejected this approach and instead came up with a simple and elegant philosophy: "Don't try to add relational/transactional items into a Cube."

Custom, non-vendor solutions to this problem exist, such as a system that stores data in relational tables with custom web-based forms for data entry. That data is loaded into Cubes where calculations happen. Once calculated, data then moves back to another set of relational tables for reporting.

This approach is difficult because it involves multiple products, and the different skillsets of multidimensional databases, relational tables, and reporting from both technologies. OneStream solves the issue of multiple products and different interfaces for the End-User by combining the relational with the Cube directly in one product.

This blend of data architectures has two primary use cases:

1. Supplementing data with more information.
2. Planning at a detailed level.

Supplemental Data

If you have used legacy solutions, you will likely have heard about the terms **supporting detail**, **text members**, and **attributes**. OneStream supports all three concepts in a highly flexible manner.

Coffee, Coffee, Coffee Everywhere, is There a Drop to Drink?

As part of its reporting process, our fictional C&C Coffee Company reports its coffee sales by state.

Figure 4.2

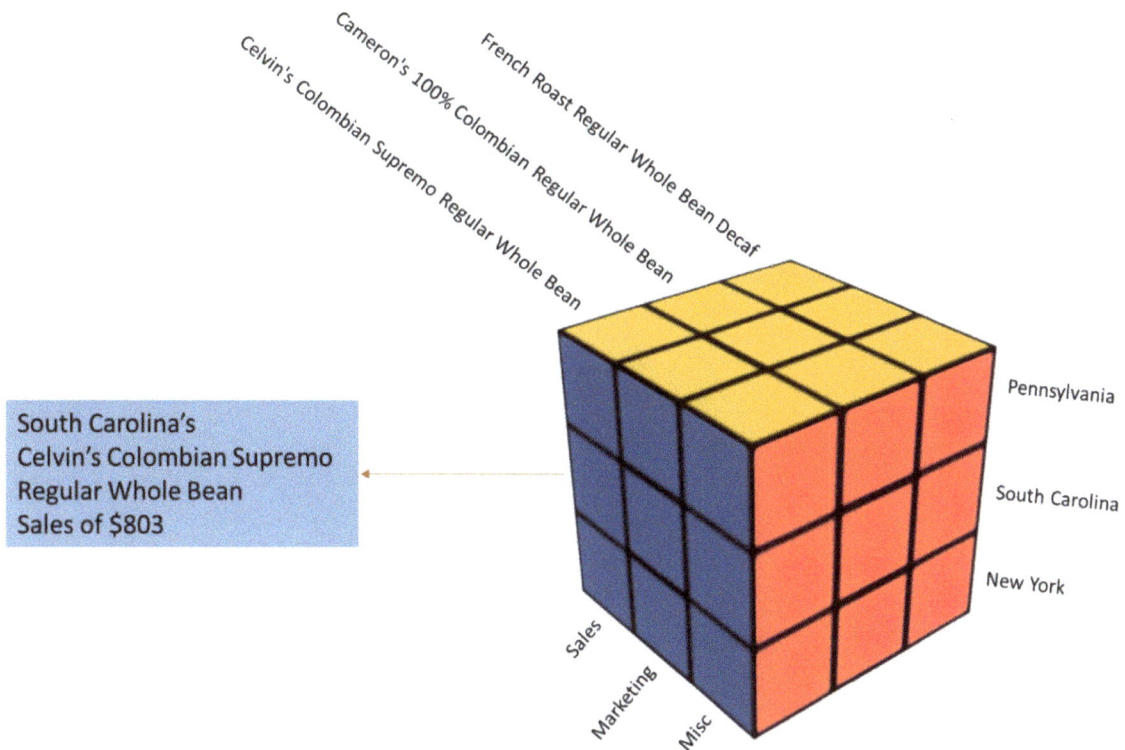

South Carolina's
Celvin's Colombian Supremo
Regular Whole Bean
Sales of $803

Figure 4.3

Sales figures (and other Accounts) are captured at a detailed level by Sales Representatives by Product by City. At a Cube level, the data is summarized to the Product and State level; Sales Representative and City are not carried in the Cube.

Imagine Celvin as a Sales Representative selling his very own *Celvin's Colombian Supremo Regular Whole Bean* to a store in Charleston, South Carolina in August 2021. Cameron is an enthusiastic analyst in FP&A that needs this detailed information to analyze and understand C&CCC's sales performance.

Use that Staging Area

How does OneStream store information that is not in a Cube? Sales Representative and City are not carried in the Cube.

Cube data *cannot* be loaded directly from any sort of external data source, whether it be Excel, text, or relational. Instead, it *must* go through a data staging space, commonly called **Stage**, that acts as a clearing house for data. As a pictorial metaphor, the below image shows the gatekeeper role of Stage.

Figure 4.4

There is no way to import data into OneStream Cubes without getting a pass from Stagealf (or Stage).

Stage data supports 20 text and 12 value attributes for loading additional information to complement Cube data. Think of these as **data attributes** since these are tied to data, not the Cube itself.

The last two lines of the below data file show the `Sales_Rep` and `City` attributes for Celvin's August 2021 sales:

UD1	Entity	Time	Scenario	Flow	Measures	Data	Sales_Rep	City
10_020	Pennsylvania	2021M8	Actual	EndBal_input	Sales	93		
10_010	Pennsylvania	2021M8	Actual	EndBal_input	Sales	120		
10_020	South_Carolina	2021M8	Actual	EndBal_input	Sales	678	Celvin Kattookaran	Charleston
10_020	South_Carolina	2021M8	Actual	EndBal_input	Sales	125	Celvin Kattookaran	Columbia

Figure 4.5

We can load this file and its additional `Sales_Rep` and `City` fields by enabling two text attributes for the Actual Scenario Type in the Cube Integration tab. If all data files/connectors with this Scenario Type use the same attributes, an alias can be added to aid User comprehension.

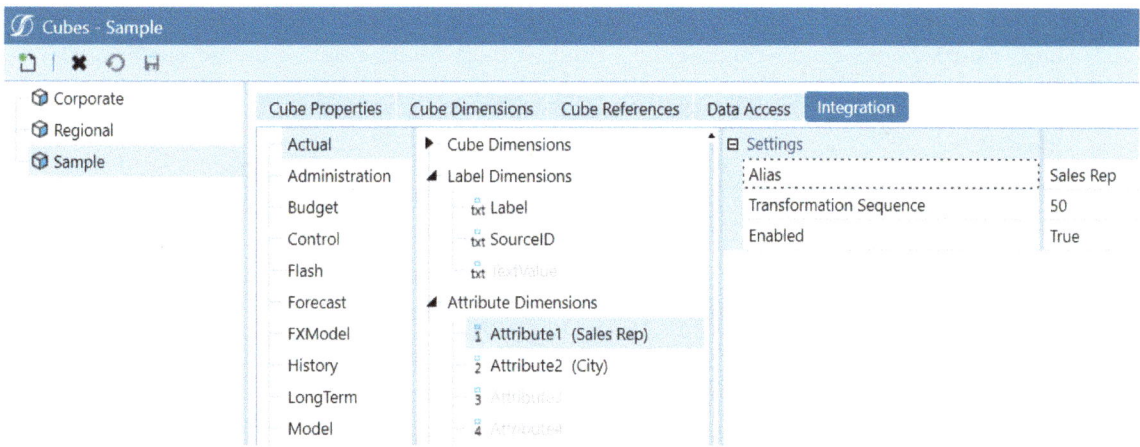

Figure 4.6

Stage Attribute Dimensions are selectable by Scenario Type, allowing more or less supplemental data as needed.

NB: Attribute Dimensions and Attribute Value Dimensions are not enabled by default.

Within the data source definition for this file, a simple match of field column to Attribute Dimension is all that is required to load data for Dimensions that do not exist in any Cube.

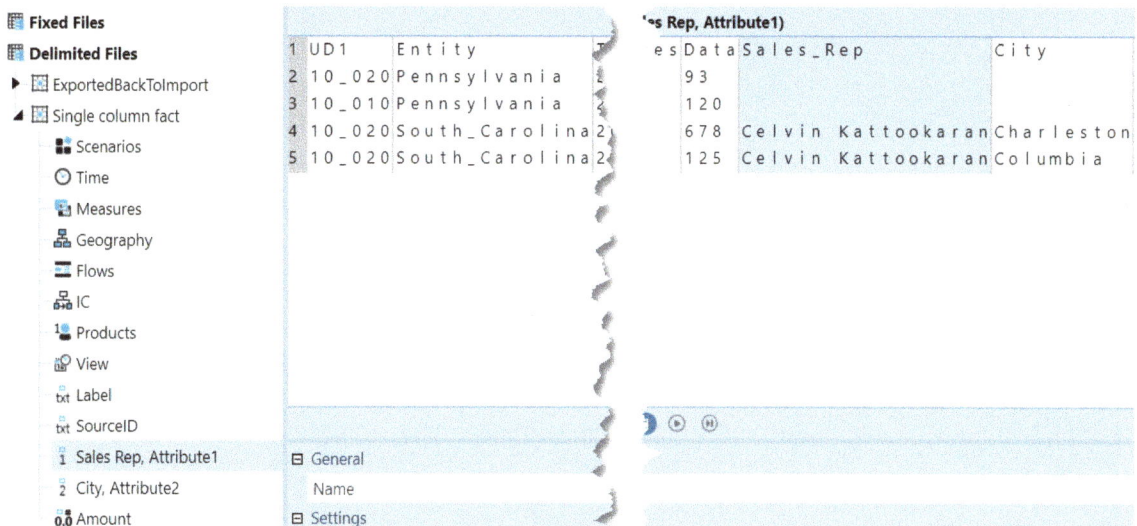

Figure 4.7

On Import, the Attributes can be observed as part of the data load.

Figure 4.8

The Validation step shows you the summarized view of those last two South Carolina records into one, and suppresses the Attribute Dimensions; validation is a Cube construct and thus cannot show Stage Attribute Dimensions.

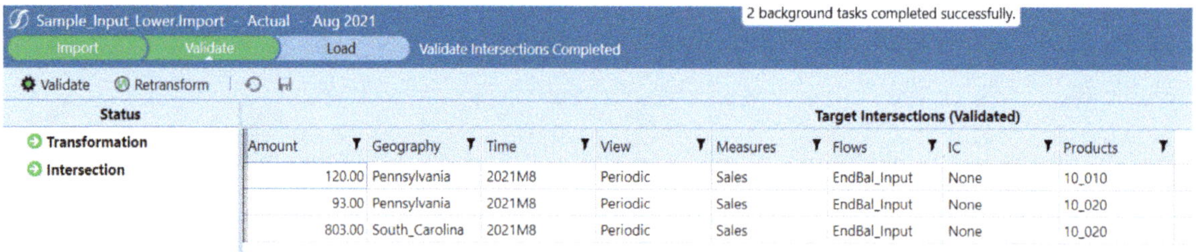

Figure 4.9

Once loaded, Cameron can now perform his analysis using Drill Downs and drill backs.

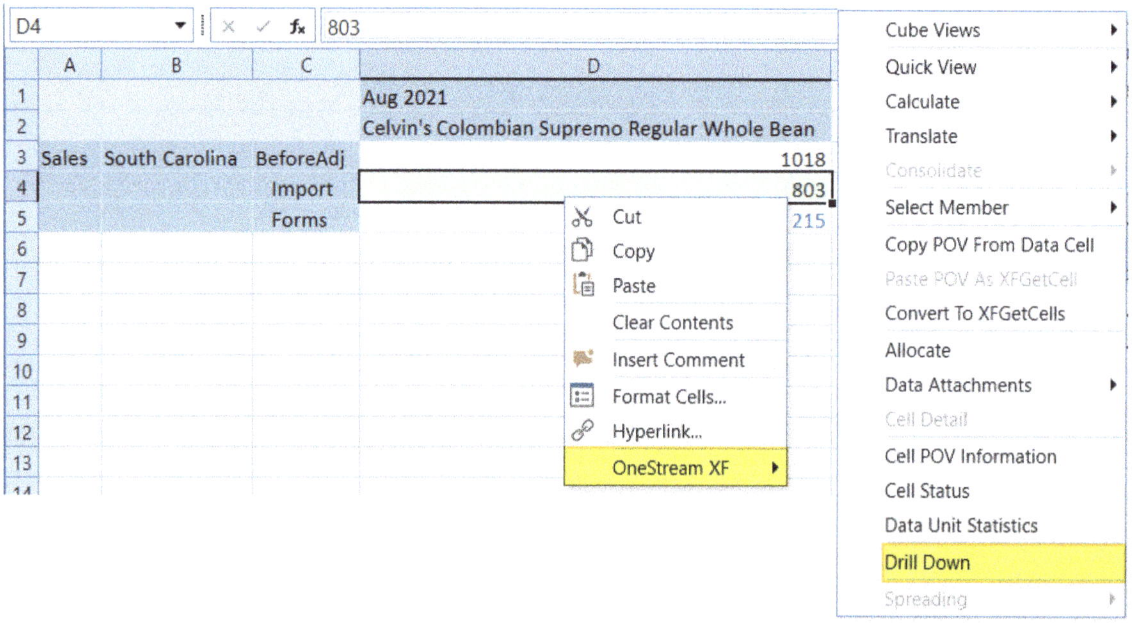

Figure 4.10

Drill Down

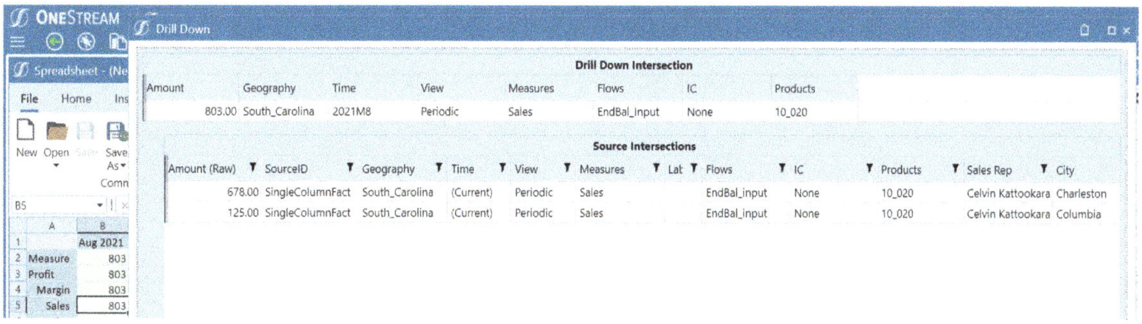

Figure 4.11

Cameron is happy (for those who know Cameron, this is quite the accomplishment). The analytical requirement of going beyond the limits of the Cube has been fulfilled.

Back to the Cube

The above example shows the reporting of Cube and supplemental data but does not illustrate the *merging* of Cube and supplemental relational data as both cannot be seen at the same time. Cube data is available in one interface, non-Cube data is viewed in a similar albeit different way. Those data points are still separate and one must still drill down to get the details.

How can both the Cube numbers and the details be viewed in the same Report? Your author has an answer for that. Well, he has multiple answers. If he is trying to be more accurate, he is behaving like his younger (much younger) self, who is raising his hand and jumping up and down in his seat.

"Relational Blending!" he wants to shout.

What is Relational Blending? Is it a Mind-Bending Trick?

Relational Blending is just what it says: it is a way to blend relational data with Cube data. OneStream provides functions to support that blend of data Types.

Relational Blending API Methods

The following Methods query/calculate blend data:

- GetStageBlendTextUsingCurrentPOV
- GetStageBlendTextUsingCurrentPOV
- GetStageBlendText
- GetStageBlendNumberUsingCurrentPOV
- GetStageBlendNumber
- GetStageBlendDataTableUsingCurrentPOV
- GetStageBlendDataTable
- GetCustomBlendDataTableUsingCurrentPOV
- GetCustomBlendDataTable

What information is being blended – and where that data is located – drives the function selection.

Our use case is blending external table-based text information with Cube data, so the function to use is GetCustomBlendDataTableUsingCurrentPOV.

```
Public Function GetCustomBlendDataTableUsingCurrentPOV(ByVal
cacheLevel As BlendCacheLevelTypes, ByVal cacheName As String, ByVal
sourceDBLocation As String, ByVal sourceSQL) As DataTable
```

Cache Levels

After choosing the correct function, we need to find out what cache level is needed for the formula.

The following cache levels are available for Relational blending API.

- `WfProfileScenarioTime`

- `WfProfileScenarioTimeEntity`

- `WfProfileScenarioTimeAccount`

- `WfProfileScenarioTimeEntityAccount`

- `Custom` – only use with the custom blend API because, in that context, the custom SQL drives the cache

Why is cache level important? Let me explain through a daily chore that anyone with young children can relate to. (For those of you who do not have children or who have mercifully forgotten the following because of the passage of time, you have missed out on some not-entirely-minor physical pain, but the idea is easy to grasp.)

A Childhood Analogy

Those Little Plastic Blocks From Denmark are a wonderful educational toy. Children love them because they are a blank slate upon which they can build; parents look on approvingly because they are not a video game or television. After a while, however, said parents might start thinking those snap-together building blocks are evil because of their ability to camouflage their location and their little sharp (and strong) corners when stepped upon with bare feet. Those little buggers hide and hurt in places where it hurts the most, clog vacuum cleaners, and then add insult to not-inconsiderable injury by making the victims dig them out from the dust pile within the vacuum bag. Ugh.

A way to sort and segregate and select these blocks from Hell would be nice. Sadistic (and hopelessly unrealistic) parents, of course, turn immediately to the idea of having their kids clean them up and sort them by color. Yellow bricks go and stay in the yellow box, red ones in the red box, and so on. Once sorted, it is easier to find a brick instead of dumping them all onto the floor, although there will, of course, remain the usual moderate level of natural anarchy and entropy 😊.

If the plastic building block gods smile upon you, those wee little rascals could sort the bricks by size/shape (getting them to colored boxes itself is a big deal). It is now easier to find a square yellow brick from the color-size/shape box compared to dumping the whole colored box.

Relational blend caches are similar to those boxes except for the plastic, the physical pain, and the unhappy children who have strangely satisfied parents.

Think of `WFProfileScenarioTime`, `WFProfileScenarioEntity`, `WFProfileScenarioAccount` as the colored boxes. Supplemental information needed from Stage based on Profile, Scenario, and Time/Entity/Account can be stored in separate boxes and queried there instead of searching the whole staging area.

Similarly, `WFProfileScenarioTimeEntityAccount` is our color-size/shape sorted box. It is a more granular level where you can easily get to the supplemental items.

It is important to pick the right cache level, as it is directly related to the performance of the query (and directly related to the pain it can cause, as with the case of those damnable little plastic bricks). When dealing with the relational world, the less you query the source tables, the better the performance, because of the time OneStream spends creating and closing connections, on a cell-by-cell basis, when it queries relational data in a grid.

In our example, we are looking for the details of a State, Account, and Product from the relational store, then the choice of cache is only one. You can only use `Custom` as your cache if you are using a custom blend. When using the `CustomBlendDataTable` Method, the SQL used to get the data defines the cache for you.

Back to the Cube

With the cache defined as custom, we can create a Dimension Member (we have arrived at the blend) to retrieve the Sales Rep details.

The UD8 Dimension can be used to add these analysis-based Members, even though they are not part of the Cube, so long as they are formulas and refer to the default U8#None Member.

When OneStream stores data in its fact tables, it stores it for each User-Defined Dimension, whether or not it is part of the Cube. If a Dimension is not part of the Cube (by default, the RootDimensions, e.g., Root<DimType>Dim becomes the Cube Dimension), OS stores the data against the default None Member.

A note about hierarchies in Dimension Types not assigned to the Cube: OneStream's Dimension editor allows the creation of an unlimited number of Dimensions and hierarchies within Dimension *Types*. The presence of a Dimension in, for instance, Dimension Type UD8, does not mean it is addressable in a Cube until it is explicitly made part of that Cube. There is a somewhat confusing exception to this rule in that dynamic Member Formulas in a non-Cube Dimension against None are allowed – think of them as reporting elements.

Relational Blend Formula in U8#Sales_Representative

The *blend* part of Relational Blend now becomes clear: a Member Formula in UD8 will query relational data, display it in a Cube View or Quick View, use the dimensionality of the other Dimensions to drive the retrieve (both on grid and POV), and then retrieve the relational data alongside Cube data.

To display the sales detail textual data, the Member U8#Sales_Representative is created with the formula Type of DynamicCalc. Since this is *text*, the formula should only execute when the V#Annotation Type Member is used.

```
If api.View.IsAnnotationType Then
```

The data is only valid at the lowest level of Cube data. The code example, below, checks whether the Entity and UD1 Members in the Quick View/Cube View are Base Members of Entity and UD1. Check for this condition using the following metadata test:

```
If Not api.Entity.HasChildren And
api.Members.GetMembersUsingFilter(api.pov.UD1Dim.DimPk, "U1#" &
productName & ".Base").Count = 1 Then
```

This formula should execute only when there is data in U8#None. To return text information, the View Dimension Member must be Annotation. The formula queries U8#None:V#Periodic's IsRealData status by using the VB.Net function Replace to substitute U8#None for U8#SalesRep or U8#SalesOrderNumber and V#Periodic for V#Annotation and then testing for U8#None:V#Periodic's data status.

This check is performed in the following way.

```
If
api.Data.GetDataCell(api.pov.GetDataCellPk.GetMemberScript(api).Replac
e("SalesRep", "None").Replace("SalesOrderNumber",
"None").Replace("Annotation", "Periodic")).CellStatus.IsRealData
```

We now have all of our checks and balances in place. The task of generating the SQL for getting the Sales Rep name begins with declaring the Text.StringBuilder variable to hold the query and retrieving the POV Members for Product, Geography, and Account.

```
Dim sql As New Text.StringBuilder
Dim productName As String = api.Pov.UD1.Name
Dim geographyName As String = api.Pov.Entity.Name
Dim accountName As String = api.Pov.Account.Name
```

149

Your author likes using `StringBuilder` for generating statements, but it is purely a personal preference. You can use a string and then append to it, or use string interpolation to achieve the same result.

Data Mart Schema

After all of the above as prologue, blending relational data alongside Cube data is now just a matter of `SELECT`, `JOIN`, and `WHERE` clauses.

This schema diagram shows the table layout in C&CCC's sales data mart.

Table Layout

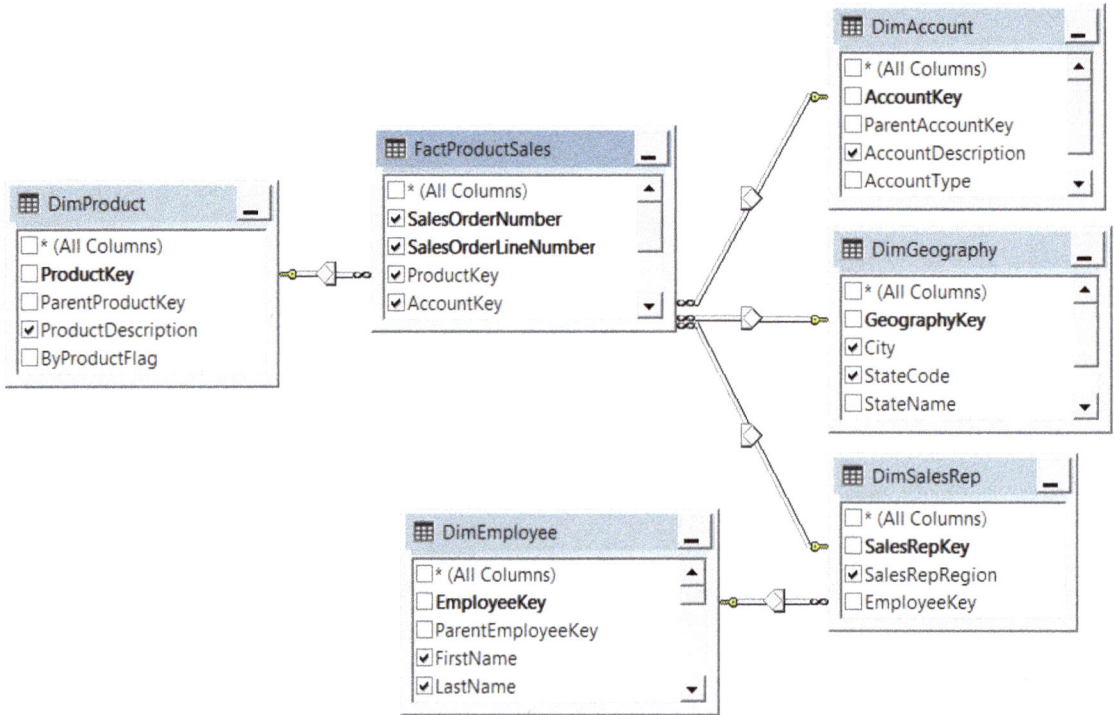

Figure 4.12

Data

	SalesOrderNumber	SalesOrderLineNumber	ProductKey	AccountKey	Geogr..	StateCode	ProductDescription	SalesRegionK.
1	00110010120	1	10_010	3	4	PA	Cameron's 100% Colombian Regular Whole Bean	1
2	00110010130	1	10_020	3	2	SC	Celvin's Colombian Supremo Regular Whole Bean	2
3	00110010135	1	10_020	3	3	SC	Celvin's Colombian Supremo Regular Whole Bean	2
4	00110010120	2	10_020	3	4	PA	Celvin's Colombian Supremo Regular Whole Bean	1
5	00110010130	2	10_020	3	2	SC	Celvin's Colombian Supremo Regular Whole Bean	2
6	00110010130	3	10_020	3	2	SC	Celvin's Colombian Supremo Regular Whole Bean	2
7	00110010130	4	10_020	3	2	SC	Celvin's Colombian Supremo Regular Whole Bean	2
8	00110010130	5	10_020	3	2	SC	Celvin's Colombian Supremo Regular Whole Bean	2

Figure 4.13

SQL

The SQL to retrieve the `Sales Rep` (representative) information is a linking process of all related keys in the central `FactProductSales` table:

```
sql.Appendline("SELECT f.FirstName + ' ' + f.LastName as 'SalesRep'")
sql.Appendline("FROM FactProductSales a")
sql.Appendline("LEFT OUTER JOIN DimAccount b On a.AccountKey =
b.AccountKey")
sql.Appendline("LEFT OUTER JOIN DimGeography c ON
a.GeographyKey=c.GeographyKey")
sql.Appendline("LEFT OUTER JOIN DimProduct d ON
a.ProductKey=d.ProductKey")
sql.Appendline("LEFT OUTER JOIN DimSalesRep e ON a.SalesRepKey =
e.SalesRepKey")
sql.Appendline("LEFT OUTER JOIN DimEmployee f ON e.EmployeeKey =
f.EmployeeKey")
```

We are returning the first and last name of the Sales Representative. Even if there is no Sales Representative for a product, the code needs to return a result, hence the LEFT OUTER JOIN.

The filters to get Geography, Account, and Product combination is shown below.

```
sql.AppendLine("WHERE c.StateAlternateName='" & geographyName & "'")
sql.AppendLine("AND b.AccountDescription='" & accountName & "'")
sql.AppendLine("AND d.ProductKey='" & productName & "'")
```

When the SQL is complete, it is ready to be run against the relational database.

Connections, Connections, Connections

Retrieving this data takes three steps:

1. Use relational blend formula to fetch the SalesRep information.

2. Confirm that data was actually retrieved.

3. Return a comma-delimited list of Sales Representatives.

```
Dim dt As DataTable = api.Functions.GetCustomBlendDataTable( _
BlendCacheLevelTypes.Custom, "RepName" & geographyName & productName &
accountName, "AVBS Warehouse", sql.ToString)
If dt.Rows.Count > 0 Then
   Dim salesRepList As List(Of String) =
dt.AsEnumerable().Select(Function(x)
x("SalesRep").toString()).ToList()
   Return  String.join(", ", salesRepList.Distinct)
End If
```

Once we have the list of Sales Representatives, we now return the unique comma-separated string to the target Quick View/Cube View.

Here is the full formula in all its glory:

```
24   If api.View.IsAnnotationType
25       Dim productName As String = api.Pov.UD1.Name
26       ' run only for base entities and base ud1
27       If Not api.Entity.HasChildren And _
28           api.Members.GetMembersUsingFilter(api.pov.UD1Dim.DimPk, "U1#" & productName & ".Base").Count = 1 Then
29           If api.Data.GetDataCell(api.pov.GetDataCellPk.GetMemberScript(api)).Replace("SalesRep", "None").Replace _
30           ("SalesOrderNumber", "None").Replace("Annotation", "Periodic")).CellStatus.IsRealData
31               Dim sql As New Text.StringBuilder
32               Dim geographyName As String = api.Pov.Entity.Name
33               Dim accountName As String = api.Pov.Account.Name
34
35               sql.Appendline("SELECT f.FirstName + ' ' + f.LastName as 'SalesRep'")
36               sql.Appendline("FROM FactProductSales a")
37               sql.Appendline("LEFT OUTER JOIN DimAccount b On a.AccountKey = b.AccountKey")
38               sql.Appendline("LEFT OUTER JOIN DimGeography c ON a.GeographyKey=c.GeographyKey")
39               sql.Appendline("LEFT OUTER JOIN DimProduct d ON a.ProductKey=d.ProductKey")
40               sql.Appendline("LEFT OUTER JOIN DimSalesRep e ON a.SalesRepKey = e.SalesRepKey")
41               sql.Appendline("LEFT OUTER JOIN DimEmployee f ON e.EmployeeKey = f.EmployeeKey")
42
43               sql.AppendLine("WHERE c.StateAlternateName='" & geographyName & "'")
44               sql.AppendLine("AND b.AccountDescription='" & accountName & "'")
45               sql.AppendLine("AND d.ProductKey='" & productName & "'")
46
47               Dim dt As DataTable = api.Functions.GetCustomBlendDataTable( _
48               BlendCacheLevelTypes.Custom, "RepName" & geographyName & productName & accountName, "AVBS Warehouse", sql.ToString)
49               If dt.Rows.Count > 0 Then
50                   Dim salesRepList As List(Of String) = dt.AsEnumerable().Select(Function(x) x("SalesRep").toString()).ToList()
51                   Return  String.join(", ", salesRepList.Distinct)
52               End If
53           End If
54       End If
55   End If
```

A similar formula (not documented but practically identical save for the fields) can provide a list of Sales Order numbers as well.

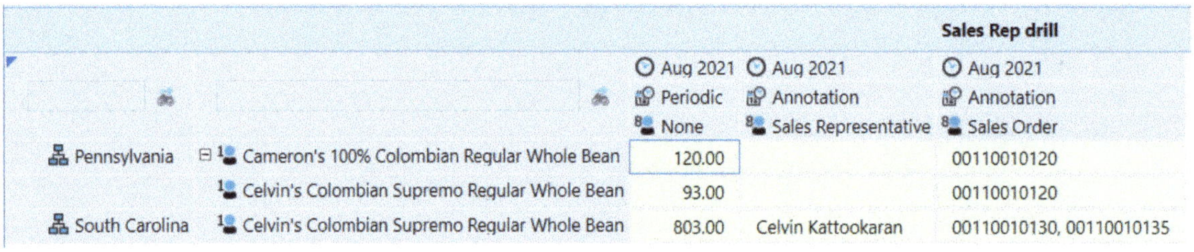

			Sales Rep drill		
			⊙ Aug 2021	⊙ Aug 2021	⊙ Aug 2021
			Periodic	Annotation	Annotation
			None	Sales Representative	Sales Order
Pennsylvania	⊟ Cameron's 100% Colombian Regular Whole Bean		120.00		00110010120
	Celvin's Colombian Supremo Regular Whole Bean		93.00		00110010120
South Carolina	Celvin's Colombian Supremo Regular Whole Bean		803.00	Celvin Kattookaran	00110010130, 00110010135

Figure 4.14

An Alternate View

Multiple items for a single data point can be hard to read when combined in a cell. Some Users are okay with it, and some are not.

For those who are not happy looking at lengthy text, an option might be to mimic the drill back on a single two-panel Dashboard, as shown below.

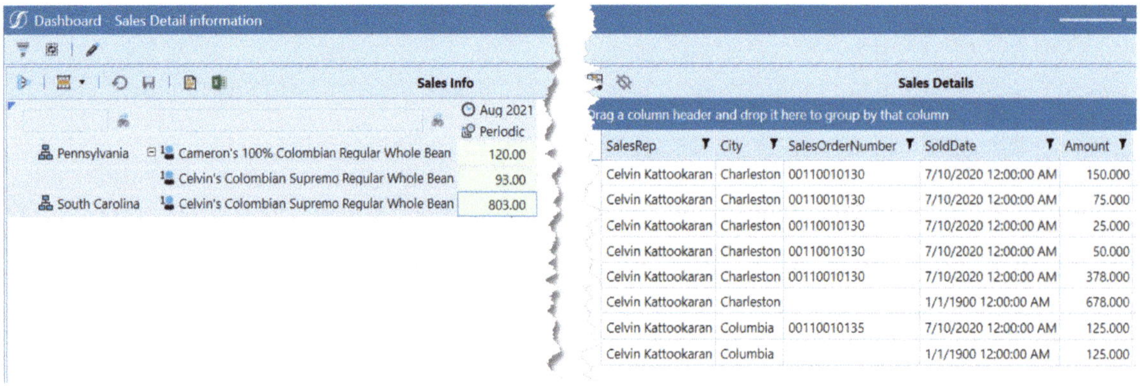

Figure 4.15

We now have a way to blend relational and Cube data for analysis in a seamless and agile fashion. OneStream has delivered functionality and flexibility that no other product can boast of.

But that melding of relational and Cube is only for reporting and this, after all, is a book about Planning. Let us now look at how we can plan at a detailed relational level in OneStream without bringing that detail into the Cube.

Planning at a Detailed Level Without the Detail

How is it possible to plan at a detailed level without the detail? Is it trickery? Black magic?

The answer is OneStream's **Specialty Planning**.

Think of Specialty Planning as a type of "relational blending", but in this case there are no out-of-the-box functions; it is a solution delivered by OneStream's MarketPlace.

Before we start looking at the MarketPlace solutions, let's look at what makes Specialty Planning special.

A Little Bit of This, a Little Bit of That

The recipe for Specialty Solutions (for this chapter, we will look only at solutions that allow Plan data at a more granular level than the Cube level) is simple. You store (how the solution is configured, how it is calculated, or how the data is stored) the details of the solution in its tables and sprinkle a few Dashboards on top of it. A Specialty solution is born. What could possibly be easier?

A note about the rest of this chapter. It does not (because it cannot) cover every nuance of what is, after all, a highly customizable and very broad set of functionality. Think of the following as a set of specific and necessarily limited use cases, documented as fully as space allows.

Where to Go, and What to Do with the Specialty Solutions

Specialty Solutions are *not* natively part of OneStream. They are instead optional modules that customers deploy on an as-needed basis, eschewing Components that are not pertinent for a given application, e.g., Accounts Reconciliation is an unlikely (although not unheard of in Planning if combined with a Consolidations Component) solution for a Planning application, as is People Planning in a financial reporting-only application. The advantage of all MarketPlace solutions is that their functionality is incorporated only when needed.

You might have already heard of (or used) OneStream's MarketPlace to download tools like Table Data Manager and the Excel Metadata Builder. All of OneStream's optional modules that are available in the MarketPlace are called Specialty Solutions, and the ones which help to Plan, are called Specialty Planning solutions or, in some cases, Specialty Planning.

Connect to the MarketPlace, log in (OneStream provides the access), and when you are in the MarketPlace Solution Center, navigate to Planning.

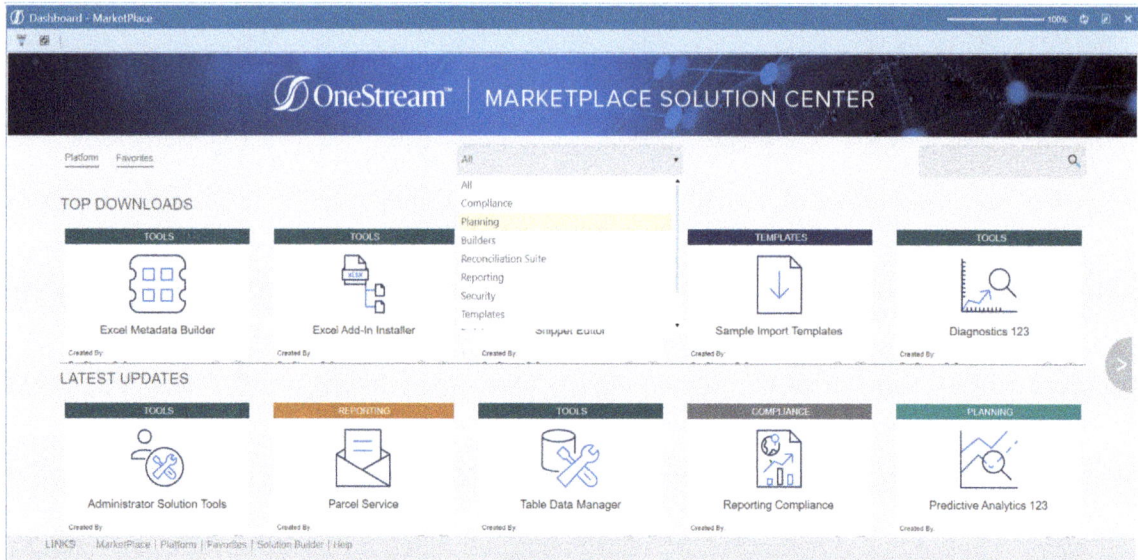

Figure 4.16

Once you are in the Planning section of MarketPlace, all seven (as of writing this book) Specialty Planning solutions are available.

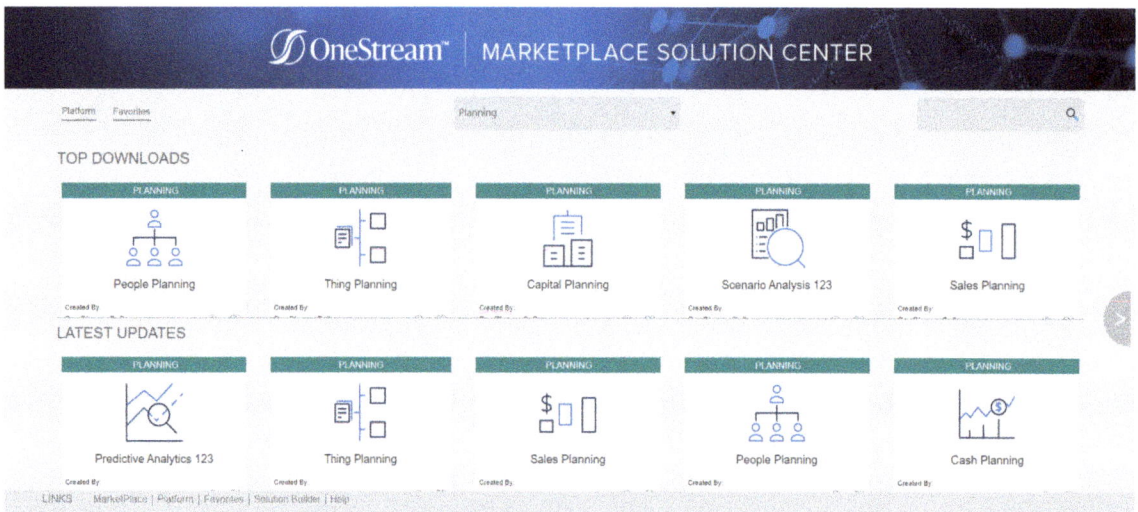

Figure 4.17

Once you find the solution you want, just go ahead and download it. Easy peasy lemon squeezy!

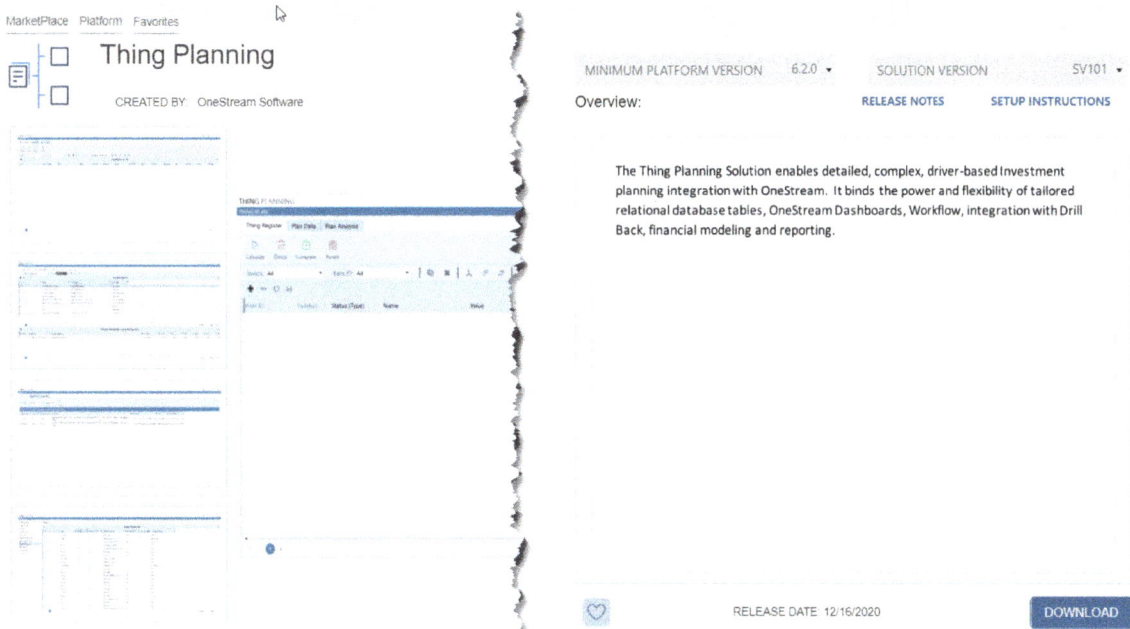

Figure 4.18

Installing a Specialty Solution is outside the scope of this chapter as it is well covered in every Specialty solution help guide.

You can find help using the upper right-hand corner ? icon in every Specialty Solution.

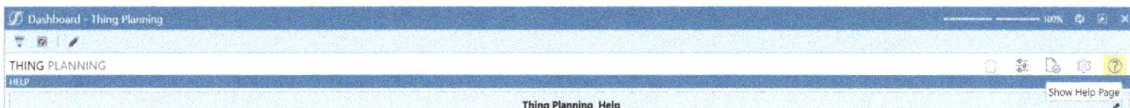

Figure 4.19

Special Considerations on Configuration

While the configuration of Specialty Planning solutions is covered in the help guide, your author would like to share some of the wisdom he has learned through his implementations.

Dashboard Profile Access

Once the solution is set up, change the visibility of the XFW Thing Planning (TLP) Dashboard Profile to Workflow from OnePlace.

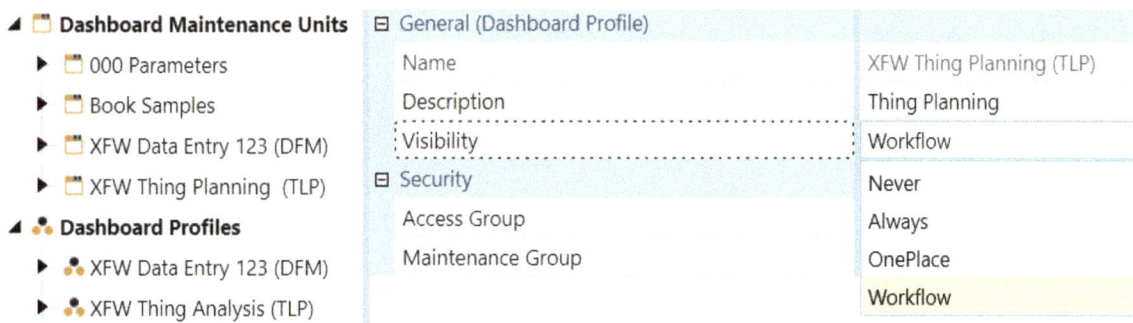

Figure 4.20

All Specialty Planning solutions add the current Workflow Profile, Scenario, and Time to the Register table. If the Dashboard Profile from OnePlace is used to access the solution instead of via a Workflow, there might be records saved against a Workflow that have nothing to do with Specialty Planning.

For example, C&CCC's Volume Planning Workflow has the following setup:

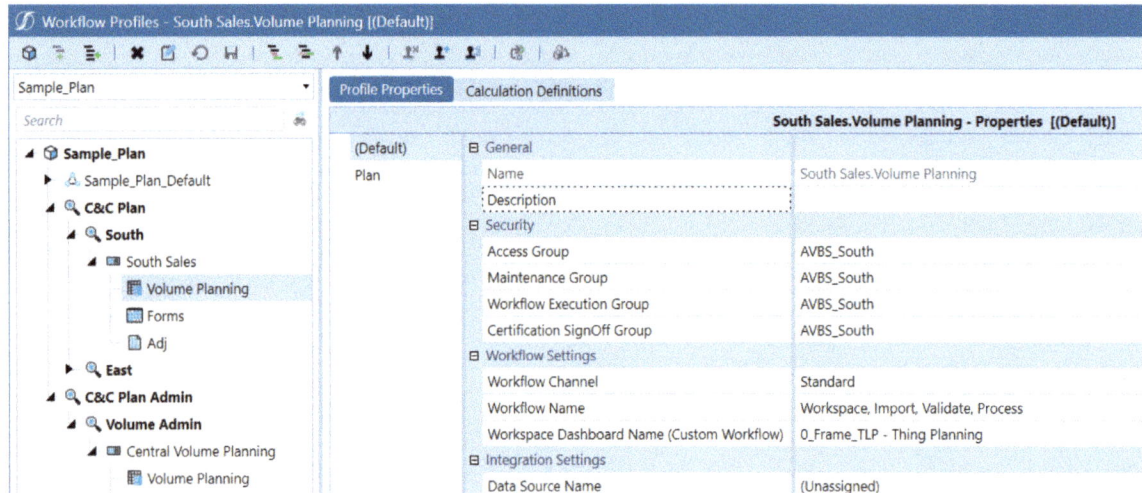

Figure 4.21

All the sales volume details are captured in Thing Planning against this Workflow. If an Administrator who was loading 2021M8 Actual values accidentally entered some details in Thing Planning via…

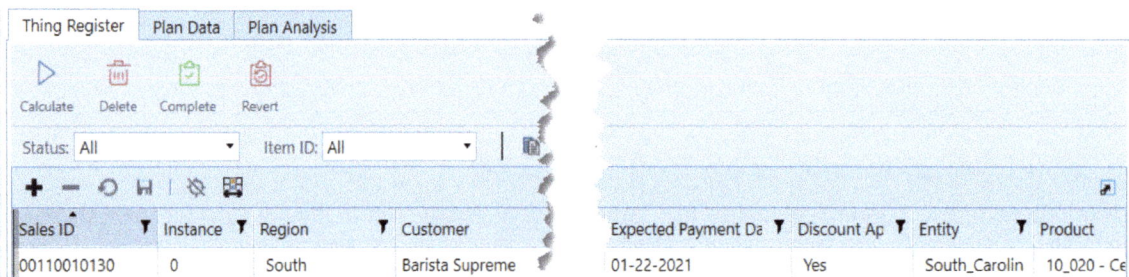

Figure 4.22

…the record is stored in the Register.

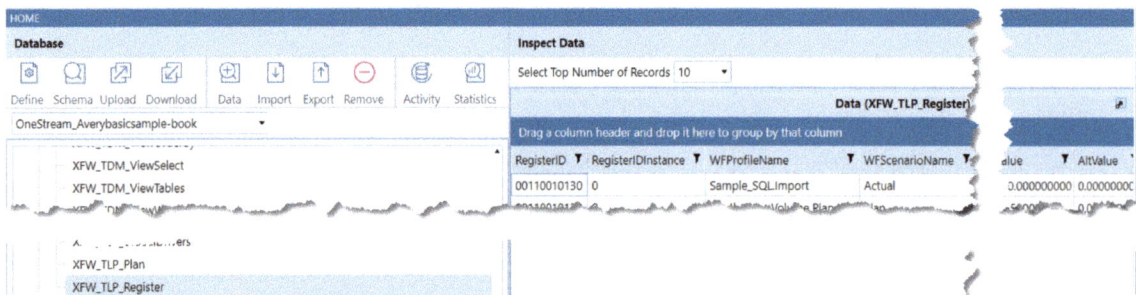

Figure 4.23

156

The record shows up as long as Thing Planning is not accessed from the Workflow Profile. However, that record will not show up from the proper Plan Workflow and Scenario, because it was recorded against the Actual Scenario.

Change that access to keep your sanity!

Control Lists

Use control lists as a way to restrict free-hand entry to the following columns:

- 12 Text fields (Code1-Code12)
- 8 Numeric fields (NCode1-NCode8)
- InCode
- OutCode
- Level

Date Field Default Values

Date fields have a default value of 1900-01-01.

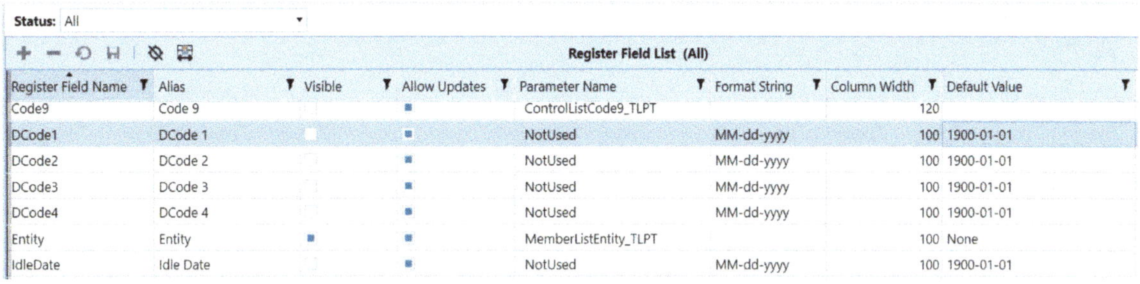

Register Field Name	Alias	Visible	Allow Updates	Parameter Name	Format String	Column Width	Default Value
Code9	Code 9		▪	ControlListCode9_TLPT		120	
DCode1	DCode 1	□	▪	NotUsed	MM-dd-yyyy	100	1900-01-01
DCode2	DCode 2		▪	NotUsed	MM-dd-yyyy	100	1900-01-01
DCode3	DCode 3		▪	NotUsed	MM-dd-yyyy	100	1900-01-01
DCode4	DCode 4		▪	NotUsed	MM-dd-yyyy	100	1900-01-01
Entity	Entity	▪	▪	MemberListEntity_TLPT		100	None
IdleDate	Idle Date		▪	NotUsed	MM-dd-yyyy	100	1900-01-01

Status: All

Register Field List (All)

Figure 4.24

If Users want to only enter YY for the year in those date fields, by default OneStream automatically fills 19 in front of it. As the 20th century has now receded into the past, always change the default to 2000-01-01.

Keep those Custom Parameters in Another Unit

If you create parameters for a MarketPlace solution, keep those parameters in a different Dashboard Unit to avoid losing them in an update of the Specialty Planning solution (most of the updates will need an uninstall of the UI, which will remove all the Components from the Dashboard Maintenance Unit).

> **Note:** For Thing Planning, suffix the custom parameters with _TLP (People Planning will be _PLP, and so on for other solutions).

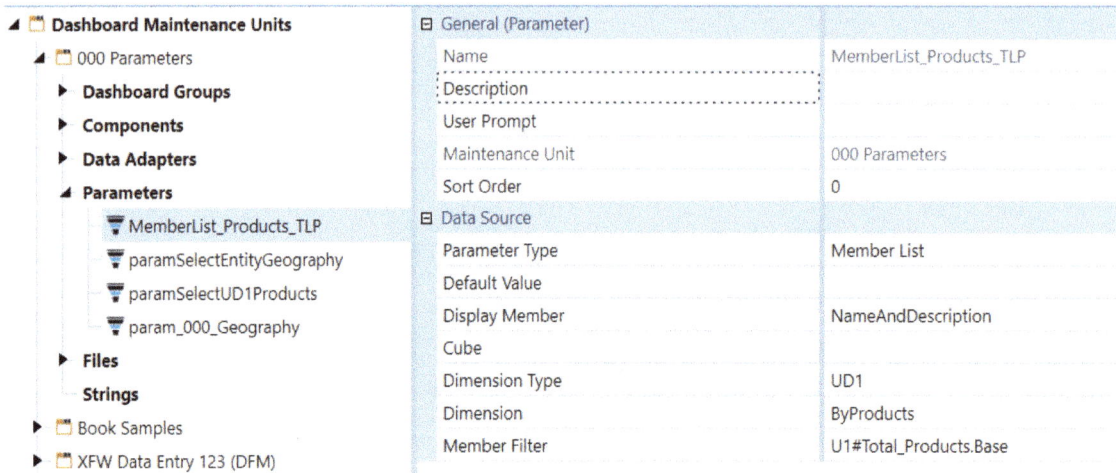

Figure 4.25

The `_TLP` suffix allows Thing Planning to see those custom parameters in the Parameter Name field:

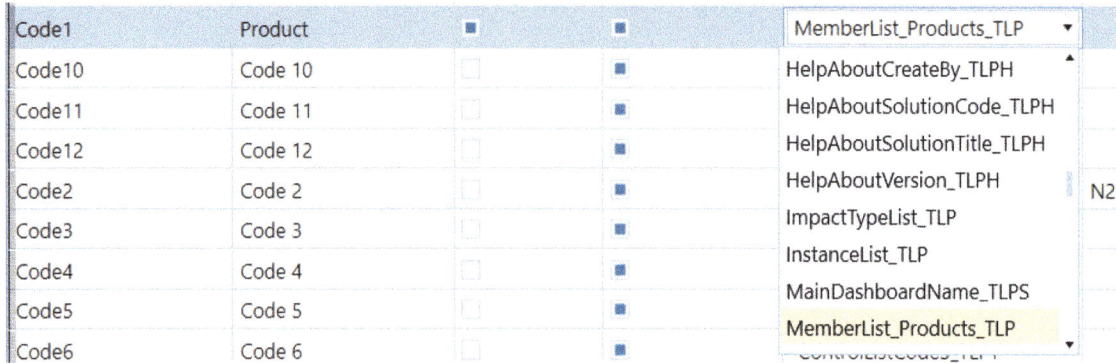

Figure 4.26

Register Field Types

While OneStream allows you to change the data Type of Code1-Code12 to Numeric/Date, be cautious because of the way the field Type is inconsistently treated in different internal tables.

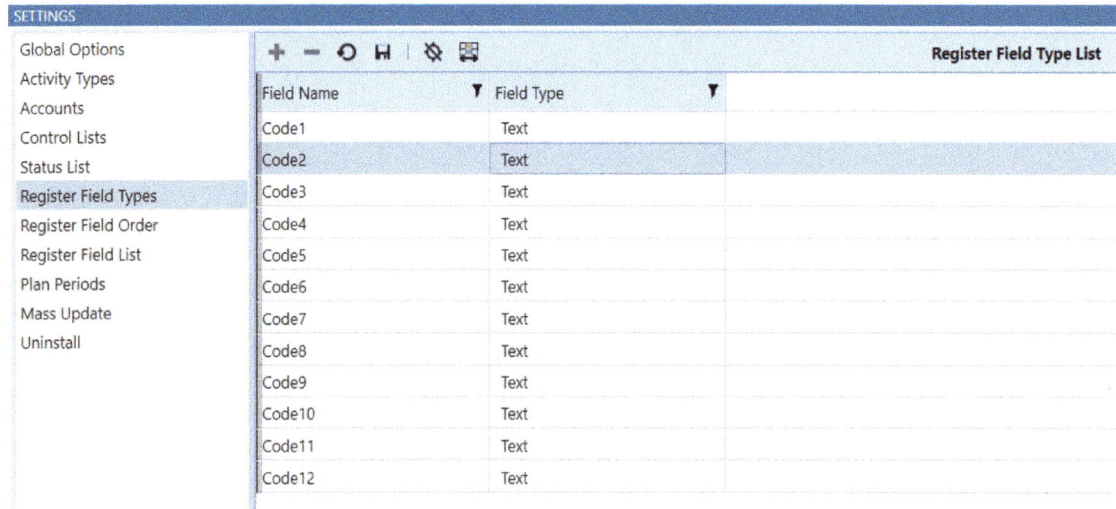

Figure 4.27

> **Note:** The database must be cleared before making any field Type change. The Plan table (where the calculated results are stored) does not reflect the changes you made on the Register. If Reports are created using the Plan table, they will not show up correctly.

Code2 to Numeric

What happens when Code2 is changed from Text to Numeric?

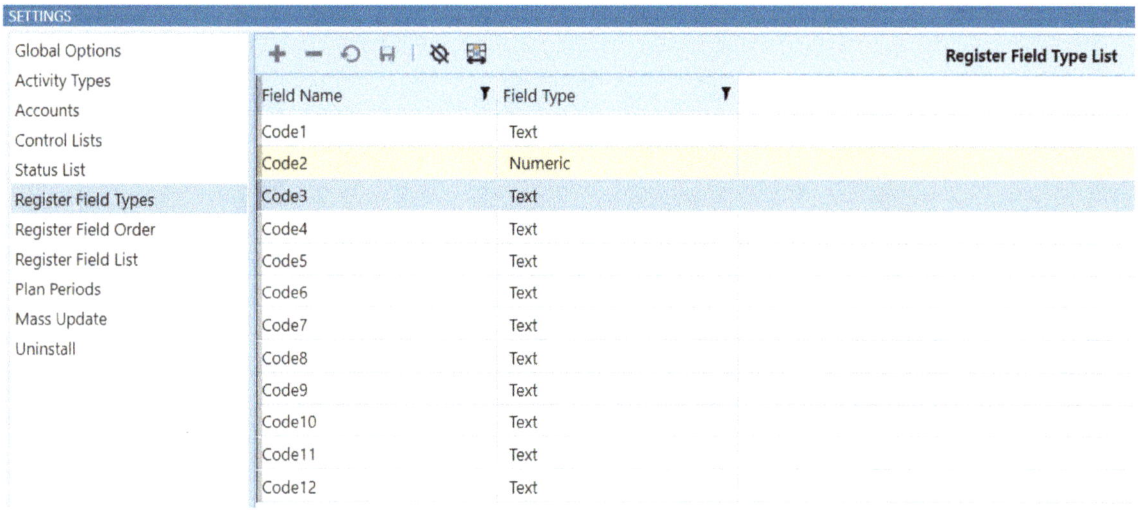

Figure 4.28

The change appears in the XFW_TLP_Register table:

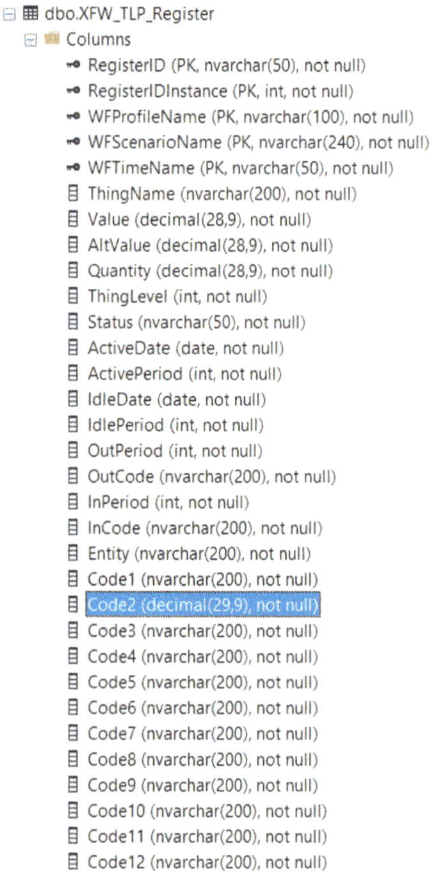

Figure 4.29

159

But not in XFW_TLP_Plan:

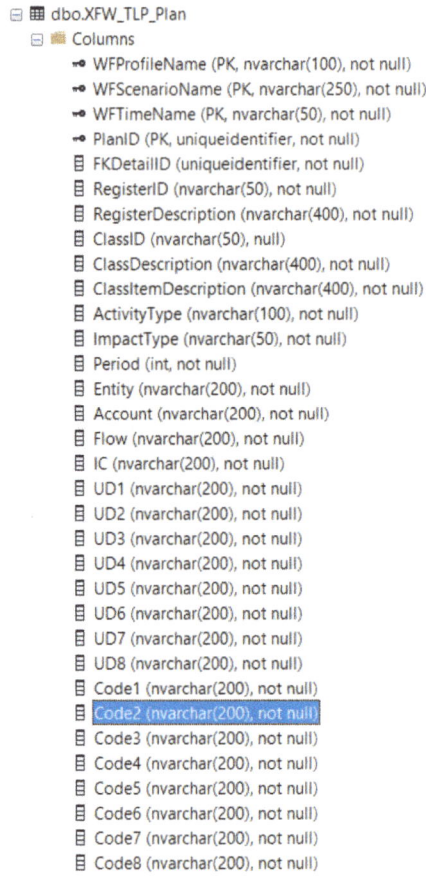

Figure 4.30

As noted, if a Report is from the Plan table, it will left-align the numbers instead of right. Change those fields if absolutely needed; else, do not.

To Use the Period or to Use the Date, that is the Question

Time, as a concept, is ubiquitous within Specialty Planning and has several definitions that are easily confused, particularly the usage of date along with period. For example, in Thing Planning, the Thing's ActiveDate along with the ActivePeriod as well as HireDate, HirePeriod, TermDate, and OutPeriod in People Planning can all be utilized. Why?

While the idea of using ActivePeriod/HirePeriod/OutPeriod to control the months in which the calculations are executed is a good one, it seems redundant to have period definitions to do this. Why cannot we use just the ActiveDate or HireDate or TermDate to drive this?

If you are using Thing Planning and want to check whether the Thing being calculated is active in the calculated period, use the Substitution Variable |dActiveMthPlan| to give you the active month based on Plan month, e.g., next year's January is 13.

MthPlan Type Substitution Variables are present in People Planning/Capital Planning, and other Specialty Planning solutions as well. As an example, you could use |dHireMthPlan| to get the plan-based hire month.

For the other dates, you can use a simple XFBR function to get the Plan month and use that in the condition execution statement.

```
|CalcPer| >= XFBR(SpecialtyPlanning_StringHelper,
GetPlanPeriodFromDate, Date=|DCode1|,CalcMonth=|CalcPerMth|)
```

`SpecialtyPlanning_StringHelper` is a custom XFBR Rule, and `GetPlanPeriodFromDate` is a custom function.

In the below XFBR, the two arguments are passed to the function. The first one passes the date field, and the second one passes the `CalcMonth` (13th period is 1st month).

```
Dim retMonth As String = String.Empty
Dim editedDate As Date =
DateTime.ParseExact(args.NameValuePairs.XFGetValue("Date"),
"yyyyMMdd",CultureInfo.InvariantCulture)
Dim calcMonth As Integer = args.NameValuePairs.XFGetValue("CalcMonth")
```

> **Note:** In the first line, an empty string is created to return the function's result.

We are converting the date field from the current row to an actual date in the second line since `|DCode1|` comes to the Rule as `yyyyMMdd` string.

The third line tells us which Calc month is getting calculated, e.g., if we are calculating the 14th period, then this variable gets a value of 2.

```
Dim wfYear As Integer =
BRApi.Finance.Time.GetYearFromId(si,si.WorkflowClusterPk.TimeKey)
Dim calcDate As New Date(wfYear, calcMonth, 1, 1, 0, 0)
```

Once we get the parameters passed and transformed, the Workflow's year must be determined.

We are calculating a calculation month field using the calc month and Workflow year information in the following `If...End If` test.

```
If wfYear = editedDate.Year Then
    retMonth = editedDate.Month
Else If wfYear > editedDate.Year Then
    'prior year, set the month to 1 based on requirement
    retMonth = 1
Else If wfYear < editedDate.Year Then
    ' future year, get the calc
    retMonth = DateDiff(DateInterval.Month, calcDate, editedDate) +
calcMonth
End If
```

If Workflow year and the parameter year are equal, then the current month should be returned. If Workflow year is greater than the checked year, the year is a prior date, so the code should return the *current* month as the *first* month so that the calculation will start there.

If the Workflow year is less than the tested year, we need to find the difference in months and then add the calc month to it, to get the year's period.

```
33    Public Function GetCalcPeriodForDateCodes(ByVal si As SessionInfo, ByVal globals As BRGlobals, ByVal args As DashboardStringFunctic
34        Try
35            Dim retMonth As String = String.Empty
36            Dim editedDate As Date = DateTime.ParseExact(args.NameValuePairs.XFGetValue("Date"), "yyyyMMdd",CultureInfo.InvariantCultur
37            Dim calcMonth As Integer = args.NameValuePairs.XFGetValue("CalcMonth")
38
39            Dim wfYear As Integer = BRApi.Finance.Time.GetYearFromId(si,si.WorkflowClusterPk.TimeKey)
40            Dim calcDate As New Date(wfYear, calcMonth, 1, 1, 0, 0)
41
42            If wfYear = editedDate.Year Then
43                retMonth = editedDate.Month
44            Else If wfYear > editedDate.Year Then
45                'prior year, set the month to 1 or 0 based on requirement
46                retMonth = 1
47            Else If wfYear < editedDate.Year Then
48                ' future year, get the calc
49                retMonth = DateDiff(DateInterval.Month, calcDate, editedDate) + calcMonth
50            End If
51
52            Return retMonth
53
54        Catch ex As Exception
55            Throw ErrorHandler.LogWrite(si, New XFException(si, ex))
56        End Try
57    End Function
```

Here is the whole function. If you wonder about where the **ActiveDate Substitution Variables** came from and how they are defined, read on as they will be covered in the *Viewing the Substitution Variables* section.

Use those System Fields where Possible

There is a limited set of columns (43) available in Specialty Planning solutions. However, if you are creative, you can use some of the system columns like InPeriod, OutPeriod for recording an integer value or even tie it to a control list that shows the User a list of choices.

Plan your column usage by counting the number of columns needed by the application by Type:

1. Get the count of pure text columns.

2. Get the count of decimal columns.

3. Get the count of columns that can be a pick-list.

4. Get the count of date columns.

With this list, identify which of the 26 code fields (Code1-Code12, NCode1-NCode8, DCode1-DCode4, Annot1-Annot2) can be refined, based on the application's needs. You can then fit all possible items identified earlier into these 26 code fields.

Reserve the annotation fields for columns that have longer text, as these two columns have a `NVARCHAR(MAX)` as data Type. You can store up to 2 GB of data in there. (Approximately one billion characters which your author hopes is sufficient.)

What if there are more text columns than numeric columns? If you can make some of the text columns as a pick-list, you can use the numeric columns (including the NCodes) substitutes for those textual values.

Creating a pick-list on those NCode columns is tricky as they are treated as decimal numbers in SQL.

I have got some handy dandy code that I use to do this.

```
Dim dt As New DataTable()
dt.Columns.Add("Name")
dt.Columns.Add("Value")
```

To solve this issue, create a Name Value Pair table to return as bound list parameters in lines 1-3.

This function can be called as shown below:

General (Parameter)	
Name	paramSelectCustomerTypes_TLP
Description	
User Prompt	
Maintenance Unit	000 Parameters
Sort Order	3015
Data Source	
Parameter Type	Bound List
Default Value	
Result Format String Type	Default
Result Custom Format String	
Command Type	Method
Method Type	BusinessRule
Method Query	{SpecialtyPlanning_HelperQueries}{GetDecimalList}{ItemList=[Restaurant, Hotel,Coffee shop]}
Results Table Name	
Display Member	Name
Value Member	Value

Figure 4.31

The Method Query passes an item list to the function as a comma-separated list.

```
Dim strList As String = args.NameValuePairs.XFGetValue("ItemList")
```

This code gets the value that has been passed to the function. (NameValuePairs is analogous to a dictionary where you have a key that holds some values.)

```
If Not String.IsNullOrEmpty(strList)
    Dim pickListItems As List(Of String) =
strList.Split(",").Select(Function(x) x.Trim).toList()
    Dim counter As Integer = 1
    For Each pickListItem In pickListItems
        Dim row As DataRow = dt.NewRow
        row("Name") = pickListItem
        row("Value") =
SqlTypes.SqlDecimal.ConvertToPrecScale(SqlTypes.SqlDecimal.Parse(count
er), 28, 9)
        dt.Rows.Add(row)
        counter += 1
    Next
End If
```

This code snippet must perform the following tasks:

1. Check whether the strList item list is empty or not. If it is not empty, convert this string to a list of items.

2. Split the strList list using a comma as delimiter, trim the split string, and add it to the pickListItems .

3. Create a counter for the pickListItems value.

4. Change that value's precision and scale to 28 and 9, respectively.

Here is the output of the function:

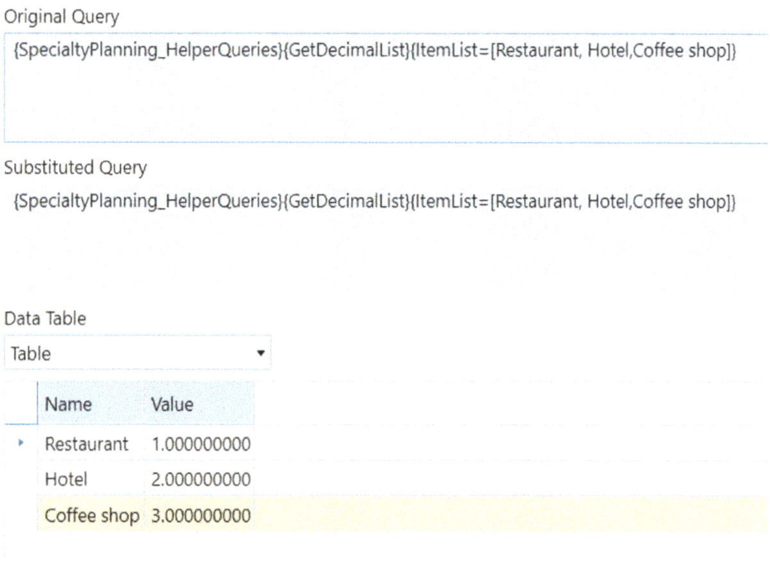

Original Query

{SpecialtyPlanning_HelperQueries}{GetDecimalList}{ItemList=[Restaurant, Hotel,Coffee shop]}

Substituted Query

{SpecialtyPlanning_HelperQueries}{GetDecimalList}{ItemList=[Restaurant, Hotel,Coffee shop]}

Data Table

Table ▼

Name	Value
Restaurant	1.000000000
Hotel	2.000000000
Coffee shop	3.000000000

Figure 4.32

Here is the function in its entirety:

```
Private Function GetDecimalList(ByVal si As SessionInfo, ByVal args As
dashboardDataSetArgs) As DataTable
    Try
        Dim dt As New DataTable()
        dt.Columns.Add("Name")
```

```
        dt.Columns.Add("Value")

        Dim strList As String =
args.NameValuePairs.XFGetValue("ItemList")
        If Not String.IsNullOrEmpty(strList)
            Dim pickListItems As List(Of String) =
strList.Split(",").Select(Function(x) x.Trim).toList()
            Dim counter As Integer = 1
            For Each pickListItem In pickListItems
                Dim row As DataRow = dt.NewRow
                row("Name") = pickListItem
                row("Value") =
SqlTypes.SqlDecimal.ConvertToPrecScale(SqlTypes.SqlDecimal.Parse(count
er), 28, 9)
                dt.Rows.Add(row)
                counter += 1
            Next
        End If

        Return dt

    Catch ex As Exception
        Throw ErrorHandler.LogWrite(si, New XFException(si, ex))
    End Try
End Function
```

Using Specialty Planning Solutions

Data Entry, the Magic of No Metadata, and Controlled Entries

Compared to a Cube-based solution, Specialty Planning solutions behave very differently when it comes to metadata. An Administrator is not needed (and indeed is not able) to add the customers, employees, assets, etc. The key thing to remember is that the Planner does it himself; no Administrator is involved. "Nothing is true; everything is permitted."

Some form of data standardization is, of course, needed; apply parameters to control data by column. These parameters must be of Types that can return a value and a display, e.g., Bound List, Member List, or Delimited List.

In this example, the division is coming from an external relational table (DimSalesRegion).

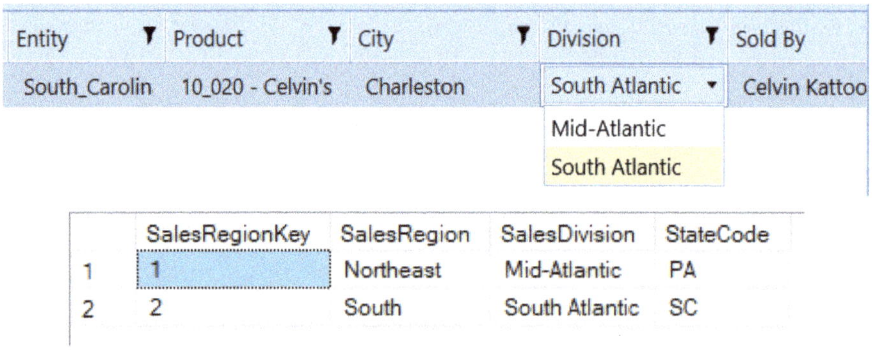

Figure 4.33

By doing so, you are now integrating the Specialty Planning solution to an external source for "metadata" using parameters. I told you it is nothing short of magical.

> **Note:** It is *not* advisable to use an extensive list with 100s of Members as this can *significantly* slow the solution's performance while presenting a difficult-to-navigate User Interface.

Security

Securing a Specialty Planning solution can be done using only Workflow Entity assignment or through a custom solution.

When Entities are assigned to the Workflow, use the default solution parameter called `MemberListEntity_TLPT`. If you are planning to use your own, use `E#Root.WFProfileEntities` as Member Filter.

Here is C&CCC's Workflow setup:

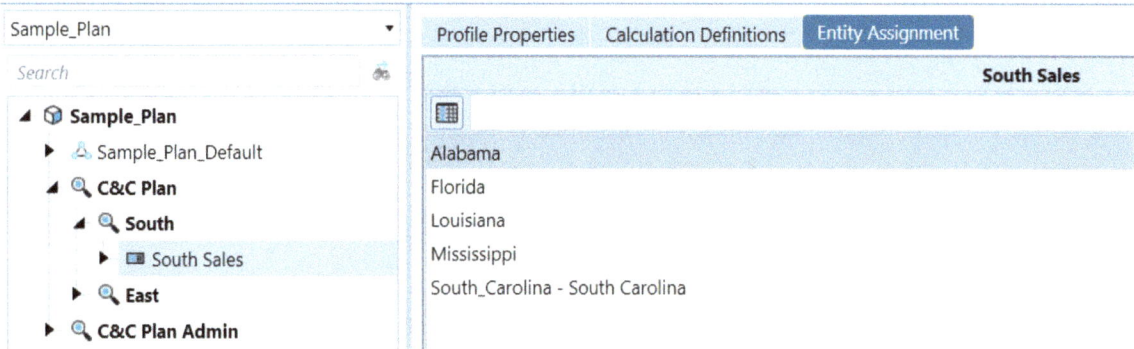

Figure 4.34

When a Planner tries to select a sales entry, they can only add the Entities that are assigned to this Workflow.

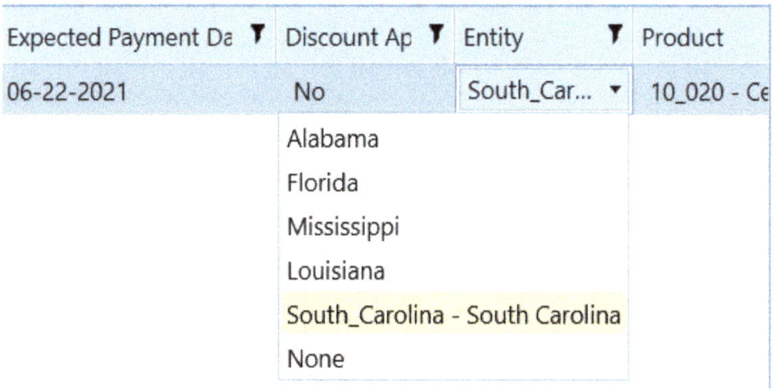

Figure 4.35

This setup will make sure that wrong Entities are not added to a Workflow if Planners are allowed to enter records in a Specialty Planning solution.

How do We See the Month's Results?

Think of the Register/data entry as a whole plan year entry. Once you enter the plan year's value, the Specialty Planning solution uses its unique Methods to calculate the plan year value into the months.

Allocation Methods

Allocation Methods are analogous to a custom Finance Business Rule that returns a value.

You can define the value that needs to be returned; also, you can add static Member intersections to this value. (This is where the data – if loaded to a Cube – will go to.)

In the example given below, Account is `Price` and Flow is `Endbal_Input`. The value is determined by a mix of conditional Ifs and an XFBR.

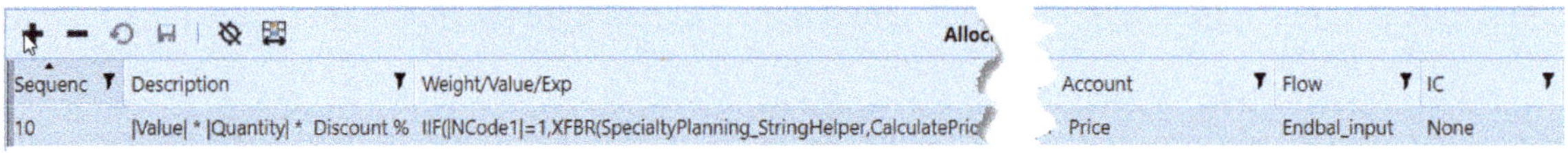

Figure 4.36

Calculating the price is done by calling an XFBR as shown below:

```
XFBR(SpecialtyPlanning_StringHelper,CalculatePrice,IsDiscounted=|InPer
|, Discount=|Restaurant
discount|,PricePerLB=|Value|,QTY=|Quantity|,Unit=|ThingLevel|)
```

You can pass the global discount rate that we defined in the *Global Drivers* section to the XFBR.

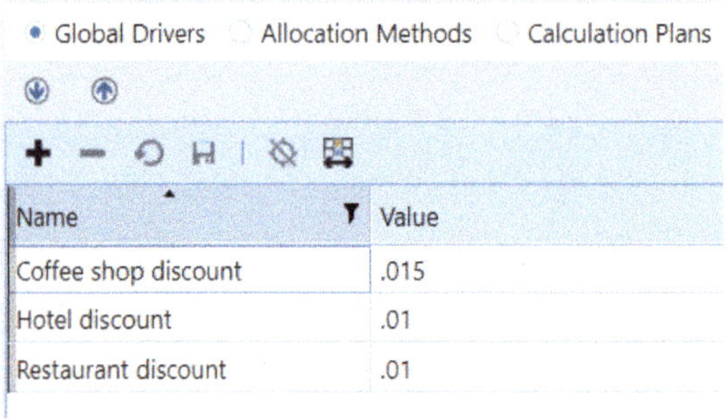

Figure 4.37

Here is the full-blown Allocation Method to check whether the customer is a coffee shop, restaurant, or hotel; based on the Type, their respective global discount rate that we defined in *Global Drivers* is passed to the XFBR.

```
IIF(|NCode1|=1,XFBR(SpecialtyPlanning_StringHelper,CalculatePrice,IsDi
scounted=|InPer|, Discount=|Restaurant
discount|,PricePerLB=|Value|,QTY=|Quantity|,Unit=|ThingLevel|),IIF(|NC
ode1|=2,XFBR(SpecialtyPlanning_StringHelper,CalculatePrice,IsDiscounte
d=|InPer|, Discount=|Hotel
discount|,PricePerLB=|Value|,QTY=|Quantity|,Unit=|ThingLevel|),IIF(|NC
ode1|=3,XFBR(SpecialtyPlanning_StringHelper,CalculatePrice,IsDiscounte
d=|InPer|, Discount=|Coffee shop
discount|,PricePerLB=|Value|,QTY=|Quantity|,Unit=|ThingLevel|),0)))/|P
EndPer|
```

The XFBR function checks where a discount is applied. If there is a discount, it does the following by looking at the unit (price is stored per lb.)

If the unit is pounds:

```
Price = Price per lb * quantity * ( 1 - Global discount based on the
customer)
```

If the unit is short tons:

```
Price = Price per lb * quantity * 2000 * ( 1 - Global discount based
on the customer)
```

If the unit is metric tons:

```
Price = Price per lb * quantity * 2204.62262 * ( 1 - Global discount
based on the customer)
```

Below is the function that does the price calculation.

```
Dim price As Decimal = 0
Dim isDiscounted As Boolean =
ConvertHelper.ToBoolean(args.NameValuePairs.XFGetValue("IsDiscounted",
0))
Dim discount As Decimal = args.NameValuePairs.XFGetValue("Discount",
0)
Dim pricePerLB As Decimal =
args.NameValuePairs.XFGetValue("PricePerLB")
Dim qty As Decimal = args.NameValuePairs.XFGetValue("QTY")
Dim unit As Integer = args.NameValuePairs.XFGetValue("Unit")

If isDiscounted Then
   Select unit
      Case 1 ' pound
         price = pricePerLB * qty * ( 1- discount)
      Case 2 ' ST
         price = pricePerLB * qty * 2000 * ( 1- discount)
      Case 3 ' Tonne
         price = pricePerLB * qty * 2204.62262 * ( 1- discount)
   End Select
Else
   Select unit
      Case 1 ' pound
         price = pricePerLB * qty
      Case 2 ' ST
         price = pricePerLB * qty * 2000
      Case 3 ' Tonne
         price = pricePerLB * qty * 2204.62262
   End Select
End If
```

Once the price is determined, it is converted to a monthly amount by using the |PEndPer| Substitution Variable.

Use Substitution Variables in the description to show the User how the calculation works. Keep in mind that it only replaces the Substitution Variable. If you use expressions in Description (as shown below)…

Sequenc ▼	Description	▼ We	Account	▼	Flow	▼
10	IIF(|NCode1=1, |Value| * |Quantity| * IIF	IV Price		Endbal_input	

Figure 4.38

…you will see something similar in the calculated data.

Amount	Period	In	Register ID	Register Description	Item Description
83,333.33	9		10112_0	Price @1.00	IIF(1=1, 1000 * 1000 * Discount=.01, IIF(1=2,1000 * 1000 * Discount=.01,0),0
83,333.33	10		10112_0	Price @1.00	IIF(1=1, 1000 * 1000 * Discount=.01, IIF(1=2,1000 * 1000 * Discount=.01,0),0
83,333.33	11	I	10112_0	Price @1.00	IIF(1=1, 1000 * 1000 * Discount=.01, IIF(1=2,1000 * 1000 * Discount=.01,0),0
83,333.33	12	I	10112_0	Price @1.00	IIF(1=1, 1000 * 1000 * Discount=.01, IIF(1=2,1000 * 1000 * Discount=.01,0),0

Figure 4.39

Now that we have the price, let us add it to a Calculation Plan.

Calculation Plans

If the Allocation Method is a custom Finance Business Rule, the Calculation Plan is the Data Management Step that calls that Rule.

The following Calculation Plan runs the price Allocation Method.

Calculation Plans

Plan ID	Description
DistributionCalc	Distribution Calculation
PriceCalc	Price calculation

Calculation Plan (PriceCalc, Price calculation)

Sequenc	Allocation Method	Description	Weight/Count/Exp	Period Divisor/Exp	Period Filter	Conditional Execution Statement	Entity Override
10	Price	Price	1	1	|PStartPer|-|PEndPer|	|CalcPer| >= XFBR(SpecialtyPlanning_StringHelper, GetPlanPeriodFr |Entity|

Figure 4.40

Calculation weighting can be defined by assigning a percentage or a number. However, it is only applied if the Allocation Method's value Type is Fixed Value or Value Percentage.

The **Period Divisor** can also be used to get a monthly rate provided the Allocation Method's value Type is Value Percentage.

In this example, a **zero suppressed expression** (Expression (ZP)) is used so the monthly price must be calculated, hence the divide by end period Substitution Variable.

Calculation Plans are extremely useful to define which periods the calculation should execute; conditional checks on those filtered periods can be performed as well.

The calculation begins at the Plan start period (1) through to the Plan end period. Once those periods are defined, they are filtered using a conditional expression as created in the *To use the period or to use the date* section of this chapter. These conditional expressions check whether the period from the period filter is greater than, or equal to, the payment start period.

Overrides can also store the Register row values as Member values using Substitution Variables (the Allocation Method stores a static value).

Execution List

Execution lists are like a Data Management Sequence that calls Data Management Steps (Calculation Plans). Calculation plans can be executed based on Workflow, Scenario, and Status in an execution list.

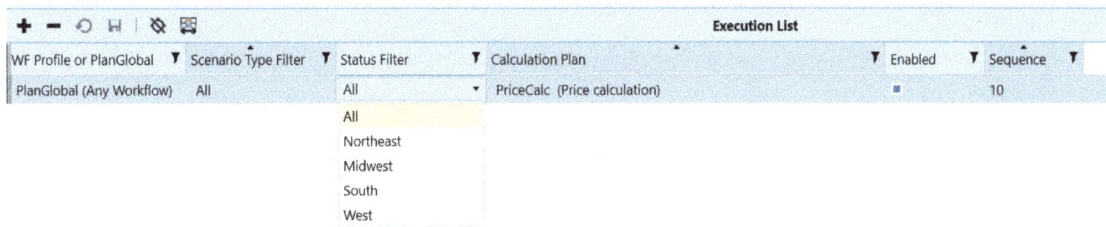

Figure 4.41

This use case has different Allocation Methods and Calculation Plans based on regions. The status filter executes them on demand.

Sequences and their Importance

Sequences in Allocation Methods, Calculation Plans, and execution lists define their execution order. Lower sequence items get written to the Register cache first.

This plays a significant role when you are going to use a calculated result to derive another calculation. A source Calculation Plan should have a lower sequence number to get the correct results.

Loading the Data

The Workflow Profile Type Workspace, Import, Load, and Process automatically load the data when the Workflow is completed. This example used the default Connector Rule to create a data source and added a Transformation Profile to transform Accounts and Time.

Figure 4.42

Drill Back and Drill Down

Once the data is loaded, drill downs are free, and the default connector comes with a few drill back options. Drill backs are also free.

When performing a drill back on a Base level, the following drill back options appear:

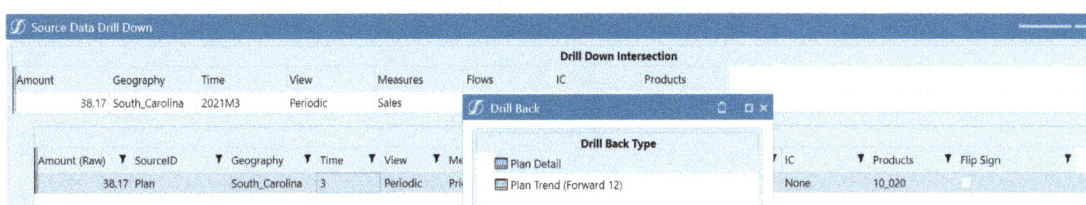

Figure 4.43

Plan Detail drill back will take you to the following Report, which will provide the Calculation Plan and the 26 custom fields used in the Register. (If you wish, you can change the SQL query in the connector.)

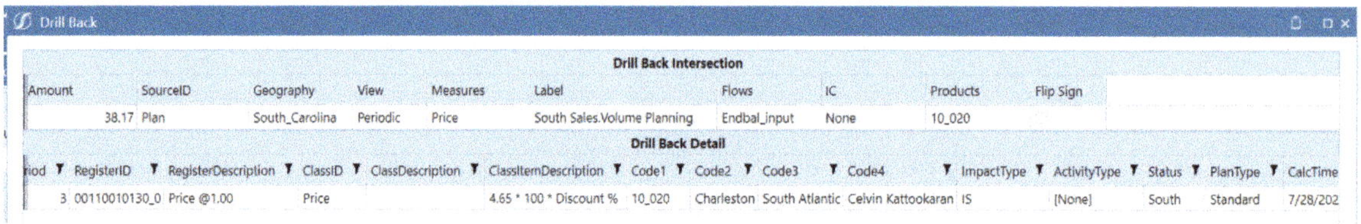

Figure 4.44

Plan Trend (Forward 12) drill back provides the following Report:

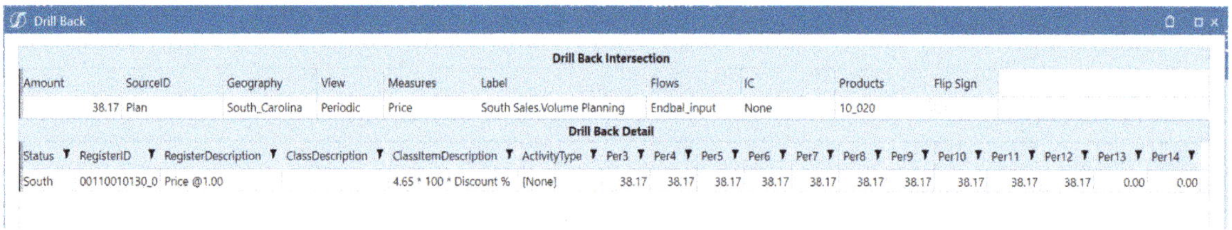

Figure 4.45

A Bit More than Basic

This section covers Specialty Planning's core architecture and functionality. Hold on to your metaphorical hat.

Peeling Away the Wrapping

Creating Tables on Install

Have you ever wondered how the solution is "setup" when you click on the Setup Tables button? Of course you do, else you would have jumped right over this section. Continue reading to understand why Specialty Planning behaves as it does.

Most of the MarketPlace Specialty solutions come with a `TableSetup` file embedded in the Dashboard.

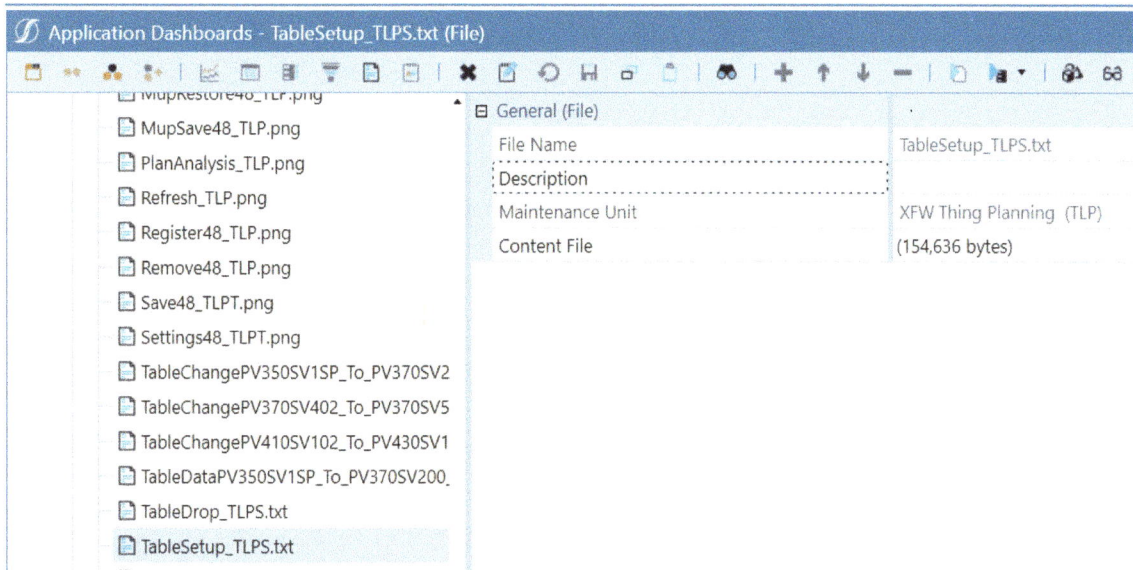

Figure 4.46

That file contains SQL DML and DDL statements. The Setup Tables button reads those statements from this file and executes them against the application database.

Using Templates for Calculation Definitions?

Templates to load calculation definitions can be used for:

1. Global drivers

2. Allocation Methods

3. Calculation Plans

4. Execution lists

Although this can be done in a Specialty Planning application directly, Excel is easier to work with because formulas can derive some of the columns.

You can download the existing templates for Allocation Methods and Calculation Plans from the Specialty Planning solution's Dashboard Unit File System.

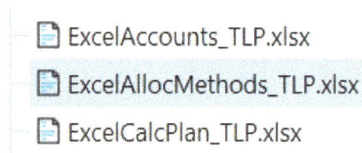

Figure 4.47

Viewing the Substitution Variables

Use the toolbar in the Allocation Methods and Calculation Plans to use the different Substitution Variables in their respective fields.

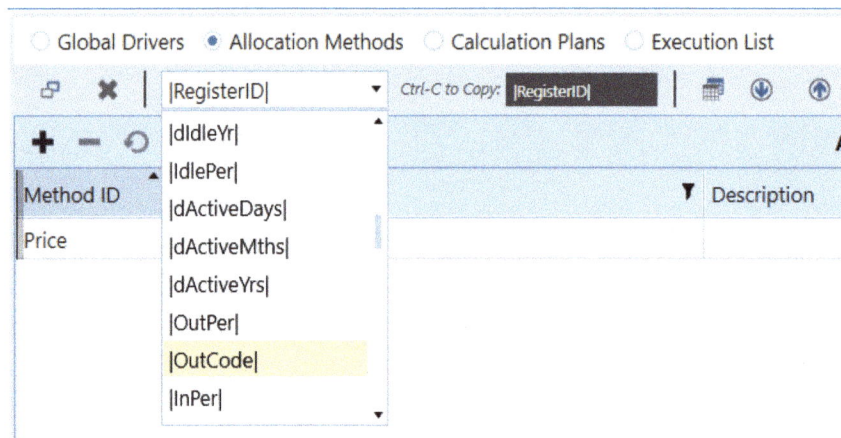

Figure 4.48

Select the variable and then the text from the text box on the right to copy it to the field.

Explore these variables as there are hidden gems like dActiveDays that returns how many days a Thing was active. This variable even looks at whether a Thing was idle and processes it using the idle date. People Planning has something similar called dEmployedDays, which returns how long the employee was employed.

Copy Allocation Methods and Calculation Plans

If you want to replicate a calculation definition and change a field or two, create the target Allocation Method/Calculation Plan, save the Method, select its row, and use the Open Copy button to copy from a source.

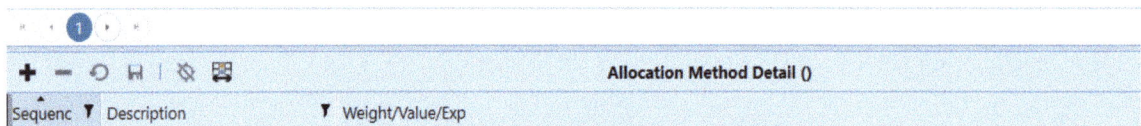

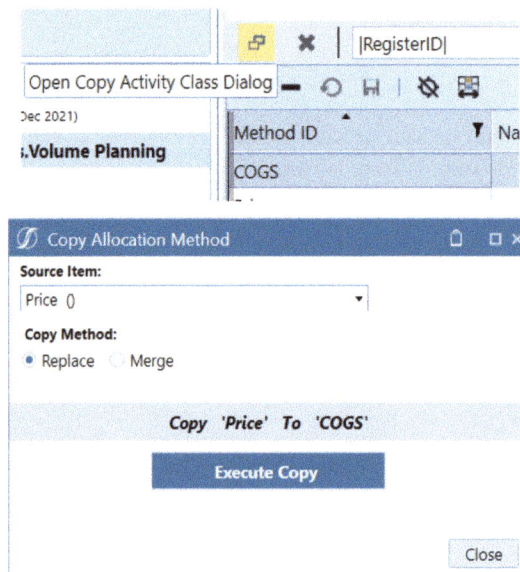

Figure 4.49

Execute the copy and it will duplicate the details.

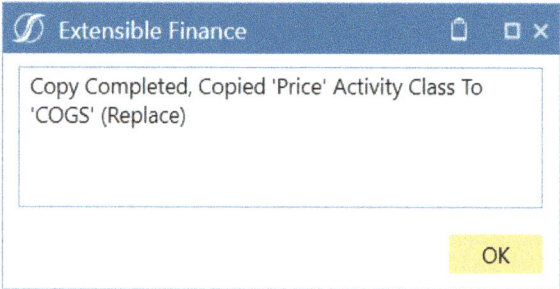

Figure 4.50

Figure 4.51

How does the Navigation Bar Type Solution Work, and How Can You Use It?

Thing Planning and similar Specialty Planning solutions use navigation buttons that take you to different sections of the solution.

The screen change on button click has a pretty ingenious approach that can be expanded to a custom solution.

At a bare minimum, this type of solution only makes sense when four or more Dashboards are required. In that instance, the main Dashboard will have two embedded Dashboards in it. One of them acts as the navigation bar (the one with the navigation buttons that open other Dashboards), and the other one acts as the content holder.

The content Dashboard has your custom embedded Dashboard as the Component.

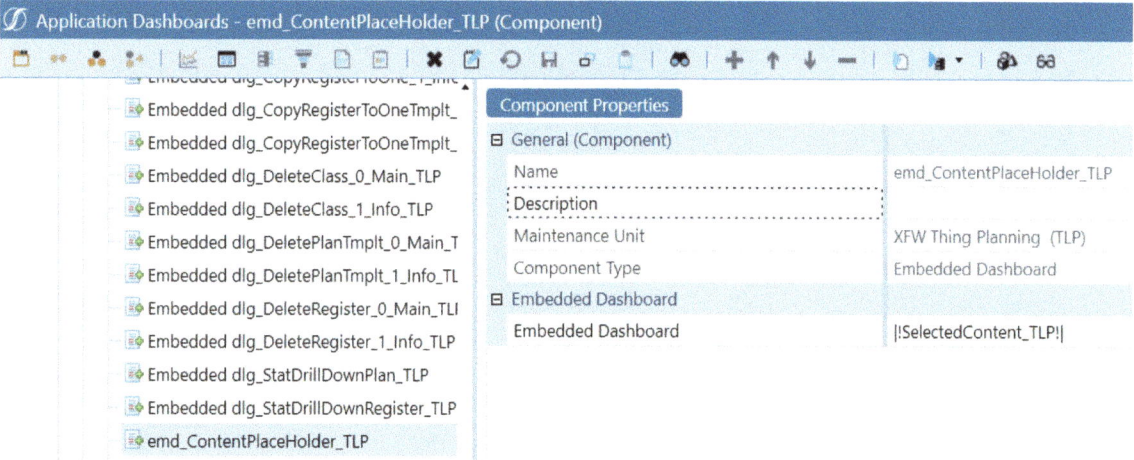

Figure 4.52

Chapter 4

Create an Input Value parameter (`!SelectedContent_TLP!`) as the embedded Dashboard. The navigation bar buttons will set the value of the parameter selected above and assign a value of an existing Dashboard to it.

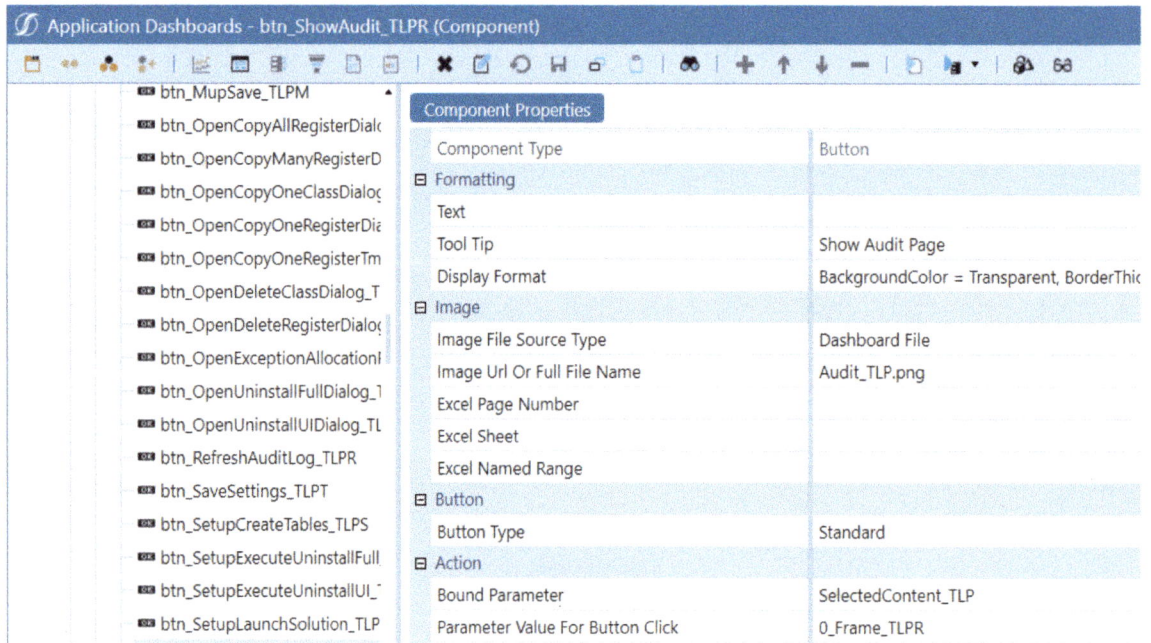

Figure 4.53

Add a User Interface action of Refresh and add the Content Dashboard for refreshing.

Figure 4.54

Let's see how it works.

There are five buttons in the Thing Planning (or similar Planning solutions).

1. `btn_ShowThingPlan_TLP` – opens the Thing Planning page.

2. `btn_ShowStandardActivityPlans_TLP` – opens the calculation definition page.

3. `btn_ShowAudit_TLPR` – opens the audit page.

4. `btn_ShowSettings_TLPT` – opens the solution settings page.

5. `btn_ShowHelp_TLPH` – opens the solution help page.

If you are a User changing an existing (or adding a new) item in the Volume Planning page (the Register) and wanted to look at the calculation definitions:

174

Figure 4.55

All you do is click on the Show Calculation Definition Page, and the screen magically changes to the Definitions page.

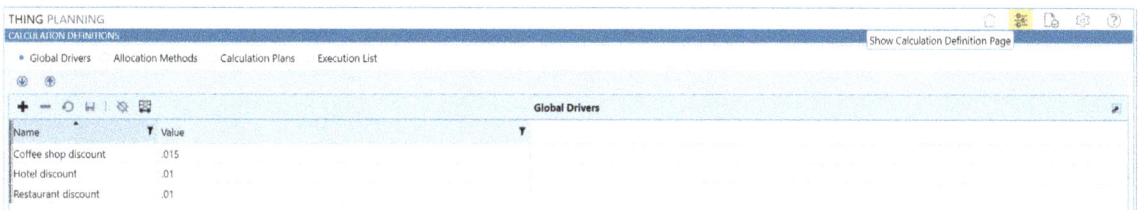

Figure 4.56

You can navigate to any of the pages listed above, by using the navigation buttons while staying on the same screen.

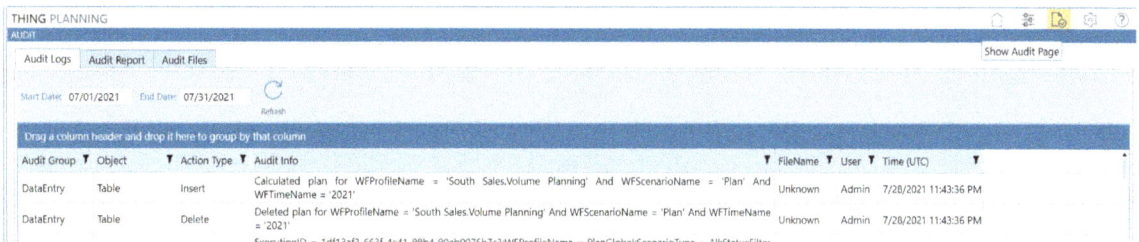

Figure 4.57

What is the Difference between Multiple Specialty Planning Solutions like Thing Planning, Capital Planning, and People Planning?

In the beginning, there was only water. Millions of years passed, then land started to form. Wait. No. This is not in a geology lesson but instead a Specialty Planning genealogy. The product line started with People Planning and has been expanded for specific use cases such as Capital Planning. As more and more demands for doing detailed level Planning came up, Thing Planning was born.

Interestingly, apart from a few additional specific columns and specific Allocation Method value Types, all of the products are the same. If they are the same, the question presents itself: should you be using Thing Planning for People Planning? No. People Planning is optimized for Workforce Planning. As a developer, you could customize Thing Planning to match People Planning's functionality, but why reinvent the wheel?

> If none of the Specialty Planning solutions meet your needs, go with Thing Planning.

Event Handlers

You might be wondering why do I ever need an Event Handler. I can do stuff on my own 😊

What is an Event Handler? It is simply a code function that fires when a specific product event occurs.

As an example, C&CCC's Volume Planning has a requirement to calculate the payment date from the selling date. For coffee shops, the payment date is two months after the selling date. For hotels, it is after 15 days, and restaurants should pay after a month.

You saw that calculated results are stored in the Plan table. How do we run a calculation on Register items?

Here is where an Event Handler script is useful. Download the Template Rule provided with the solution.

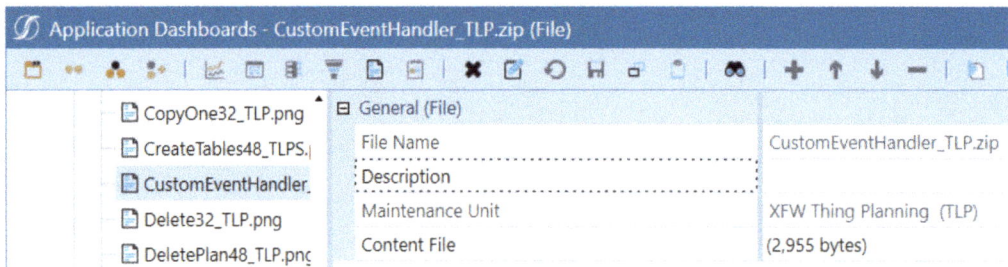

Figure 4.58

You can edit the XML file if you want to change the name of the Rule. Upload the zip, and a new Dashboard Extender Rule will now be in the application.

Once the Rule is imported, Event Handler functions can be used for Component selection changes/Table Editor saves. From PV620-SV100 version onwards, a custom filter on the Register items can be added before calculating them instead of using a conditional expression.

To calculate the payment date, a custom function in the Event Handler Rule was added as shown below:

```
For Each xfRow As XFEditedDataRow In saveDataTaskInfo.EditedDataRows
    If xfRow.InsertUpdateOrDelete = DbInsUpdateDelType.Insert OrElse
xfRow.InsertUpdateOrDelete = DbInsUpdateDelType.Update Then
        Dim soldDate As Date = xfrow.ModifiedDataRow.Item("ActiveDate")
        Dim customerType As Decimal =
xfRow.ModifiedDataRow.Item("NCode1")
        If customerType = 3 Then 'coffee shop
            xfrow.ModifiedDataRow.SetValue("IdleDate",
soldDate.AddMonths(2), XFDataType.DateTime)
        ElseIf customerType = 2 Then ' hotel
            xfrow.ModifiedDataRow.SetValue("IdleDate",
soldDate.AddDays(15), XFDataType.DateTime)
        ElseIf customerType = 1 Then ' restaurant
            xfrow.ModifiedDataRow.SetValue("IdleDate",
soldDate.AddMonths(1), XFDataType.DateTime)
        Else
            xfrow.ModifiedDataRow.SetValue("IdleDate", soldDate,
XFDataType.DateTime)
        End If
    End If
Next
```

For every edited row (new or updated), the code checks the customer Type and calculates the payment date from the sold date accordingly.

```
Using dbConn As DbConnInfo = BRApi.Database.CreateDbConnInfo(si,
saveDataTaskInfo.SqlTableEditorDefinition.DbLocation,
saveDataTaskInfo.SqlTableEditorDefinition.ExternalDBConnName)
    dbConn.BeginTrans()
    BRApi.Database.SaveDataTableRows(dbConn,
saveDataTaskInfo.SqlTableEditorDefinition.TableName,
saveDataTaskInfo.Columns, saveDataTaskInfo.HasPrimaryKeyColumns,
saveDataTaskInfo.EditedDataRows, True, False, True)
    dbConn.CommitTrans()
End Using

result.IsOK = True
result.ShowMessageBox = False
result.CancelDefaultSave = False
```

Once calculated, only the changed entries are saved to the Register. Once the entries are saved, the default save feature is cancelled.

Here is the full function used for this requirement.

```
278    Public Sub TLPAfterRegisterSaveEvent(ByVal si As SessionInfo, ByVal globals As BRGlobals, _
279    ByVal args As DashboardExtenderArgs, ByVal result As XFSqlTableEditorSaveDataTaskResult)
280        Try
281            Dim saveDataTaskInfo = New XFSqlTableEditorSaveDataTaskInfo
282            saveDataTaskInfo = args.SqlTableEditorSaveDataTaskInfo
283
284            For Each xfRow As XFEditedDataRow In saveDataTaskInfo.EditedDataRows
285                If xfRow.InsertUpdateOrDelete = DbInsUpdateDelType.Insert _
286                    OrElse xfRow.InsertUpdateOrDelete = DbInsUpdateDelType.Update Then
287                    Dim soldDate As Date = xfrow.ModifiedDataRow.Item("ActiveDate")
288                    Dim customerType As Decimal = xfRow.ModifiedDataRow.Item("NCode1")
289                    If customerType = 3 Then 'coffee shop
290                        xfrow.ModifiedDataRow.SetValue("IdleDate", soldDate.AddMonths(2), XFDataType.DateTime)
291                    ElseIf customerType = 2 Then ' hotel
292                        xfrow.ModifiedDataRow.SetValue("IdleDate", soldDate.AddDays(15), XFDataType.DateTime)
293                    ElseIf customerType = 1 Then ' restaurant
294                        xfrow.ModifiedDataRow.SetValue("IdleDate", soldDate.AddMonths(1), XFDataType.DateTime)
295                    Else
296                        xfrow.ModifiedDataRow.SetValue("IdleDate", soldDate, XFDataType.DateTime)
297                    End If
298                End If
299            Next
300
301        Catch ex As Exception
302            Throw ErrorHandler.LogWrite(si, New XFException(si, ex))
303        End Try
304    End Sub
```

Add this function to the AfterSaveDataEvent for the SaveRegisterRows function, as shown below.

```
Public Sub AfterSaveDataEvent(ByVal si As SessionInfo, ByVal globals As BRGlobals, ByVal
    Try

        'AFTER
        '******************************************************************************
        'Specialty Planning Save Data Events
        If (args.FunctionName.XFEqualsIgnoreCase("SaveRegisterRows")) Then
            TLPAfterRegisterSaveEvent(si, globals, args, result)
        Else If (args.FunctionName.XFEqualsIgnoreCase("SaveCalcPlanDetailRows")) Then

        Else If (args.FunctionName.XFEqualsIgnoreCase("SaveStatusRows")) Then
```

What is BRGlobals, and How Does it Help in Specialty Planning Solutions Calculations?

Imagine a driver-based Planning process that uses the Entity Dimension. Its detailed Planning employs Specialty Planning.

This approach could store the driver for a given Entity/Account combination in the Cube and retrieve the value for Specialty using an XFBR in an Allocation Method. Alternatively, the driver could be stored in a relational table.

Merging Cube Data with Specialty Planning

Using the example of C&CCC's Volume Planning, I can perform a detailed Distribution calculation using a Distribution Rate stored in the Sample Cube.

		Jan 2021	Feb 2021	Mar 2021	Apr 2021	May 2021	Jun 2021	Jul 2021	Aug 2021	Sep 2021	Oct 2021	Nov 2021	Dec 2021
2 Alabama	Distribution_Rate												
3 Florida	Distribution_Rate												
4 Mississippi	Distribution_Rate												
5 Louisiana	Distribution_Rate												
6 South Carolina	Distribution_Rate	0.0445	0.044	0.04	0.0445	0.044	0.04	0.0445	0.044	0.04	0.0445	0.044	0.04
8 Distribution = 205 * Rate		9.1225	9.02	8.2	9.1225	9.02	8.2	9.1225	9.02	8.2	9.1225	9.02	8.2

Figure 4.59

What happens when there are 1,000 sales items for South_Carolina in the Register?

What happens during the calculation process is the distribution rate that is stored against South_Carolina is fetched 1000 * 12 times. Is this really necessary, or could it instead be retrieved just 12 times?

This is where BRGlobals comes into play as it allows you to set a global value and retrieve it elsewhere so long as all processes are called sequentially. (Or in pure VB.Net terms; in the same thread.)

Using the Event Handler described in the previous section, a BeforeSelectionChangedEvent for CalculatePlan that pulls the values for all Workflow Profile Entities and saves them as a Dictionary object can be set up. If this is a value that needs multiple combinations, it can be added as a DataTable to BRGlobals.

```
Else If (args.FunctionName.XFEqualsIgnoreCase("CalculatePlan"))
            Dim dt As DataTable =
BRApi.Import.Data.FdxExecuteDataUnit(si, "Sample",
"E#Root.WFProfileEntities", "Local", ScenarioTypeId.Plan, "S#Plan",
"T#WF.Months", "Periodic", True, "Account='Distribution_Rate' AND
UD1='None' AND Flow='Endbal_Input' AND Origin='Forms'", 8, False)
            globals.SetObject("DistributionRateTable", dt)
```

The FDX operator is used to extract the Data Unit for all Profile Entities. Once extracted, an in-memory table similar to the one below is created:

Cube	Entity	Parent	Cons	Scenario	Time	View	Account	Flow	Origin	IC	UD1	UD2	UD3	UD4	UD5	UD6	UD7	UD8	Amount
Sample	South_Carolina		USD	Plan	2021M1	Periodic	Distribution_Rate	EndBal_Input	Forms	None	None	None	None	None	None	None	None	None	0.0445

Figure 4.60

A function in the XFBR Rule calculates Distribution:

```
Dim distribution As Decimal = 0
Dim sales As Decimal = args.NameValuePairs.XFGetValue("Sales")
Dim calcMonth As Integer = args.NameValuePairs.XFGetValue("CalcMonth")
Dim entity As String = args.NameValuePairs.XFGetValue("Entity")
```

```
Dim distRateDT As DataTable =
globals.GetObject("DistributionRateTable")
```

The first line initiates a variable as the return of this function.

The second, third, and fourth lines receive the parameters passed to this function.

In the fifth line, the `DistributionRateTable` from `BRGlobals` is retrieved.

```
Dim wfYear As Integer =
BRApi.Finance.Time.GetYearFromId(si,si.WorkflowClusterPk.TimeKey)
If Not distRateDT Is Nothing
   Dim distRateRow As DataRow()= distRateDT.Select("Entity='" & entity
& "' AND Time='" & wfYear & "M" & calcMonth & "'")
   If distRateRow.Count = 1 Then
      distribution = sales * distRateRow(0)("Amount")
   End If
End If
```

This code snippet determines the Workflow year. Once calculated, we know the year and are now querying the in-memory table using a filter, as seen in line three.

In line four, the code ensures that an entry for that Entity and Time period exists in the `DataTable`. If true, the code derives the distribution rate and calculates the Distribution.

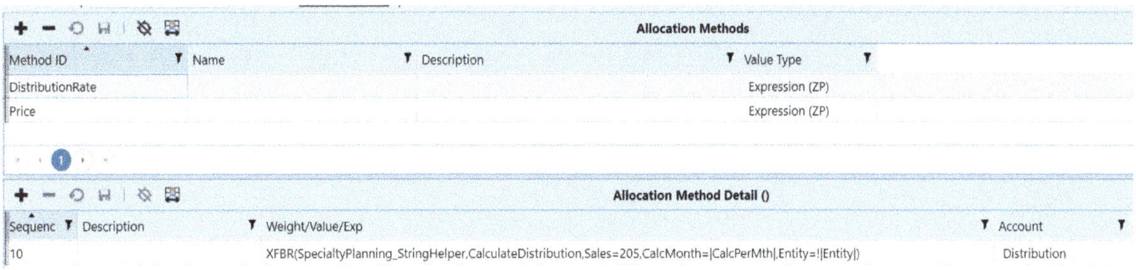

Allocation Methods

Method ID	Name	Description	Value Type
DistributionRate			Expression (ZP)
Price			Expression (ZP)

Allocation Method Detail ()

Sequenc	Description	Weight/Value/Exp	Account
10		XFBR(SpecialtyPlanning_StringHelper,CalculateDistribution,Sales=205,CalcMonth=|CalcPerMth|,Entity=!|Entity|)	Distribution

Figure 4.61

In the allocation Rule, `!|Entity|` is used as the Substitution Variable. If `!` is used with a Substitution Variable, the value will not be enclosed in single quotes.

Here is the result of the calculation:

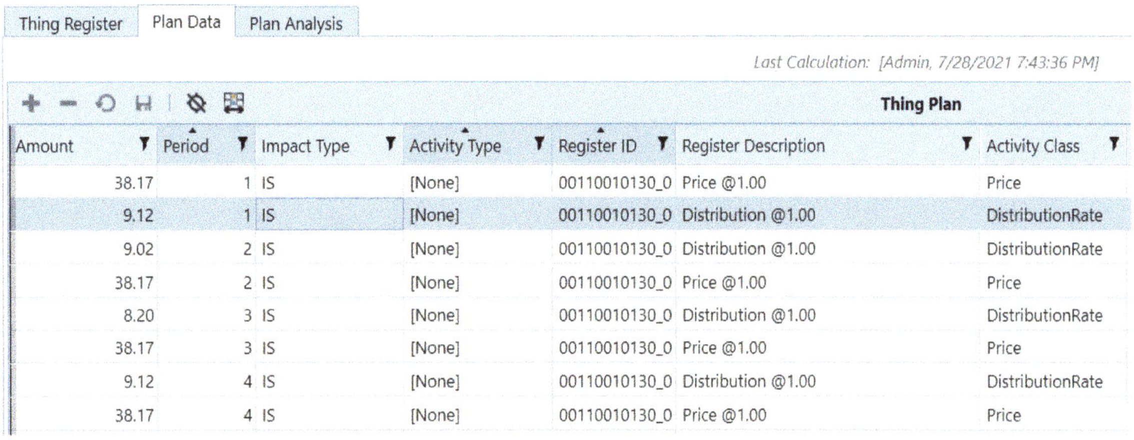

Amount	Period	Impact Type	Activity Type	Register ID	Register Description	Activity Class
38.17	1	IS	[None]	00110010130_0	Price @1.00	Price
9.12	1	IS	[None]	00110010130_0	Distribution @1.00	DistributionRate
9.02	2	IS	[None]	00110010130_0	Distribution @1.00	DistributionRate
38.17	2	IS	[None]	00110010130_0	Price @1.00	Price
8.20	3	IS	[None]	00110010130_0	Distribution @1.00	DistributionRate
38.17	3	IS	[None]	00110010130_0	Price @1.00	Price
9.12	4	IS	[None]	00110010130_0	Distribution @1.00	DistributionRate
38.17	4	IS	[None]	00110010130_0	Price @1.00	Price

Figure 4.62

Real-world applications that use a similar relational table driver storage model have been observed to provide four times better performance than non in-memory Methods.

If you are going to use Substitution Variables for comparison then it is easier to use the ones without the single quotes. The following codes are available to use without the single quote wrapping:

1. `!|OutCode|`
2. `!|InCode|`
3. `!|Entity|`
4. `!|Code1|`
5. `!|Code2|`
6. `!|Code3|`
7. `!|Code4|`
8. `!|Code5|`
9. `!|Code6|`
10. `!|Code7|`
11. `!|Code8|`
12. `!|Code9|`
13. `!|Code10|`
14. `!|Code11|`
15. `!|Code12|`
16. `!|Annot1|`
17. `!|Annot2|`

Does Anyone Here Know the Guy Called RegisterCache?

As we saw in the previous section, caching makes a lot of difference in the relational world. If you have looked at the Dashboard Extender Rule for Specialty Planning solutions, you might have noticed another class in this Rule called `RegisterCacheItem`.

This class plays an important role in the efficiency of Specialty Planning calculations. The calculation is done in parallel, and it is done on a row by row basis. The calculated row is written to an in-memory table, and it is then saved to the Plan table.

`RegisterCacheItem` is the class that is helping out – behind-the-scenes – to achieve the process. It is also the class that gets used in many out-of-the-box XFBR Rules.

Custom Functions in Specialty Planning

The following custom functions are available in out-of-the-box XFBR Rules:

- `GetTimeSpan` – returns the difference between two dates (you can return the time span in days, months, years).

- `GetRegValue` [deprecated] – returns the value of a Register field (use Substitution Variables for this purpose).

- `GetLimitResidual` – returns the residual amount by supplying a limit value.

- `GetSumPer` – returns the sum of an Account for a given period and a Register ID.

- `GetSumCum` – returns the cumulative sum of an Account until a given period and a Register ID.

- `GetSumCustom` – returns the sum based on criteria mentioned for a given Register ID.

- `GetMin` – returns the minimum value of an Account for a given period and a Register ID.

- `GetMinCustom` - returns the minimum value based on the criteria mentioned for a given Register ID.

- `GetMax`

- `GetMaxCustom`

- `GetAvg`

- `GetAvgCustom`

If you are going to create custom functions that are going to fetch a calculated row, create them based on the available functions.

Specialty Planning Solution vs. a Custom Solution

OneStreamers often say, "Oh, that's a Thing Planning solution" when faced with a set of Planning requirements that are not good fits for the more specialized Specialty Planning modules. But is it? What determines suitability?

Fitness for Purpose

Consider C&CCC's requirement for capturing Sales information. They need to capture sales across cities in the USA by Sales Representative. While Thing Planning could do that, it is akin to a sledgehammer used to crack a nut.

The following are some areas where Thing Planning is overkill or cannot meet specific requirements:

1. Reporting information is captured but not planned.

2. Planning drivers vary by Thing.

3. Plan is entered and calculated by months.

Could Thing Planning be used in this context? Yes, but with several disadvantages.

1. Thing Planning's overhead is incurred but not used.

2. Thing Planning's model does not cleanly support different drivers by Thing if they vary by month or if you've used all the numeric columns.

3. While a Scenario with monthly input could be created and calculate a single month, this approach requires 12 Workflows, thus repeating the same "Thing" 12 times.

The Custom Way

A truly custom solution can scare off practitioners because of the complexity of creating SQL scripts to create the backbone of a relational system. This effort has been reduced with the introduction of a new tool in MarketPlace called **Table Data Manager** (TDM). It makes creating custom solutions (or just creating custom tables) a breeze.

Using TDM for Sales Information

On initial installation, TDM can interrogate the databases that are present in the Application Server Configuration File (including the external databases) to reveal table schema and data for tables not created using TDM.

This screenshot shows a `DimEmployee` that was not created by TDM; TDM-created tables have an `_XFC` suffix.

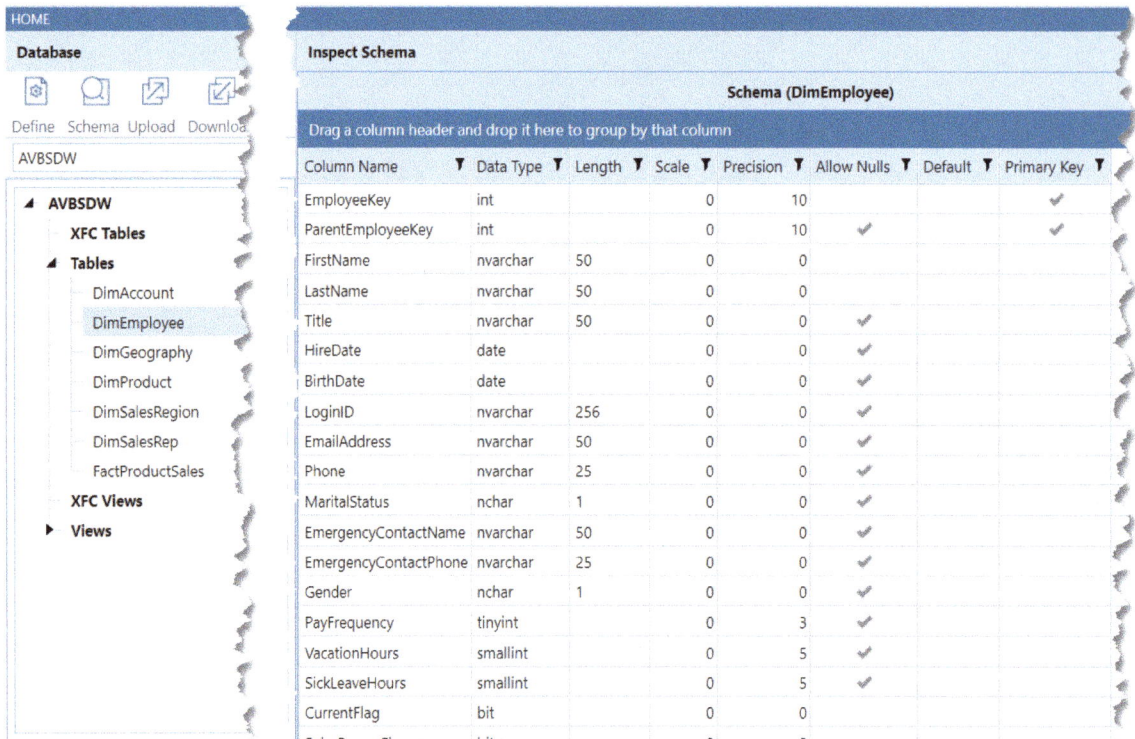

Figure 4.63

Creating a Custom Sales Table

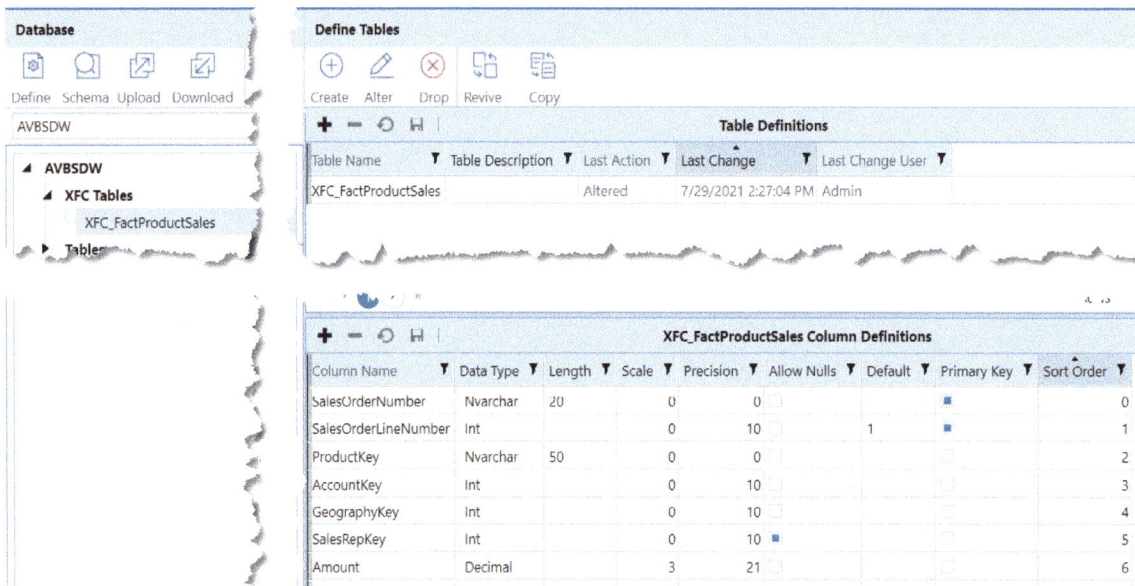

Figure 4.64

A few things that must be kept in mind when creating the tables:

1. You can upload a DDL file to create the table.

2. You cannot add indexes/foreign keys.

3. If you use a DDL file to create the table with indexes/foreign keys, TDM will create them. However, a download of the definition will not include them.

4. Copying tables also ignores the indexes/foreign keys.

5. You cannot use [ ] in table names, so do not use spaces in table names.

Importing Data

Data imports to an XFC table requires an XML file. The format of the file is straightforward:

1. `<DocumentElement>` is the root element.

2. `<TableName>` is the only Parent node and repeats for each data row.

3. `<ColumnNames>` defines the field Child nodes.

4. Data is encapsulated in the `<ColumnNames>` nodes.

```xml
1   <?xml version="1.0" encoding="utf-8" ?>
2   <DocumentElement>
3     <XFC_FactProductSales>
4       <SalesOrderNumber>00110010120</SalesOrderNumber>
5       <SalesOrderLineNumber>1</SalesOrderLineNumber>
6       <ProductKey>10_010</ProductKey>
7       <AccountKey>3</AccountKey>
8       <GeographyKey>4</GeographyKey>
9       <SalesRepKey>1</SalesRepKey>
10      <Amount>120.000</Amount>
11      <SoldDate>5/10/2020 12:00:00 AM</SoldDate>
12      <SalesRegionKey>1</SalesRegionKey>
13    </XFC_FactProductSales>
14  </DocumentElement>
```

Once the table is created, a Dashboard with a SQL editor Component can be used to enter data into this table.

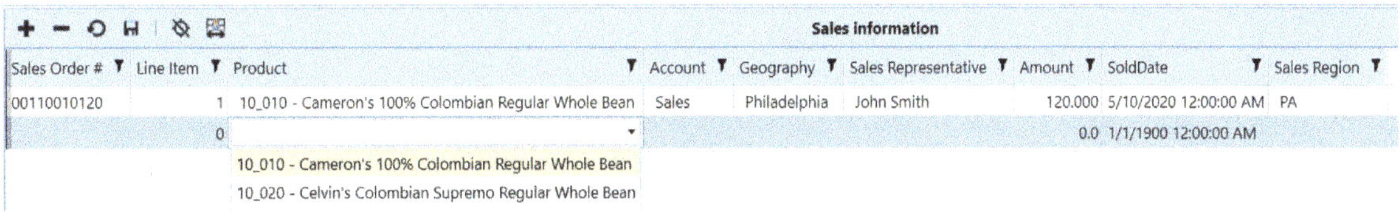

Figure 4.65

These custom tables can be used as an integration point, or as a piece of detailed information for Specialty Planning solutions if the required column count exceeds the maximum number supplied.

For example, you can just add the Sales Order Number and Line Item (provided they are unique) in the Specialty Planning solution and create a custom button to show the details from this table. The possibilities are endless.

Conclusion

Hopefully, this chapter has shown that Specialty Planning solutions are special in their own way. They let you plan and analyze data at a detailed level by bringing the relational and multidimensional worlds together. Use them.

5

All Data Points Lead to Reporting and Analysis

Calculating plan data must be the bedrock of any planning application. Understanding and acting upon that information, within OneStream and without, is the true purpose of any performance management system and is realized only through reporting and analysis.

This chapter will examine:

1. Planning with Dashboards.

2. Performing faster data exports from OneStream for external consumption.

3. Analyzing large volumes of data related/unrelated to OneStream.

Planning with Dashboards

The nature of this book is Planning, not dashboarding. But all work and no play makes Jack a dull boy; data comprehension is aided when supplemented by "pretty" Dashboards that highlight key financial information at a glance. OneStream adds its own flavor to these Dashboards by letting the OneStream practitioner make them interactive.

Planning mostly avoids a lot of dashboarding because we Planners think that we are all about numbers. Dashboards *are* about the numbers. Even though this section covers Dashboards, it is deeply rooted in the data and the numbers that Planning and Budgeting requires.

Data Management Sequences

As we mentioned in the *Theory, Philosophy, and Practice* chapter, Custom Calculate Finance Business Rules run business models in Planning. In the following examples, two Data Management Sequences will be used to execute the calculations from a Dashboard button and from a Dashboard Extender Rule.

The Sequences `CopyToPennsylvania` and `DistributionCalculation` are as shown in Data Management.

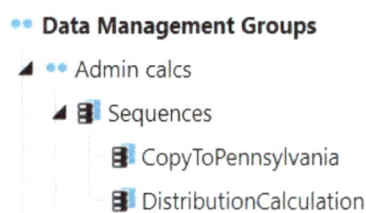

Figure 5.1

Run on Save

A common Planning Scenario is executing a rule after entering driver numbers. In this example, C&CCC's Planners want to calculate the Distribution after entering a distribution rate for a product.

If a Finance Business Rule is being used to execute the distribution calculation (and it should be in preference to formulas or rules attached to a Cube to run on Consolidation), a Custom Finance Business Rule to execute the distribution calculation on save can be performed through a simple Dashboard.

Your author always finds it helpful to draw the Dashboard, even with his poor artistic skills, to have a clear idea of the User's needs.

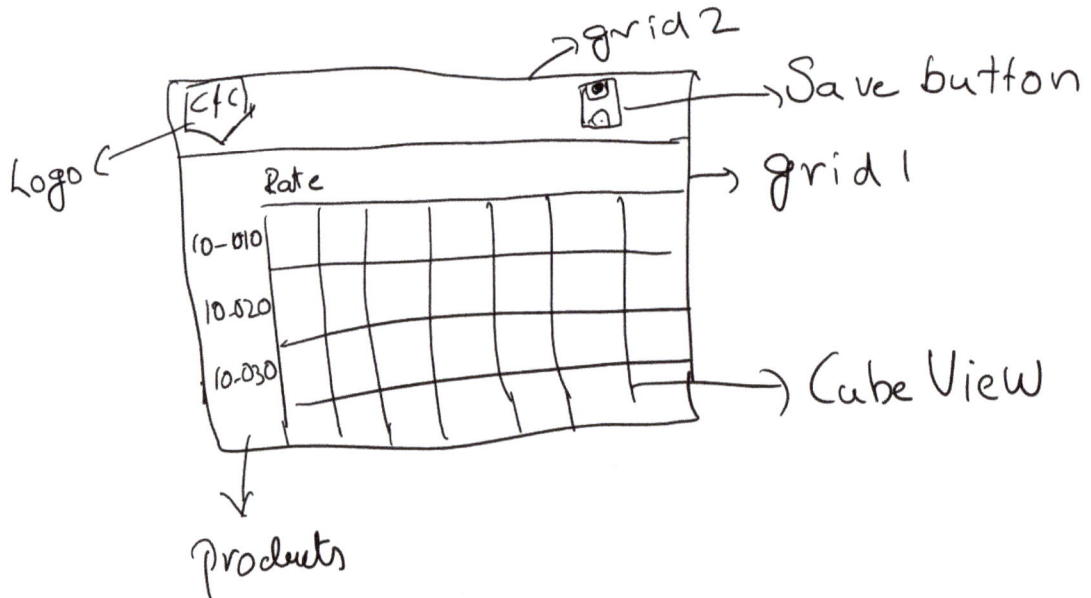

Figure 5.2

Components

This rough design sketch will need the following Components to become a fully-fledged Dashboard:

1. One Cube View

2. A button to execute a DM job

3. An image

From these Components, and looking at the rough layout of the picture to create a Dashboard similar to the picture, the following are needed:

1. A dock-type Dashboard with a left-docked image (Logo) and a right-docked button (Save Button).

2. A Dashboard to hold the Cube View.

3. A Dashboard with two rows to hold Dashboards 1 and 2 (above).

Cube View

Cube Views can be used as Dashboard Components for data entry and reporting. The Products Dimension in rows, Time in a Column, and every other Dimension is in the POV. If you do not choose a Cube View POV Member, it takes it from the Cube POV. It is almost always a good practice to fully define the POV within the Cube View.

An alias is used on the Time Member to aid User comprehension.

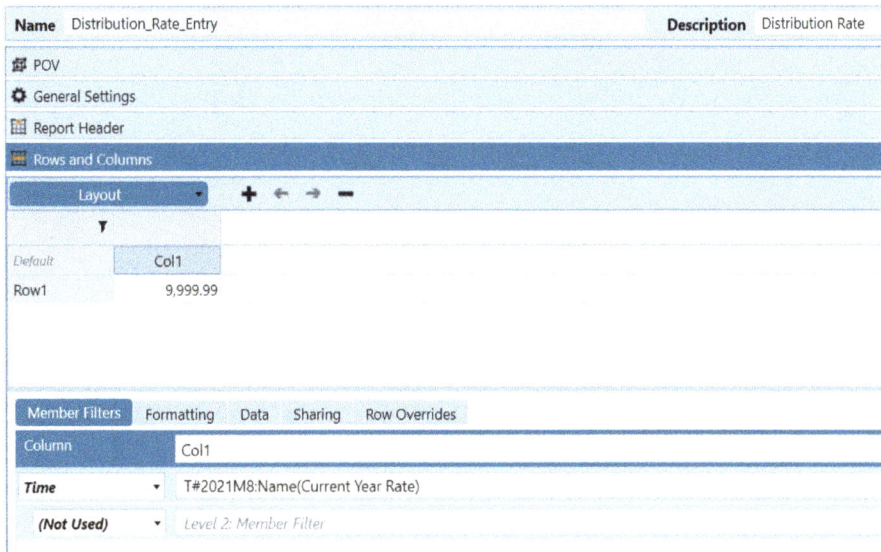

Figure 5.3

This Cube View `Distribution_Rate_Entry` is added as a Cube View Component in the Dashboard Maintenance Unit.

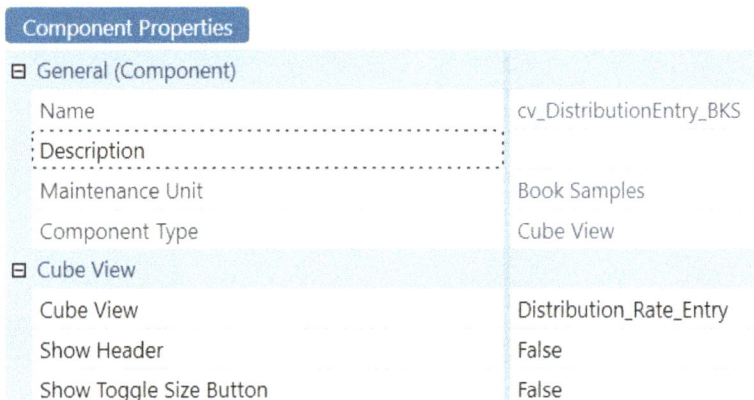

Figure 5.4

By making the Show Header property False, the default Cube View buttons are removed from the Dashboard.

Button – to Run the Model

In OneStream Dashboarding, Buttons play a major role. They can be used to download objects, upload a file to a location, run Business Rules, or run Data Management sequences. This section illustrates how to use a button to execute a Data Management sequence.

> **Note:** Component property descriptions are given in the order they appear in OneStream.

An image file – `Save_Button.png` – saved as Dashboard File is used. Images are not required for Buttons to work, but they aid understanding. There are many public domain Open, Save, Print, etc. icon files on the web; use one or subscribe to an image library.

Component Properties	
⊟ General (Component)	
Name	btn_Run_on_Save_BKS
Description	
Maintenance Unit	Book Samples
Component Type	Button
⊟ Formatting	
Text	
Tool Tip	Save and Calculate
Display Format	BackgroundColor = Transparent, BorderThickness = 0, HorizontalAlignment = Right, VerticalAlignment = Center
⊟ Image	
Image File Source Type	Dashboard File
Image Url Or Full File Name	Save_Button.png

Figure 5.5

Since an image is used in the Button, it should (this is your author's design choice) appear as a part of the Dashboard and not stand out as a separate Component; a transparent background color is used. A border thickness of zero ensures no border is added to the Button, and the right alignment makes it dock to the right.

In the Button action section, a click will fire the Save Data for All Components action for the Selection Changed Save Action. This means that on a button click, all open Cube Views, Spreadsheet Quick Views, etc., will be saved to the Cube.

On the Selection Changed Server Task, running the Data Management Sequence {Distribution Calculation}{} executes the Finance Business Rule. Note the set of empty curly braces – these are used to pass parameters to the sequence and required whether parameters are passed or not.

Action	
Bound Parameter	
Parameter Value For Button Click	
Apply Selected Value To Current Dashboard	True
Save Action	
Selection Changed Save Action	Save Data For All Components
Selection Changed Save Arguments	
POV Action	
Selection Changed POV Action	No Action
Selection Changed POV Arguments	
Server Task	
Selection Changed Server Task	Execute Data Management Sequence
Selection Changed Server Task Arguments	{DistributionCalculation}{}

Figure 5.6

Image

The image Component shows an image on the Dashboard. The source graphics file that comprises an image can be stored in multiple locations; since this image is specific to this Dashboard board, it is uploaded as a Dashboard file.

If an image is reused multiple times in an application, it is recommended to store it as an **Application Database file**.

Component Properties	
⊟ General (Component)	
Name	img_CCCC
Description	
Maintenance Unit	Book Samples
Component Type	Image
⊟ Formatting	
Tool Tip	
Display Format	Height = 30, HorizontalAlignment = Left, MarginLeft = 5, VerticalAlignment = Center, Width = 30
⊟ Image	
File Source Type	Dashboard File
Url Or Full File Name	C&C logo.png
Excel Page Number	
Excel Sheet	
Excel Named Range	

Figure 5.7

Since the header row width is small in the main Dashboard, the image's width and height are fixed at 30.

Header Dashboard

Dashboard Properties	Dashboard Components
⊟ General (Dashboard)	
Name	1_Run_On_Save_Rules_Header_BKS
Description	
Page Caption	
Dashboard Group	Run on Save
⊟ Formatting	
Layout Type	Dock
Is Initially Visible If Embedded	True
Display Format	
⊟ Literal Parameter Values	
Name Value Pairs (e.g., Param1=Value1, …)	
⊟ Action (Primary Dashboard Only)	
Server Task	
Load Dashboard Server Task	No Task
Load Dashboard Server Task Arguments	

Figure 5.8

Image Components and the Save Button Component go here.

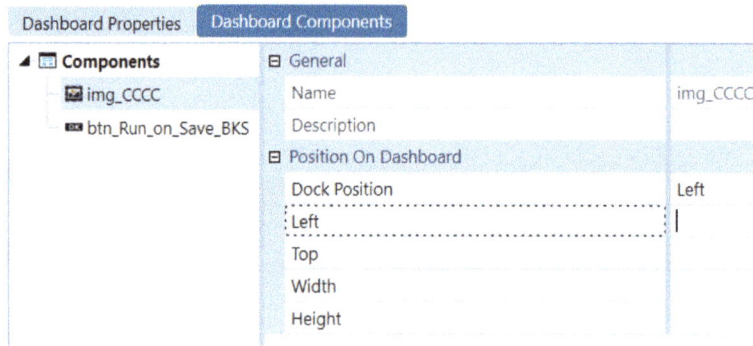

Figure 5.9

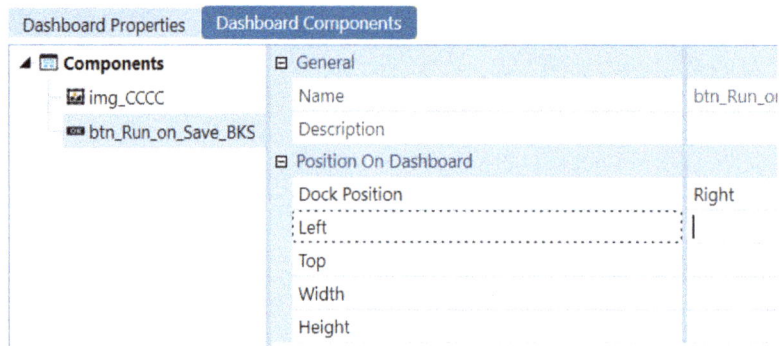

Figure 5.10

Cube View Dashboard

A Dashboard that contains just this single Cube View is not required since that Cube View is the only Component. However, creating what seems to be a redundant Dashboard is a way of future-proofing to allow more Components to be added (if needed) to this Dashboard at a later point in time.

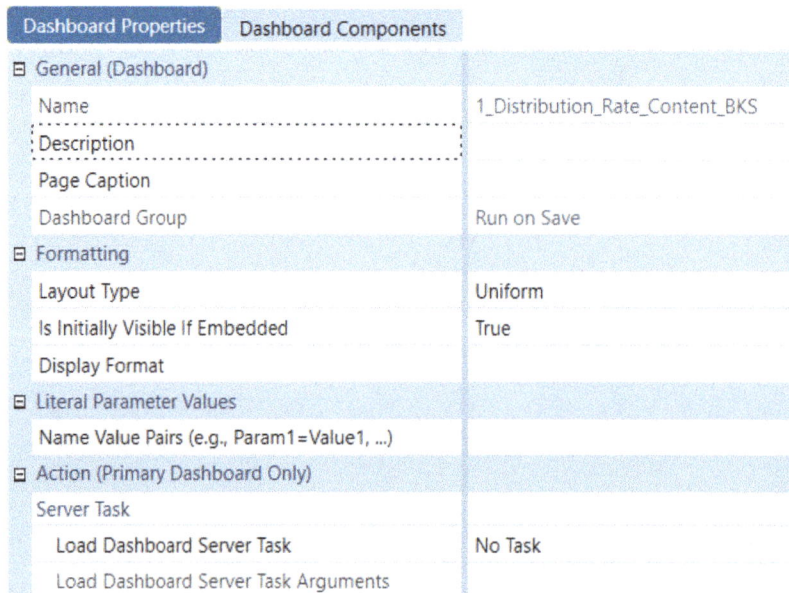

Figure 5.11

Main Dashboard

Now that all the Components are ready, it is now just a matter of housing the above two Dashboards into a single one.

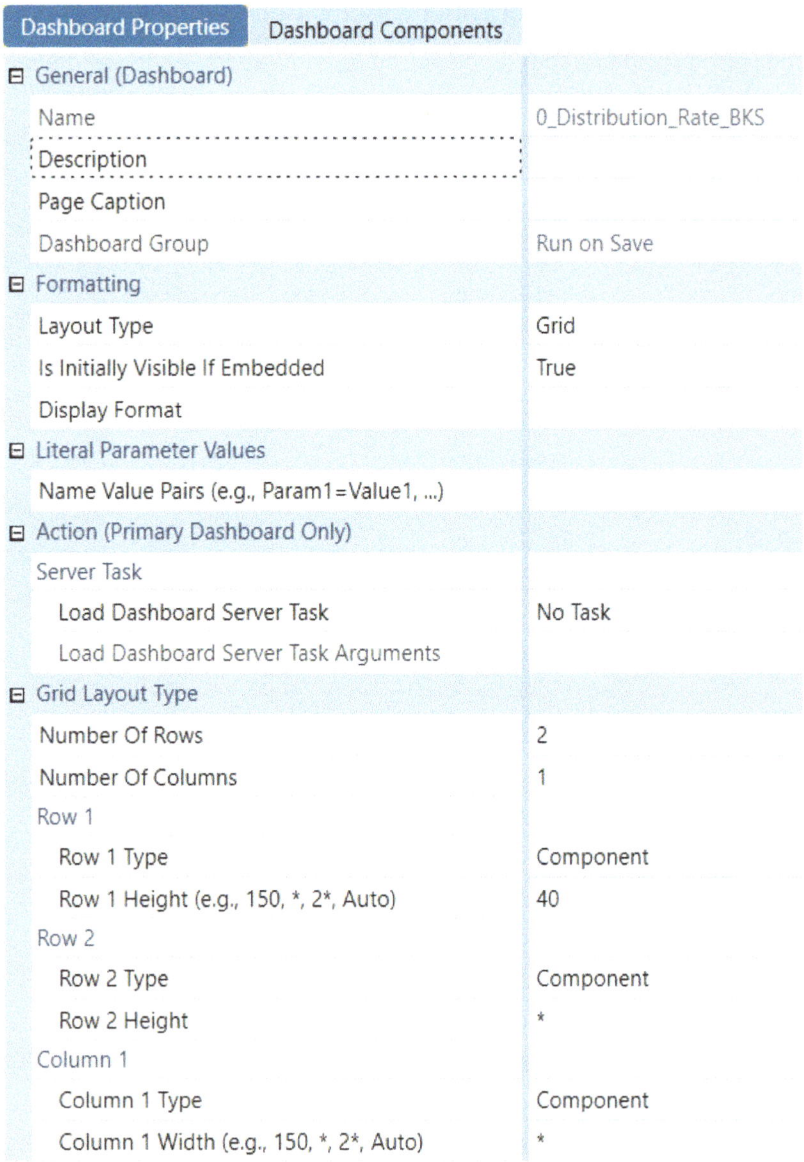

Dashboard Properties	Dashboard Components	
⊟ General (Dashboard)		
Name		0_Distribution_Rate_BKS
Description		
Page Caption		
Dashboard Group		Run on Save
⊟ Formatting		
Layout Type		Grid
Is Initially Visible If Embedded		True
Display Format		
⊟ Literal Parameter Values		
Name Value Pairs (e.g., Param1=Value1, ...)		
⊟ Action (Primary Dashboard Only)		
Server Task		
Load Dashboard Server Task		No Task
Load Dashboard Server Task Arguments		
⊟ Grid Layout Type		
Number Of Rows		2
Number Of Columns		1
Row 1		
Row 1 Type		Component
Row 1 Height (e.g., 150, *, 2*, Auto)		40
Row 2		
Row 2 Type		Component
Row 2 Height		*
Column 1		
Column 1 Type		Component
Column 1 Width (e.g., 150, *, 2*, Auto)		*

Figure 5.12

The header Dashboard is given a height of 40 (as it works perfectly for line headers), and the rest of the space is occupied by the Cube View Dashboard.

Here is how it looks when viewed as a Dashboard.

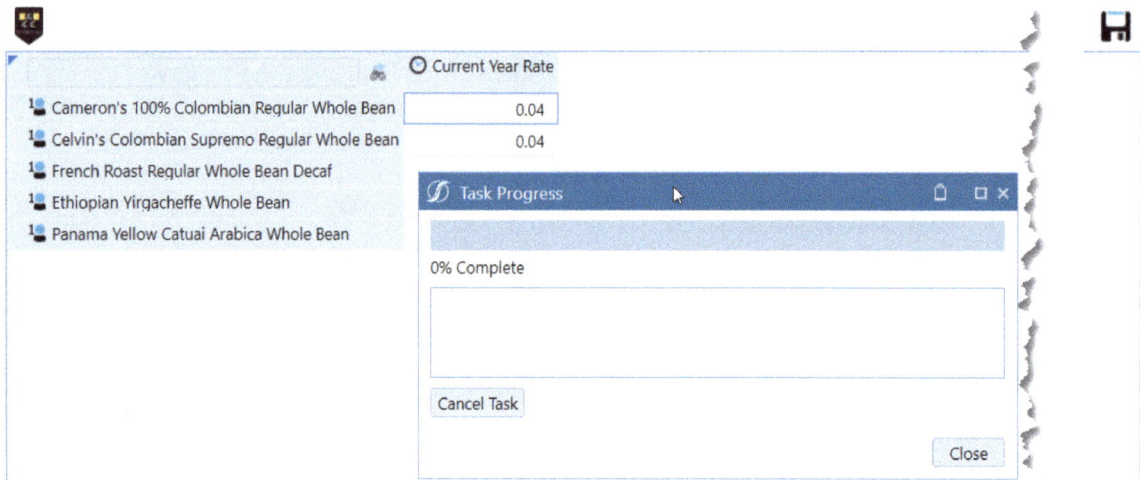

Figure 5.13

Select and Run Multiple Rules

C&CCC's Planners want choice when it comes to running Business Rules. Who does not want choice in life, huh?

What they want – what they need – is a list of rules to be presented on-screen while entering data (with a default selection). From this list, the Planners can select the ones to execute.

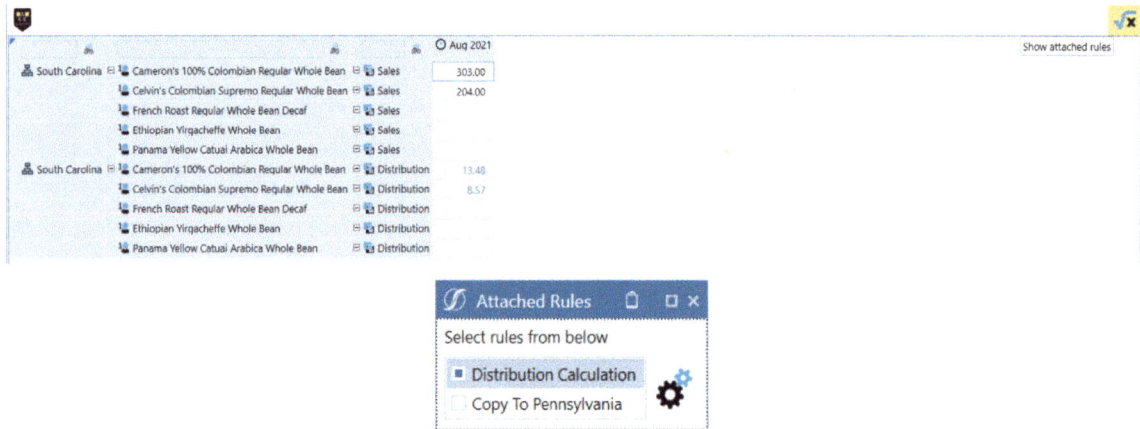

Figure 5.14

This is a perfect use case for a **multi-select option**. The following Components allow multi-select:

1. Combo Box
2. List Box
3. Grid View
4. SQL Table Editor

Components

This use case's Dashboard follows a similar structure as our previous one, and will need the following Components:

1. One Cube View
2. A button to show the rule list

3. An image

4. A dock-type Dashboard with a left-docked image, and a right-docked button to separate the header

5. A delimited parameter with the list of DM jobs

6. A List Box to show the list of rules

7. A Button to execute the selected rules

8. A dialog Dashboard to show the List Box and the rule execution Button

9. A grid-type Dashboard with two rows to hold the Cube View and the header Dashboard

Cube View

A Cube View is created to record Sales data. A calculated Distribution is in the rows. To prevent any data modification, it is marked as read-only (Can Modify Data – False).

Cube View Properties	Point Of View	Headers	Columns	Rows	
Sales	⊟ General				
Distribution	Row Name				Distribution
	Can Modify Data				False
	⊞ Cube View Sharing				
	⊞ Formatting				
	⊞ Navigation Links				
	⊟ Row Members				
	Member Expansion 1				
	Primary Dimension Type				Entity
	Member Filter				E#South_Carolina
	Indent Level				0
	Nested Member Expansion 2				
	Primary Dimension Type				UD1
	Member Filter				U1#Whole_Bean.Base
	Nested Member Expansion 3				
	Primary Dimension Type				Account
	Member Filter				A#Distribution
	Nested Member Expansion 4				
	Primary Dimension Type				(Not Used)
	Member Filter				

Figure 5.15

This Cube View is now added as a Cube View Component in the Dashboard Maintenance Unit.

⊟ General (Component)	
Name	cv_SalesDistribution_BKS
Description	
Maintenance Unit	Book Samples
Component Type	Cube View
⊟ Cube View	
Cube View	Sales_Distribution
Show Header	False
Show Toggle Size Button	False

Figure 5.16

By making the Show Header property False, the default Cube View Buttons are removed from the Dashboard.

Button – to Show the Rule Dashboard

An image is used for this Button to show that there are rules associated with the Cube View.

Component Properties	
⊟ General (Component)	
Name	btn_Run_on_Save_BKS
Description	
Maintenance Unit	Book Samples
Component Type	Button
⊟ Formatting	
Text	
Tool Tip	Save and Calculate
Display Format	BackgroundColor = Transparent, BorderThickness = 0, HorizontalAlignment = Right, VerticalAlignment = Center
⊟ Image	
Image File Source Type	Dashboard File
Image Url Or Full File Name	Save_Button.png

Figure 5.17

In the Button Action section, the Save Action property is set to Save Data For All Components.

When a selection is changed (in this case, a button click), a dialog Dashboard is opened to show the associated rules for the Cube View.

⊟ Action	
Bound Parameter	
Parameter Value For Button Click	
Apply Selected Value To Current Dashboard	True
Save Action	
Selection Changed Save Action	Save Data For All Components
Selection Changed Save Arguments	
POV Action	
Selection Changed POV Action	No Action
Selection Changed POV Arguments	
Server Task	
Selection Changed Server Task	No Task
Selection Changed Server Task Arguments	
User Interface Action	
Selection Changed User Interface Action	Open Dialog With No Buttons, Apply Changes, And Refresh
Dashboards To Redraw	
Dashboards To Show	
Dashboards To Hide	
Dashboard To Open In Dialog	1_Choose_Rules_BKS
Navigation Action	
Selection Changed Navigation Action	No Action
Selection Changed Navigation Arguments	

Figure 5.18

Parameter

General (Parameter)	
Name	BRChoices_BKS
Description		
User Prompt	
Maintenance Unit	Book Samples
Sort Order	0
Data Source	
Parameter Type	Delimited List
Default Value	DistributionCalculation
Display Items (comma delimited)	Distribution Calculation,Copy To Pennsylvania
Value Items (comma delimited)	DistributionCalculation,CopyToPennsylvania

Figure 5.19

A delimited list-type parameter is used to show the rules associated with the Cube View. The values for this parameter are the Data Management Sequence names used to run the Custom Finance Rules.

List Box

A List Box shows the Business Rules that a Planner can execute. To achieve this, the List Box is bound to the parameter we created above.

Component Properties	
General (Component)	
Name	lbx_BRChoices_BKS
Description	
Maintenance Unit	Book Samples
Component Type	List Box
Formatting	
Text	
Tool Tip	
Display Format	HorizontalAlignment = Left, IsMultiSelect = True, MarginLeft = 7, VerticalAlignment = Center
Action	
Bound Parameter	BRChoices_BKS
Apply Selected Value To Current Dashboard	True

Figure 5.20

Setting the Display Format property of IsMultiSelect to True makes this List Box a selectable one, where Planners can choose one or more rules to execute.

Button – to Execute the Selected Rules

This Button is similar to the one shown in the previous example.

Component Properties	
Text	
Tool Tip	Save and Calculate
Display Format	BackgroundColor = Transparent, BorderThickness = 0, Height = 48, HorizontalAlignment = Left, VerticalAlignment = Center, Width = 48
⊟ Image	
Image File Source Type	Dashboard File
Image Url Or Full File Name	Calculate_BKS.png
Excel Page Number	
Excel Sheet	
Excel Named Range	
⊟ Button	
Button Type	Standard
⊟ Action	
Bound Parameter	
Parameter Value For Button Click	
Apply Selected Value To Current Dashboard	True
Save Action	
Selection Changed Save Action	Save Data For All Components
Selection Changed Save Arguments	
POV Action	
Selection Changed POV Action	No Action
Selection Changed POV Arguments	
Server Task	
Selection Changed Server Task	Execute Dashboard Extender Business Rule (General Server)
Selection Changed Server Task Arguments	{BookRules}{RunChosenRules}{Rules=[!!BRChoices_BKS!]}
User Interface Action	
Selection Changed User Interface Action	No Action
Dashboards To Redraw	

Figure 5.21

Given that the Planner can select multiple Data Management Sequences, there is no option available that can directly receive the selection. This is where a **Dashboard Extender Rule** comes into play. When the Planner makes the selection, the Bound Parameter can now pass the selection as a comma-separated string to the Rule.

When the Button's Selection Changed Server Task action fires, the DashboardExtenderFunctionType of ComponentSelectionChanged is tested. The passed parameter RunChosenRules fires as this is the function passed from Selection Changed User Interface Action.

```
Case Is = DashboardExtenderFunctionType.ComponentSelectionChanged
    If args.FunctionName.XFEqualsIgnoreCase("RunChosenRules") Then

        Dim selectionChangedTaskResult As New
XFSelectionChangedTaskResult()
        selectionChangedTaskResult = Me.RunChosenRules(si, globals,
args)
        Return selectionChangedTaskResult
    End If
```

RunChosenRules returns a new XFSelectionChangedTaskResult object back to the Dashboard.

```
Dim selectionChangedTaskResult As New XFSelectionChangedTaskResult()
Dim strChosenRules As String = args.NameValuePairs.XFGetValue("Rules")
```

Next, we get the value of the Data Management Sequences selected by the User.

```
If Not(String.IsNullOrEmpty(strChosenRules) OrElse
StringHelper.DoesStringContainCustomSubstVarsOrSubstVarStringFunctions
(strChosenRules))
    Dim listChosenRules As List(Of String) =
strChosenRules.Split(",").Select(Function(x) x.Trim).ToList()
    For Each chosenRule In listChosenRules
        Dim params As New Dictionary(Of String, String)
        BRApi.Utilities.StartDataMgmtSequence(si, chosenRule, params) '
task gets executed in background
```

```
     Next
End If
```

This code block checks whether `strChosenRules` is empty (the Planner did not select a rule) or whether the parameter is evaluated (if it is not evaluated, then the parameter will come to the rule as `|!BRChoices_BKS!|`).

The Method `DoesStringContainCustomSubstVarsOrSubstVarStringFunctions` can check whether the supplied parameter value has a substitution variable (|) or a parameter (|!) in the string.

If the check passes, the function then splits the string using a comma as a delimiter, and it also trims each string, e.g., if the User selected both options, the string value is `DistributionCalculation, CopyToPennsylvania`. For each selected Data Management Sequence, the function will start the sequence as a background job that runs in parallel. If there are dependent rules, use `BRApi.Utilities.ExecuteDataMgmtSequence` to start them sequentially.

Note: The above Method of splitting and trimming the string can be used for all the Components that support multi-select like Grid Views, SQL Table Editors, List Boxes, and Combo Boxes. For Grid Views and SQL Table Editors, a bound parameter and a bound column is required to make this work.

Full function below:

```
Private Function RunChosenRules(ByVal si As SessionInfo, ByVal globals
As BRGlobals, ByVal args As DashboardExtenderArgs) As
XFSelectionChangedTaskResult
   Try
      Dim selectionChangedTaskResult As New
XFSelectionChangedTaskResult()
      Dim strChosenRules As String =
args.NameValuePairs.XFGetValue("Rules")
      If Not(String.IsNullOrEmpty(strChosenRules) OrElse
StringHelper.DoesStringContainCustomSubstVarsOrSubstVarStringFunctions
(strChosenRules))
         Dim listChosenRules As List(Of String) =
strChosenRules.Split(",").Select(Function(x) x.Trim).ToList()
         For Each chosenRule In listChosenRules
            Dim params As New Dictionary(Of String, String)
            BRApi.Utilities.StartDataMgmtSequence(si, chosenRule,
params) ' task gets executed in background
         Next
      Else
         selectionChangedTaskResult.IsOK = False
         selectionChangedTaskResult.ShowMessageBox = True
         selectionChangedTaskResult.Message = "Select a rule to
execute."
      End If
      selectionChangedTaskResult.IsOK = True
      selectionChangedTaskResult.ShowMessageBox = True
      selectionChangedTaskResult.Message = "Calculation started" &
vbCrLf & "Please check the status in ""Task Activity"""

      Return selectionChangedTaskResult
   Catch ex As Exception
      Throw ErrorHandler.LogWrite(si, New XFException(si, ex))
   End Try
End Function
```

Dialog Dashboard

When a Planner clicks on the Show Associated Rules button, the below Dashboard with the List Box and execution button is shown.

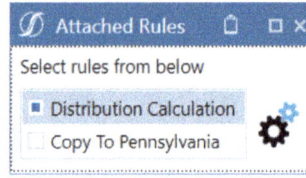

Figure 5.22

This Dashboard is created, as shown below.

Dashboard Properties	Dashboard Components
⊟ General (Dashboard)	
Name	1_Choose_Rules_Content_BKS
Description	
Page Caption	
Dashboard Group	Run on Save
⊟ Formatting	
Layout Type	Grid
Is Initially Visible If Embedded	True
Display Format	
⊟ Literal Parameter Values	
Name Value Pairs (e.g., Param1=Value1, ...)	
⊟ Action (Primary Dashboard Only)	
Server Task	
Load Dashboard Server Task	No Task
Load Dashboard Server Task Arguments	
⊟ Grid Layout Type	
Number Of Rows	1
Number Of Columns	2
Row 1	
Row 1 Type	Component
Row 1 Height (e.g., 150, *, 2*, Auto)	*
Column 1	
Column 1 Type	Component
Column 1 Width (e.g., 150, *, 2*, Auto)	Auto
Column 2	
Column 2 Type	Component
Column 2 Width	50

Figure 5.23

The header Dashboard, Cube View Dashboard, and main Dashboard follow the same structure as the previous example.

Here is how it looks when everything is done.

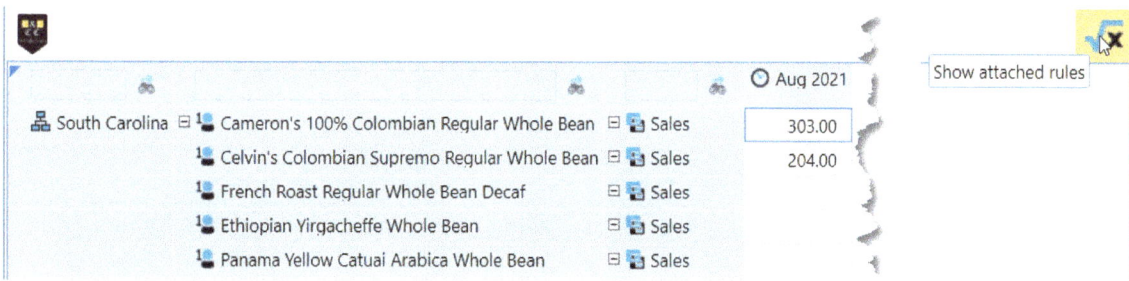

Figure 5.24

Dashboard Design Mode

The Dashboard Design Mode can be used to fine-tune any Components (spacing, margins, etc.).

To launch a Dashboard in Design mode, select the required Dashboard and set it as the Default Dashboard (this applies to the Design Mode only).

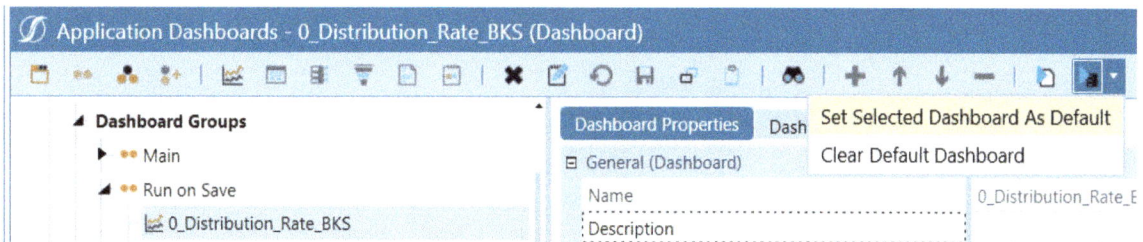

Figure 5.25

Once the Dashboard is set as default, launch the Design Mode using the *database + media play* icon.

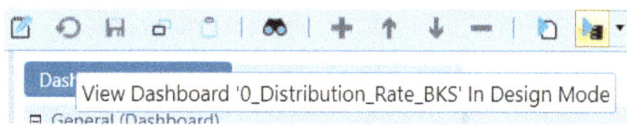

Figure 5.26

This launches the Dashboard in Design Mode. It is extremely useful because it shows the Components with a red triangle in the top corner. Selecting each Component within the design mode will navigate to the Dashboard it is a part of.

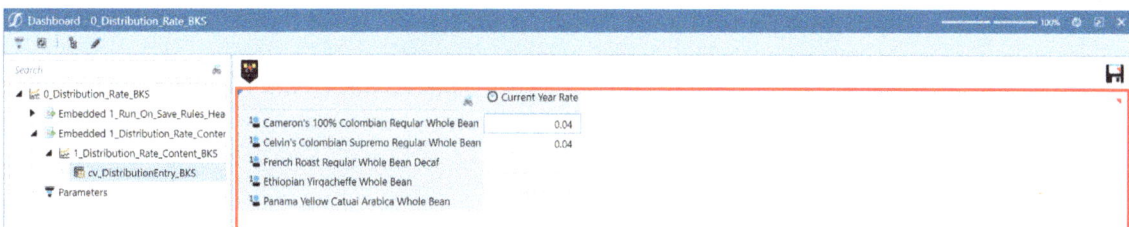

Figure 5.27

Parameters (if any) within the Dashboard can be viewed in this way, alongside their runtime values. Hovering on a parameter will show the value as a tooltip.

Form Profile

Presenting this information to the Planner for data entry can be done in multiple ways.

1. A Workspace Workflow Profile

2. A Forms Workflow Profile

In this example, C&CCC's Planners have multiple data entry Cube Views; hence, a **Forms Workflow Profile** option is needed. To do this, a Form Template with Form Type as Dashboard is created and added to a template profile.

While there are multiple Form Types (Cube View, Dashboard, and Spreadsheet), your author prefers to use the Dashboard Type when multiple Forms, or dependent Combo boxes (a Combo box driving another Combo box), or buttons need to be used in a Form.

This example uses a tabbed Dashboard to combine both examples as a single Dashboard.

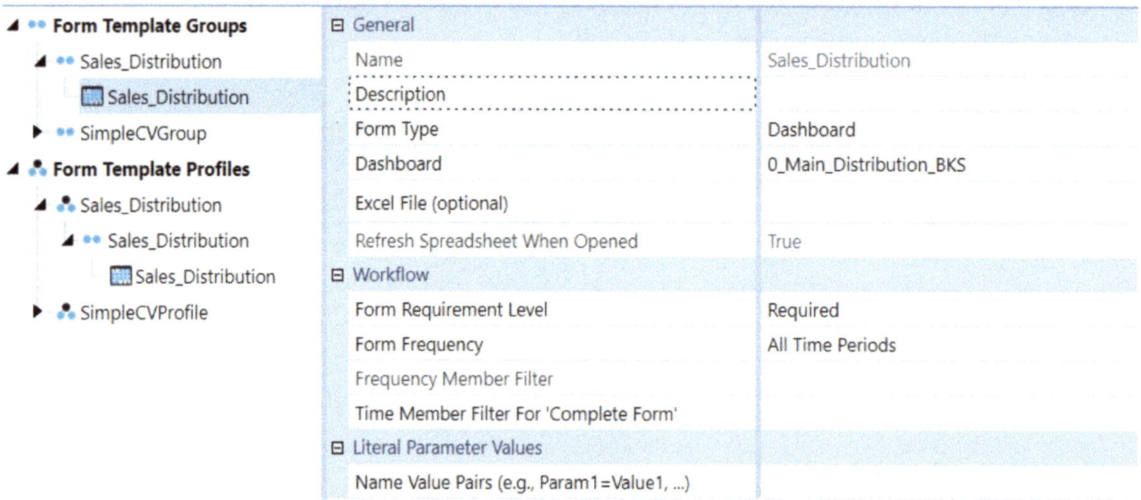

Figure 5.28

This profile is added as the Input Forms Profile Name in the Forms Workflow Child.

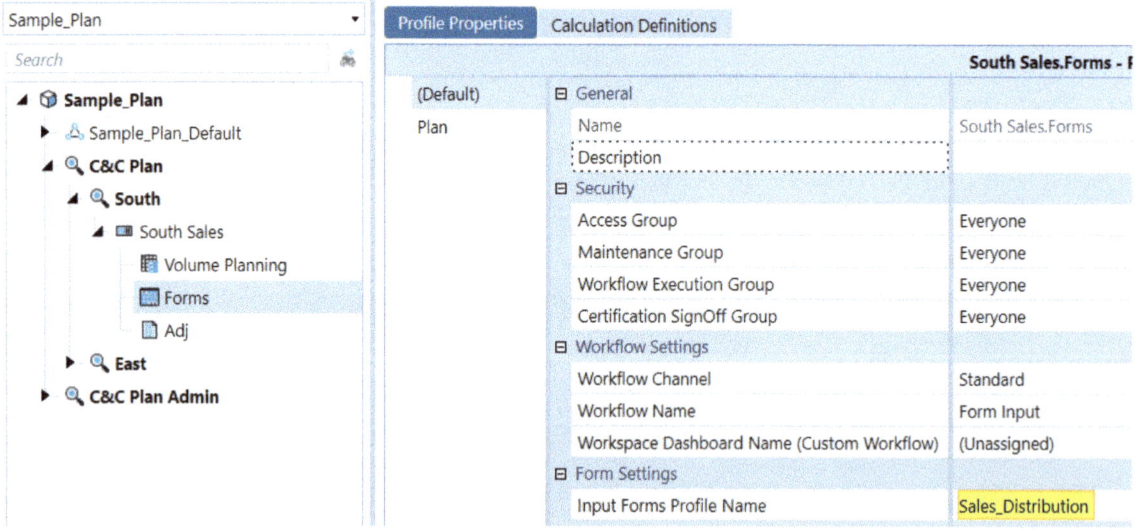

Figure 5.29

It will manifest in the Workflow as below:

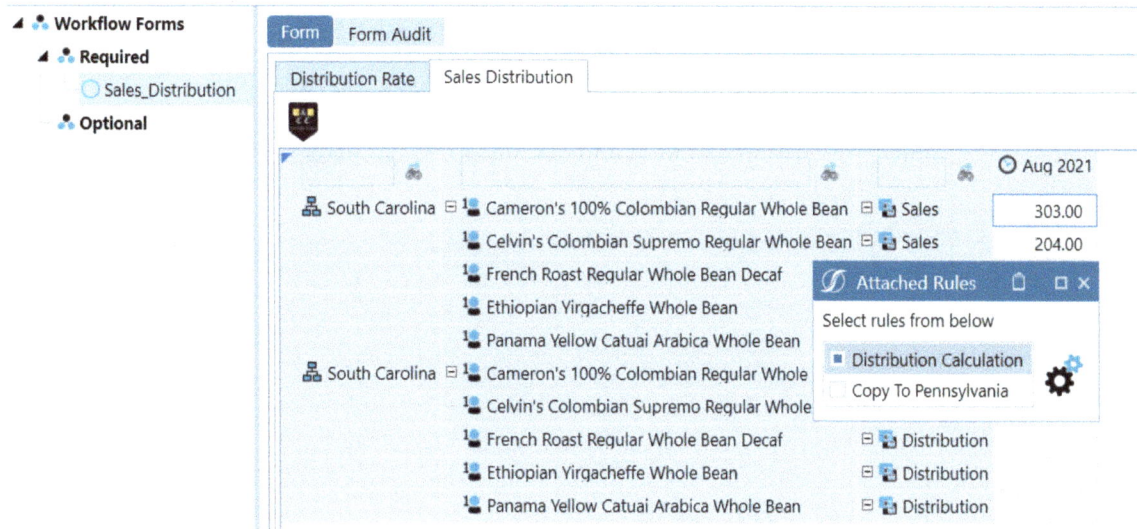

Figure 5.30

Planners can now select multiple rules and execute them.

Note: Keep in mind that a refresh on a tabbed Report refreshes the whole Dashboard, not just the active Cube View. Once the refresh operation is complete, it will return to the first Cube View's tab. To avoid this, buttons could appear (think of this as mimicking the tabbed Dashboard interface, but with a custom showing and hiding of controls) as tabs and refresh just the active Report. Some utilities like the MindStream Metadata Manager, which can be used to update Metadata (manually or automatically) from flat files and external relational tables, use this Method versus the regular tabbed Method.

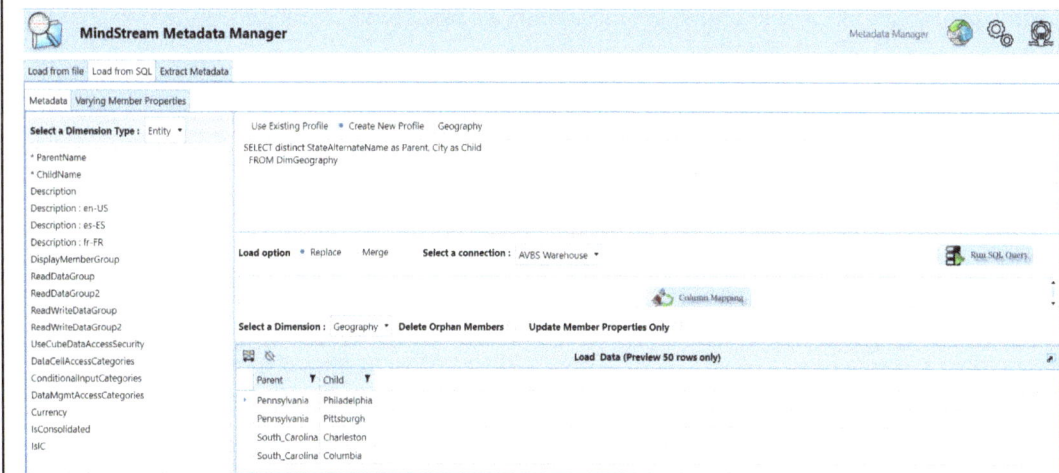

Figure 5.31

Performing Faster Data Exports from OneStream for External Consumption

Fast Data Exports that extract data from OneStream, through parallelism and in-memory processing, were introduced in the 5.3 release.

An in-memory Data Table is generated as a result of an FDX export and can be easily transformed if needed. This flexibility, when combined with parallelism, makes FDX export triumph over the regular *Export Data* Data Management sequences.

FDX APIs can extract data using:

1. Cube Views
2. Data Units
3. Stage Workflow Imports
4. External sources

When Should I Use FDX APIs?

OneStream has myriad data export use cases. The following list contains examples but is by no means exhaustive:

1. Exporting OneStream data (and metadata) for external systems
2. Internal OneStream data transfers (Planning Cubes with different Departments as Entity Dimensions moving data to Corporate Cubes with real Entity Dimensions)
3. Exporting dynamically-calculated results
4. Extracting data from external systems

Who, after all, eschews better performance?

Which FDX APIs Should I Use?

C&CCC's Planners need to send data from OneStream to external systems for invoicing purposes. They also need the information from Volume Sales Planning (Thing Planning) and Cube data to perform a reconciliation process outside OneStream, using external systems.

To extract Cube data, either of the following approaches can be used. Their selection is driven by how external systems handle Time Dimensions.

FDXExecuteDataUnit or FDXExecuteDataUnitTimePivot

FDXExecuteDataUnit

FDX Data Unit extract API Methods do what they say: extract data from a OneStream Cube using its Data Units.

The Time Pivot API (`FDXExecuteDataUnitTimePivot`) Method acts like `FDXExecuteDataUnit` with the difference that Time will appear as columns.

To illustrate, this use case will extract Sales data from the Cube so that it can be sent to an external relational table via an Extender Rule.

C&CCC's database team set up a table for the Cube data that looks like the following.

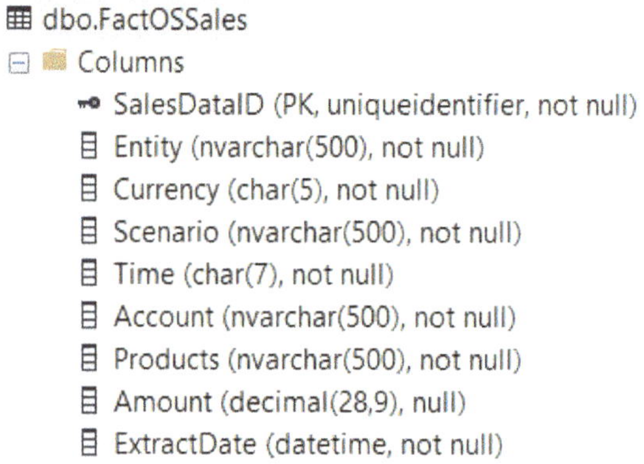

```
⊞ dbo.FactOSSales
⊟ 🗀 Columns
      ⇢● SalesDataID (PK, uniqueidentifier, not null)
      ⊟ Entity (nvarchar(500), not null)
      ⊟ Currency (char(5), not null)
      ⊟ Scenario (nvarchar(500), not null)
      ⊟ Time (char(7), not null)
      ⊟ Account (nvarchar(500), not null)
      ⊟ Products (nvarchar(500), not null)
      ⊟ Amount (decimal(28,9), null)
      ⊟ ExtractDate (datetime, not null)
```

Figure 5.32

```
Dim strPlanYear As String =
BRApi.Dashboards.Parameters.GetLiteralParameterValue(si, False,
"paramstrPlanYear")
Dim lstOriginBase As List(Of String) =
BRApi.Finance.Metadata.GetMembersUsingFilter(si, "Origin",
"O#Top.Base", True, Nothing, Nothing).Select(Function(x)
x.Member.Name).ToList()
Dim dt As datatable = BRApi.Import.Data.FdxExecuteDataUnit(si,
"Sample", "E#Root.Base", "Local", ScenarioTypeId.Plan, "S#Plan", "T#"
& strPlanYear & ".Months", "Periodic", True, "Account='Sales' AND
Flow='Endbal_Input' AND " & SqlStringHelper.CreateInClause("Origin",
lstOriginBase, True, True), 8, False)
```

The Extender Rule snippet above shows that `FDXExecuteDataUnit` can be used to retrieve data from the Sample Cube using a Member selection syntax similar to defining a data buffer with `api.Data.GetDataBufferUsingFormula`.

Note: For a Range Scenario like the one below...

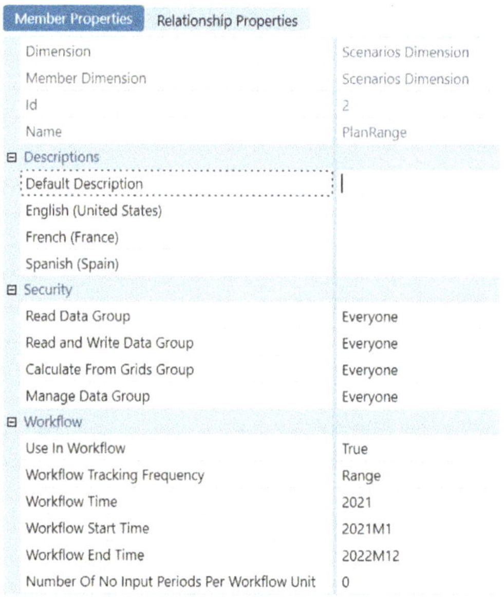

Figure 5.33

...use the Start Time and End Time properties to generate the range of periods for this Scenario as follows.

```
Dim intStartPeriod As Integer =
BRApi.Finance.Scenario.GetWorkflowStartTime(si,
BRApi.Finance.Metadata.GetMember(si, DimTypeId.Scenario,
"PlanRange").Member.MemberId)

Dim intEndPeriod As Integer =
BRApi.Finance.Scenario.GetWorkflowEndTime(si,
BRApi.Finance.Metadata.GetMember(si, DimTypeId.Scenario,
"PlanRange").Member.MemberId)

''' Select(Function(x) TimeDimHelper.GetNameFromId(x) is LINQ

''' GetIdsInRange function will give you a list of time members
from start month to the end month

Dim lstPlanPeriods As List(Of String) =
TimeDimHelper.GetIdsInRange(intStartPeriod,
intEndPeriod).Select(Function(x)
TimeDimHelper.GetNameFromId(x)).toList()
```

As the Data Unit extraction Method can only work with Base Members, Parent Members cannot be used in the filter. In order to get all the Origin Members (or with any other Dimension), use GetMembersUsingFilter to get all Base Members.

BRApi.Import.Data.FdxExecuteDataUnit uses the following parameters:

1. SessionInfo
2. Cube Name
3. Entity Filter
4. Consolidation Name
5. Scenario Type ID
6. Scenario Filter
7. Time Filter
8. View Name
9. Suppress No Data – True/False
10. Filter – Use SQL LIKE filters on the DataTable on the Dimension that is not part of the Data Unit
11. Parallel Query Count – an integer for parallel threads (cannot exceed 128)
12. Log FDX Statistics – True/False

When data is extracted using FdxExecuteDataUnit, the following columns are generated.

```
Cube,Entity,Parent,Cons,Scenario,Time,View,Account,Flow,Origin,IC,UD1,
UD2,UD3,UD4,UD5,UD6,UD7,UD8,Amount
```

Before this data can be moved to the Data Warehouse, the scope and the nature of the data must be changed.

Renaming, Removing, and Adding Columns to a DataTable

Field names must match for a seamless import to the FactOSSales table.

Rename Cons and UD1 columns to Currency and Products, respectively.

```
dt.Columns("Cons").ColumnName = "Currency"
dt.Columns("UD1").ColumnName = "Products"
```

After the rename, remove the columns that C&CCC's Data Warehouse team does not need.

```
dt.Columns.Remove("Cube")
dt.Columns.Remove("Parent")
dt.Columns.Remove("View")
dt.Columns.Remove("Flow")
dt.Columns.Remove("Origin")
dt.Columns.Remove("IC")
```

Remove the UDs that are not used using a For loop.

```
For i As Integer = 2 To 8
    dt.Columns.Remove("UD" & i)
Next
```

C&CCC's FactOSSales table leads with a UID field. Add a new column with Type GUID and make it the first column of the DataTable.

A new column for the extract date is added as the last column of the DataTable.

```
dt.Columns.Add("SalesDataID", GetType(Guid)).SetOrdinal(0)
dt.Columns.Add("ExtractDate")
```

Running Parallel Operations

We are going to add the Sales Data ID and Extract Time in parallel for efficiency.

To use parallel operations, Threading.Tasks Namespace is imported to the Business Rule, as shown below.

```
1  Imports System
2  Imports System.Data
3  Imports System.Data.Common
4  Imports System.IO
5  Imports System.Collections.Generic
6  Imports System.Globalization
7  Imports System.Linq
8  Imports Microsoft.VisualBasic
9  Imports System.Windows.Forms
10 Imports OneStream.Shared.Common
11 Imports OneStream.Shared.Wcf
12 Imports OneStream.Shared.Engine
13 Imports OneStream.Shared.Database
14 Imports OneStream.Stage.Engine
15 Imports OneStream.Stage.Database
16 Imports OneStream.Finance.Engine
17 Imports OneStream.Finance.Database
18 Imports System.Threading.Tasks
19
20 Namespace OneStream.BusinessRule.Extender.CCCC_ThingPlanning_Extracts
```

Figure 5.34

```
Dim currentTime As datetime = Date.Now
dt.Columns("SalesDataID").ReadOnly = False
dt.Columns("ExtractDate").ReadOnly = False
Parallel.ForEach(dt.AsEnumerable(), Function(x)
    x.BeginEdit
    x("SalesDataID") = Guid.NewGuid
    x("ExtractDate") = currentTime
    x.EndEdit
End Function)

BRApi.Database.SaveCustomDataTable(si, "AVBS Warehouse",
"FactOSSales", dt, True)
```

205

The code performs the following:

1. The current date and time are captured.

2. `SalesDataID` and `ExtractDate` columns are set as writable.

3. `SalesDataID` and `ExtractDate` columns are edited in parallel.

The resulting DataTable is then saved to the external database.

FDXExecuteDataUnitTimePivot

If the target table has Time Members defined as columns, use the TimePivot variation of DataUnit FDX.

`FdxExecuteDataUnitTimePivot` has a `useGenericTimeColNames` property that adds time intelligence to the data headers in the form of T*YYYYMmm* or a generic Time1, Time2, Time*n* value.

If `useGenericTimeColNames` is set to `False`,

```
Dim dt As datatable =
BRApi.Import.Data.FdxExecuteDataUnitTimePivot(si, "Sample",
"E#Root.Base", "Local", ScenarioTypeId.Plan, "S#Plan", "T#" &
strPlanYear & ".Months", "Periodic", True, False, "Account='Sales' AND
Flow='Endbal_Input' AND " & SqlStringHelper.CreateInClause("Origin",
originBase, True, True), 8, False)
```

the following data is generated:

```
Cube,Entity,Parent,Cons,Scenario,View,Account,Flow,Origin,IC,UD1,UD2,U
D3,UD4,UD5,UD6,UD7,UD8,T2021M1,T2021M2,T2021M3,T2021M4,T2021M5,T2021M6
,T2021M7,T2021M8,T2021M9,T2021M10,T2021M11,T2021M12
Sample,South_Carolina,,USD,Plan,Periodic,Sales,EndBal_Input,Forms,None
,10_010,None,None,None,None,None,None,None,0,0,0,0,0,0,0,303.000000000
,0.000000000,0.000000000,0.000000000,0.000000000
Sample,South_Carolina,,USD,Plan,Periodic,Sales,EndBal_Input,Forms,None
,10_020,None,None,None,None,None,None,None,0,0,0,0,0,0,0,204.000000000
,0.000000000,0.000000000,0.000000000,0.000000000
Sample,South_Carolina,,USD,Plan,Periodic,Sales,EndBal_Input,Import,Non
e,10_020,None,None,None,None,None,None,None,38.168750000,38.168750000,
38.168750000,38.168750000,38.168750000,38.168750000,38.168750000,38.16
8750000,38.168750000,38.168750000,38.168750000,38.168750000
```

If `useGenericTimeColNames` is set to `True`,

```
Dim dt As datatable =
BRApi.Import.Data.FdxExecuteDataUnitTimePivot(si, "Sample",
"E#Root.Base", "Local", ScenarioTypeId.Plan, "S#Plan", "T#" &
strPlanYear & ".Months", "Periodic", True, True, "Account='Sales' AND
Flow='Endbal_Input' AND " & SqlStringHelper.CreateInClause("Origin",
originBase, True, True), 8, False)
```

the following data is generated:

```
Cube,Entity,Parent,Cons,Scenario,View,Account,Flow,Origin,IC,UD1,UD2,U
D3,UD4,UD5,UD6,UD7,UD8,Time1,Time2,Time3,Time4,Time5,Time6,Time7,Time8
,Time9,Time10,Time11,Time12
Sample,South_Carolina,,USD,Plan,Periodic,Sales,EndBal_Input,Forms,None
,10_010,None,None,None,None,None,None,None,0,0,0,0,0,0,0,303.000000000
,0.000000000,0.000000000,0.000000000,0.000000000
Sample,South_Carolina,,USD,Plan,Periodic,Sales,EndBal_Input,Forms,None
,10_020,None,None,None,None,None,None,None,0,0,0,0,0,0,0,204.000000000
,0.000000000,0.000000000,0.000000000,0.000000000
Sample,South_Carolina,,USD,Plan,Periodic,Sales,EndBal_Input,Import,Non
e,10_020,None,None,None,None,None,None,None,38.168750000,38.168750000,
```

```
38.168750000,38.168750000,38.168750000,38.168750000,38.168750000,38.16
8750000,38.168750000,38.168750000,38.168750000,38.168750000
```

FDXExecuteCubeView

Cube Views can be used to extract data from OneStream, and a Cube View comes in handy for the following Scenarios:

1. Extract Parent-level information (for Dimensions other than Entity)

2. Export dynamically-calculated Members

3. Export cell text information (only the ones attached to a View Member get exported)

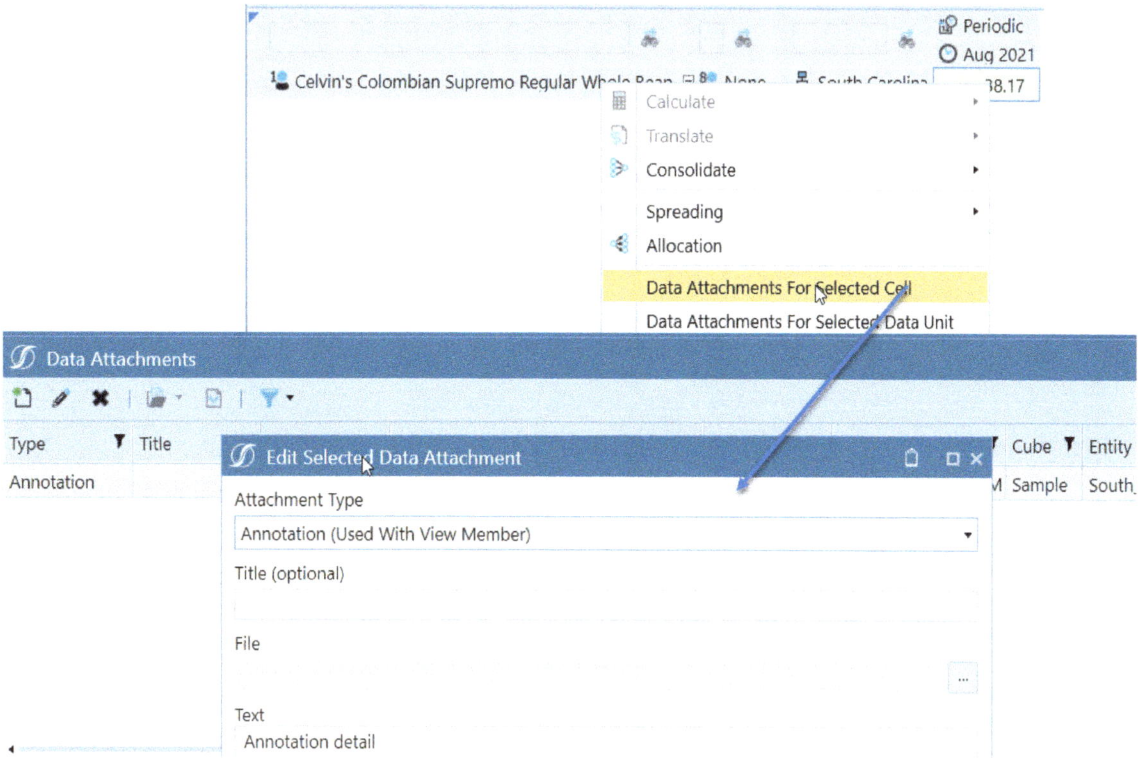

Figure 5.35

```
Dim dt As DataTable = BRApi.Import.Data.FdxExecuteCubeView(si, "Sales
Rep", "Geography", "", "Scenarios", "", "", Nothing, True, False, "",
8, False)
```

We can extract data using a Cube View by providing the following parameters.

1. SessionInfo

2. Cube View name

3. Entity Dimension Name – will use the Cube View values if nothing is provided

4. Entity Filter – will use the Cube View values if nothing is provided

5. Scenario Dimension Name – will use the Cube View values if nothing is provided

6. Scenario Filter – will use the Cube View values if nothing is provided

7. Time Member Filter – will use the Cube View values if nothing is provided

8. A Name Value parameter object – this can be used if additional parameters are used in the Cube View

9. Include Text columns – True/False (can be used to show the Cell-level annotation)

10. Use Standard Fact Table fields – True/False (can be used to use the Dimension Names to be in the columns)

11. Filter – Use SQL `LIKE` filters on the DataTable on the Dimension that is not part of the Data Unit

12. Parallel Query Count – An integer for parallel threads (cannot exceed 128)

13. Log FDX Statistics – True/False

What a Difference Switches and Levers Make

These seemingly minor Methods and properties can have a disproportionate effect on usefulness. Keep them in mind when going for that extra bit of functionality.

Extract Cell Text

Extract the cell text by using the `includeCellTextCols` option.

```
Dim dt As DataTable = BRApi.Import.Data.FdxExecuteCubeView(si, "Sales
Info", "", "", "", "", "", Nothing, True, True, "", 8, False)
```

This code snippet directs the function to extract the cell text and use the standard fact tables.

```
Cube,Entity,Parent,Cons,Scenario,Time,View,Account,Flow,Origin,IC,UD1,
UD2,UD3,UD4,UD5,UD6,UD7,UD8,RowHdr0ParentName,V2021M8,Col0Annotation,C
ol0Assumptions,Col0AuditComment,Col0Footnote,Col0VarianceExplanation
Sample,Pennsylvania,,Local,Actual,2021M8,Periodic,Sales,EndBal_Input,I
mport,None,10_010,None,None,None,None,None,None,None,East,120.00000000
0,Annotation detail,,,,
Sample,Pennsylvania,,Local,Actual,2021M8,Periodic,Sales,EndBal_Input,I
mport,None,10_020,None,None,None,None,None,None,None,East,93.000000000
,,,,,
Sample,South_Carolina,,Local,Actual,2021M8,Periodic,Sales,EndBal_Input
,Import,None,10_020,None,None,None,None,None,None,None,South,803.00000
0000,,,,,
```

Cube	Entity	Pare...	o	Time	V...		UD1	UD...	.8	RowHdr0ParentName	V2021M8	Col0Annotation
Sample	Pennsylvania		..l	2021M8	Pe	ie	10_010	Non	n	East	120.000000000	Annotation detail
Sample	Pennsylvania		.	2021M8	Pe	ne	10_020	Non...	une	East	93.000000000	
Sample	South_Carolina		.	2021M8		ie	10_020	Nc	e	South	803.000000000	

Figure 5.36

Since there was an annotation added to the View Member, the cell text got extracted.

Difference Between Standard Fact Columns and Cube View Columns

When the standard fact column (10th parameter) is not used, the column headers are different and there are extra columns.

```
PovCubeName,Pov00EntityName,Pov01ConsolidationName,Pov02ScenarioName,P
ov03TimeName,Pov04ViewName,Pov05AccountName,Pov06FlowName,Pov07OriginN
ame,Pov08ICName,Pov09UD1Name,Pov10UD2Name,Pov11UD3Name,Pov12UD4Name,Po
v13UD5Name,Pov14UD6Name,Pov15UD7Name,Pov16UD8Name,RowHdr0_Entity,RowHd
r0ParentName,RowHdr1_UD1,RowHdr2_UD8,ColVal0_2021M8,Col0Annotation,Col
0Assumptions,Col0AuditComment,Col0Footnote,Col0VarianceExplanation
Sample,Total_Geography,Local,Actual,2021M8,Periodic,Sales,EndBal_Input
,Import,None,None,None,None,None,None,None,None,None,Pennsylvania,East
,10_010,None,120.000000000,Annotation detail,,,,
Sample,Total_Geography,Local,Actual,2021M8,Periodic,Sales,EndBal_Input
,Import,None,None,None,None,None,None,None,None,None,Pennsylvania,East
,10_020,None,93.000000000,,,,,
```

```
Sample,Total_Geography,Local,Actual,2021M8,Periodic,Sales,EndBal_Input
,Import,None,None,None,None,None,None,None,None,South_Carolina,So
uth,10_020,None,803.000000000,,,,,
```

Entity, Scenario and Time Member Filters

Entity, Scenario, and Time Member Filters can be used to extract data from a Cube View.

However, use caution when using these Member Filters. If these Members are already mentioned in the Cube View, passing a different set will *not* override what is already in the Cube View.

Let us look at what happens using the Cube View from the previous example.

Using the sample Cube View, here are the following Dimension selections in the Row definitions.

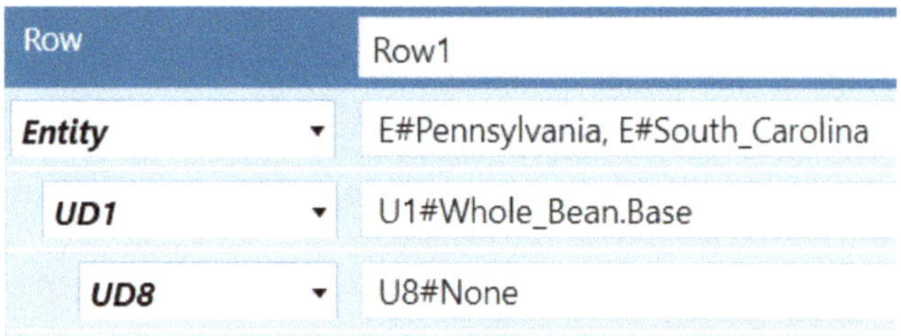

Row	Row1
Entity ▾	E#Pennsylvania, E#South_Carolina
UD1 ▾	U1#Whole_Bean.Base
UD8 ▾	U8#None

Figure 5.37

What happens if FdxExecuteCubeView is executed to extract the Base Members of East?

```
Dim dt As DataTable = BRApi.Import.Data.FdxExecuteCubeView(si, "Sales
Info", "Geography", "E#East.base", "", "", "", Nothing, True, True,
"", 8, False)
```

When the Rule runs, the Cube View gets called four times (four Base Members for East).

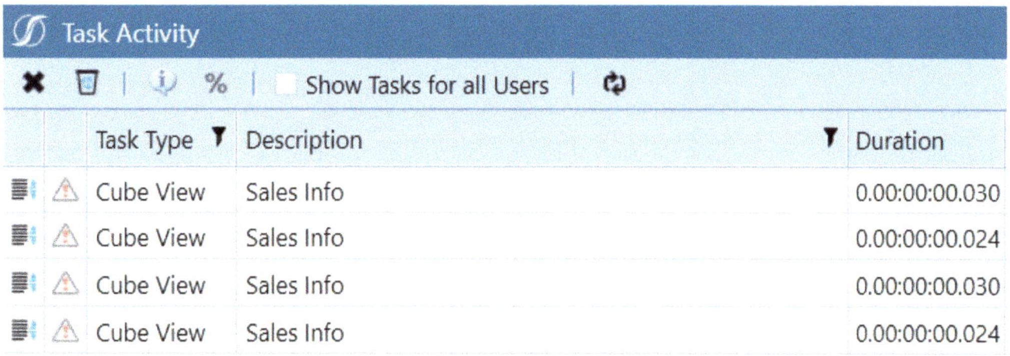

	Task Type ▼	Description		Duration
▤ ⚠	Cube View	Sales Info		0.00:00:00.030
▤ ⚠	Cube View	Sales Info		0.00:00:00.024
▤ ⚠	Cube View	Sales Info		0.00:00:00.030
▤ ⚠	Cube View	Sales Info		0.00:00:00.024

Task Activity — Show Tasks for all Users

Figure 5.38

Did it work?

The code extracts the data for Pennsylvania and South Carolina four times, replicating the data.

```
Cube,Entity,Parent,Cons,Scenario,Time,View,Account,Flow,Origin,IC,UD1,
UD2,UD3,UD4,UD5,UD6,UD7,UD8,RowHdr0ParentName,VPeriodic,Col0Annotation
,Col0Assumptions,Col0AuditComment,Col0Footnote,Col0VarianceExplanation
Sample,Pennsylvania,,Local,Actual,2021M8,Periodic,Sales,EndBal_Input,I
mport,None,10_010,None,None,None,None,None,None,None,East,120.00000000
0,,,,,
Sample,Pennsylvania,,Local,Actual,2021M8,Periodic,Sales,EndBal_Input,I
mport,None,10_020,None,None,None,None,None,None,None,East,93.000000000
,,,,,
```

```
Sample,South_Carolina,,Local,Actual,2021M8,Periodic,Sales,EndBal_Input
,Import,None,10_020,None,None,None,None,None,None,None,South,803.00000
0000,,,,,
Sample,Pennsylvania,,Local,Actual,2021M8,Periodic,Sales,EndBal_Input,I
mport,None,10_010,None,None,None,None,None,None,None,East,120.00000000
0,,,,,
Sample,Pennsylvania,,Local,Actual,2021M8,Periodic,Sales,EndBal_Input,I
mport,None,10_020,None,None,None,None,None,None,None,East,93.000000000
,,,,,
Sample,South_Carolina,,Local,Actual,2021M8,Periodic,Sales,EndBal_Input
,Import,None,10_020,None,None,None,None,None,None,None,South,803.00000
0000,,,,,
Sample,Pennsylvania,,Local,Actual,2021M8,Periodic,Sales,EndBal_Input,I
mport,None,10_010,None,None,None,None,None,None,None,East,120.00000000
0,,,,,
Sample,Pennsylvania,,Local,Actual,2021M8,Periodic,Sales,EndBal_Input,I
mport,None,10_020,None,None,None,None,None,None,None,East,93.000000000
,,,,,
Sample,South_Carolina,,Local,Actual,2021M8,Periodic,Sales,EndBal_Input
,Import,None,10_020,None,None,None,None,None,None,None,South,803.00000
0000,,,,,
Sample,Pennsylvania,,Local,Actual,2021M8,Periodic,Sales,EndBal_Input,I
mport,None,10_010,None,None,None,None,None,None,None,East,120.00000000
0,,,,,
Sample,Pennsylvania,,Local,Actual,2021M8,Periodic,Sales,EndBal_Input,I
mport,None,10_020,None,None,None,None,None,None,None,East,93.000000000
,,,,,
Sample,South_Carolina,,Local,Actual,2021M8,Periodic,Sales,EndBal_Input
,Import,None,10_020,None,None,None,None,None,None,None,South,803.00000
0000,,,,,
```

Entity, Scenario, and Time are part of the Data Unit, and in this case, it is no different. If two different Scenarios are passed for the override, it will run the Cube View eight times (four Entities and two Scenarios), again with redundant data.

So, when and how then should this override function be used?

To make use of these three overrides, employ the following parameters.

1. FDXEntity

2. FDXScenario

3. FDXTime

Add these parameters to the POV (Member expansion is not supported), as shown below.

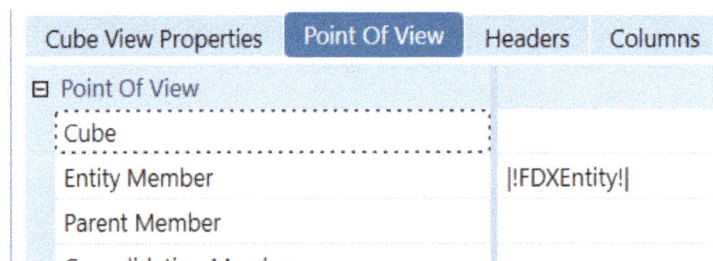

Figure 5.39

```
Dim dt As DataTable = BRApi.Import.Data.FdxExecuteCubeView(si, "Sales
Info", "Geography", "E#South_Carolina", "", "", "", Nothing, True,
True, "", 8, False)
```

Running that code results in just one Entity.

```
Cube,Entity,Parent,Cons,Scenario,Time,View,Account,Flow,Origin,IC,UD1,
UD2,UD3,UD4,UD5,UD6,UD7,UD8,RowHdr0ParentName,VPeriodic,Col0Annotation
,Col0Assumptions,Col0AuditComment,Col0Footnote,Col0VarianceExplanation
Sample,South_Carolina,,Local,Actual,2021M8,Periodic,Sales,EndBal_Input
,Import,None,10_020,None,None,None,None,None,None,None,South,803.00000
0000,,,,,
```

If a Member expansion function is passed, the Cube View will be queried four times.

```
Dim dt As DataTable = BRApi.Import.Data.FdxExecuteCubeView(si, "Sales
Info", "Geography", "E#East.base", "", "", "", Nothing, True, True,
"", 8, False)
```

Only the Cube POV's Entity will be picked up, despite the Member expansion.

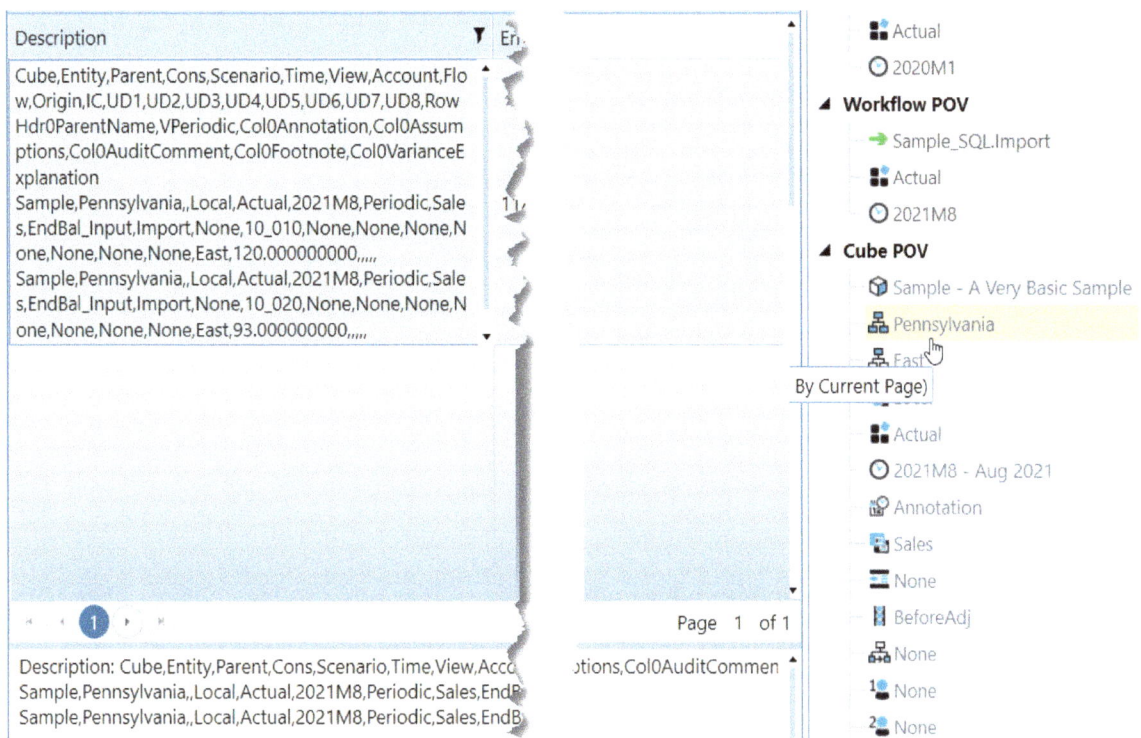

Figure 5.40

Entity can be overridden to support Member expansion using the `NameValueFormatBuilder` object. To do this, define a parameter in the Cube View.

Row	Row1
UD1 ▾	|!MyProductsParam!|
UD8 ▾	U8#None
Entity ▾	|!MyEntityParam!|

Figure 5.41

This example shows two parameters defined in the Cube View: one for UD1 and the other for Entity.

```
Dim nvb As New NameValueFormatBuilder()
nvb.NameValuePairs.Add("MyEntityParam", "E#Total_Geography.base")
nvb.NameValuePairs.Add("MyProductsParam", "U1#Total_Products.base")
Dim dt As DataTable = BRApi.Import.Data.FdxExecuteCubeView(si, "Sales
Info", "Geography", "", "", "", "", nvb, True, True, "", 8, False)
)
```

By defining a Name Value Pair format builder, the Entity and UD1 parameter used in the Cube View are passed and are then expanded to contain all of the Members in E#Total_Geography and U1#Total_Products.

The NameValueFormatBuilder object can then be passed as the eighth parameter to the function, executing the Cube View read just once, putting the expanded results into the DataTable.

Multiple Column Cube Views

The FDXExecuteCubeView function does not easily support multiple column Cube Views.

If the Cube View used in the previous examples is changed to have a dynamic Member expansion that returns multiple columns:

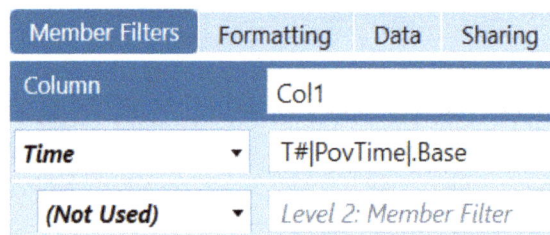

Figure 5.42

As expected, the Data Explorer will show you all the columns based on your POV (2021Q3).

Figure 5.43

And what happens when FDXExecuteCubeView is executed? Data from the correct corresponding months are extracted. However, the Time field contains 2021Q3, which is wrong, because the data values are monthly.

```
Cube,Entity,Parent,Cons,Scenario,Time,View,Account,Flow,Origin,IC,UD1,
UD2,UD3,UD4,UD5,UD6,UD7,UD8,RowHdr2ParentName,V2021M7,Col0Annotation,C
ol0Assumptions,Col0AuditComment,Col0Footnote,Col0VarianceExplanation,V
2021M8,Col1Annotation,Col1Assumptions,Col1AuditComment,Col1Footnote,Co
l1VarianceExplanation,V2021M9,Col2Annotation,Col2Assumptions,Col2Audit
Comment,Col2Footnote,Col2VarianceExplanation
Sample,Pennsylvania,,Local,Actual,2021Q3,Periodic,Sales,EndBal_Input,I
mport,None,10_010,None,None,None,None,None,None,None,East,0.000000000,
,,,,,120.000000000,Annotation detail,,,,,,0.000000000,,,,,
```

```
Sample,Pennsylvania,,Local,Actual,2021Q3,Periodic,Sales,EndBal_Input,I
mport,None,10_020,None,None,None,None,None,None,None,East,0.000000000,
,,,,,93.000000000,,,,,,0.000000000,,,,,
Sample,South_Carolina,,Local,Actual,2021Q3,Periodic,Sales,EndBal_Input
,Import,None,10_020,None,None,None,None,None,None,South,0.0000000
00,,,,,,803.000000000,,,,,,0.000000000,,,,,
```

Entity	Parent	Cons	Scenario	Time
Pennsylvania		Local	Actual	2021Q3
Pennsylvania		Local	Actual	2021Q3
South_Carolina		Local	Actual	2021Q3

Figure 5.44

The above table's Time field shows the POV's value (2021Q3). You will have to use the value columns (starting with a V) to figure out what the Time is.

V2021M7	Col0Annot	Col0Assun	Col0Audit(	Col0Footn	Col0Variar	V2021M8	Col1Annot	Col1Assun	Col1Audit(	Col1Footn	Col1Variar	V2021M9
0						120	Annotation detail					0
0						93						0
0						803						0

Figure 5.45

If multiple Dimensions are used in the columns, the Rule will fail as it is now trying to add three columns called VPeriodic to the DataTable.

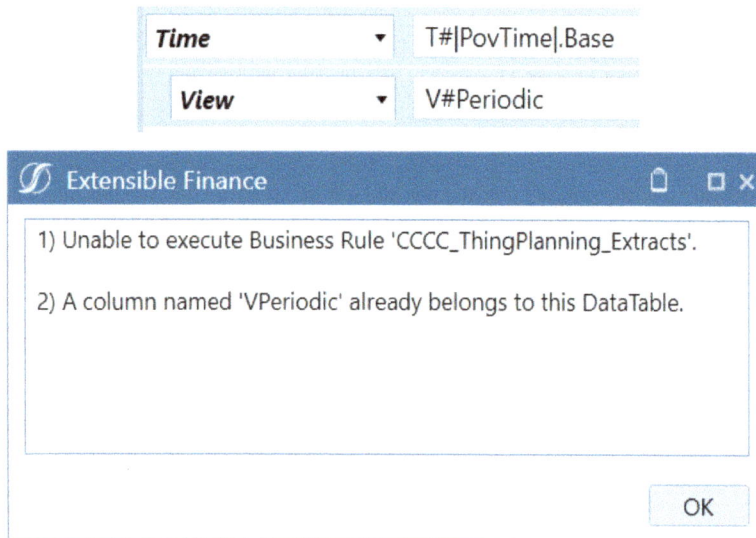

Time	▼	T#|PovTime|.Base
View	▼	V#Periodic

Extensible Finance

1) Unable to execute Business Rule 'CCCC_ThingPlanning_Extracts'.

2) A column named 'VPeriodic' already belongs to this DataTable.

OK

Figure 5.46

To get around this issue, Time could be moved to the second column Dimension definition. Doing so will result in View being picked up from the POV.

Entity	Parent	Cons	Scenario	Time	View
Pennsylvania		Local	Actual	2021Q3	**Annotation**
Pennsylvania		Local	Actual	2021Q3	**Annotation**
South_Carolina		Local	Actual	2021Q3	**Annotation**

Figure 5.47

The values columns will not even show what View was used to pull this Cube View. Whichever View Dimension was used for which column information is now lost.

V2021M7	Col0Annot	Col0Assum	Col0Audit(	Col0Footn	Col0Variar	V2021M8	Col1Annot	Col1Assum	Col1Audit(	Col1Footn	Col1Variar	V2021M9
0						120	Annotation detail					0
0						93						0
0						803						0

Figure 5.48

> **Note:** Do not use multiple column (a column with Member function included) Cube Views to extract data.

FDXExecuteStageTargetTimePivot

Exporting Stage Data

In this use case, Volume Sales information (Thing Planning) now needs to be extracted.

This can be done in two ways:

1. Use data in Stage
2. Directly pull from the Plan tables

Suppose all the required details (from the Plan table) were used in the Connector Rule that loads Thing Planning data to the Cube. If so, use FDXExecuteStageTargetTimePivot. This Method will require the following parameters to pull the data that went to the Cube from the Stage.

1. Parent Workflow Profile name (If there are multiple profiles under the Parent, use a filter)
2. Scenario Name
3. Start Time
4. End Time
5. If there are no attributes assigned in the data source, use False for the includeAttributes parameter
6. Use generic Time columns – True/False
7. Filter – Use SQL LIKE filters on the DataTable for the Dimensions that are not part of the Data Unit
8. Parallel Query Count – An integer for parallel threads (cannot exceed 128)
9. Log FDX Statistics – True/False

The below will pull data for Volume Planning.

```
Dim dt As DataTable =
BRApi.Import.Data.FdxExecuteStageTargetTimePivot(si, "C&C Plan",
```

```
"Plan", "2021M1", "2021M12", False, True, "Lb LIKE '%.Volume
Planning'", 8, False)
```

The `WFProfileName` – `Volume Planning` – is added as a Label in the data source and used to filter the Volume Planning Workflows.

Running the code produces the following data:

```
Rt,Si,Lb,Tv,EtT,PrT,CnT,SnT,VwT,AcT,FwT,OgT,IcT,U1T,U2T,U3T,U4T,U5T,U6
T,U7T,U8T,Time1,Time2,Time3,Time4,Time5,Time6,Time7,Time8,Time9,Time10
,Time11,Time12
0,Plan,East Sales.Volume
Planning,,Pennsylvania,,Local,Plan,Periodic,Distribution,EndBal_Input,
Import,None,20_010,,,,,,,,,0,0,0,0,0,0,0,0,8.200000000,9.122500000,9.02
0000000,8.200000000
0,Plan,East Sales.Volume
Planning,,Pennsylvania,,Local,Plan,Periodic,Distribution,EndBal_Input,
Import,None,40_010,,,,,,,,,0,0,0,0,0,0,0,0,8.200000000,9.122500000,9.02
0000000,8.200000000
0,Plan,East Sales.Volume
Planning,,Pennsylvania,,Local,Plan,Periodic,Sales,EndBal_Input,Import,
None,20_010,,,,,,,,,0,0,0,0,0,0,0,0,458.333333333,458.333333333,458.333
333333,458.333333333
```

FdxExecuteWarehouseTimePivot

Exporting the Plan Table to an External Database

This example will pull directly from the `XFW_TLP_Plan` table as all the information requested by C&CCC's DW team is not present in Stage.

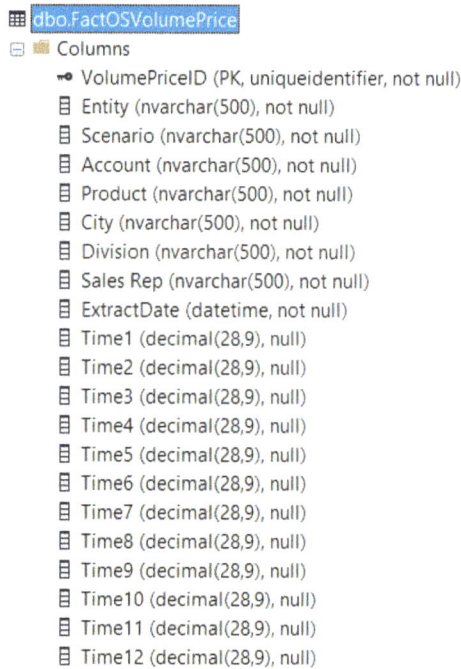

Figure 5.49

The Method to perform the retrieval of a Time-based multicolumn fact table is called `FdxExecuteWarehouseTimePivot`.

It requires the following parameters.

1. SessionInfo

2. Parallel item's column name – any column in a table can be used to parallelize the code execution

3. List of distinct items from the parallel column – used for parallelization

4. SELECT Statement

5. Queried tables– if JOIN statements are being used, include the keyword FROM here, e.g., FROM *tablename*)

6. WHERE clause – define filters (Do not use the keyword WHERE)

7. Group By – if performing Aggregations (SUM, AVG, etc.,) indicate them here by using GROUP BY

8. Order by – if sorting records, list the columns here using ORDER BY

9. Time column name – define the Time column name here (Keep in mind that this column must be a Text-type column (char, varchar, nvarchar))

10. List of distinct Time Members

11. Pivot Measure column (this is the column that has numbers in it)

12. Use generic Time columns – True/False

13. Database location – the external table name or "App" for OS internal application tables or "Framework" for OS system tables

14. Filter – Use SQL LIKE filters on the DataTable on the Dimension that is not part of the Data Unit

15. Parallel Query Count – An integer for parallel threads (this cannot exceed 128)

16. Log FDX Statistics – True/False

```
Dim strPlanYear As String =
BRApi.Dashboards.Parameters.GetLiteralParameterValue(si, False,
"paramPlanYear")
Dim lstAcc As New List(Of String)
Dim lstPlanPeriods As New List(Of String)
```

Get the plan year from the Literal Parameter paramPlanYear and create two List objects. The latter two will be used for parallelism (Account) and pivot (Time).

```
Using dbConn As DbConnInfo =
BRApi.Database.CreateApplicationDbConnInfo(si)
    lstAcc = BRApi.Database.ExecuteSqlUsingReader(dbConn, "SELECT
DISTINCT Account FROM XFW_TLP_Plan WHERE WFTimeName='" & strPlanYear &
"'", True).AsEnumerable().Select(Function(x)
x("Account").toString()).ToList()
    lstPlanPeriods = BRApi.Database.ExecuteSqlUsingReader(dbConn,
"SELECT DISTINCT 'M'+FORMAT(Period, '00') as Period FROM XFW_TLP_Plan
WHERE WFTimeName='" & strPlanYear & "'",
True).AsEnumerable().Select(Function(x)
x("Period").toString()).ToList()
End Using
```

A database connection is initiated to get the distinct Account and Period values.

SQL gets the distinct list of Accounts present in the Plan table, and a LINQ query is used to convert the rows from the DataTable to a List.

SQL gets the distinct list of Periods present in the Plan table. Note that months are converted to Text and are formatted as MM.

If they are not formated as MM, the following will happen: Month 2 is going to get Month 10's data, Month 3 will get Month 11's, Month 4 will get Month 12's, and Month 5 will get Month 2's.

Confused? Your author spent quite a bit of time trying to figure out what was going on. It is the omnipresent issue of Periods following the M*m* and M*mm* naming pattern, (e.g., M1 and M10).

This can be seen in SQL:

Figure 5.50

When Period is Text, SQL arranges them just as it arranges any Text column: M10 comes after M1. Forcing a FORMAT command to make the Period number two digits, with a leading "0" for Periods 1 through 9, fixes the issue.

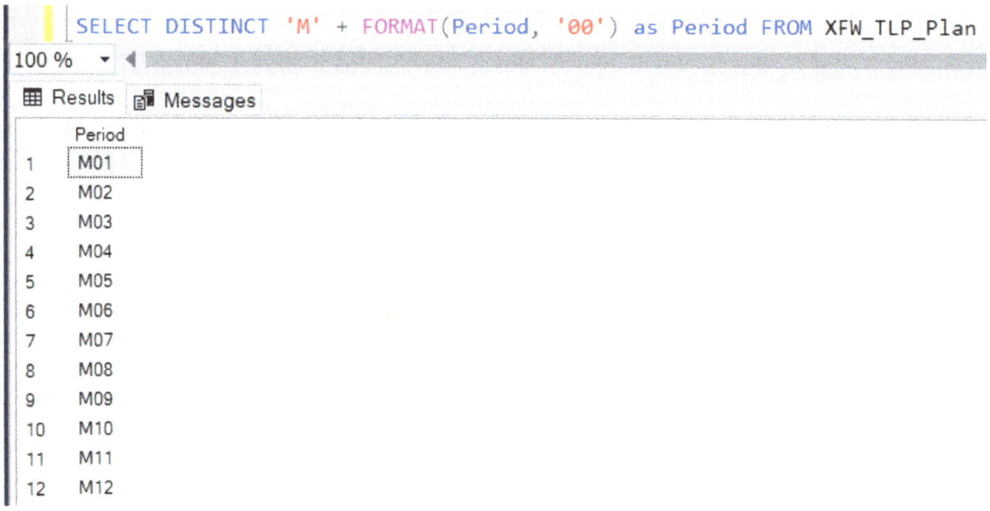

Figure 5.51

```
Dim selectStmt As New Text.StringBuilder
selectStmt.AppendLine("SELECT NEWID() as VolumePriceID, Entity,
WFScenarioName as Scenario, Account, Code1 as Product,")
selectStmt.AppendLine("Code2 as City, Code3 as Division, Code4 as
'Sales Rep',")
selectStmt.AppendLine("Amount, GETDATE() as ExtractDate,
'M'+FORMAT(Period, '00') as Period")
```

In the StringBuilder's SQL, a new GUID is generated using the NEWID() function (note that the rows do not need to be edited to add a GUID like the FDXExecuteDataUnit *or* FDXExecuteDataUnitTimePivot examples).

The current date populates the extract date column, with the Period as two-digit months prefixed with "M".

```
Dim strSelectFrom As String = "FROM XFW_TLP_Plan" ' Need FROM
Dim strSelectCriteria As String = "Account='Price' AND
WFScenarioName='Plan' AND WFTimeName='" & strPlanYear & "'" ' do not
use WHERE
Dim strGroupByStmt As String = "" ' Need Group by
Dim strOrderByStmt As String = "Order by Entity" ' Need ORDER by
```

The table name is defined in the strSelectFrom string variable.

Since only Price data is being sent, that selection is defined in strSelectCriteria.

An ORDER BY statement is used to order the rows by Entity in strGroupByStmt.

```
Dim dt As DataTable =
BRApi.Import.Data.FdxExecuteWarehouseTimePivot(si, "Account", lstAcc,
_
selectStmt.ToString, strSelectFrom, strSelectCriteria, strGroupByStmt,
strOrderByStmt, "Period", _
lstPlanPeriods, "Amount", True, "App", "", 8, True)
BRApi.Database.SaveCustomDataTable(si, "AVBS Warehouse",
"FactOSVolumePrice", dt, True)
```

FDXExecuteWarehouseTimePivot is used to generate a DataTable which is saved to the external table using SaveCustomDataTable.

Extract OneStream Dimension to an External Database or How to Generate a Custom FdxExecuteWarehouse Function

Some Dimensions will exist only in OneStream, (e.g., Scenario). In these cases, if downstream systems consume OneStream data, Scenario's metadata will have to be sent along with the data.

FDXExecuteWarehouseTimePivot's name implies that it needs a Time column to perform a pivot. This poses a significant problem when the target system is a single-column Fact table.

The solution is to make FDXExecuteWarehouseTimePivot act like it does not have to pivot on Time.

```
Dim lstProducts As List(Of String) =
BRApi.Finance.Metadata.GetMembersUsingFilter(si, "Products",
"U1#Total_Products.DescendantsInclusive", True).Select(Function(x)
x.Member.MemberId.ToString).toList()
Dim lstPlanPeriods As New List(Of String) From {"Time1"}
```

GetMembersUsingFilter gets the Member IDs of the inclusive descendants of Total_Products so that the Parent Product Members can act as the parallel item.

The Method requires a Time Dimension column and Time Members to work. Since that requirement cannot be bypassed, create a ghost column with a single value in it, in the List lstPlanPeriods.

```
Dim selectStmt As New Text.StringBuilder
selectStmt.AppendLine("WITH ProductTree AS")
selectStmt.AppendLine("(SELECT ChildId, ParentId, 'Time1' as Period, 1
as Amount FROM Relationship MbrRelation WITH (NOLOCK), Member Mbr WITH
(NOLOCK), Dim AppDimension WITH (NOLOCK)")
selectStmt.AppendLine("WHERE Mbr.MemberId=MbrRelation.ParentId and")
selectStmt.AppendLine("Mbr.Name = 'Total_Products' and")
selectStmt.AppendLine("MbrRelation.DimId=AppDimension.DimId and")
selectStmt.AppendLine("AppDimension.Name = 'Products'")
selectStmt.AppendLine("UNION ALL ")
selectStmt.AppendLine("SELECT MbrRelation.ChildId,
MbrRelation.ParentId, 'Time1' as Period, 1 as Amount")
selectStmt.AppendLine("FROM Relationship as MbrRelation WITH (NOLOCK),
ProductTree, Dim AppDimension WITH (NOLOCK)")
selectStmt.AppendLine("WHERE ProductTree.ChildID =
MbrRelation.ParentId and")
selectStmt.AppendLine("MbrRelation.DimId=AppDimension.DimId and")
selectStmt.AppendLine("AppDimension.Name = 'Products')")
selectStmt.AppendLine("SELECT Mbr.Name as Child, ParentMbr.Name as
Parent, Mbr.Description, Period, Amount")
```

Create the StringBuilder selectStmt to capture the required SQL.

This code snippet uses **Recursive Common Table Expressions** to get the Members of the Product Dimension in a Parent-Child format.

The following tables are used to generate the required Parent-Child format:

1. Relationship – this table holds the relationship between Members (Parent-Child).

2. Member – this table holds Member-related properties (Name, ID, Description, Security).

3. Dim – this table holds the Dimension IDs and their Types.

> **Note:** SQL NOLOCK hint must be used when you are going against Application or System tables.

Note the 'Time1' as Period, 1 as Amount SELECT criteria to create two ghost columns (Period with a default value of Time1, and Amount with a default value of 1).

All the tables required to fetch the SELECT statements are mentioned in the FROM string to perform an implied JOIN.

Criteria is mentioned to pull the data from the CTE, and it is joined with the Member table (twice – once to get the Child's Name, and another time to get the Parent's name).

```
Dim strSelectFrom As String = "FROM ProductTree, Member Mbr WITH
(NOLOCK), Member ParentMbr WITH (NOLOCK)" ' Need FROM
Dim strSelectCriteria As String = "ProductTree.ChildId=Mbr.MemberId
AND ProductTree.ParentId=ParentMbr.MemberId" ' Cannot use WHERE
Dim strGroupByStmt As String = "" ' Need Group by
Dim strOrderByStmt As String = "" ' Need ORDER by
```

Generate a new DataTable with the SQL, removing the Time column.

```
Dim dt As DataTable =
BRApi.Import.Data.FdxExecuteWarehouseTimePivot(si, "ParentId",
lstProducts, _
selectStmt.ToString, strSelectFrom, strSelectCriteria, strGroupByStmt,
strOrderByStmt, "Period", _
```

```
lstPlanPeriods, "Amount", True, "App", "", 8, False)

dt.Columns.Remove("Time1")
```

Use an external database connection to delete the existing Product Dimension.

Once deleted, save the new information to the external table DimOSProduct.

```
Using dbConn As DbConnInfo =
BRApi.Database.CreateExternalDbConnInfo(si, "AVBS Warehouse")
    BRApi.Database.ExecuteActionQuery(dbConn, "DELETE FROM
DimOSProduct", True, True)
End Using
BRApi.Database.SaveCustomDataTable(si, "AVBS Warehouse",
"DimOSProduct", dt, True)
```

After the execution of this code, DimOSProduct is as shown below:

```
/****** Script for SelectTopNRows command from SSMS  ******/
SELECT TOP (1000) [Child]
      ,[Parent]
      ,[Description]
   FROM [AVBSDW].[dbo].[DimOSProduct]
```

100 %

Results   Messages

	Child	Parent	Description
1	10_010	Whole_Bean	Cameron's 100% Colombian Regular Whole Bean
2	10_020	Whole_Bean	Celvin's Colombian Supremo Regular Whole Bean
3	10_030	Whole_Bean	French Roast Regular Whole Bean Decaf
4	10_040	Whole_Bean	Ethiopian Yirgacheffe Whole Bean
5	10_050	Whole_Bean	Panama Yellow Catuai Arabica Whole Bean
6	20_010	Ground_Coffee	Premium Blend
7	20_020	Ground_Coffee	100% Colombian Decaf
8	20_030	Ground_Coffee	Royal Kona Blend
9	20_040	Ground_Coffee	Jack Benny House Masterblend
10	40_010	Single_Cup	House Blend
11	40_020	Single_Cup	Breakfast Blend
12	40_030	Single_Cup	Dark Kenya AA
13	30_010	Filter	Regular Filter Pack
14	30_020	Filter	Decaf Filter Pack-1.5oz
15	30_030	Filter	Hot Shoppes Regular Filter Pack Decaf
16	10_030	Decaf	French Roast Regular Whole Bean Decaf
17	20_020	Decaf	100% Colombian Decaf
18	30_020	Decaf	Decaf Filter Pack-1.5oz
19	Decaf	Total_Products	Decaf
20	Filter	Total_Products	
21	Groun...	Total_Products	Ground Coffee
22	No_Pr...	Total_Products	
23	Single...	Total_Products	Single Cup
24	Whole...	Total_Products	Whole Bean

Figure 5.52

The FDX APIs support multiple export Types: Cube Data, Specialty Data, and Cube Metadata for consumption by external systems in an elegant, efficient, and unified manner.

Analyzing Large Volumes of Data, Both Related and Unrelated, to OneStream

When OneStream started out as a Financial Intelligence platform, no one would have imagined a need to analyze large volumes of data. This was somewhat myopic as almost all financial operations are – at some point – transactional in nature.

All businesses perform daily activities that are recorded; the act of entering them daily (sometimes even hourly) makes such data transactional.

When it comes to Financial Data Analysis, Planners do not generally concern themselves with transactional details. However, there are use cases where higher-level plan data must be analyzed alongside transactional data. Some examples center around how the market is behaving, or how the weather is driving the intersection between sales incentives and customer spending patterns. There are endless possibilities that require a dive into data that sits "below" OneStream.

OneStream's data orientation, scalability, and architecture are not centered on transactional-level detail, yet the need still exists. Its solution to the problem of transactional analytics is in the feature called BI Blend, also colloquially called Analytic Blend.

What is BI Blend?

BI Blend is a read-only columnar database, or more properly, it is a framework and architecture for creating columnar databases using OneStream dimensionality. Once created, BI Blend differs from the traditional Cube in that Planners cannot enter data, nor can they consume the data in a traditional Cube View. The concepts of aggregating dimensionality and calculations (extremely limited in the case of BI Blend, and in a different form than the Cube's or Specialty Planning's Calculation Engines and languages) are the same; practically everything else is different. Architectural differences aside, its purpose is the same as OneStream's other Engines: provide a way for Planners to analyze and understand data.

In contrast to a Cube or Specialty Planning's Register, think of a BI Blend database as a write-once database. When a "Blend" process is completed, it completely overwrites the existing table with new information; there is no concept of load and modify.

How Can I Use BI Blend?

C&CCC has, in reaction to the ruthlessly competitive coffee market, decided to use their agribusiness domain expertise to expand into the burgeoning localtarian Farmers Markets movement. This use case will use C&CCC's OneStream application to perform analysis on Farmers Markets in two states (your author jokes that he is a farmer first and a OneStream practitioner second, so his bias towards farming examples in this chapter is understandable). Data will be retrieved using a REST API *USDA National Farmers Market Directory API*.

A BI Blend table (or simply put, BI Blend) must be generated through a Workflow. Blend can be a Workflow Profile Child or can even be an entire Workflow review tree like the one below for Blend only.

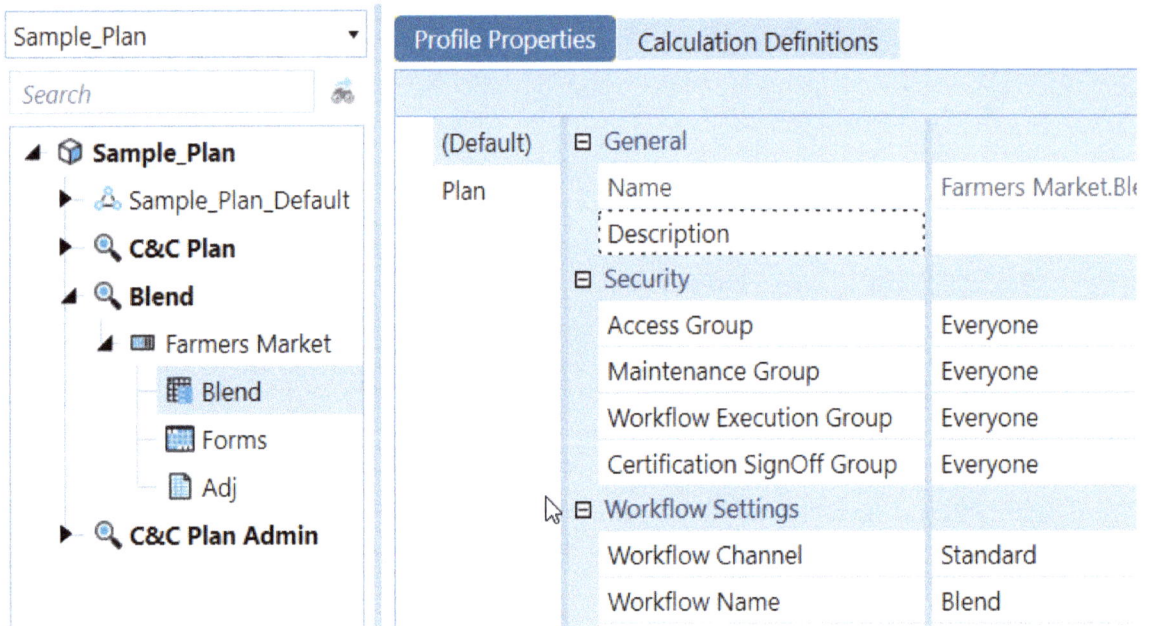

Figure 5.53

There are three Types of Workflow names available for Blend operations.

1. Blend

2. Blend – Workspace (A Dashboard can be added after Blend operations)

3. Workspace – Blend (A Dashboard to view/upload files before Blend operations)

Once a Workflow Profile is defined as Blend (or any other related Blend Type), the parameters for BI Blend are defined under BI Blend Settings.

Figure 5.54

What are the BI Blend Settings?

In contrast to practically every other facet of OneStream, BI Blend is a code-free Component, and its configuration is enacted through simple settings.

There are three types of settings:

1. Data Controls

2. Aggregation Controls

3. Performance Controls

Data Controls

Data Controls are the building blocks to BI Blend that decide where the Blend is going to be created and how many columns it will have.

Measure Type

Measure Type is the control responsible for the layout of Time columns in the Blend. Even though the name says Measure – it controls Time.

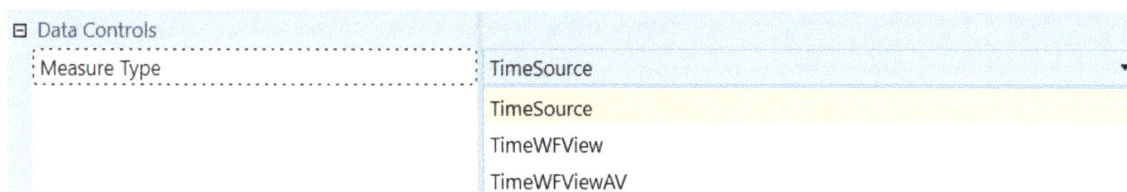

Figure 5.55

There are three Types: TimeSource, TimeWFView, and TimeWFViewAV.

1. TimeSource – BI Blend looks at the data (depending on the data source configuration) and generates the required Time columns.

2. TimeWFView – BI Blend looks at the Scenario's Workflow frequency and generates the Time columns.

3. TimeWFViewAV – BI Blend uses the Attribute Value Dimension (1-12) with each Attribute Value Dimension associated with a Time column. Think of this like a traditional Cube Matrix Data Source.

Content Type

Content Type is the control responsible for the layout of the rest of the metadata columns in the Blend except for the following default columns.

1. Rt

2. SourceID – coming from the data source

3. Label

4. TextValue

5. AccountType

There are four content Types to pick from:

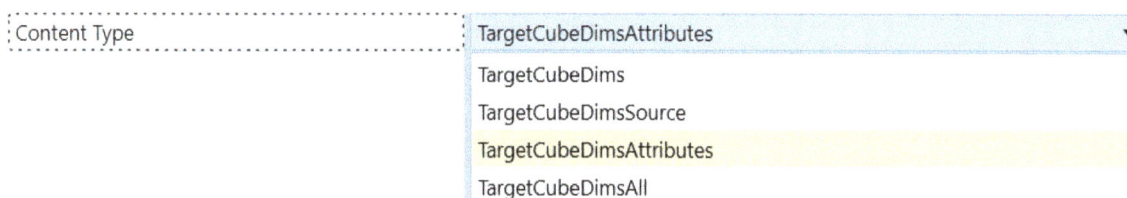

Figure 5.56

1. TargetCubeDims – Along with the defaults, the Blend table will only have the Dimensions present in the Cube.

2. TargetCubeDimsSource – Along with the defaults, the Blend table will have the Cube Dimensions and the source Dimensions from the source.

3. TargetCubeDimsAttributes – Along with the defaults, the Blend table will have the Cube Dimensions and the attribute Dimensions (if used in the data source).

4. TargetCubeDimsAll – The Blend table will have all the columns (defaults, Cube, source, and attribute Dimensions)

Star Schema

BI Blend can create a Star Schema of the host OneStream Application with data and metadata.

On generating a Star Schema, OneStream will create the following:

1. Fact table; named as
   `BIB_<AppName>_<WorkflowName>_<WFScenarioName>_<WFTimeName>`

2. Dimension tables; named as
   `BIB_<AppName>_<WorkflowName>_<WFScenarioName>_<WFTimeName>_Dim<Stag eDimensionName>` (`Et` for Entity, `Ac` for Account, and so on)

3. A View that joins the Dimensions with fact tables; named as `v_<FactTableName>`

Database Location

Blend information cannot reside in the Application database. Configure an external connection for BI Blend.

OneStream will create the tables (and the view uses Star Schema) needed in that external connection. Multiple databases/connections are not required for each Blend Scenario.

Data Explosion Adjustor

Despite its dramatic name, there is little to do with this setting because OneStream estimates the size of the rows after the first learning mode.

The first execution of the Blend profile (the Analytic Blend log file (`.xfl` text file)) executes a learning mode to figure out the explosion and adjusts this number accordingly.

```
BEFORE AGGREGATION
*******************************************************************************
BI-BLEND ENGINE STATISTICS
_____
Blend Unit Dimemsion: F#
Bypassed Base Rows: 2,300
Page Count: 1
    EndBal_Input
        Partitions: 1
        Base Page Rows (Observed): 840      [Parent Factorial: 1]
        Base Page Size (Estimate): 628,320  [Bytes/Row (Estimate): 748]
        ---------------------------------------------------------------
        Explosion Factor Adjuster: 1.0
        Explosion Factor (Observed): 2.0
        ---------------------------------------------------------------
        Exploded Page Rows: 1,680
        Exploded Page Size: 1,256,640
```

Figure 5.57

```
0: AFTER AGGREGATION
0: *****************************************************************************
0: BI-BLEND ENGINE STATISTICS
0:
0: _____
0:     EndBal_Input
0:         Partitions: 1
0:         Base Page Rows (Observed): 840        [Parent Factorial: 1]
0:         Base Page Size (Estimate): 628,320  [Bytes/Row (Estimate): 748]
0:         ----------------------------------------------------------------
0:         Explosion Factor (Observed): 1.0
0:         ----------------------------------------------------------------
0:         Exploded Page Rows (Observed): 840          I
0:         Exploded Page Size: (Observed): 628,320
0:
```

Figure 5.58

Column Aliases

Default Stage columns can be aliased to User-friendly descriptions.

In C&CCC's case the following is used as Column Alias

```
EtT=Geography, AcT=MarketID, Si=Address, Lb=MarketName, A1=ZipCode,
A2=Measure, A3=GoogleLink, A4=Products, A5=Schedule
```

After processing the Blend, here is the output from the underlying fact table.

⊞ dbo.BIB_Averybasicsamplebook_FarmersMarketBlend_Plan_2021
  ⊟ 📁 Columns
      🗒 Rt (int, not null)
      🗒 Address (nvarchar(250), not null)
      🗒 MarketName (nvarchar(250), not null)
      🗒 TextValue (nvarchar(250), not null)
      🗒 Geography (nvarchar(250), not null)
      🗒 Cons (nvarchar(250), not null)
      🗒 Scenario (nvarchar(250), not null)
      🗒 View (nvarchar(250), not null)
      🗒 MarketID (nvarchar(250), not null)
      🗒 Flow (nvarchar(250), not null)
      🗒 Origin (nvarchar(250), not null)
      🗒 IC (nvarchar(250), not null)
      🗒 UD1 (nvarchar(250), not null)
      🗒 ZipCode (nvarchar(250), not null)
      🗒 Measure (nvarchar(250), not null)
      🗒 GoogleLink (nvarchar(250), not null)
      🗒 Products (nvarchar(250), not null)
      🗒 Schedule (nvarchar(250), not null)
      🗒 AccountType (nvarchar(250), null)
      🗒 2021M1 (decimal(29,9), null)

Figure 5.59

Note: You cannot use spaces in the aliases; if they are used, BI Blend will ignore them.

Aggregation Controls

Aggregation controls help you control Aggregation. It also contains a very important item in the whole Blend creation process: **Blend Unit**.

Aggregation Controls		
Translate	NotUsed	
Blend Unit Dimension Token	F#	
Entity Aggregation Info	NotUsed	...
Account Aggregation Info	NotUsed	...
IC Aggregation Info	NotUsed	...
Flow Aggregation Info	EndBal_Input	...
UD1 Aggregation Info	NotUsed	...
UD2 Aggregation Info	NotUsed	...

Figure 5.60

Translate

Simple FX translations can be performed in Blend.

⬭ BI-Blend Settings		
⊟ Data Controls		
Measure Type	TimeSource	
Content Type	TargetCubeDimsAttributes	
Create Star Schema	False	
Database Location / External Connection	OneStream Analytics Blend	
Data Explosion Adjustor	1	
Column Aliases (Name Value Pairs)	EtT=Geography, AcT=Market ID, Si=Address, Lb=Market Name, A1=Zip C(	
⊟ Aggregation Controls		
Translate	NotUsed	▼
Blend Unit Dimension Token	NotUsed	
Entity Aggregation Info	AED	
Account Aggregation Info	AFN	
IC Aggregation Info	ALL	
Flow Aggregation Info	AMD	

Figure 5.61

Since there is nothing to translate in the Farmers Market directory, it is left as NotUsed.

Blend Unit Dimension Token

Blend Unit is similar to a Data Unit, although that similarity starts and ends with the fact that it defines a logical coupling (grouping) of Members within the data.

If your data contains Members other than what is defined (Members in a source file or table are filtered using the Aggregation information of the Blend Unit) in the Blend Dimension Aggregation, these data values are skipped.

> **Note:** No error message is provided if a Member is skipped from the data because of the Blend Unit.

Blend Unit is used to group the data, and that grouping leads to partitions (along with Source ID); partitions lead to parallel Aggregations; parallelism drives performance; performance drives happiness, and we all want to be as happy as we can be.

Any Dimension (except IC and Account) can be a Blend Unit. However, only *one* Dimension can be the Blend Unit.

Blend Unit plays a role in aggregating the Blend Dimension. It *must* have a corresponding Aggregation Info property other than NotUsed.

Read further about the Blend Unit in the *BI Blend Platform Guide*.

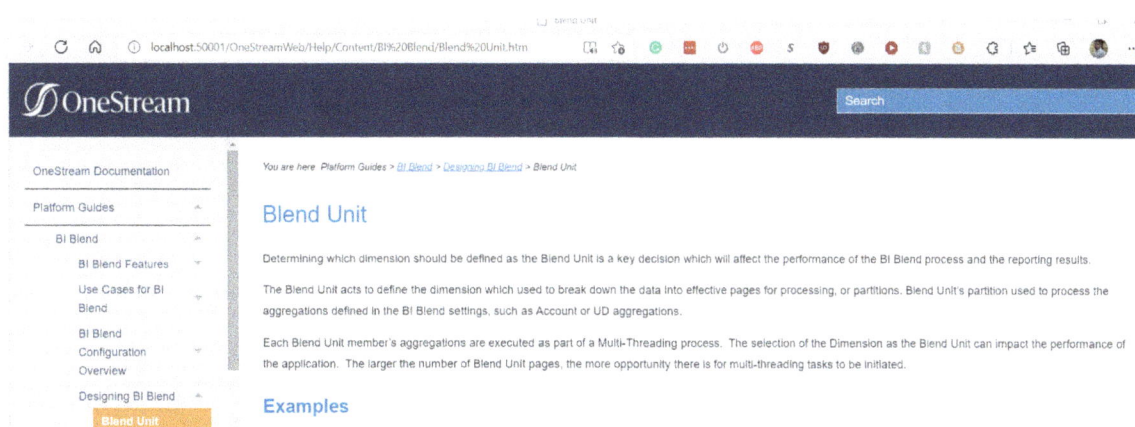

Figure 5.62

Despite the discussion of grouping and partitions, sometimes an Aggregation on the Blend Unit is *not* needed.

Consider the Scenario where C&CCC wants to analyze their hourly transactions (all sent to OneStream as flat files) and a summarized level of this information is loaded to the Cube.

In this Scenario, instead of loading millions of records to analyze a few columns, that data could be loaded to a Blend database, and then BI Blend can be used as the source for loading to the Cube. Summarizing data on a columnar database is blazingly fast.

In this Scenario, Stage is not being burdened (refer to the topic *Supplemental Data Analysis Without Wreaking Havoc on Stage* in the next chapter) with millions of records, as this data is stored only in Blend.

With Blend as the source, the Stage Engine will hand over everything to the BI Blend cache once the Transformation and Derivative Rules are executed.

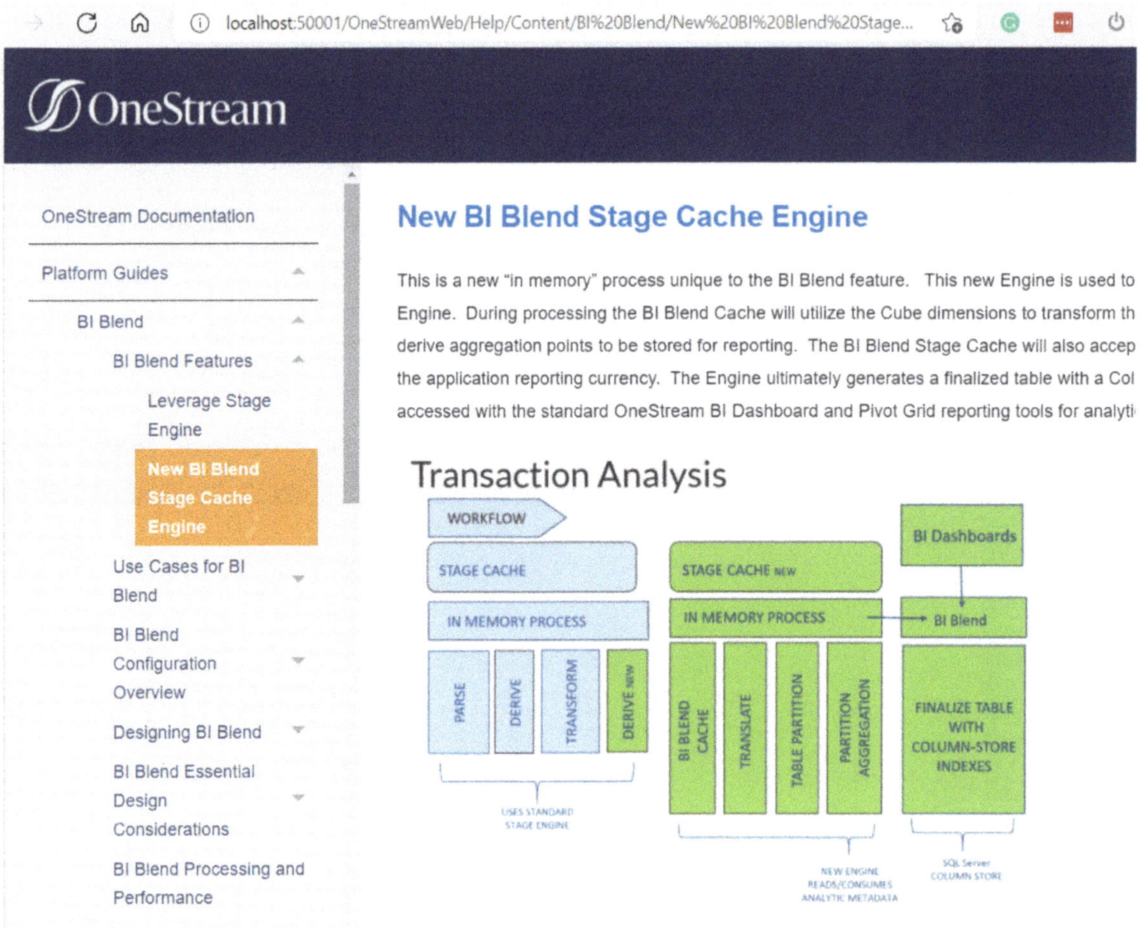

Figure 5.63

In this case, aggregated data that corresponds to Parents in Cube Dimensions are not needed because you cannot load data to upper-level Members in the Cube. Instead, pick a static Dimension (only one Member from that Dimension is present in the data) to be your Blend Unit Dimension.

In this example, a fixed Flow Dimension Member `EndBal_Input` is being loaded.

Translate	NotUsed
Blend Unit Dimension Token	F#
Entity Aggregation Info	NotUsed
Account Aggregation Info	NotUsed
IC Aggregation Info	NotUsed
Flow Aggregation Info	EndBal_Input

Figure 5.64

If there are multiple Members of the Flow Dimension present in the data, they are ignored as the Flow Aggregation Info property mentions only `EndBal_Input`.

There is a performance tradeoff because the absence of grouping prevents parallelism. Regardless, BI Blend performs the heavy lifting.

The Big One – Aggregation Info

Your author is conflicted between calling either Aggregation Info or the Blend Unit as the Big One as they are both equally important when creating a highly performant BI Blend model.

Aggregation Info is used to define how materialized Aggregations are done in a BI Blend and it also plays a role in generating the metadata if used along with Create Star Schema.

Aggregation Behavior

The Members contained in the BI Blend table are based on the Member selection defined in each Aggregation Info property.

1. NotUsed – no Parent Members are included in the BI Blend (all level 0)

2. Member selection – All Members (Descendants Inclusive) under this Parent will be included in the BI Blend

Aggregation Info can be filtered to add more granularity to the selection process. The following filters are available:

1. `Member`

2. `Member.Children` (inclusive)

3. `Children` (non-inclusive)

4. `TreeDescendants` (non-inclusive)

5. `Member.TreeDescendants` (inclusive)

When a filter is used in Aggregation Info, the Aggregation behavior changes for Blend Unit Dimensions and others.

If Entity was picked as the Blend Unit in the Farmers Market blend, the following Member Filter selections are possible.

1. `Total_Geography` – All Members under Total_Geography will be present

2. `Total_Geography;Member` – Only Total_Geography will be present

3. `Total_Geography;Member.Children` – Only East, West, Mid_West, and South will be present

What happens if Entity is **not** the Blend Unit

1. `Total_Geography` – All Members under Total_Geography will be present

2. `Total_Geography;Member` – Total_Geography and all the Base Members of Total_Geography will be present

3. `Total_Geography;Member.Children` – East, West, Mid_West, South, all the Base Members of the Parents will be present

Labels

Labels in Aggregation Info change how Member names are populated:

The following labels are supported.

1. `N` Member name (default)

2. `D` Member description

3. `ND` Member name and description

Labels can be specified by adding them after the filter (e.g., `Total_Geography;;ND` – the Blend table will be populated with Member name and descriptions for the Entity Dimension).

StarSchemaControls

SSOnly

Use the **SSOnly token** if non-Blend Unit Dimensions should not be aggregated in the Star Schema.

> **Note:** Blend Unit Dimensions are always aggregated.

Pick a static Member Dimension, as explained in the *Blend Unit Dimension Token* section, to have a non-aggregated Star Schema fact table.

Metadata extraction is also dependent on the Member selection done in Aggregation Info.

East;;;SSOnly will result in only East and its descendants being present in the Entity Dimension table.

If a Dimension is flagged as NotUsed, no Dimension tables are created for this Dimension.

SSLeveled

The SSLeveled token can be used to create hierarchy levels in the Dimension tables. When this token is used, even with the performance impact, BI Blend will produce something similar to the table below.

MemberName	MemberDesc	NameAndDesc	ParentName	IndentLevel	IsBase	MemberSeq	IsBaseBiBlend	Level_0	Level_1	Level_2
Alabama	Alabama	Alabama	South	2	1	24	1	Total_Geography	South	Alabama
Arizona	Arizona	Arizona	West	2	1	9	1	Total_Geography	West	Arizona
California	California	California	West	2	1	10	1	Total_Geography	West	California
Delaware	Delaware	Delaware	East	2	1	4	1	Total_Geography	East	Delaware
East	East	East	Total_Geography	1	0	2	0	Total_Geography	East	XFStored
Florida	Florida	Florida	South	2	1	23	1	Total_Geography	South	Florida
Indiana	Indiana	Indiana	Mid_West	2	1	19	1	Total_Geography	Mid_West	Indiana
Louisiana	Louisiana	Louisiana	South	2	1	25	1	Total_Geography	South	Louisiana
Michigan	Michigan	Michigan	Mid_West	2	1	16	1	Total_Geography	Mid_West	Michigan
Mid_West	Mid West	Mid_West - Mid West	Total_Geography	1	0	15	0	Total_Geography	Mid_West	XFStored
Minnesota	Minnesota	Minnesota	Mid_West	2	1	18	0	Total_Geography	Mid_West	Minnesota
Mississippi	Mississippi	Mississippi	South	2	1	26	1	Total_Geography	South	Mississippi
Montana	Montana	Montana	West	2	1	12	1	Total_Geography	West	Montana
New_Jersey	New Jersey	New_Jersey - New Jersey	East	2	1	5	1	Total_Geography	East	New_Jersey
New_York	New York	New_York - New York	East	2	1	6	1	Total_Geography	East	New_York

Figure 5.65

The entire hierarchy can then be displayed in a Report if needed.

An **XFStored level** is a Member created by BI Blend to show there is no Level 2 Member (for the legacy folks, this is generation) for East. Think of this as a form of dimensional evenness required by relational (or, in this case, columnar) databases.

IsBaseBiBlend will also tell you whether these are Members inserted by BI Blend. (0 means they are made up names.)

Attribute Dimensions

By virtue of Stage supporting an Attribute Dimension, BI Blend inherits the Attribute Dimensions. However, it puts a different spin on things by treating them as additional User-Defined Dimensions in UD8 and uses it in Aggregation Info. For example, an additional Dimension called Distance is created in UD8 with the following structure and is used in the Attribute 2 Aggregation Info.

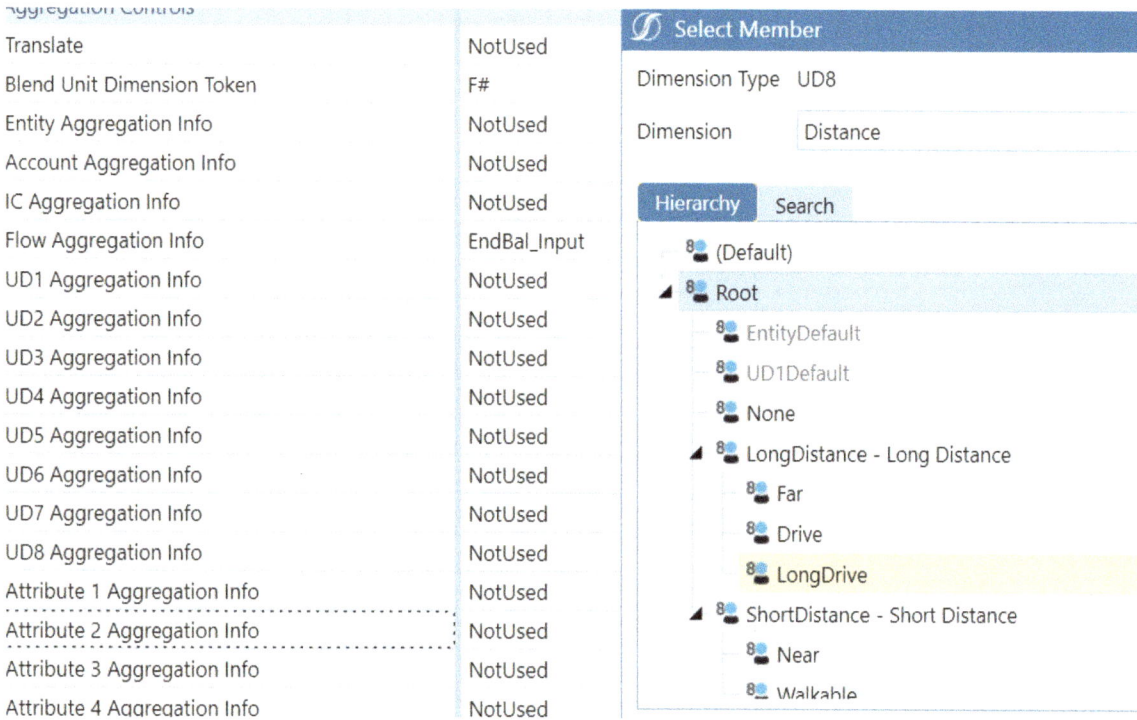

Aggregation Controls	
Translate	NotUsed
Blend Unit Dimension Token	F#
Entity Aggregation Info	NotUsed
Account Aggregation Info	NotUsed
IC Aggregation Info	NotUsed
Flow Aggregation Info	EndBal_Input
UD1 Aggregation Info	NotUsed
UD2 Aggregation Info	NotUsed
UD3 Aggregation Info	NotUsed
UD4 Aggregation Info	NotUsed
UD5 Aggregation Info	NotUsed
UD6 Aggregation Info	NotUsed
UD7 Aggregation Info	NotUsed
UD8 Aggregation Info	NotUsed
Attribute 1 Aggregation Info	NotUsed
Attribute 2 Aggregation Info	NotUsed
Attribute 3 Aggregation Info	NotUsed
Attribute 4 Aggregation Info	NotUsed

Select Member

Dimension Type UD8

Dimension Distance

Hierarchy | Search

- (Default)
- ▲ Root
  - EntityDefault
  - UD1Default
  - None
  - ▲ LongDistance - Long Distance
    - Far
    - Drive
    - LongDrive
  - ▲ ShortDistance - Short Distance
    - Near
    - Walkable

Figure 5.66

This Dimension is used to perform Aggregation or Star Schema creation. In essence, BI Blend treats the 20 Stage Attribute Dimensions as "real" additional Dimensions.

Performance Controls

The degree of parallelism can be controlled using the following settings:

Performance Controls	
Max Degree of Parallelism (No SQL)	8
Max Degree of Parallelism (SQL)	4
Row Limit	10,000,000
Shrink After Finalize	True
Application Servers (optional, use commas and *? '	...

Figure 5.67

> **Note:** BI Blend limits the number of rows in a Blend Table (Aggregation included) to 500 million rows.

Shrink After Finalize is used to compress the columnar table after the Blend creation.

Use the Application Servers setting to change BI Blend process execution. By default, it runs on the Stage Server.

REST API and BI Blend

A REST API Connector Rule is used to fetch the Farmers Market details from USDA's directory into BI Blend.

By providing the Zip code to the API, the Market IDs nearby are returned. With that key, the Market details can be extracted.

In the Connector Rule, the following Namespaces are imported to aid this. Newtonsoft (a OneStream-provided external dll used for REST API JSON processing) is shipped with OneStream.

```
' To help with the HTTP requests
Imports System.Net
Imports System.Net.Http
Imports System.Net.Http.Headers

' To Parse JSON objects
Imports Newtonsoft.Json
Imports Newtonsoft.Json.Linq
```

A list of columns is returned under the GetFieldList case section. These fields are mapped to different Dimensions in a data source that uses this Connector Rule.

```
Case Is = ConnectorActionTypes.GetFieldList

    'Get the list of field names
    Dim fieldList As New List(Of String) From {"ID", "ZipCode",
"Distance", "Apart", "Name", "Address", "GoogleLink", "Products",
"Schedule"}
    Return fieldList
```

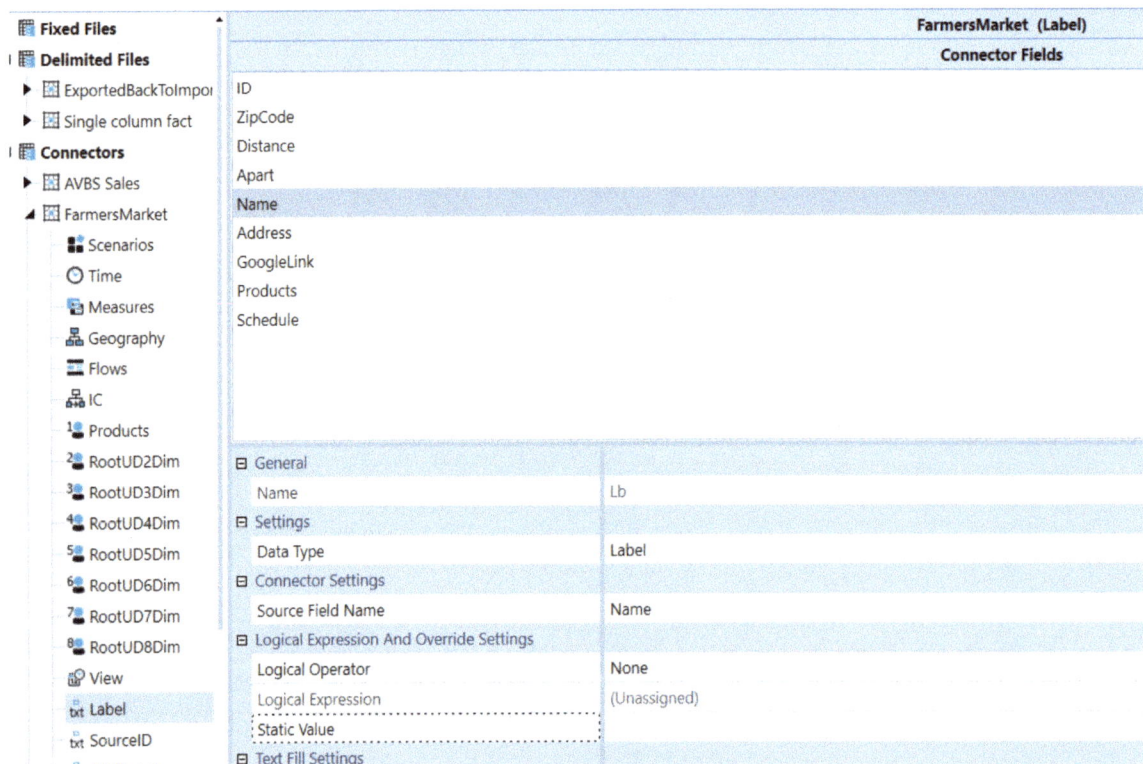

Figure 5.68

The GetFarmersMarketInfo function is used to return a DataTable with the Market information. It is then processed using the ProcessDataTable Method.

```
Case Is = ConnectorActionTypes.GetData
    Dim marketDetails As DataTable = GetFarmersMarketInfo(si)
    api.Parser.ProcessDataTable(si, marketDetails, False,
api.ProcessInfo)
```

A List of Zip Codes is created to use in the function.

A DataTable is created with the columns used in GetFieldList.

```
Dim zipCodeList As New List(Of Integer) From {48307, 94065}
Dim marketDetails As New DataTable()
marketDetails.Columns.Add("ID", GetType(Integer))
marketDetails.Columns.Add("ZipCode", GetType(Integer))
marketDetails.Columns.Add("Distance", GetType(Decimal))
marketDetails.Columns.Add("Apart")
marketDetails.Columns.Add("Name")
marketDetails.Columns.Add("Address")
marketDetails.Columns.Add("GoogleLink")
marketDetails.Columns.Add("Products")
marketDetails.Columns.Add("Schedule")
```

The Zip Code is used to generate the endpoint URL for the REST API.

A string is created to hold the static part of the endpoint.

Loop through the Zip Codes to get the Market ID and Market Name.

An HTTPClient is created to get a response from the endpoint.

Capture the result from the HTTP GET Method.

```
Dim strSearchURL As String =
"http://search.ams.usda.gov/farmersmarkets/v1/data.svc/"
For Each zipCode In zipCodeList
    Dim marketRequestClient As New HttpClient()
    Dim marketInfoResult As HttpResponseMessage =
marketRequestClient.GetAsync(strSearchURL & "zipSearch?zip=" &
zipCode).Result
```

If the response was successful, read the result contents.

Since this response is a JSON object, parse the information as a JObject.

```
If marketInfoResult.IsSuccessStatusCode Then
    Dim strMarketInfoContent As String =
marketInfoResult.Content.ReadAsStringAsync().Result
    Dim marketJSONResult As JObject =
JObject.Parse(strMarketInfoContent)
```

After a successful query, the JSON object looks like the below:

```
1   {
2       "results": [
3           {
4               "id": "1021420",
5               "marketname": "10.0 City of St. Clair Shores Farmers Market"
6           },
7           {
8               "id": "1019725",
9               "marketname": "19.7 New Baltimore Farmers Market"
10          },
11          {
12              "id": "1019305",
13              "marketname": "20.4 Sowing Seeds Growing Futures Farmers Market"
14          },
```

Since the JObject can be treated as a Dictionary, and all the results are kept under a key called results, loop through the values of results (Market information).

Another query is used to fetch the market details using the Market ID.

If the response was successful, read the contents and parse the content as a JSON object.

```
For Each marketID In marketJSONResult("results")
    Dim marketDetailsResult As HttpResponseMessage =
marketRequestClient.GetAsync(strSearchURL & "mktDetail?id=" &
marketID("id").tostring).Result
    If marketDetailsResult.IsSuccessStatusCode Then
        Dim strMarketDetailsContent As String =
marketDetailsResult.Content.ReadAsStringAsync().Result
        Dim marketDetailsJSONResult As JObject =
JObject.Parse(strMarketDetailsContent)
```

The market details JSON object looks similar to the one below.

```
1  {
2      "marketdetails": {
3          "Address": "24800 Jeffereson, St. Clair Shores, Mi, Michigan, 48080",
4          "GoogleLink": "http://maps.google.com/?q=42.6958071%2C%20-82.932268%20
               (%22City+of+St.+Clair+Shores+Farmers+Market%22)",
5          "Products": "Baked goods; Crafts and/or woodworking items; Fresh
               fruit and vegetables; Honey; Prepared foods (for immediate
               consumption); Soap and/or body care products",
6          "Schedule": "05/23/2021 to 05/23/2021 Thu: 5:00 PM-9:00 PM;Sun: 8:00
               AM-2:00 PM;<br> <br> <br> "
7      }
8  }
```

The table can now be populated with the information from the JSON object.

A new DataRow is created, and the Market ID and the Zip code are added to their respective columns.

The market name comes with the distance from the Zip code that was provided, in this case the Zip code of OneStream Headquarters to the Farmers' market location, so separate the distance from the name by splitting the name using spaces.

Since the name also contains spaces, and only the distance needs to be removed from it, join the string array back by skipping only the first one.

Perform a distance measurement to classify the distance as long or short distances.

Loop through the multiple JProperty items under marketdetails and assign their name as the column name and cell value.

Replace the HTML characters
 (break) with a null. Since BI Blend will only allow the cells to have 250 characters, we are using a Left operation after trimming and replacing.

This row is then added to the table.

The data source can now be added to the Workflow Profile.

```
Dim dr As DataRow = marketDetails.NewRow
dr("ID") = Trim(marketID("id"))
dr("ZipCode") = zipCode
Dim strMarketNameAndDistance As String() =
marketID("marketname").ToString.Split(" ")
dr("Name") = Trim(String.Join(" ", strMarketNameAndDistance.Skip(1)))
Dim decDistance As Decimal = strMarketNameAndDistance(0)
dr("Distance") = decDistance
```

```
If decDistance <= 1
    dr("Apart") = "Walkable"
Else If decDistance > 1 And decDistance <= 5
    dr("Apart") = "Near"
Else If decDistance > 5 And decDistance <= 20
    dr("Apart") = "Far"
Else If decDistance > 20 And decDistance <= 50
    dr("Apart") = "Drive"
Else If decDistance > 50
    dr("Apart") = "LongDrive"
End If
For Each marketInfo As JProperty In
marketDetailsJSONResult("marketdetails")
    dr(marketInfo.Name) =
Left(Trim(marketInfo.Value.ToString).Replace("<br>",""), 100)
Next
marketDetails.Rows.Add(dr)
```

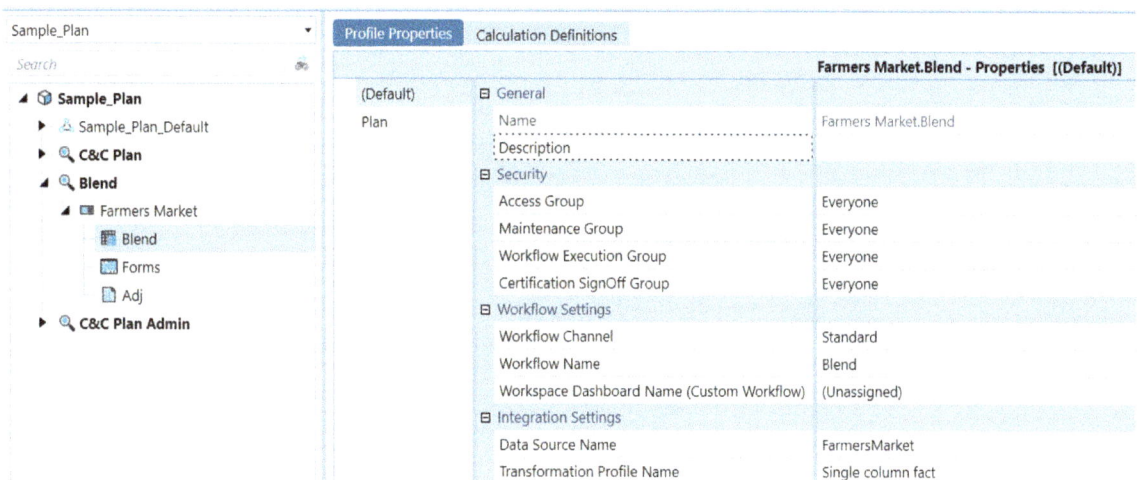

Figure 5.69

A successful execution will create the following tables in the Blend database.

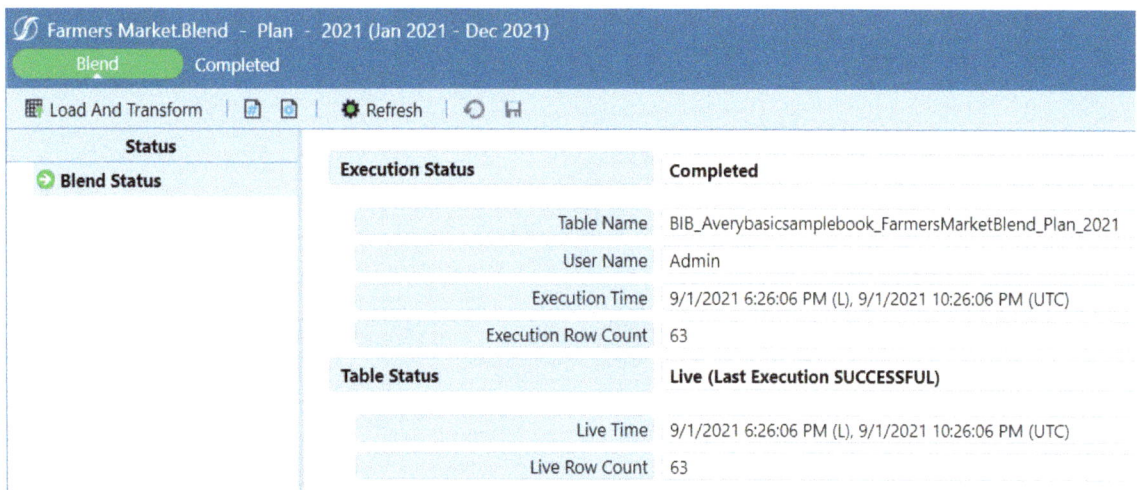

Figure 5.70

⊞ dbo.BIB_Averybasicsamplebook_FarmersMarketBlend_Plan_2021
⊞ dbo.BIB_Averybasicsamplebook_FarmersMarketBlend_Plan_2021_DimA2
⊞ dbo.BIB_Averybasicsamplebook_FarmersMarketBlend_Plan_2021_DimFw
⊞ dbo.BIB_Averybasicsamplebook_FarmersMarketBlend_Plan_2021_ME

Figure 5.71

Since Flow is picked as the Blend Unit, a Dimension table was created for the Flow Dimension with only `Endbal_Input` in it because it is in the Aggregation Info.

Attribute 2 was tagged to use a UD8 Dimension and a Dimension table was created for the attribute Dimension.

MemberName	MemberDesc	NameAndDesc	ParentName	IndentLevel	IsBase	MemberSeq
Drive	Drive	Drive	LongDistance	1	1	6
EntityDefault	EntityDefault	EntityDefault	Root	0	1	1
Far	Far	Far	LongDistance	1	1	5
LongDistance	Long Distance	LongDistance - Long Distance	Root	0	0	4
LongDrive	LongDrive	LongDrive	LongDistance	1	1	7
Near	Near	Near	ShortDistance	1	1	9
None	None	None	Root	0	1	3
ShortDistance	Short Distance	ShortDistance - Short Distance	Root	0	0	8
UD1Default	UD1Default	UD1Default	Root	0	1	2
Walkable	Walkable	Walkable	ShortDistance	1	1	10

Figure 5.72

Once complete, the view or the fact tables are available for reporting.

Address	MarketName	MarketID	ZipCode	Measure
On Washington Street between Main & Front Streets...	New Baltimore Farmers Market	1019725	48307	Far
18917 Joy Road, Detroit, Michigan, 48228	Sowing Seeds Growing Futures Farmers Market	1019305	48307	Drive
Warren and Woodward Ave, Detroit , Michigan, 48202	Wayne State University Farmers Market	1012485	48307	Drive
24800 Jeffereson, St. Clair Shores, Mi, Michigan, 48...	City of St. Clair Shores Farmers Market	1021420	48307	Far
4201 Central Parkway, Dublin, California, 94568	Dublin	1005358	94065	Drive

Figure 5.73

I Have The Honor to Report

To have value to the people who use a OneStream Planning application, data – once created – must be made available to them through a rich and powerful User Experience, by exposing OneStream data to external systems, and via analysis on large datasets within OneStream.

The next – and last – chapter also concerns itself with reporting analysis, focusing on the other major component of Planning in OneStream: Specialty Planning.

6

Specialty Planning Analysis

Note that this section, in its power, flexibility, and sophistication is not necessarily an everyday use case. Instead, it illustrates how intricate and demanding requirements can be fulfilled – and more – within a OneStream application.

This chapter differs from the others in its depth, complexity, and highly code-oriented nature. To best understand its content, read it while examining a live instance of the A Very Basic Sample application, and treat the following as what may quite possibly be the best technical documentation ever.

Gentle Reader, in this chapter you have reached the culmination/the grand finale/the end of the saga of the previous chapters. All of those calculation Methods, models, and data points we discussed lead to a formatted Report or an unstructured analysis sheet or a graphical Dashboard. But data can only become actionable information if it is understood.

In this chapter, we shall cover:

1. Performing analysis using Pivot Grids.

2. Performing analysis and modifying Specialty data in the OneStream client Spreadsheet.

3. Supplemental data analysis without wreaking havoc on Stage.

Specialty Planning Data Analysis

A true analytic capability was lacking for Specialty Planning solutions until the release of OneStream 5.2. Your author considers slicing, dicing, and the ability to pick rows and columns of your choice to be the core of analysis (like an Excel pivot table). Yes, there were Grid Views, charts, and graphs, but really they were more like Reports; they were very limited in the way of analytic capabilities.

This absence of true analytical functionality spawned creative solutions. Your ever-curious author wonders how a solution like the one below (it did exist) might be valued by you, Gentle Reader.

In that wild world of not-that-long-ago, the below add-in could retrieve data from Specialty Planning relational tables (any relational tables, application or external) directly into Excel.

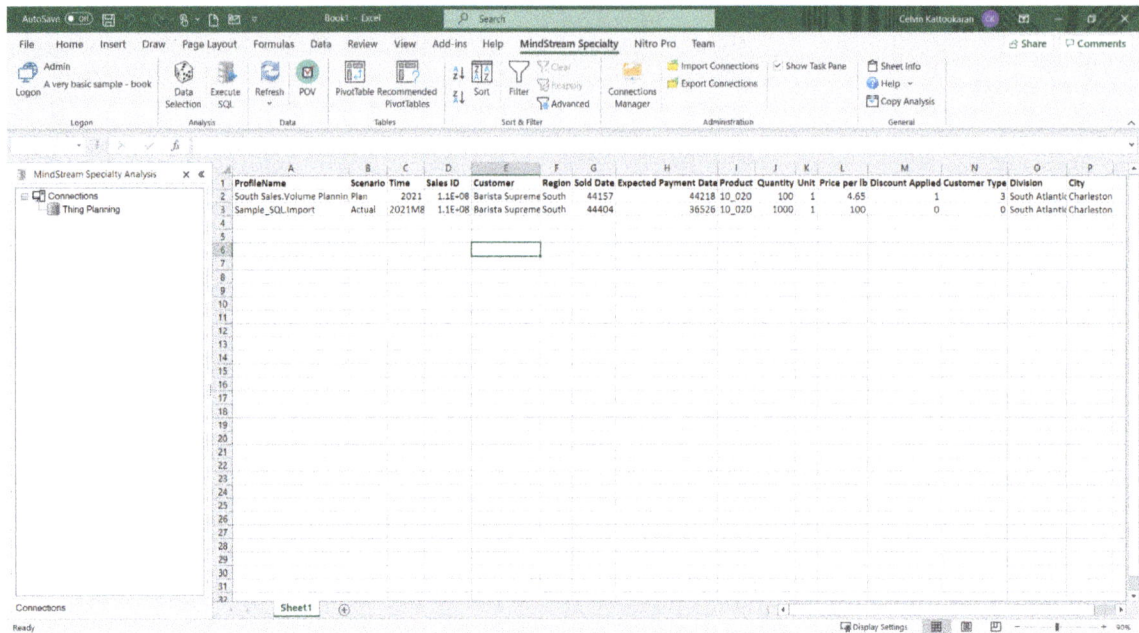

Figure 6.1

Once retrieved, Specialty Planning's fields could be dragged, dropped, filtered, and sorted in a pivot table User Interface.

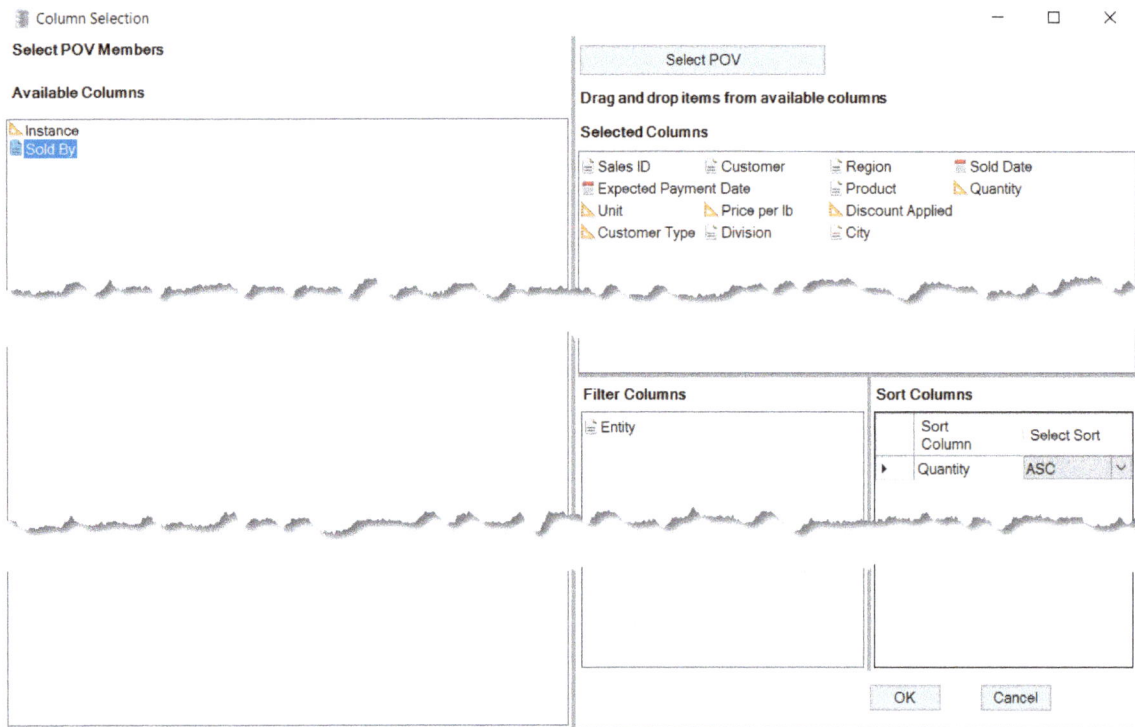

Figure 6.2

This add-in had a POV selector that worked in concert with the row and column editor.

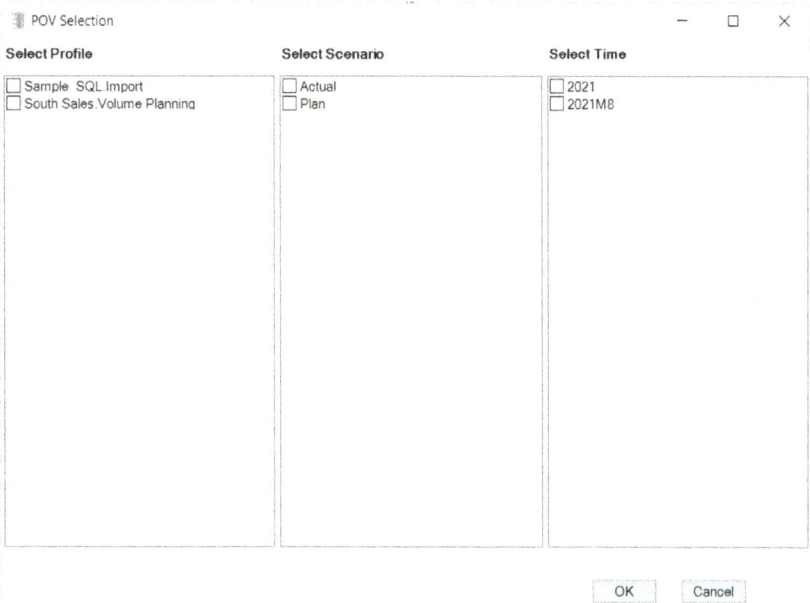

Figure 6.3

Once retrieved, the query data and metadata were stored in the Workbook to allow distribution to fellow Planners. If they had access, they could refresh the sheet to view/update that analysis.

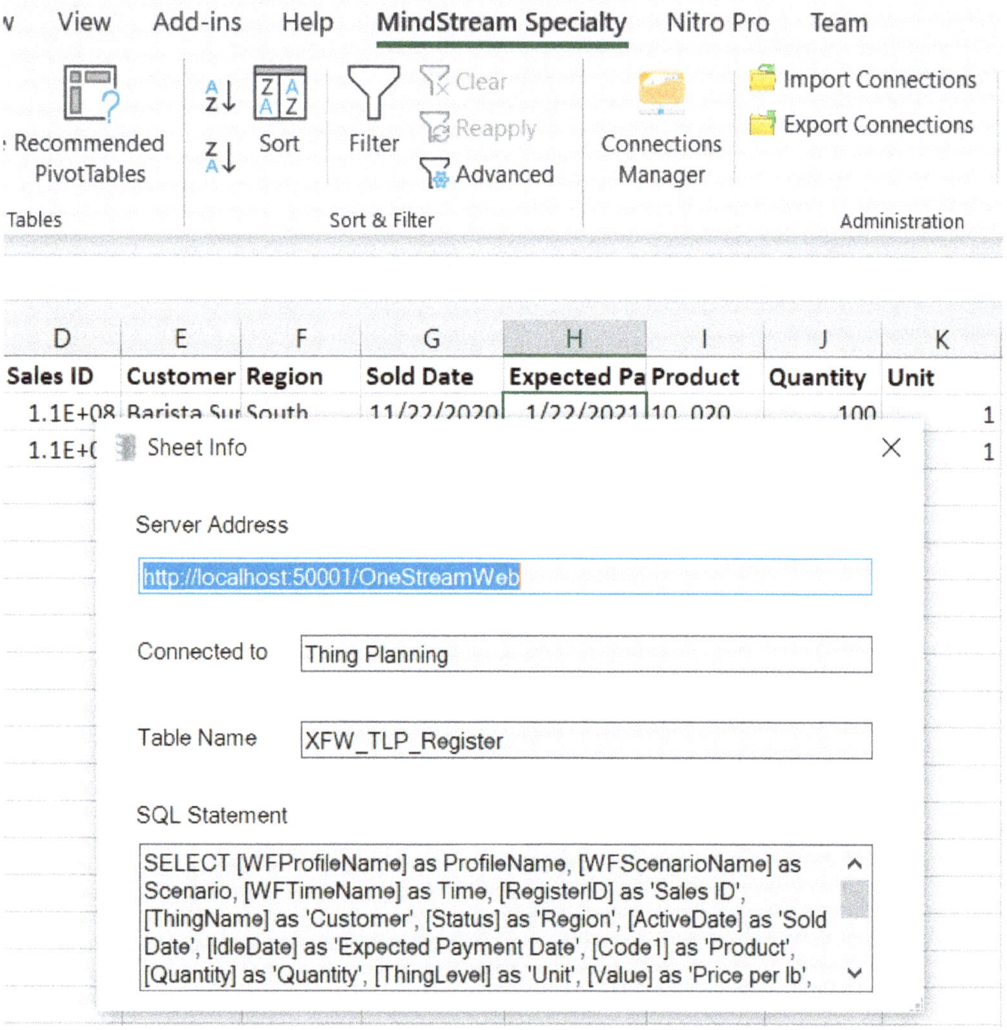

Figure 6.4

This solution, although intriguing in its possibilities, became somewhat redundant when OneStream 5.2 was released. 5.2's release introduced **Pivot Grids** and **Table Views** and added some flexibility to Grid Views and SQL Table Editors.

That redundancy aside, an Excel-based data analysis canvas has its uses. Your author's curiosity around the potential use of an add-in, such as the above, continues. Contact Celvin via LinkedIn or other means, and let him know your thoughts.

Grids and Interaction

Prior to version 5.2, Grid Views could be used to show data in a grid/table format. SQL Table Editor – while doing the same – also allowed you to edit the underlying data coming from a relational table. However, as a User, you could not change the appearance of what was shown on the columns of a Grid View/SQL Table Editor; you were always at the mercy of whoever created the view for you, hence making these two options "rigid". That "rigidity" changed after the **Save State** option was added to the SQL Table Editor and Grid Views.

Grid View	
Table Name	
Show Header	True
Show Column Settings Button	True
Show Deselect All Button	True
Allow Column Reorder	True
Show Toggle Size Button	True
Show Group Panel	True
Show Row Headers	True
Show Column Headers	True
Show Horizontal Grid Lines	True
Show Vertical Grid Lines	True
Default For Columns Are Visible	True
Retain Table Column Order	True
Column Name For Bound Parameter	
Allow Multiselect	False
Save State Settings	
Save State	True
Vary Save State By	(Use Default)
Grid View Column Format	(Use Default)
Column Format 1	False
Column Format 2	Workflow Profile and Scenario

Figure 6.5

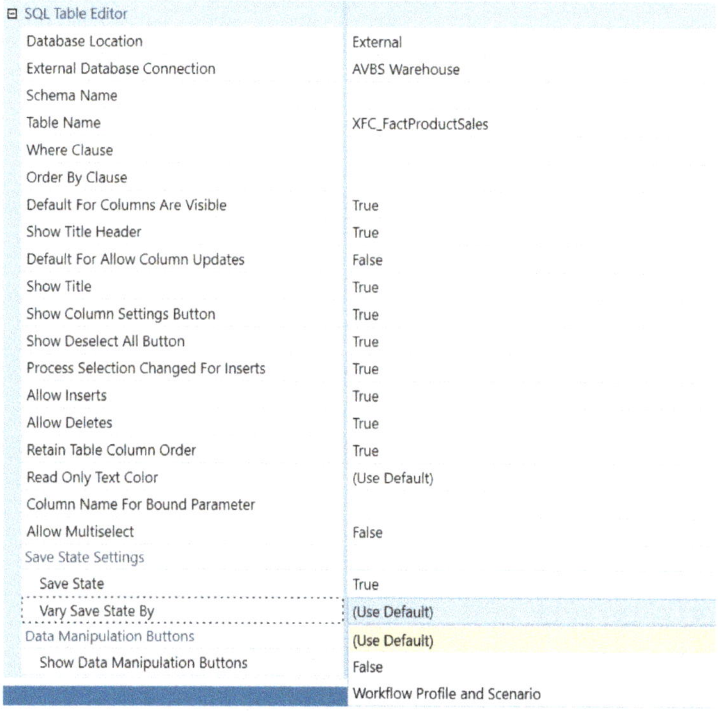

Figure 6.6

The Save State can vary by Workflow Profile and Scenario. Once enabled, Users will be able to change the order and hide/show columns.

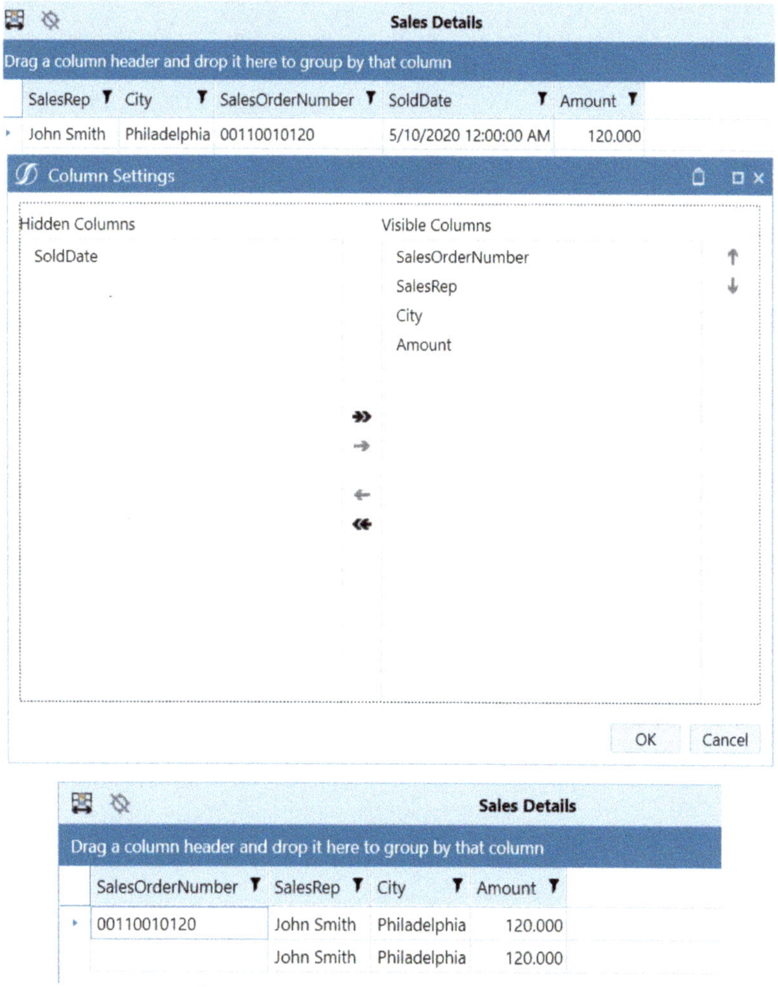

Figure 6.7

> **Note:** In the SQL Table Editor, hiding columns that do not have a stored default value can cause NULL inserts, and the save operation will fail. Keep that in mind when enabling the Save State option.

Pivot Grids

Everyone loves Pivot Grids or should. Gentle Reader, if you do not, you are missing out on a key piece of functionality that gives your Planners the ability to interactively analyze relational data in a powerful and intuitive manner.

Pivot Grids largely mimic Excel pivot tables. Given that both are addressing a normalized table (OneStream's as a table; Excel's as a worksheet, generally speaking), the use case and the interface are largely the same. They both provide a way to pivot the data against rows and columns and analyze them from different perspectives.

There are two Types of Pivot Grids in OneStream. Arguably, BI Viewer has one as well, but it does not fully fit the definition of a User-driven analysis as it is a catered Report.

1. Large Pivot Grids

2. Pivot Grids

They are both the same except that Large Pivot Grids can handle 20-40 times more data than Pivot Grids. Large Pivot Grids query the data directly from the tables/views, whereas Pivot Grids use a data adapter to get the data. Large Pivot Grids can support more data as they query on the fly. The Pivot Grid's data adapter pulls all the data upfront, and hence supports a limited number of rows (100K rows).

When to Use Large versus Regular

Apart from the volume difference, there are other use cases that force a decision between Large and Regular Pivot Grids.

Consider a use case where you want to show data from two different tables, or you want the columns to have more sensible names (Product instead of UD1) or show Member descriptions. In this situation, the obvious choice is to create a data adapter and use the regular Pivot Grid. However, if you are going against a large volume of data – and still want to achieve this – you will have to create a SQL view to perform transformations. Only then can a Large Pivot Grid be used.

How It Looks and What It Does

How does a Pivot Grid help analyze data?

Regular and Large Pivot Grids

When creating a Pivot Grid, one can provide Users with a starting point by assigning SQL columns to rows/columns/data fields and grouping properties.

Component Properties	Data Adapters
⊟ General (Component)	
Name	pg_Thing_Plan_BKS
Description	
Maintenance Unit	Book Samples
Component Type	Pivot Grid (Windows App Only)
⊟ Pivot Grid	
Show Toggle Size Button	True
Row Fields	
Column Fields	
Data Fields	
Field Groups	
Save State	False

Figure 6.8

Alternately, Users could have a clean slate when opening a Pivot Grid to let them fully define its properties by leaving those fields and groupings blank.

Large Pivot Grids

Large Pivot Grids allow the exclusion of columns from the analysis; regular Pivot Grids do not, as you are already controlling the columns using a data adapter.

Component Properties	
⊟ General (Component)	
Name	lpg_Thing_Plan_BKS
Description	
Maintenance Unit	Book Samples
Component Type	Large Data Pivot Grid (Windows App Only)
⊟ Large Data Pivot Grid	
Show Toggle Size Button	True
Database Location	Application
External Database Connection	(Select One)
Table Name	
Row Fields	
Column Fields	
Data Fields	
Filter Fields	
Where Clause	
Data Field Aggregation Types	
Excluded Fields	
Page Size	500
Save State	False

Figure 6.9

Chapter 6

Documentation and Further Reading

Use the *Platform Guides* documentation to learn more about the Component settings.

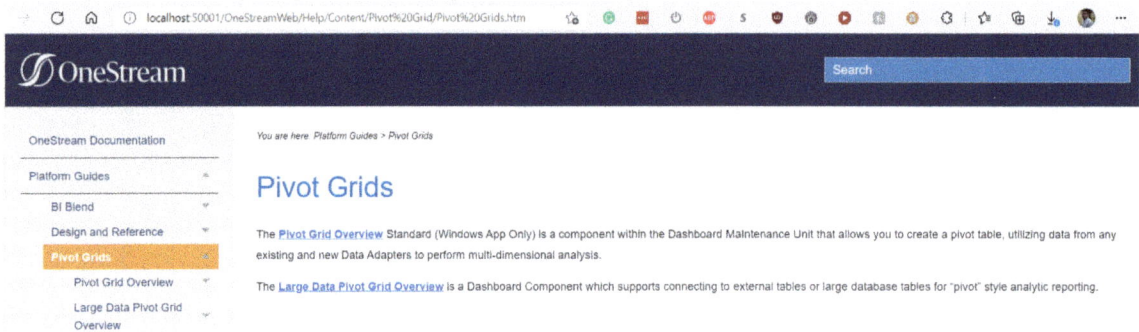

Figure 6.10

Dragging and Dropping

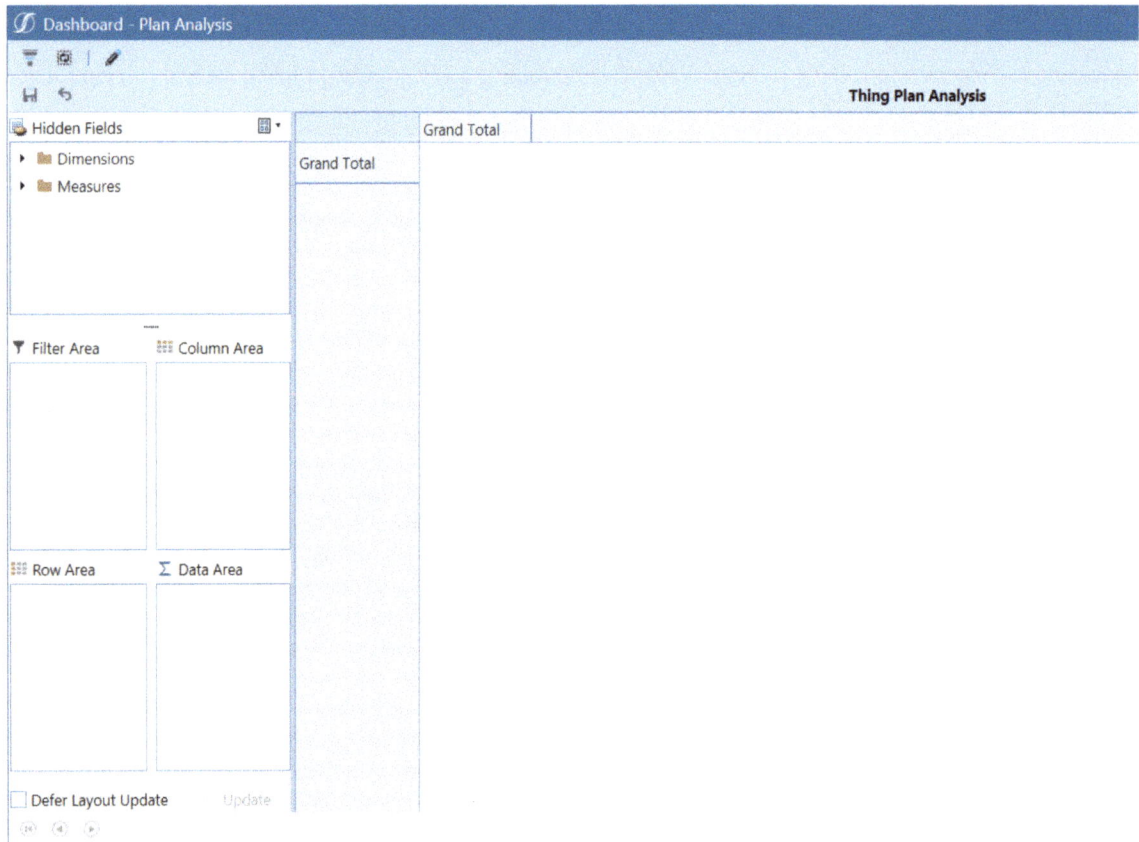

Figure 6.11

Both Types of Pivot Grids support dragging and dropping Dimensions to a Row/Column/Filter Area, and Measures to a Data Area.

If Save State is enabled, Planners can save their version of Analysis.

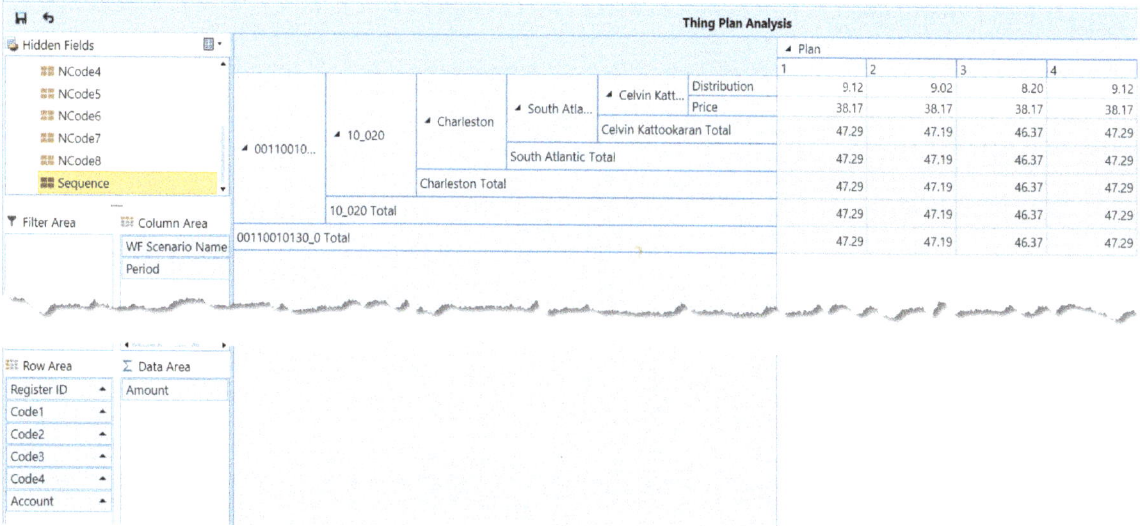

Figure 6.12

If they wish to return to the default setting, the Reset Pivot Grid to Component's setting reverts things back to the Pivot Grid's original state.

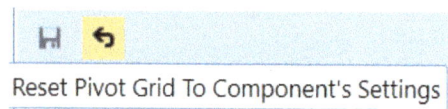

Reset Pivot Grid To Component's Settings

Figure 6.13

Adding Security to a Pivot Grid

C&CCC's Users love their analyses, and they want to look at Volume Planning (Thing Planning) data and create their own versions of Reports while working within the company's strict data security policies (defined in Slice Security (Data Cell Security) as discussed in the *Core Planning II – Command and Control the Cube* chapter. As an added security measure, Planners not involved in Volume Planning must have no access to this information.

The out-of-the-box analysis Reports that are part of Specialty Planning solutions are not appropriate for C&CCC's Users because of the following reasons:

1. Plan Data is shown as an unalterable fixed grid.

2. Much of the information in the Register is not shown, e.g., Quantity, Expected Pay Date, etc.

3. Security is only by Entity.

4. Column names are not User-friendly.

With these requirements, this use case is a perfect example to drive the solution by going with a regular Pivot Grid, as discussed above, because a Large Pivot Grid requires creating individual SQL Views per User to fulfill the security requirements.

This view can now be complex with multiple UNION ALL statements to honor the Data Cell Security. These complex queries can lead to memory issues depending on the length of the UNION Statements.

A much more acceptable approach (other than saying it is not possible 😊) is to use a regular Pivot Grid, which uses a data adapter to fetch all of the rows that the current User can see, to satisfy the first and third use case requirements.

Chapter 6

How to Achieve This?

Now that we have finalized the Component to use (Regular Pivot Grid), we need to provide a data adapter for the Pivot Grid to show the data to be analyzed.

A data adapter can be created using five Command Types:

1. Cube View

2. Cube View Multidimensional

3. Method – an astounding 35 Method Types can be used. Most of them are documented in the data adapters section in the Platform guide.

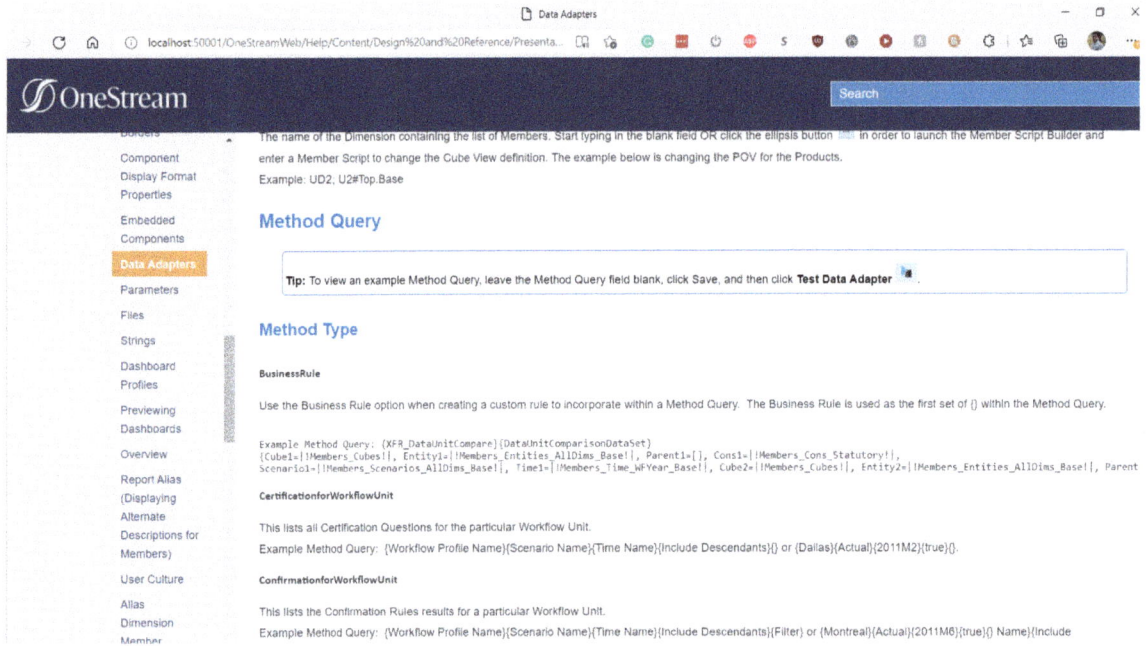

Figure 6.14

4. SQL

5. BI Blend

We are going to use Method as the Command Type and a Business Rule as the Method Type. This choice is made since the SQL required to generate the information is dynamic (it is based on the current User) in nature, and needs OneStream's scripting capability for generating the SQL. The Business Rule that can be used in a data adapter is called as a **Dashboard Dataset Rule**.

Why This Rule and What Is It Doing?

A Dashboard Data Set Business Rule can return a DataTable back to the calling Component; in this case the data adapter.

We need to get the current User to read that User's Entity access rights. With C&CCC's strict security policies, the implementation of Data Cell Access Security requires that rule to read the slice information as well as to generate the retrieval SQL.

To facilitate C&CCC's second requirement of analyzing Register-only information – like Expected Payment dates and Quantity – the Register Table (inputted or loaded data) must be joined with the Plan Table (the calculated results).

The fourth requirement of showing User-friendly column names is satisfied by aliasing the default columns to what is shown in the Register.

Here are the columns that are visible for a Planner in the Thing Planning Register.

Register Field Name ▲ ▼	Alias ▼	Visible ▼	Allow Updates ▼	
ActiveDate	Sold Date	■	■	
Code1	Product	■	■	
Code2	City	■	■	
Code3	Division	■	■	
Code4	Sold By	■	■	
Entity	Entity	■	■	
IdleDate	Expected Payment Date	■	☐	
InPeriod	Discount Applied	■	■	
NCode1	Customer Type	■	■	
Quantity	Quantity	■	■	
RegisterID	Sales ID	■	■	
RegisterIDInstance	Instance	■	■	
Status	Region	■	■	
ThingLevel	Unit	■	■	
ThingName	Customer	■	■	
Value	Price per lb	■	■	

Figure 6.15

Aliasing the Columns and Joining the Tables

Details from the Register column and details from the Dimensions (Entity is Geography, UD1 is Products) as used to generate User-friendly columns.

Time and Scenario information are derived from the Planner's Workflow. The Cube's name is passed as a parameter to the Business Rule.

The next step is to generate a **StringBuilder** that can hold the columns and table information. This SQL acts as a universal column and table information for all Planners and Administrators alike.

```
Dim strTimeName As String =
TimeDimHelper.GetNameFromId(si.WorkflowClusterPk.TimeKey)
Dim strScenarioName As String = ScenarioDimHelper.GetNameFromId(si,
si.WorkflowClusterPk.ScenarioKey)
Dim strCubeName As String = args.NameValuePairs.XFGetValue("CubeName")
Dim sqlColumns As New Text.StringBuilder
sqlColumns.AppendLine("a.Entity as Geography, a.UD1 as Products,
a.Account, a.Amount, b.Value as 'Price per Lb',")
sqlColumns.AppendLine("b.Quantity, a.Code2 as City, a.Code3 as
Division, a.Code4 as 'Sold By', b.IdleDate as 'Expected Payment
Date',")
sqlColumns.AppendLine("b.ActiveDate as 'Sold Date',")
```

Transformations

We need to perform a few transformations as the Register uses Control columns to show fields as dropdowns. Some of the fields like Discount Applied show as a Yes/No dropdown in the Register; however, a value of 1 is stored for Yes, and 0 for No.

SQL CASE statements are employed to convert the backend control values back to display values.

```
sqlColumns.AppendLine("CASE WHEN b.InPeriod = 1 THEN 'Yes' ELSE 'No'
END as 'Discount Applied',")
```

247

```
sqlColumns.AppendLine("CASE WHEN a.NCode1 = 1 THEN 'Restaurant' WHEN
a.NCode1 = 2 THEN 'Hotel' WHEN a.NCode1= 3 THEN 'Coffee Shop' END as
'Customer Type',")
sqlColumns.AppendLine("a.Status as Region, b.ThingName as Customer,")
sqlColumns.AppendLine("CASE WHEN b.ThingLevel = 1 THEN 'Pounds' WHEN
b.ThingLevel = 2 THEN 'Short Tons' WHEN b.ThingLevel = 3 THEN 'Tonne'
END as Unit,")
sqlColumns.AppendLine("CASE WHEN Period=1 THEN 'Jan' WHEN Period=2
THEN 'Feb' WHEN Period=3 THEN 'Mar'")
sqlColumns.AppendLine("WHEN Period=4 THEN 'Apr' WHEN Period=5 THEN
'May' WHEN Period=6 THEN 'Jun'")
sqlColumns.AppendLine("WHEN Period=7 THEN 'Jul' WHEN Period=8 THEN
'Aug' WHEN Period=9 THEN 'Sep'")
sqlColumns.AppendLine("WHEN Period=10 THEN 'Oct' WHEN Period=11 THEN
'Nov' WHEN Period=12 THEN 'Dec' END as Months")
```

The table values of 1 and 0 are transformed to Yes/No for Discount Applied (this is the repurposed InPeriod column in the Register).

For the Customer Type, NCode1 is changed to the following names.

Name	Value
Restaurant	1.000000000
Hotel	2.000000000
Coffee shop	3.000000000

Figure 6.16

ThingLevel is used to show Units.

Stored Value	Display Value
1	Pounds
2	Short Tons
3	Tonne

Figure 6.17

The Period column is converted to Month Name using the Month numbers present in the Plan table.

Joining the Tables

Once the required aliasing and transformations are done, we need to join the Register Table (inputted/loaded data) and the Plan table (calculated results).

```
sqlColumns.AppendLine("FROM XFW_TLP_Plan a, XFW_TLP_Register b")
sqlColumns.AppendLine("WHERE a.WFTimeName='" & strTimeName & "'")
sqlColumns.AppendLine("AND a.WFScenarioName='" & strScenarioName &
"'")
sqlColumns.AppendLine("AND a.RegisterID=
CONCAT(CONCAT(b.RegisterID,'_'), b.RegisterIDInstance)")
sqlColumns.AppendLine("AND a.WFTimeName=b.WFTimeName")
sqlColumns.AppendLine("AND a.WFScenarioName=b.WFScenarioName")
sqlColumns.AppendLine("AND a.WFProfileName=b.WFProfileName")
```

The Plan and Register tables are joined using `RegisterID`, `RegisterIDInstance`, `Profile`, `Time`, and `Scenario`. We are also showing the information from the current Workflow Time and Workflow Scenario.

Admins are Special

Administrators are not constrained by security as Planners are. The `BRApi.Security.Authorization.IsUserInAdminGroup(si)` Method determines if a username is in the default Administrator's group or not.

```
Dim dt As New DataTable()

Using dbConn As DbConnInfo =
BRApi.Database.CreateApplicationDbConnInfo(si)
    If BRApi.Security.Authorization.IsUserInAdminGroup(si)
        dt = BRApi.Database.ExecuteSqlUsingReader(dbConn, "SELECT " &
sqlColumns.ToString, True)
```

Creating The DataTable

Once the column information is populated, a new DataTable must be created to return the output of this function.

An application database connection is opened using the `Using` statement, which allows the querying of the application tables.

Administrators can see all of the information that is present in the Plan and the Register tables, which is why no additional `WHERE` statements are added to the StringBuilder. The same is not true of all other Users.

Users are Special, too

In the case of Users, C&CCC's strict security policy does not allow anyone other than Volume Planning Users to read the detailed Volume Planning information. C&CCC's Volume Planners are all part of a group called `TLP_ALL_USERS`.

```
Else ' if the user is not an Admin
    If BRApi.Security.Authorization.IsUserInGroup(si, "TLP_ALL_USERS")
Then
        Dim cloneSQL As New Text.StringBuilder
        cloneSQL.AppendLine("SELECT Top (1)")
        cloneSQL.AppendLine(sqlColumns.ToString)
        dt = BRApi.Database.ExecuteSqlUsingReader(dbConn,
cloneSQL.ToString, True).Clone ' to set the structure for DT
```

If the User is not an Administrator, the code must check if they are Volume Planners.

Since the `DataTable` was created as a blank DataTable, it now needs the columns and their data Types. An easy way to perform this step is to run a query that returns that metadata.

To minimize the performance impact caused by pulling all the records to get the structure, issue a `SELECT TOP 1` statement using the column information created above. Once a row is retrieved, the `Clone` Method applies the structure to the DataTable `dt` without copying the rows that are present in the source table.

If the User is not a Volume Planner, he or she will not get access, and the `else` condition is handled at the end of the code.

Read Entity Access and Data Cell Access Security

Once we confirm that the User is a Volume Planner, we need the Entity Access (Metadata security) information for the current User and the Data Cell Access security.

This information is added to a WHERE clause, and it acts as the security gatekeeper for the Pivot Grid.

```
Dim userWhereClause As New Text.StringBuilder
```

Once this test is complete, create another StringBuilder to add the User-specific WHERE clauses.

```
Dim lstParentGroups As List(Of Guid) =
BRApi.Security.Admin.GetUser(si,
si.UserName).ParentGroups.Keys.Select(Function(x) x).toList()
```

Identify all the groups the current User is a part of, in order to get the Entities the User can view.

> **Note:** You could use AncestorGroups to get the nested group information if needed.

```
Dim objCubeInfo As CubeInfo = BRApi.Finance.Cubes.GetCubeInfo(si,
strCubeName)
```

The next step is to read the Data Cell Access items. To perform this, get the Cube information.

```
Dim userSliceAccess As List(Of CubeDataAccessItem) =
objCubeInfo.Cube.CubeDataCellAccessItems.Where(Function(x)
(x.AccessLevelInGrpInFilter = 1 OrElse x.AccessLevelInGrpInFilter = 2)
And lstParentGroups.Contains(x.GroupUniqueID)).ToList()
```

Retrieve all the data cell access lines that are Read (1) or All Access (2) that are assigned to a group that the User is a part of.

Entities in Data Cell Access Security

C&CCC's slice security information is done by a combination of Entity and Products (UD1) Dimension. The following code is going to read both Entity and UD1 Member Filters from the Data Cell Access categories the User is a part of, and adds them to a collection for further processing.

```
If userSliceAccess.Count > 0 Then
    For Each objCubeDataCellAccessItem In userSliceAccess
```

Check whether the User is part of the Data Cell Access Security rows. If so, then loop through those items.

```
Dim lstEntity As New List(Of String)
```

A list for holding the Entities from Data Cell Access and the Entities the User has access to is created.

```
If Not
String.IsNullOrEmpty(objCubeDataCellAccessItem.MemberFilters.Entity)
    For Each entityFilter In
objCubeDataCellAccessItem.MemberFilters.Entity.Split(",").Select(Funct
ion(x) x.Trim)

    lstEntity.AddRange(BRApi.Finance.Metadata.GetMembersUsingFilter(si,
"Geography", entityFilter, True, Nothing, Nothing).Select(Function(z)
z.Member.Name).ToList())
    Next
```

Check whether any of those Entities are part of the Data Cell Access Security. If an Entity is present, then split the information using a comma and loop through them. Use the GetMembersUsingFilter Method to expand the Member Filter and add that to the Entity list.

West_Decaf Data Cell Access Security Category

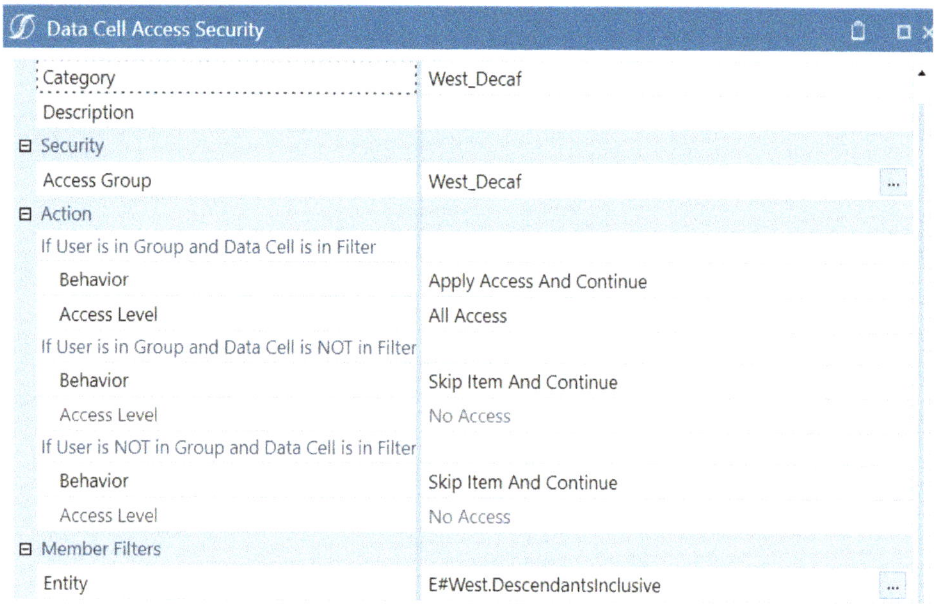

Figure 6.18

Using the example above, after the operation the Entity list will contain the following.

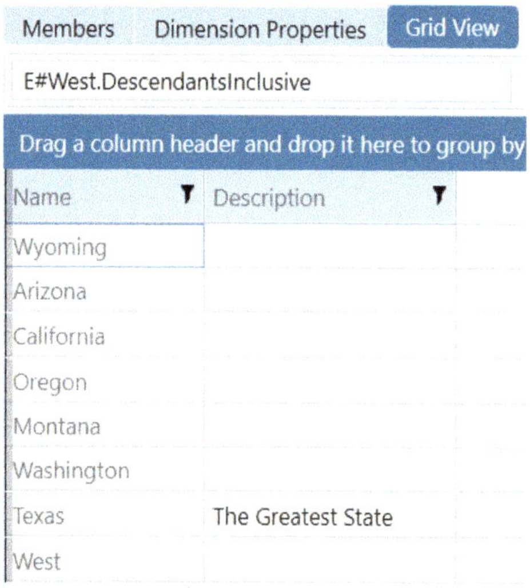

Figure 6.19

```
Else
    For Each entMbrInfo As MemberInfo In
BRApi.Finance.Metadata.GetMembersUsingFilter(si, "Geography",
"E#Root.base", True, Nothing, Nothing).Where(Function(x) _
    (lstParentGroups.Contains(x.Member.ReadDataGroupUniqueID) OrElse
lstParentGroups.Contains(x.Member.ReadDataGroupUniqueID2) _
    OrElse
lstParentGroups.Contains(x.Member.ReadWriteDataGroupUniqueID) OrElse
lstParentGroups.Contains(x.Member.ReadWriteDataGroupUniqueID2)) And
x.Member.UseCubeDataAccessSecurity).toList()
        lstEntity.Add(entMbrInfo.Member.Name)
    Next
End If
```

Chapter 6

Chapter 6

Where there are no Entities in the Data Cell Access row, the User's Entities must be interrogated, alongside whether these Entities are flagged to use Cube Data Access Security. The Entities that match both criteria are added to the list.

Adding to the WHERE Clause

Once the Entities from the Data Cell Access security are collected, they go to the WHERE clause.

```
If lstEntity.Count > 0 Then
    userWhereClause.AppendLine("AND " &
SqlStringHelper.CreateInClause("a.Entity",
lstEntity.Distinct.ToList(), True, True))
End If
```

A SQLStringHelper is employed to create an IN clause. Your author finds this an easier approach than a String.Join Method as it is simpler to wrap the SQL items in single quotes (1st parameter) and escape SQL text (2nd parameter).

Similar steps are repeated for UD1 to get the Products that are part of the slice.

```
If lstUD1.Count > 0 Then
    userWhereClause.AppendLine("AND " &
SqlStringHelper.CreateInClause("a.UD1", lstUD1.Distinct.ToList(),
True, True))
End If
Dim userSQL As New Text.StringBuilder
userSQL.AppendLine("SELECT ")
userSQL.AppendLine(sqlColumns.ToString)
userSQL.AppendLine(userWhereClause.ToString)
Dim dt1 As DataTable = BRApi.Database.ExecuteSqlUsingReader(dbConn,
userSQL.ToString, True)
For Each dr1 As DataRow In dt1.Rows
    dt.ImportRow(dr1)
Next

userSQL.Clear
userWhereClause.Clear
```

Once both Entity and Product information from the slice are added, add the details to StringBuilder's WHERE clause by checking whether the Entity and UD1 list is empty or not.

A new SQL statement is created by adding SELECT, the sqlColumns StringBuilder, and the WHERE clause StringBuilder.

This SQL is used to fetch information to a temporary DataTable dt1, and later added to the main DataTable dt. This process is preferred to a UNION ALL SQL statement as this prevents a huge SQL query that can cause a memory issue.

Once the rows are added to the main table, clear the userSQL and userWhereClause StringBuilders within the FOR loop so that they are not used for the following items.

No Pie for You

When a User is not part of Data Cell Access security, we need to allow these Users to view the Volume Planning information based on the Entity Dimension's security.

```
Else ' get Access based on entity read, read2, read and write, read
and write 2
```

If there are no Data Cell Access Security rows for the current User, allow the User to view the Entities they can access.

```
Dim lstEntity As New List(Of String)
```

Create a list to hold the User's Entities.

```
Dim userSQL As New Text.StringBuilder
```

A new StringBuilder is added to generate the SQL for this condition.

```
userSQL.AppendLine("SELECT " & sqlColumns.ToString)
For Each entMbrInfo As MemberInfo In
BRApi.Finance.Metadata.GetMembersUsingFilter(si, "Geography",
"E#Root.base", True, Nothing, Nothing).Where(Function(x) _
lstParentGroups.Contains(x.Member.ReadDataGroupUniqueID) OrElse
lstParentGroups.Contains(x.Member.ReadDataGroupUniqueID2) _
OrElse lstParentGroups.Contains(x.Member.ReadWriteDataGroupUniqueID)
OrElse
lstParentGroups.Contains(x.Member.ReadWriteDataGroupUniqueID2)).toList
()
    lstEntity.Add(entMbrInfo.Member.Name)
Next
```

Read the security information of the Base Members of the Geography Dimension to check if the User is part of the Read Data Group, Read Data Group 2, Read and Write Data Group, and Read and Write Data Group 2 group assignment. If the User is part of any of these groups, that Entity is added to the list of accessible Entities.

```
    userWhereClause.AppendLine("AND " &
SqlStringHelper.CreateInClause("a.Entity",
lstEntity.Distinct.ToList(), True, True))
    userSQL.AppendLine(userWhereClause.ToString)
    dt = BRApi.Database.ExecuteSqlUsingReader(dbConn, userSQL.ToString,
True)
    userSQL.Clear
    userWhereClause.Clear
End If
```

Combine the SELECT statement from the preceding code snippet, the sqlColumns StringBuilder, and the WHERE clause StringBuilder to populate the Main DataTable as that is the only valid condition for this User.

Clear the SQL and the WHERE clause StringBuilders after the DataTable is populated.

Entities Not Using Data Cell Access Security

Not all (most likely in real-world Scenarios) Entities are included in Data Cell Access Security. Check the Entities that are not using Data Cell Access and include them in the Planner's access if Entity-specific security should grant it.

```
Dim lstEntityNoUseCubeDataAccess As New List(Of String)
```

A list for holding the Planner's Entities where Use Cube Data Access Security is False is created.

```
For Each entMbrInfo As MemberInfo In
BRApi.Finance.Metadata.GetMembersUsingFilter(si, "Geography",
"E#Root.base", True, Nothing, Nothing).Where(Function(x)
(lstParentGroups.Contains(x.Member.ReadDataGroupUniqueID) OrElse
lstParentGroups.Contains(x.Member.ReadDataGroupUniqueID2) _
OrElse lstParentGroups.Contains(x.Member.ReadWriteDataGroupUniqueID)
OrElse lstParentGroups.Contains(x.Member.ReadWriteDataGroupUniqueID2))
And Not x.Member.UseCubeDataAccessSecurity).toList()
    lstEntityNoUseCubeDataAccess.Add(entMbrInfo.Member.Name)
Next
```

Read the security information of the Base Members of the Geography Dimension to check if the current User is part of the Read Data Group, Read Data Group 2, Read and Write Data Group, and Read and Write Data Group 2 group assignment. If the User is part of any of these groups and the current Entity is flagged not to use Cube Data Access Security, it is added to the accessible list of Entities.

```
If lstEntityNoUseCubeDataAccess.Count > 0 Then ' if there are entities
that are not using Data Cell Access
    Dim userSQL As New Text.StringBuilder
    userSQL.AppendLine("SELECT " & sqlColumns.ToString)
    userWhereClause.AppendLine("AND " &
SqlStringHelper.CreateInClause("a.Entity",
lstEntityNoUseCubeDataAccess.Distinct.ToList(), True, True))
    userSQL.AppendLine(userWhereClause.ToString)
    Dim dt1 As DataTable = BRApi.Database.ExecuteSqlUsingReader(dbConn,
userSQL.ToString, True)
    For Each dr1 As DataRow In dt1.Rows
        dt.ImportRow(dr1)
    Next

    userSQL.Clear
    userWhereClause.Clear
End If
```

If Entities are not using Data Cell Access, generate a SQL statement using SELECT, the sqlColumns StringBuilder, and the WHERE clause StringBuilder.

Populate the temporary DataTable dt1 and add to the DataTable dt.

Clear the SQL and the WHERE clause StringBuilders once the DataTable dt is populated.

Users that are Not Part of Thing Planning

This step is performed to ensure that Planners who are not part of the Volume Sales (Thing Planning) group cannot see the data.

If the Planner is not part of the Volume Planning group (TLP_ALL_USERS), then add a single column to the NoAccess DataTable.

```
                Else ' User is not part of TLP
                    dt.Columns.Add("NoAccess")
                End If
            End If
        End Using
        dt.TableName = "ThingPlanData"
        Return dt
```

Actually Analyzing Data

The Business Rule is the long prelude; it needs to be tied to a data adapter, a Pivot Grid, and finally a Dashboard.

Data Adapter

The data adapter's Method Query references that SpecialtyPlanning_HelperQueries rule. Since the Dashboard Dataset Rule can have multiple datasets…

```
Select Case args.FunctionType

    Case Is = DashboardDataSetFunctionType.GetDataSet
        If args.DataSetName.XFEqualsIgnoreCase("GetDivisions") Then
            Return Me.GetDivisions(si, globals, args)
        Else If args.DataSetName.XFEqualsIgnoreCase("GetDecimalList") Then
            Return Me.GetDecimalList(si, args)
        Else If args.DataSetName.XFEqualsIgnoreCase("GetSliceAccess") Then
            Return GetSliceAccess(si, globals, args)
        End If
End Select
```

…we are passing the dataset name as the second parameter.

General (Data Adapter)	
Name	grd_UserPlanData_BKS
Description	|
Maintenance Unit	Book Samples
Data Source	
Command Type	Method
Method Type	BusinessRule
Method Query	{SpecialtyPlanning_HelperQueries}{GetSliceAccess}{CubeName=|WFCube|}
Results Table Name	ThingPlanData

Figure 6.20

The current Workflow Cube is passed to gather the Data Cell Access security information.

Pivot Grid

That Pivot Grid uses the previous data adapter.

Component Properties	**Data Adapters**	
General (Component)		
Name	pg_Thing_Plan_BKS	
Description	Thing Planning Analysis	
Maintenance Unit	Book Samples	
Component Type	Pivot Grid (Windows App Only)	
Pivot Grid		
Show Toggle Size Button	True	
Row Fields	Geography,Products,Account	
Column Fields	Months	
Data Fields	Amount	
Field Groups	Customer, Customer Type	
Save State	True	

Figure 6.21

C&CCC's Users are given a starting point where Geography, Products, and Account are added to rows. Months are added to columns, and Amount to the Data field.

Since Customer and Customer Type are used together, these two are grouped as a single column.

Users can save their analysis with the Save State set to True.

Dashboard

A simple Dashboard is created for the Users to access this information by adding the Pivot Grid as a Component.

The Volume Sales Register records are as below.

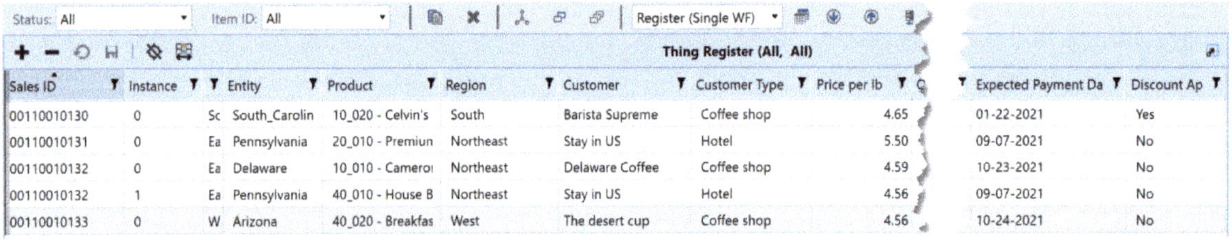

Sales ID	Instance		Entity	Product	Region	Customer	Customer Type	Price per lb	Expected Payment Da	Discount Ap
00110010130	0	Sc	South_Carolin	10_020 - Celvin's	South	Barista Supreme	Coffee shop	4.65	01-22-2021	Yes
00110010131	0	Ea	Pennsylvania	20_010 - Premiun	Northeast	Stay in US	Hotel	5.50	09-07-2021	No
00110010132	0	Ea	Delaware	10_010 - Cameroı	Northeast	Delaware Coffee	Coffee shop	4.59	10-23-2021	No
00110010132	1	Ea	Pennsylvania	40_010 - House B	Northeast	Stay in US	Hotel	4.56	09-07-2021	No
00110010133	0	W	Arizona	40_020 - Breakfas	West	The desert cup	Coffee shop	4.56	10-24-2021	No

Figure 6.22

Access by Planner

Natalie, the Vice President of FP&A will see all of the Entities and Products, per her view of `Total_Geography` (Dimensional Access) and its descendants as well as all Products (`Product_Total` Category – Data Cell Access row).

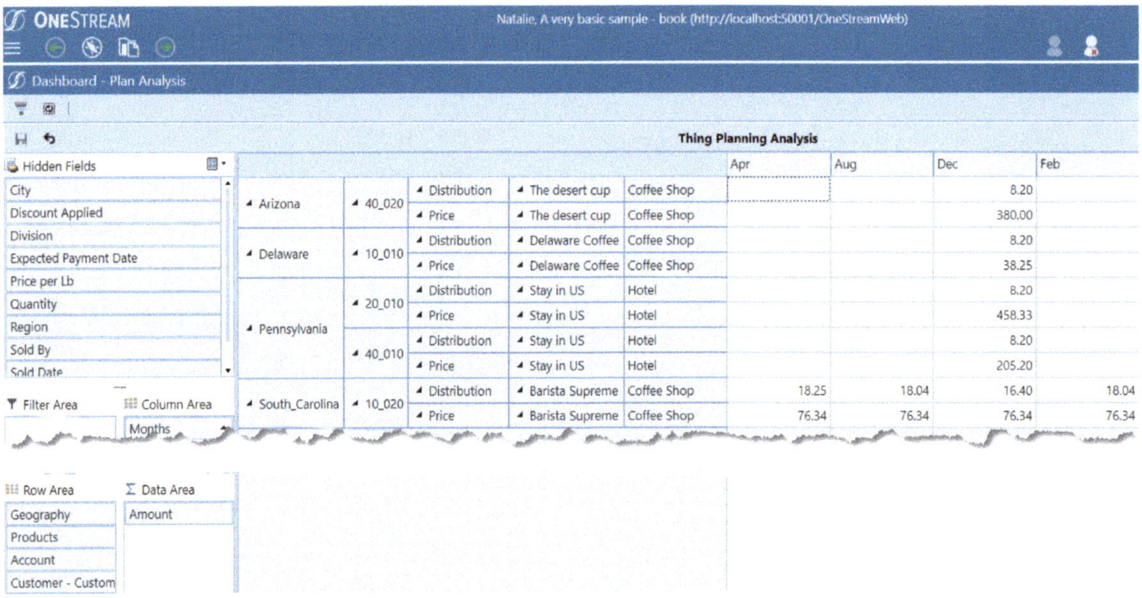

					Apr	Aug	Dec	Feb
Arizona	40_020	Distribution	The desert cup	Coffee Shop			8.20	
		Price	The desert cup	Coffee Shop			380.00	
Delaware	10_010	Distribution	Delaware Coffee	Coffee Shop			8.20	
		Price	Delaware Coffee	Coffee Shop			38.25	
Pennsylvania	20_010	Distribution	Stay in US	Hotel			8.20	
		Price	Stay in US	Hotel			458.33	
	40_010	Distribution	Stay in US	Hotel			8.20	
		Price	Stay in US	Hotel			205.20	
South_Carolina	10_020	Distribution	Barista Supreme	Coffee Shop	18.25	18.04	16.40	18.04
		Price	Barista Supreme	Coffee Shop	76.34	76.34	76.34	76.34

Figure 6.23

Jessica can see all Entities under `West` (Dimensional Access) and all Products (`Product_Total` Category – Data Cell Access row).

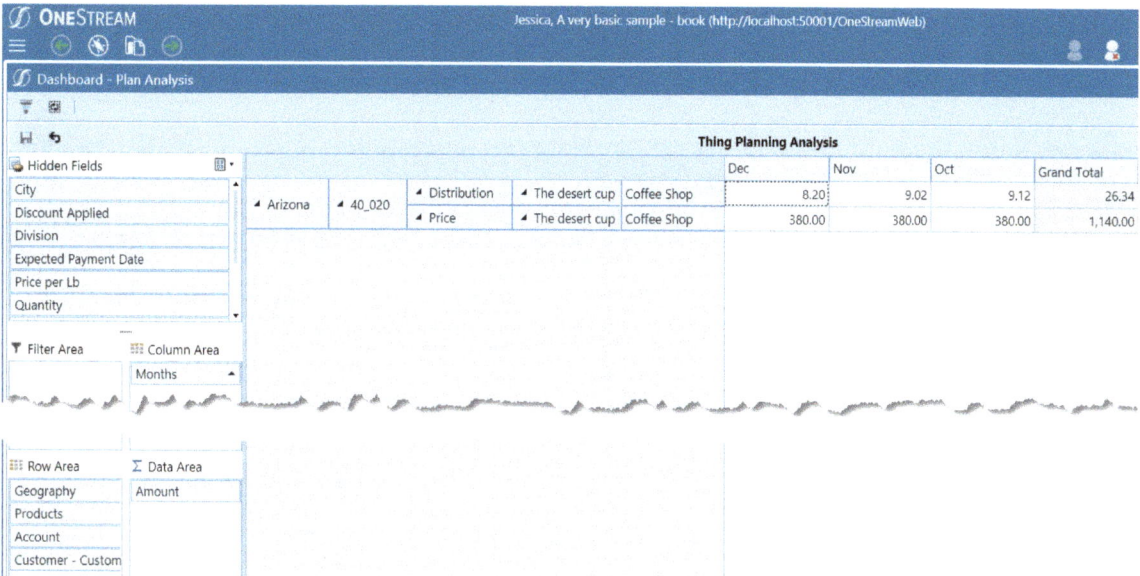

Figure 6.24

Tiffany can see all Ground Coffee Products under East Entities (Ground_Coffee_East Category – Data Cell Access row), all Decaf Products under West Entities (West_Decaf Category – Data Cell Access row), all Whole Bean Products under East Entities (Whole_Bean_East Category – Data Cell Access row).

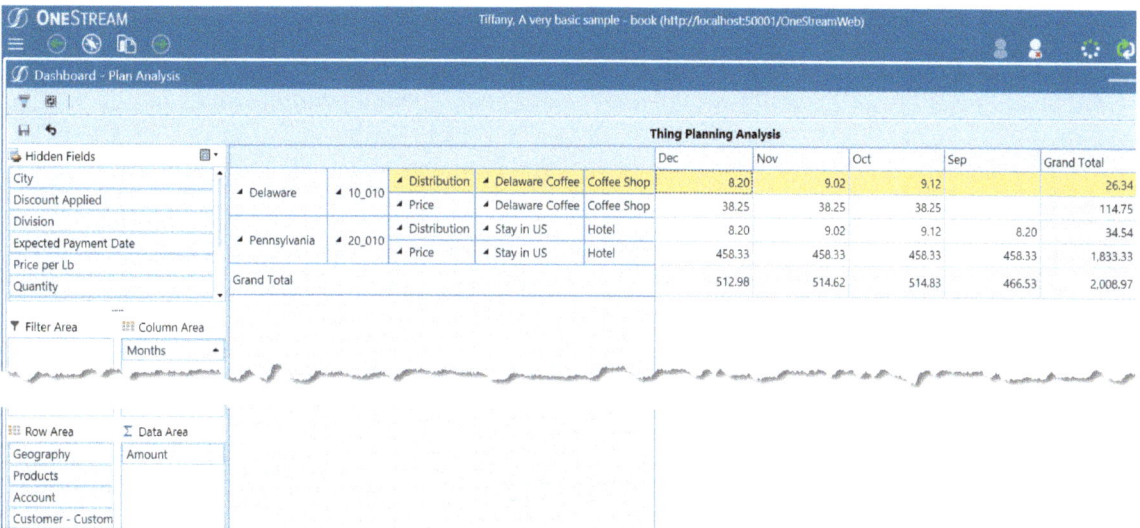

Figure 6.25

Sandra has left C&CCC's FP&A group. Although her username still exists, she has been removed from the `AVBS_South` group and so cannot analyze any information.

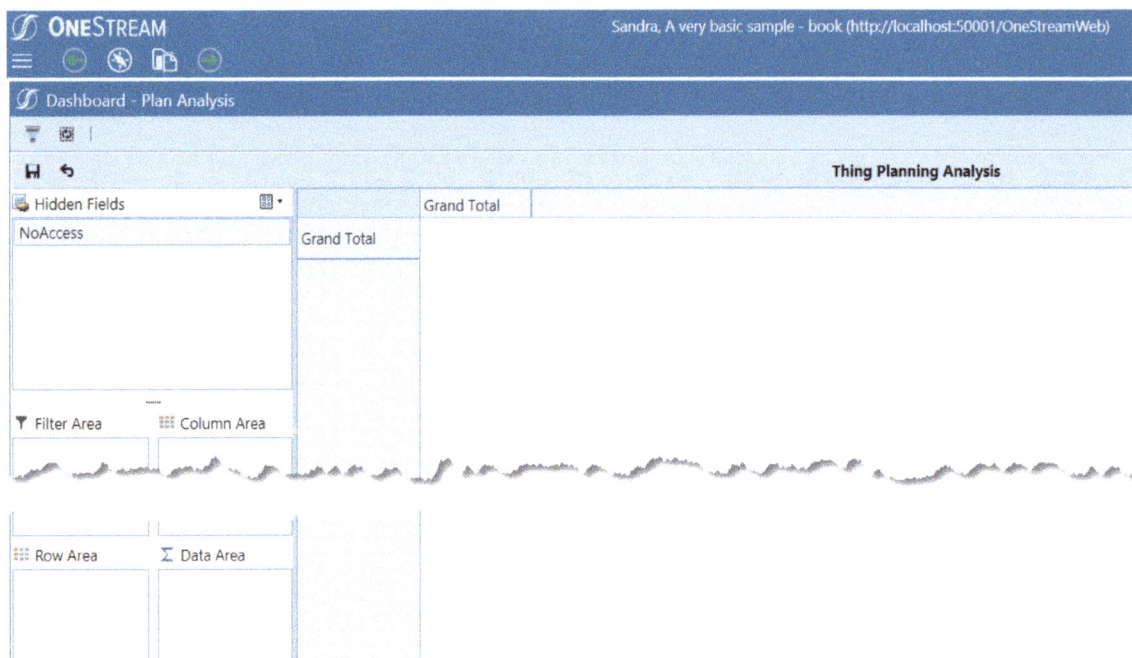

Figure 6.26

Table Views

C&CCC's *FP&A live in Excel*. They love the way Specialty Planning works. They, like all semi-reasonable Users, want to do more, and want to do it in Excel. The business has spoken. On its face, "Can we perform Volume Sales Planning (Thing Planning) in Excel?" seems like a reasonable request. Is it?

If the data was Cube-based, multiple Cube Views embedded in an Excel workbook would fulfill the requirement of planning Volume Sales in Excel. However, since this is done in relational tables, another approach must be taken.

OneStream's 5.2 release debuted the much anticipated/requested Table Views that can be used to analyze relational data in the Spreadsheet. The release, coincidently, made your author's Excel add-in useless.

Using a Spreadsheet Business Rule, Planners can analyze and update data in relational sources.

Thing Planning in Spreadsheet

To give Planners the ability to query, display, and update Register data in a Spreadsheet, the Spreadsheet Rule must perform the following:

1. Fetch the data from Thing Planning Register based on the filters (if any).

2. Modify the Thing Planning Register based on the User actions in the Spreadsheet.

A Spreadsheet Rule supports three function Types in the following order:

1. Allow Users to apply filters on underlying data using bound-Type parameters. This operation is supported in `GetCustomSubstVarsInUse` function Type.

2. Show the filtered data (if using any parameter). This operation is supported in `GetTableView` function Type.

3. If data modification is allowed in the Table View, the modification process is supported by `SaveTable View` function Type.

How to Let the User Filter Data in Table Views

Add parameters to a Spreadsheet Rule using the `GetCustomSubstVarsInUse` function Type.

```
Select Case args.FunctionType

   Case Is = SpreadsheetFunctionType.Unknown

   Case Is = SpreadsheetFunctionType.GetCustomSubstVarsInUse
       Return Me.TLPSearchParameters(si,
args.CustSubstVarsAlreadyResolved)
```

The code above uses a function to return a list of parameters that will be used in this Spreadsheet Rule.

```
Private Function TLPSearchParameters(ByVal si As SessionInfo, ByVal
custSubstVarsAlreadyResolved As Dictionary(Of String, String)) As
List(Of String)
     Try
         ' Prompt for status. You can use parameters here
         '
         Dim list As New List(Of String)
         list.Add("StatusList_TLP")

         Return list
     Catch ex As Exception
        Throw ErrorHandler.LogWrite(si, New XFException(si, ex))
     End Try
  End Function
```

C&CCC's Users filter data using regions (the Status column in Register), using the out-of-the-box `StatusList_TLP` parameter.

When a parameter is added to a Spreadsheet Rule connected to a Table View, the Table View will always prompt the User after a refresh and a save.

This parameter pop-up is often not desired, and can be suppressed after a refresh using the following.

Suppress Parameter Pop-up in Table Views
For background information, see the instructions in the *Suppress Cube View Parameter Popup in Spreadsheet or Excel Add-in Upon Refresh* section in the OneStream *Design and Reference Guide*.

Spreadsheet Instructions
Volume Planning makes use of dropdowns in the Register. However, the lack of support for dropdowns in data columns for a Table View can be mitigated by adding an instructions sheet to the Spreadsheet.

The instruction sheet, as shown below, helps provide the required information to Users about the dropdowns in the Register and what values they need to use in the Spreadsheet (as of OneStream 6.5, Table Views do not support dropdowns in data columns).

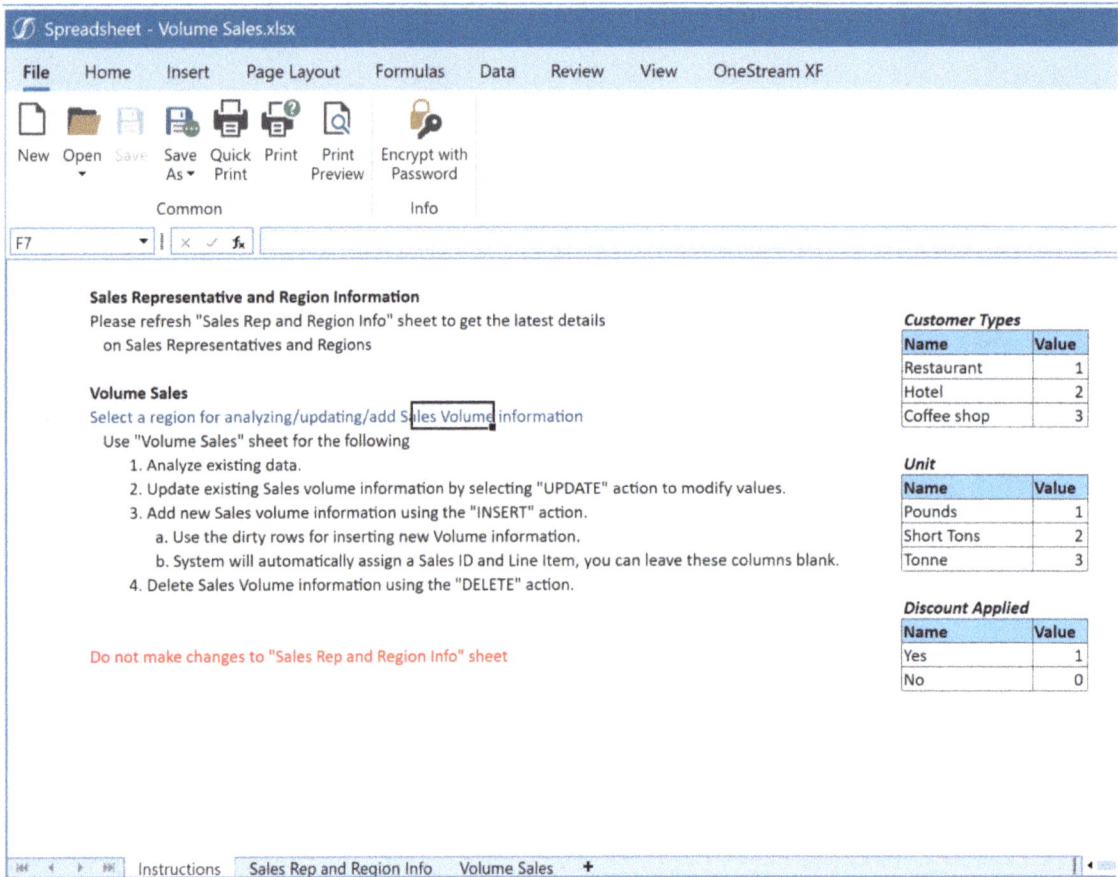

Figure 6.27

Sales Representative and Region

A sheet with two Table View sections pulls Sales Representative and Sales Volume Region information.

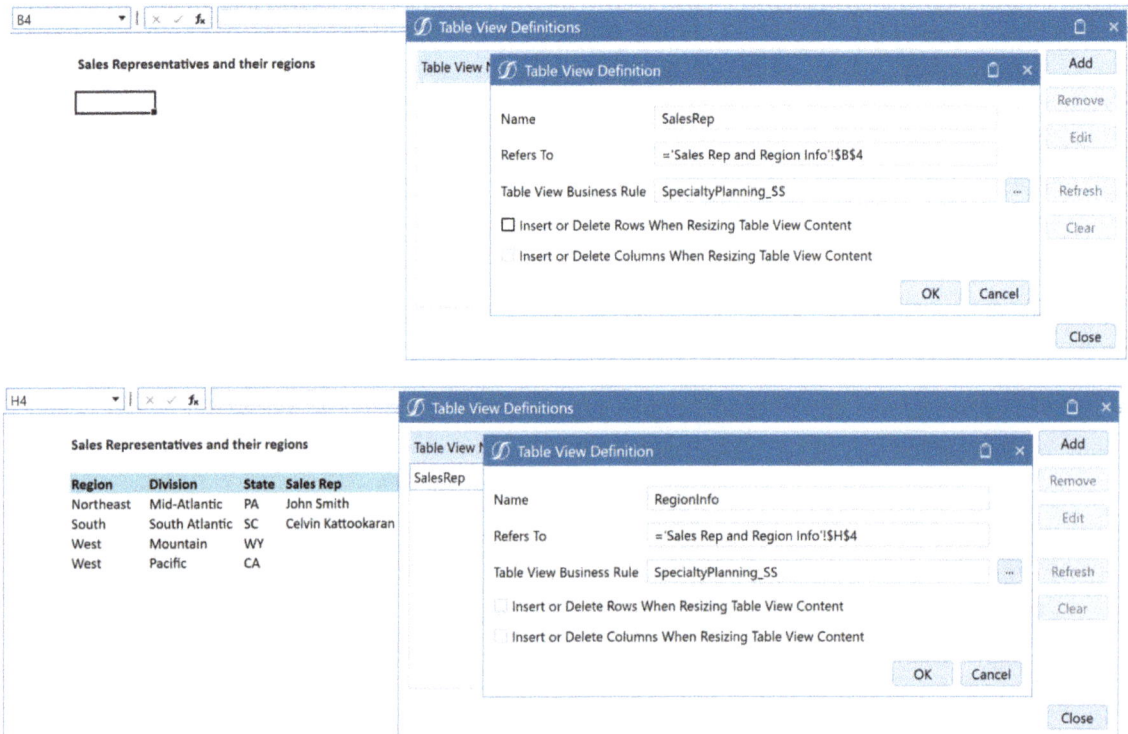

Figure 6.28

As two Table Views are on this sheet, uncheck the Insert or Delete Rows When Resizing Table View Content check box.

Note: If the default option of allowing the Table View to Insert or Delete Rows is checked, the following will happen.

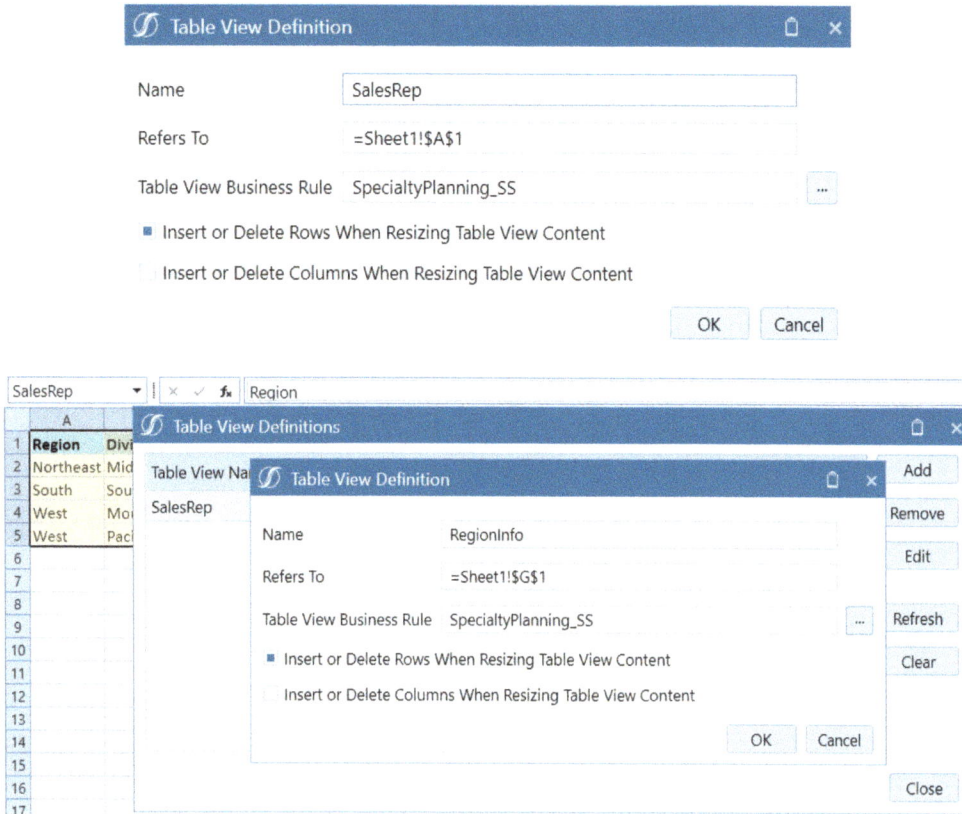

Figure 6.29

When the second Table View is added, it will push the rows of the first Table View to accommodate its rows.

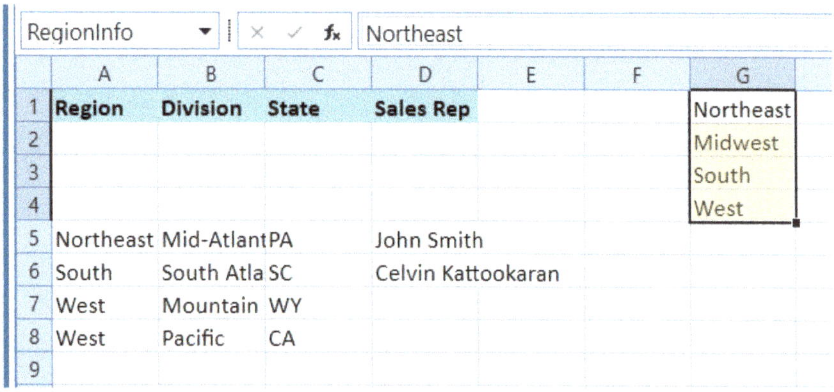

Figure 6.30

Sales Representatives are retrieved from a custom external table so that Users get up-to-date information on the Sales Representatives. Note that this table is completely outside of Thing Planning and is an example of the supplemental relational data that OneStream can support in a solution.

Sales Volume Region is pulled from Thing Register.

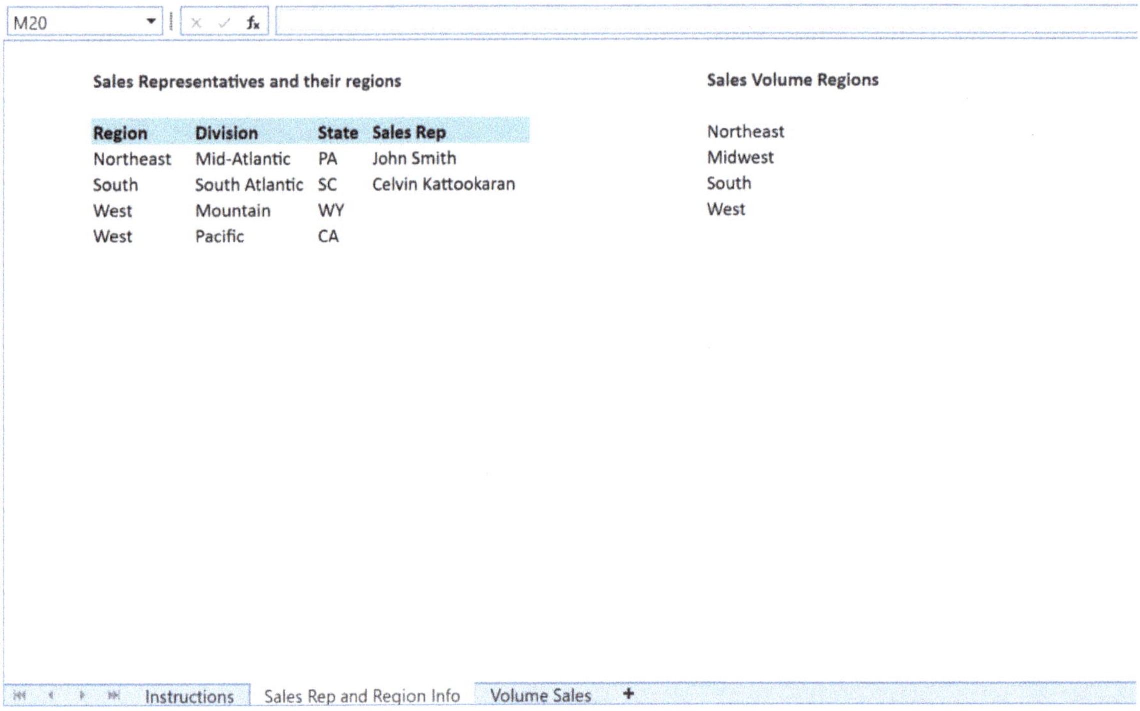

Sales Representatives and their regions

Region	Division	State	Sales Rep
Northeast	Mid-Atlantic	PA	John Smith
South	South Atlantic	SC	Celvin Kattookaran
West	Mountain	WY	
West	Pacific	CA	

Sales Volume Regions

Northeast
Midwest
South
West

Instructions | Sales Rep and Region Info | Volume Sales +

Figure 6.31

While a name can be defined for the Table Views in a rule, it is instead recommended to use a single Spreadsheet Rule/no Table View name for User analysis Table View operations. We are providing this suggestion as there is no option to list the names of the Table Views included in a Spreadsheet Rule, and it can be hard for Users to remember all the different names in a Spreadsheet Rule.

This use case has multiple Table Views in a single Spreadsheet Rule.

```
Case Is = SpreadsheetFunctionType.GetTableView
    If args.TableViewName.XFEqualsIgnoreCase("RegionInfo") Then
        Return Me.GetRegionInformation(si)
    Else If args.TableViewName.XFEqualsIgnoreCase("SalesRep") Then
        Return Me.GetSalesRepInformation(si)
    Else
        Return Me.GetVolumeSalesInformation(si, globals, args.CustSubstVarsAlreadyResolved)
    End If
```

The SalesRep and RegionInfo Table Views are not being exposed for User analysis; they are there to provide the supplemental information to the Users and no more.

After adding the Table Views, OneStream automatically creates named ranges in the Spreadsheet.

Sales Volume Regions

Northeast
Midwest
South
West

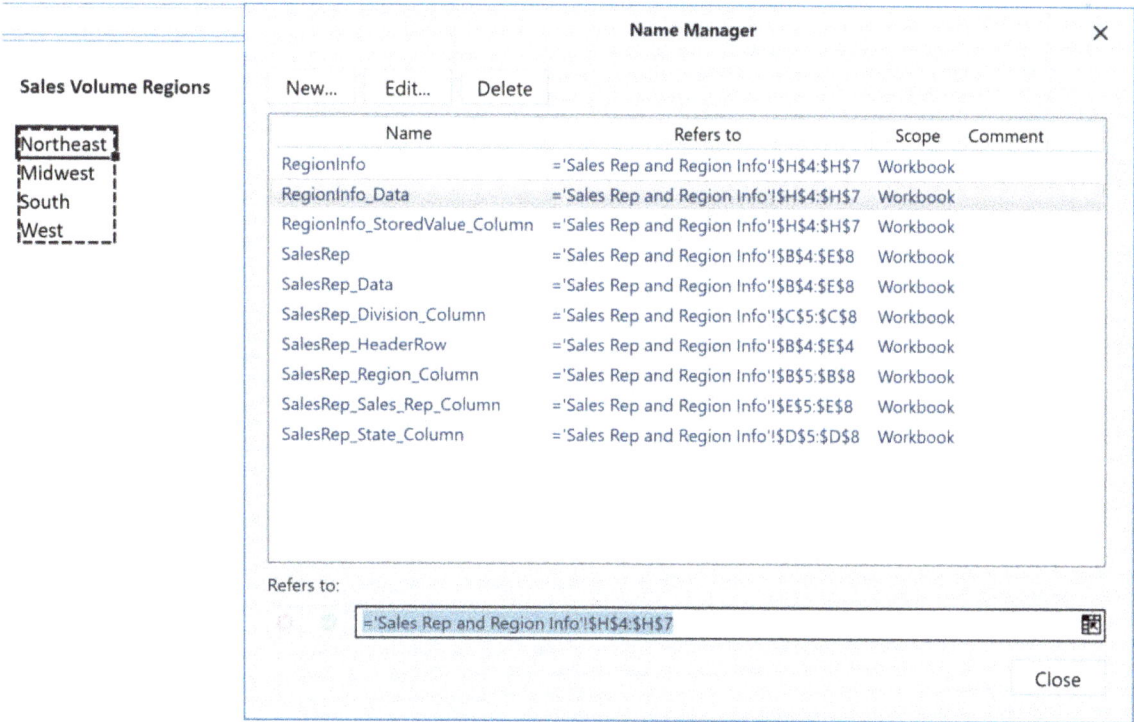

Figure 6.32

Use the RegionInfo_Data-named range to add a dropdown in the Volume Sales sheet.

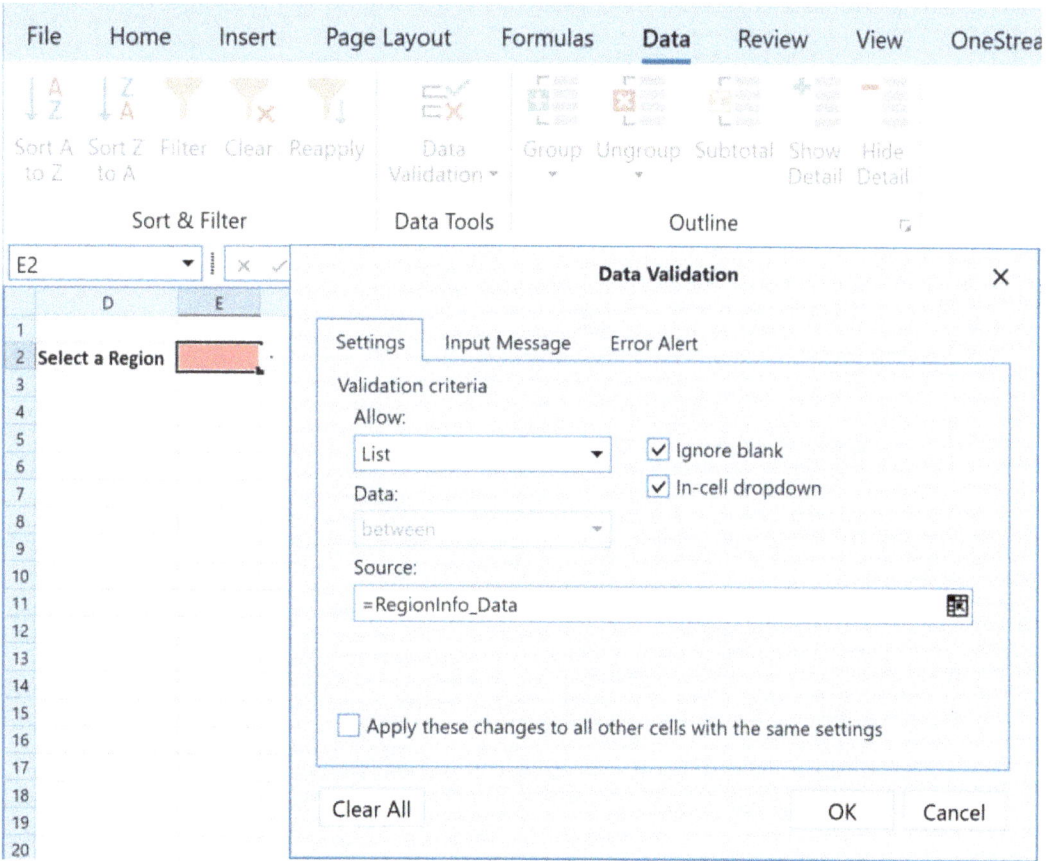

Figure 6.33

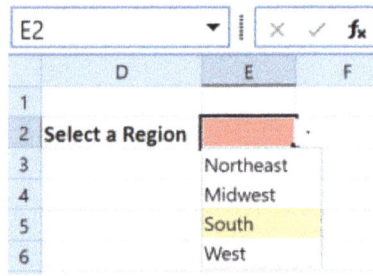

Figure 6.34

Once the list is set up, name this cell with the parameter name. In this example, cell E2 is named StatusList_TLP.

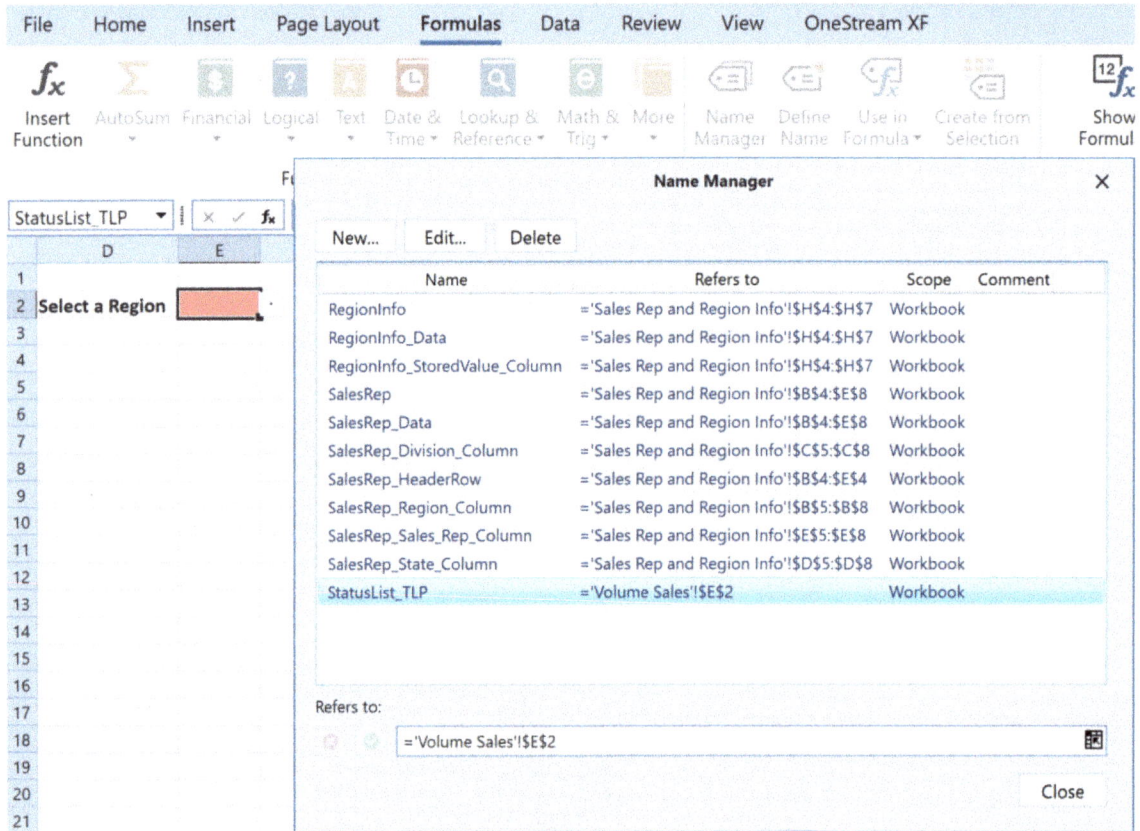

Figure 6.35

By doing this, the cell's Named Range value feeds the parameter value from the Spreadsheet, and the pop-up remains hidden. By using a Table View to pull the Status from Register, only the valid Statuses in Thing Planning are displayed.

How to Get Data in a Table View

Data in Table View is shown to the User with the help of GetTableView function Type.

```
Case Is = SpreadsheetFunctionType.GetTableView
    If args.Table ViewName.XFEqualsIgnoreCase("RegionInfo") Then
        Return Me.GetRegionInformation(si)
    Else If args.Table ViewName.XFEqualsIgnoreCase("SalesRep") Then
        Return Me.GetSalesRepInformation(si)
    Else
        Return Me.GetVolumeSalesInformation(si, globals,
args.CustSubstVarsAlreadyResolved)
    End If
```

264

Multiple Table Views in a Spreadsheet Rule are possible. However, it is recommended to limit one Table View per Spreadsheet, although there is a place for more than one in administrative functions.

Data from External Tables

Sales Representative information is retrieved from an external table using the following function.

```
Dim salesRepInfoView As New TableView()
salesRepInfoView.CanModifyData = False

Using dbConn As DbConnInfo =
BRApi.Database.CreateExternalDbConnInfo(si, "AVBS Warehouse")
    Dim sql As New Text.StringBuilder
    sql.AppendLine("SELECT SalesRegion as Region")
    sql.AppendLine(",SalesDivision as Division")
    sql.AppendLine(",StateCode as State")
    sql.AppendLine(", c.FirstName + ' ' + c.LastName as 'Sales Rep'")
    sql.AppendLine("FROM DimSalesRegion a")
    sql.AppendLine("LEFT OUTER JOIN DimSalesRep b ON
a.SalesRegionKey=b.SalesRegionKey")
    sql.AppendLine("LEFT OUTER JOIN DimEmployee c ON
b.EmployeeKey=c.EmployeeKey")

    Dim dt As DataTable = BRApi.Database.ExecuteSqlUsingReader(dbConn,
sql.ToString, True)
    salesRepInfoView.PopulateFromDataTable(dt, True, True)
    Dim tblHeaderFormat As New TableViewFormat()
    tblHeaderFormat.IsBold = True
    tblHeaderFormat.BackgroundColor = XFColors.LightBlue
    salesRepInfoView.HeaderFormat = tblHeaderFormat

End Using

Return salesRepInfoView
```

The code performs the following steps:

1. Instantiate a new unmodifiable Table View.

2. Create an external database connection information (this database is already added as an external source in the OneStream Application Server configuration). Three tables from the AVBS Warehouse are joined to get the required information on Regions, Divisions, States, and their Sales Representatives.

   Populate the Table View using the `dt` DataTable. Show the column headers (1st Boolean parameter) and use DataTypes in the Table View (2nd Boolean parameter) using `salesRepInfoView.PopulateFromDataTable`.

3. Format the headers to make them pretty.

Status from Thing Planning

Regions are shown in the Spreadsheet using the following function.

```
Dim regionInfoView As New TableView()
regionInfoView.CanModifyData = False

Using dbConn As DbConnInfo =
BRApi.Database.CreateApplicationDbConnInfo(si)
    Dim sql As New Text.StringBuilder
    sql.AppendLine("SELECT StoredValue")
    sql.AppendLine("FROM XFW_TLP_ControlListItems")
    sql.AppendLine("WHERE FieldName='StatusValues'")
    sql.AppendLine("ORDER BY DisplayValue")
```

```
    Dim dt As DataTable = BRApi.Database.ExecuteSqlUsingReader(dbConn,
sql.ToString, True)
    regionInfoView.PopulateFromDataTable(dt, False, True)
End Using

Return regionInfoView
```

Specialty Planning solutions store Status information in a table called
XFW_TLP_ControlListItems. Statuses are stored with a FieldName value of StatusValues.
The values shown in the Status List of Thing Planning are fetched using this function.

Figure 6.36

Since there is only one column, the column headers are suppressed via
regionInfoView.PopulateFromDataTable.

Register Data in Spreadsheet

The Else condition below reflects not using a Table View Name for the Register information.

```
Case Is = SpreadsheetFunctionType.GetTableView
    If args.Table ViewName.XFEqualsIgnoreCase("RegionInfo") Then
        Return Me.GetRegionInformation(si)
    Else If args.Table ViewName.XFEqualsIgnoreCase("SalesRep") Then
        Return Me.GetSalesRepInformation(si)
    Else
        Return Me.GetVolumeSalesInformation(si, globals,
args.CustSubstVarsAlreadyResolved)
    End If
```

The Planner can use this rule to perform analysis by selecting the Table View Business Rule only.
(The name, in this case, is automatically filled by the selection process, it must be left as is for the
rules without a Table View name.)

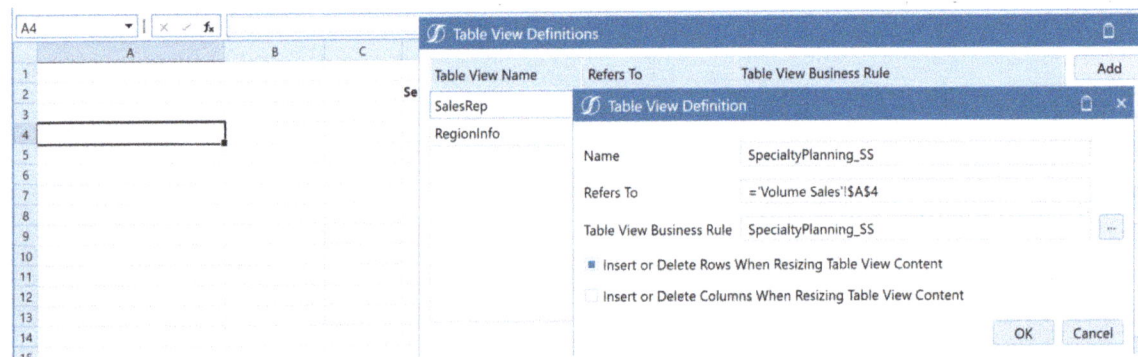

Figure 6.37

266

C&CCC's Users' desire to perform Volume Planning in Excel is satisfied by closely replicating what the Register does.

Planners can use the region filter to pull data from the Register, as shown below.

Select a Region												
Actions	Sales ID	Instance	Region	CustoCustomer Type	Price per lb	Quantity		Unit	Sold Date	Expected Payme	Discount A	Entity
	00110010130		0 South	Barist	3	4.65		100	1 11/22/2020 12:0	1/22/2021 12:0		1 South_Caroli

Figure 6.38

Apart from the Actions columns, it is a replica of the Thing Planning Register.

Columns Based on Region (Status) Selection

To replicate the Register in Spreadsheet, we need to get the Time and Scenario information from the Workflow. This also involves getting the columns that are active and their aliases based on the Region (Status) selected by the User.

```
Dim volumeSalesView As New TableView()
Dim strScenarioName As String = ScenarioDimHelper.GetNameFromID(si,
si.WorkflowClusterPk.ScenarioKey)
Dim strTimeName As String =
BRApi.Finance.Time.GetNameFromId(si,si.WorkflowClusterPk.TimeKey)
```

To bring the Register information to the Spreadsheet, a Table View must be created by querying the Scenario and Time from the current Workflow.

```
If custSubstVarsAlreadyResolved.ContainsKey("StatusList_TLP")
    Dim strStatus As String =
custSubstVarsAlreadyResolved("StatusList_TLP")
    'Create a dictionary of Register Columns and Aliases
    Dim codeDict As Dictionary(Of String, String) =
Me.GetRegisterColAliases(si, strStatus)
```

Check whether the Status substitution variable is resolved (this is done to use the Status value in the SQL WHERE clause), then create a Dictionary that will hold the alias values of the columns that are visible in the Register.

Register column values are stored using a FieldName value of RegCol suffixed with the Status. Each status can have its own set of columns enabled. E.g., the Midwest region can capture more detail than the Northeast region (like a customer address).

267

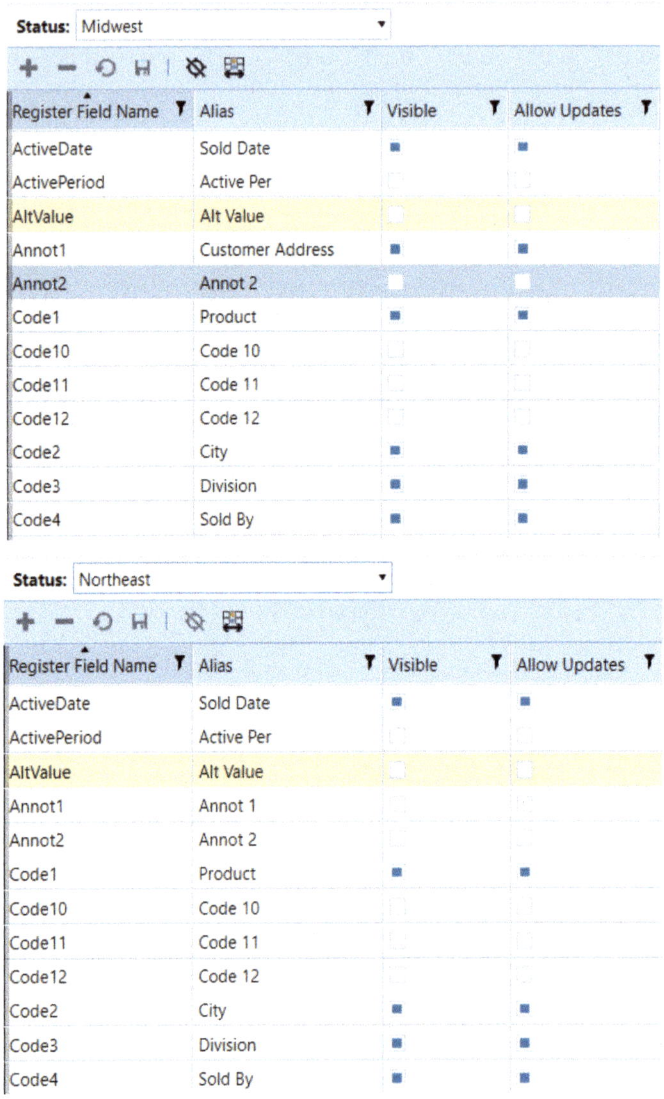

Register Field Name	Alias	Visible	Allow Updates
ActiveDate	Sold Date	■	■
ActivePeriod	Active Per		
AltValue	Alt Value		
Annot1	Customer Address	■	■
Annot2	Annot 2		
Code1	Product	■	■
Code10	Code 10		
Code11	Code 11		
Code12	Code 12		
Code2	City	■	■
Code3	Division	■	■
Code4	Sold By	■	■

Status: Midwest

Register Field Name	Alias	Visible	Allow Updates
ActiveDate	Sold Date	■	■
ActivePeriod	Active Per		
AltValue	Alt Value		
Annot1	Annot 1		
Annot2	Annot 2		
Code1	Product	■	■
Code10	Code 10		
Code11	Code 11		
Code12	Code 12		
Code2	City	■	■
Code3	Division	■	■
Code4	Sold By	■	■

Status: Northeast

Figure 6.39

In C&CCC's case, there are the following column and alias value combinations, ignoring the default *All* and *Exception* statuses.

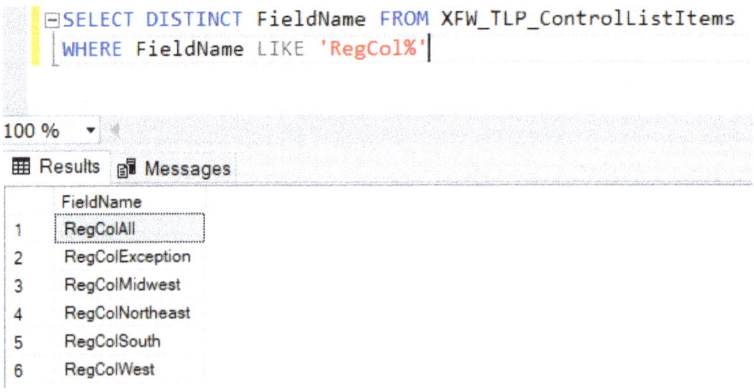

```sql
SELECT DISTINCT FieldName FROM XFW_TLP_ControlListItems
WHERE FieldName LIKE 'RegCol%'
```

100 %

Results | Messages

	FieldName
1	RegColAll
2	RegColException
3	RegColMidwest
4	RegColNortheast
5	RegColSouth
6	RegColWest

Figure 6.40

The code is pulling all valid columns for each Region.

Function for Getting Register Information

A function is created for getting the Register information as this part of the code is re-used.

Use the Register's column names (Register Field Names) as the Dictionary key.

```
Private Function GetRegisterColAliases(ByVal si As SessionInfo, ByVal
strStatus As String) As Dictionary(Of String, String)
   Try
        Dim codeDict As New Dictionary(Of String, String)
        Using dbConn As DBConnInfo =
BRAPi.Database.CreateApplicationDbConnInfo(si)
            Dim codeNameSQL As New Text.StringBuilder
            codeNameSQL.AppendLine("SELECT CASE WHEN
a.DisplayValue='' THEN a.StoredValue ELSE a.DisplayValue END as
DisplayValue")
            codeNameSQL.AppendLine(",a.StoredValue")
            codeNameSQL.AppendLine(", CAST(colOrder.StoredValue as
int) as SortOrder")
            codeNameSQL.AppendLine("FROM XFW_TLP_ControlListItems a
WITH (NOLOCK)")
```

The code performs the following steps:

1. Create a new Dictionary to hold the column names and their aliases.

2. Create database connection information to get the Register column information.

3. Instantiate a new StringBuilder to capture the required SQL.

4. As discussed earlier, the Control List table (XFW_TLP_ControlListItems) holds a handful of information. In this case, we use the columns shown on Register using the Region (Status) selected by the User.

5. StoredValue is the column that holds the column name; DisplayValue holds the alias value. If an alias is not supplied, use StoredValue as the alias.

Column Order from Register

Since this Table View is getting created as a replica of the Register, the code also needs to get the columns in the order they are shown in the Register.

Register column order is stored in the Control List table with a FieldName of RegisterFieldOrder.

Position	Field Name
	Register Field Order List
3	Status
4	ThingName
5	NCode1
6	Value
7	Quantity
8	ThingLevel
9	ActiveDate
10	ActivePeriod
11	IdleDate
12	IdlePeriod
13	OutPeriod
14	OutCode
15	InPeriod
16	InCode
17	Entity
18	Code1
19	Code2
20	Code3
21	Code4

Figure 6.41

This is how the table stores the Register Field Order.

```sql
SELECT FieldName, DisplayValue, StoredValue FROM XFW_TLP_ControlListItems
WHERE FieldName = 'RegisterFieldOrder'
ORDER BY CAST(StoredValue as int)
```

100 % ▼

Results | **Messages**

	FieldName	DisplayValue	StoredValue
1	RegisterFieldOrder	RegisterID	1
2	RegisterFieldOrder	RegisterIDInstance	2
3	RegisterFieldOrder	Status	3
4	RegisterFieldOrder	ThingName	4
5	RegisterFieldOrder	NCode1	5
6	RegisterFieldOrder	Value	6
7	RegisterFieldOrder	Quantity	7
8	RegisterFieldOrder	ThingLevel	8
9	RegisterFieldOrder	ActiveDate	9
10	RegisterFieldOrder	ActivePeriod	10
11	RegisterFieldOrder	IdleDate	11
12	RegisterFieldOrder	IdlePeriod	12

Figure 6.42

```vb
    codeNameSQL.AppendLine("LEFT JOIN XFW_TLP_ControlListItems colOrder
WITH (NOLOCK) on colOrder.DisplayValue=a.StoredValue")
    codeNameSQL.AppendLine("WHERE a.FieldName='RegCol" & strStatus &
"'")
    codeNameSQL.AppendLine("AND (a.Active=1)")
    codeNameSQL.AppendLine("AND
colOrder.FieldName='RegisterFieldOrder'")
    codeNameSQL.AppendLine("ORDER BY SortOrder")
    Dim codeDT As DataTable = BRApi.Database.ExecuteSql(dbConn,
codeNameSQL.ToString, False)

    For Each codeNameDr As DataRow In codeDT.Rows
      codeDict.Add(codeNameDr("StoredValue"),codeNameDr("DisplayValue"))
    Next
End Using

Return codeDict
```

The code performs the following steps:

1. A SELF JOIN on DisplayValue and StoredValue to get column order.

2. Filter the columns based on the Region information (Status).

3. Show only columns that are visible for each Region.

4. Order the columns by the column order.

Once the information is populated in the DataTable, populate the Dictionary with the column names as key, and alias as value, and return it to the calling Component.

Perform Register Actions in Spreadsheet

Users can perform the following actions in a Register.

1. Add new volume information

2. Update existing information

270

3. Delete volume information

For the Spreadsheet Rule to mimic these actions, and to capture the type of action, we are going to make use of the Spreadsheet Status column (not to be confused with the Register status).

```
Using dbConn As DBConnInfo =
BRAPi.Database.CreateApplicationDbConnInfo(si)
    ' Allow table view to update data
    volumeSalesView.CanModifyData = True

    ' Add status columns to table view so that users can interact with
it.
    volumeSalesView.EnableStatusColumn(True, "Actions", 3,
"INSERT,UPDATE,DELETE")
```

A database connection is created for fetching the Register data.

Users can modify the Table View, so set the CanModifyData property of the Table View to True.

Planners must pick an action as there are no buttons on the Spreadsheet (unlike the Register) to find out whether a User wants to DELETE, INSERT, or UPDATE on each row they are changing.

Once enabled (1st parameter), a status column allows adding multiple values as a dropdown list (4th parameter). Set a name for the status column (2nd parameter) and mention where the column will show up in Spreadsheet (3rd parameter, this follows zero-based indexing).

Allowing Row Inserts in Table View

If a Table View is set to allow modifications, you can add empty rows to the Table View (An Excel menu action of Insert > Rows will not work in Table Views) by allowing a certain set of empty rows to be added along with the existing data.

Users want to add new Volume sales information; they are allowed to add up to 15 rows at a time. To distinguish between the existing rows and new rows, a different background color (a custom color is used in this example) is applied to the empty rows.

```
' Add empty columns for inserting data
volumeSalesView.NumberOfEmptyRowsToAdd = 15
volumeSalesView.EmptyRowsBackgroundColor =
XFColors.GetOrCreateColor("#FFFCE4D6")
```

Getting the Data and Adding it in Table View

We are going to make use of the Register columns (stored as Keys in the Dictionary) and their aliases (stored as Values in the Dictionary) to generate the SQL.

```
    Dim sql As New Text.StringBuilder
    sql.AppendLine("SELECT WFProfileName as ProfileName, WFScenarioName
as ScenarioName, WFTimeName as TimeName,")
    sql.AppendLine(String.Join("," ,codeDict.Select(Function(x) x.Key &
" as '" & x.Value & "'").toList()))
    sql.AppendLine("FROM XFW_TLP_Register")
    sql.AppendLine("WHERE Status ='" & strStatus & "'")
    sql.AppendLine("AND WFTimeName='" & strTimeName & "'")
    sql.AppendLine("AND WFScenarioName='" & strScenarioName & "'")

    Dim dt As DataTable = BRApi.Database.ExecuteSqlUsingReader(dbConn,
sql.ToString, True)
    volumeSalesView.PopulateFromDataTable(dt, True, True)

End Using
```

A StringBuilder is created to generate the required SQL.

Workflow `ProfileName`, `ScenarioName`, and `TimeName` are pulled (these columns will be hidden in the Spreadsheet, which is why the Actions column in the previous section *Perform Register Actions in Spreadsheet* was as the 4th column).

Generate the SQL statement using the Dictionary's keys and values to alias the columns. The Dictionary stores values as a **Key Value Pair**: `RegisterID:Sales ID`.

Use a `String.Join` operation to join the list of values as a comma-separated string. This command will generate a string like the one below.

```
RegisterID as 'Sales ID', Code1 as 'Product', IdleDate as 'Expected Payment Date'
```

> **Note:** `ProfileName` can be used in the `WHERE` clause, if you are limiting the User's selection based on Workflows and Statuses.

Generate a `DataTable` using the SQL statement and populate the Table View using the DataTable. `PopulateFromDataTable` is a Method that was introduced in version 6.4.

Formatting Table View Columns

OneStream 6.4 added options for formatting Table View columns. We can make use of them so that particular columns can stand out for the User.

All column headers are given a light blue color using a `TableViewColumnFormat`.

```
Dim tblHeaderFormat As New TableViewFormat()
tblHeaderFormat.IsBold = True
tblHeaderFormat.BackgroundColor = XFColors.LightBlue
volumeSalesView.HeaderFormat = tblHeaderFormat
```

C&CCC's Users would like to show Price with two-digit precision. To achieve this, add a column format similar to the header format. The price column is also given a background color to indicate that it can be updated.

```
' format price per lb to two decimals
Dim priceColFormat As New TableViewColumnFormat()
priceColFormat.NumDecimals = 2
priceColFormat.BackgroundColor = XFColors.LightGoldenrodYellow
volumeSalesView.Columns(8).ColumnFormat = priceColFormat
```

Similar highlighting is added to the Quantity and Unit columns. Keep in mind that you need to refer to columns by their respective column number (9 is Column K, and 10 is Column L).

```
' change quantity, and unit color
Dim updateColFormat As New TableViewColumnFormat
updateColFormat.BackgroundColor = XFColors.LightGoldenrodYellow
volumeSalesView.Columns(9).ColumnFormat = updateColFormat
volumeSalesView.Columns(10).ColumnFormat = updateColFormat
```

Hiding Table View Columns

Profile, Time, and Scenario names are needed for updating and deleting records from the Register. However, C&CCC's Users want this to appear and function as closely to a Register as possible, hence these are hidden in the Table View.

To hide columns in a Spreadsheet, use a column width (your author has found to his chagrin that a column width of zero does not work), which equals a small decimal number. The first three columns are hidden using the code below.

```
' hide profile, scenario, time id columns
Dim hideColFormat As New TableViewColumnFormat
hideColFormat.ColumnWidth = .01
```

```
volumeSalesView.Columns(0).ColumnFormat = hideColFormat
volumeSalesView.Columns(1).ColumnFormat = hideColFormat
volumeSalesView.Columns(2).ColumnFormat = hideColFormat
```

After selecting Northeast from the region selection (currently showing South region), when the Planner performs a "Refresh Sheet" operation, the latest data is retrieved.

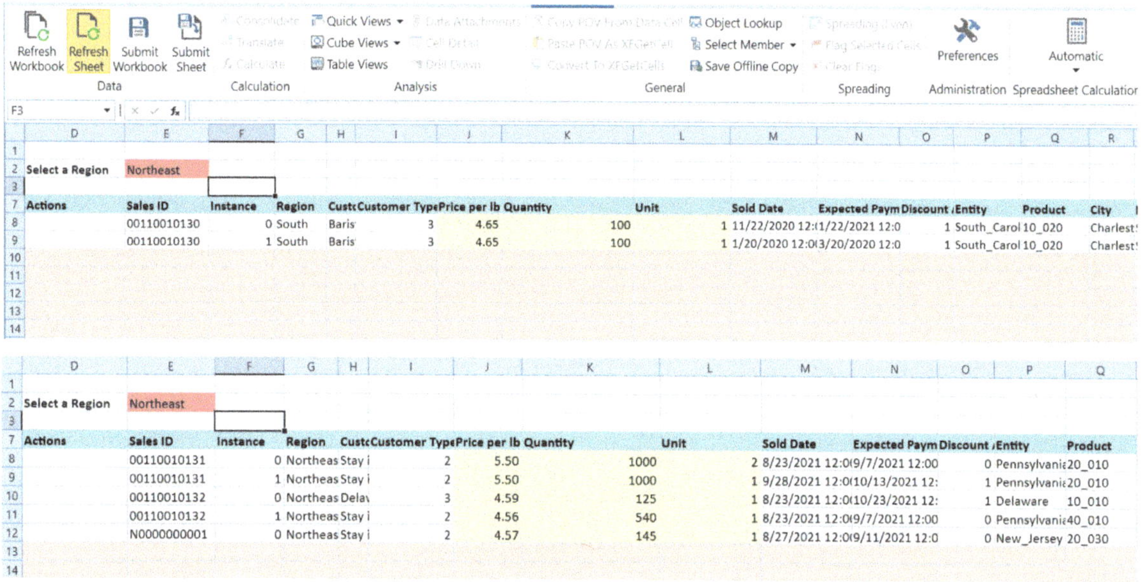

Figure 6.43

How to Update Data from a Table View

Saving a Table View can only work if you are allowing modifications to the Table View. The `SaveTable View` function Type allows Planners to modify the Register contents if `CanModifyData` is set to `True` for the Table View in question.

Here is a function to change the Register.

```
Case Is = SpreadsheetFunctionType.SaveTable View
    Return ChangeTLPRegister(si, globals,
args.CustSubstVarsAlreadyResolved, args.Table View)
```

Pass `BRGlobals`, `CustomSubVars` and the Table View from the Spreadsheet to the function.

Get Register Column Information

The function employed for fetching data is used for updating as well. (The Spreadsheet Rule does not currently support `BRGlobals` and hence the Dictionary cannot be saved as a global object and a repeated call is required to gather the Register column names and aliases information again.) Use a Boolean to flag whether the save worked or not. Generate the code Dictionary (*Register data in Spreadsheet*) to get the aliases and column names as a Dictionary.

```
Dim didSaveWork As Boolean = True
If custSubstVarsAlreadyResolved.ContainsKey("StatusList_TLP")
    Dim strStatus As String =
custSubstVarsAlreadyResolved("StatusList_TLP")
    Dim codeDict As Dictionary(Of String, String) =
    Me.GetRegisterColAliases(si, strStatus)
```

Take Action Only on Changed Rows

Similar to the Register, you can find out which rows are changed by the User, by using the `IsDirty` Method on the Table View Row. Table View is more intelligent than you think it is.

We are going to loop through all the changed rows and perform the respective action selected by the User.

```
If Not tblView Is Nothing
    Dim updateStmt As New Text.StringBuilder
    Dim deleteStmt As New Text.StringBuilder
    Using dbConn As DbConnInfo =
BRApi.Database.CreateApplicationDbConnInfo(si)
        Dim insertDT As DataTable =
BRApi.Database.ExecuteSqlUsingReader(dbConn, "SELECT Top (1) * FROM
XFW_TLP_Register", True).Clone

        For Each tblViewRow As Table ViewRow In
tblView.Rows.Where(Function (x) x.Item("Actions").IsDirty And
x.IsHeader = False)
            If
tblViewRow.Item("Actions").Value.XFEqualsIgnoreCase("INSERT")
                Me.InsertVolumeSales(si, codeDict, tblView, tblViewRow,
insertDT)

            Else If
tblViewRow.Item("Actions").Value.XFEqualsIgnoreCase("UPDATE")
                Me.UpdateVolumeSales(si, codeDict, tblViewRow, updateStmt)

            Else If
tblViewRow.Item("Actions").Value.XFEqualsIgnoreCase("DELETE")
                Me.DeleteVolumeSales(si, codeDict, tblViewRow, deleteStmt)

            End If
        Next
```

This code snippet performs the following steps:

1. Check whether the Table View that got passed is a blank Table View.

2. Two StringBuilders are created to capture the SQL statements for updating and deleting the records.

3. Database connection information is created to capture the structure of the Register table that is used to add new rows (new volume information recorded by Users in the Table View).

4. Loop through the rows in the Spreadsheet and check whether the Actions column is dirty (this check ensures that only edited rows are considered) and the changed row is not a header row).

5. Perform the corresponding action.

For each action (INSERT, UPDATE, DELETE), a specific function is used to perform the activities related to that function.

Update Register Data from Table View

Updating the changes back to the Register is performed by creating a SQL statement using the earlier-generated Register Column Alias Dictionary, and the Updated Table View Row.

The Register Column Alias Dictionary is required to reverse-engineer the Table View column name (Register Aliases) to the real Register Column names (Register Fields).

Pass the Register Column Alias Dictionary, the edited Table View row, and the StringBuilder to the UPDATE function.

```
Dim colNameValues As New Dictionary(Of String, Object)
For Each colName In codeDict.Values
......
Next
```

Create a Dictionary to capture the column name and the changed value.

To generate the SQL Update statement, we need the name of the Register Column and the Value. We are looping through the columns of the changed Table View Row.

```
    colNameValues.Add(codeDict.FirstOrDefault(Function(x)
x.Value.Equals(colName)).Key, tblViewRow.Item(colName).Value)
```

The code above is using a Method to find the key of a Dictionary using its value (Alias – Table View column name, Register Field – Key). Once we get the Register Column name, we add the column name and the value to the Dictionary.

For example, the Register Column Alias Dictionary has three Key Value Pairs: RegisterID:Sales ID, Code1:Product, Code2:City. We are looping through the Table View column names (Sales ID, Product, City) to find their respective key in the Dictionary.

> **Note:** if you want the process to be more efficient, make an additional check to determine if the User changed the value of the column by comparing tblViewRow.Item(colName).OriginalValue.Equals(tblViewRow.Item(colName).Value). To perform this additional check on different column data Types (Decimal, Integer, Date), you will need a conversion from the literal String. The original value will produce a string with precision; hence a string comparison of 125.000000000 to 125.0 will fail.

An UPDATE statement is generated for all the updated rows. The execution of this statement is only done once to maintain better performance.

```
If colNameValues.Count > 0 Then
    updateSTMT.AppendLine("UPDATE XFW_TLP_Register")
    updateSTMT.AppendLine("SET ")
    updateSTMT.AppendLine(String.Join(", ",
colNameValues.Select(Function(x) x.Key & "='" & x.Value &
"'").toList()))
    updateSTMT.AppendLine("WHERE RegisterID ='" &
tblViewRow.Item(codeDict("RegisterID")).Value & "'")
    updateSTMT.AppendLine("AND RegisterIDInstance='" &
tblViewRow.Item(codeDict("RegisterIDInstance")).Value & "'")
    updateSTMT.AppendLine("AND WFProfileName='" &
tblViewRow.Item("ProfileName").Value & "'")
    updateSTMT.AppendLine("AND WFTimeName='" &
tblViewRow.Item("TimeName").Value & "'")
    updateSTMT.AppendLine("AND WFScenarioName='" &
tblViewRow.Item("ScenarioName").Value & "'")

End If
```

This code snippet performs the following steps:

1. Check whether a column update is needed.

2. Generate the UPDATE SQL statement using the captured values.

3. Use a **LINQ** function to get the keys and values from the colNameValues Dictionary to get a list and then join them using a comma to generate a comma-separated string. As an example, if colNameValues has values like Quantity:125, Price:4.35, then the above operation generates the following String: Quantity='125', Price='4.35'

Delete Register Data from Table View

Deleting rows is done by generating a DELETE statement using the RegisterID, Instance, Profile, Time, and Scenario information from the Table View.

Pass the Register Column Alias Dictionary, the edited Table View row, and the StringBuilder to the DELETE function.

```
deleteStmt.AppendLine("DELETE FROM XFW_TLP_Register")
deleteStmt.AppendLine("WHERE RegisterID ='" &
tblViewRow.Item(codeDict("RegisterID")).Value & "'")
deleteStmt.AppendLine("AND RegisterIDInstance='" &
tblViewRow.Item(codeDict("RegisterIDInstance")).Value & "'")
deleteStmt.AppendLine("AND WFProfileName='" &
tblViewRow.Item("ProfileName").Value & "'")
deleteStmt.AppendLine("AND WFTimeName='" &
tblViewRow.Item("TimeName").Value & "'")
deleteStmt.AppendLine("AND WFScenarioName='" &
tblViewRow.Item("ScenarioName").Value & "'")
```

The code gets the RegisterID and RegisterIDInstance values from Table View and generates a DELETE SQL statement for each DELETE row.

This statement is then executed once in the main code.

Add New Records with Auto-generated RegisterIDs from Table View

There are two types of people in this world: those who love RegisterID and those who do not. Gentle Reader, you know where C&CCC's Users stand by this section's title. 😊

This step also needs to adhere to the security that is setup on the Register using Workflow Entities; as we saw in the previous chapter, *Planning without limits,* Register security is driven through the Profile Entities. While adding new Volume information, we now need to find out the correct profile name using the Entity added by the User.

We also need to generate all the default values for the columns that are not present in the Table View as many of these columns are not NULLABLE while performing an INSERT operation.

Instead of generating multiple INSERT statements, and performing them one after the other, we are going to generate a DataTable with all the required information and use a BULK upload approach.

Since we are taking a BULK upload approach, we need to grab all the columns in the Register and understand their data Types (for creating the default values).

Pass the Register Column Alias Dictionary, the Table View, the edited Table View row, and the DataTable (which has the Register Column information) to the INSERT function.

Getting the Scenario, and Time names from the current Workflow. This will be used to add the row to the Register table.

```
Dim strScenarioName As String = ScenarioDimHelper.GetNameFromID(si,
si.WorkflowClusterPk.ScenarioKey)
Dim strTimeName As String =
BRApi.Finance.Time.GetNameFromId(si,si.WorkflowClusterPk.TimeKey)
```

Get Workflow Name from the User-entered Entity

Since Users can type in the Entity Member name to the Spreadsheet (versus a dropdown based on the Profile Entities in the Register), we need to find the matching profile to send the newly created Volume information.

The code to get the profile from the Entity works as follows.

Using an ancestor (the ancestor of Volume Planning Workflows is C&C Plan) Workflow, loop through all the descendants of Type Import and get the assigned Entity information if they are used for Volume Planning.

C&CCC's Volume Planning information is under the Main review Workflow called C&C Plan, as shown below.

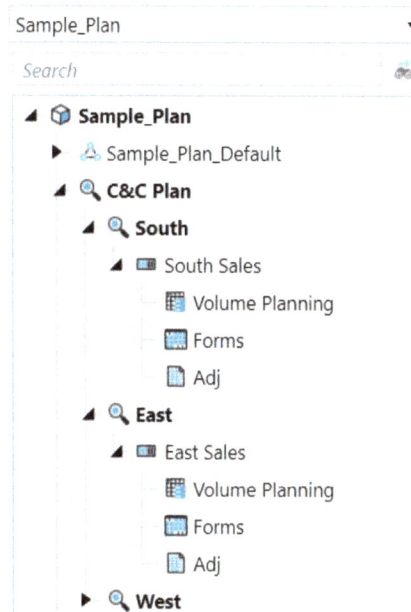

Figure 6.44

```
' Get all workflows under C&C Plan review groups
' All Volume Planning workflows are assumed to be under this parent
Dim wfClusterPk As WorkflowUnitClusterPk =
BRApi.Workflow.General.GetWorkflowUnitClusterPk(si, "C&C Plan",
strScenarioName, strTimeName)
Dim objList As List(Of WorkFlowProfileInfo) =
BRApi.Workflow.Metadata.GetRelatives(si, wfClusterPk,
WorkflowProfileRelativeTypes.Descendants,
WorkflowProfileTypes.InputImportChild)

Dim wfEntityLookup As New Dictionary(Of String, String)
For Each wfChild As WorkflowProfileInfo In objList
  Dim strWFName As String() = wfChild.Name.Split(".")
  If strWFName(1).Equals("Volume Planning") Then
    'Get the entity assignment for this wf
    Dim wfEntList As List(Of WorkflowProfileEntityInfo) =
BRApi.Workflow.Metadata.GetProfileEntities(si, wfChild.ProfileKey)
    If wfEntList.Count > 0 Then
      For Each entityAssignentValue As WorkflowProfileEntityInfo In
wfEntList
        wfEntityLookup.Add(entityAssignentValue.EntityName,
wfChild.Name)
      Next
    End If
  End If
Next
```

This code section performs the following steps:

1. Get the Workflow Unit cluster using C&C Plan, Scenario, and Time information.

2. Query the descendants of that Workflow, which are of the Type Import (Volume Planning is of Import Type).

3. Create a Dictionary to hold the Entity and Workflow information.

4. Loop the Workflow Profile information to check if the Workflow Profile is Volume Planning by splitting the Workflow name by " . "

5. For all the Volume Planning Workflows, get the profile Entities and add the Entity Name and the profile name to the Dictionary.

Generate a RegisterID

Generating a `RegisterID` can be handled in many ways. You can generate a sequential ID for every single row, or you can generate one using a combination of columns. In C&CCC's case, we want to generate a new ID for any new combination of Entity, Product, and City.

Use a combination of Entity-Product-City to auto-generate a Sales ID. If this is an existing combination, get the Sales ID (`RegisterID`) and add it as a new Instance (`RegisterIDInstance`).

This code section performs the following steps:

1. Create a database connection information to get the required information from the Register table.

2. Capture the Users' Entity, Product, and City information.

3. Get the correct profile for this new row.

```
Using dbConn As DbConnInfo =
BRApi.Database.CreateApplicationDbConnInfo(si)
    Dim strEntityName As String =
tblViewRow.Item(codeDict("Entity")).Value
    Dim strProductName As String =
tblViewRow.Item(codeDict("Code1")).Value
    Dim strCityName As String =
tblViewRow.Item(codeDict("Code2")).Value
    Dim strProfileName As String = wfEntityLookup(strEntityName)
```

This code section performs the following steps:

1. Create a StringBuilder to generate the SQL to find out the existing `RegisterID` and the `Max RegisterIDInstance` for Entity-Product-City combination.

2. Populate a `DataTable` with the information from the Register.

```
Dim salesIDInfo As New Text.StringBuilder
    salesIDInfo.AppendLine("SELECT RegisterID, MAX(RegisterIDInstance)
as RegisterIDInstance")
    salesIDInfo.AppendLine("FROM XFW_TLP_Register")
    salesIDInfo.AppendLine("WHERE WFProfileName='" & strProfileName &
"'")
    salesIDInfo.AppendLine("AND WFTimeName='" & strTimeName & "'")
    salesIDInfo.AppendLine("AND WFScenarioName='" & strScenarioName &
"'")
    salesIDInfo.AppendLine("AND Entity='" & strEntityName & "' AND
Code1='" & strProductName & "' AND Code2='" & strCityName & "'")
    salesIDInfo.AppendLine("GROUP BY RegisterID")
    Dim salesIDAndInstance As DataTable =
BRApi.Database.ExecuteSqlUsingReader(dbConn, salesIDInfo.ToString,
True)
```

If this is a new combination, the above generated `DataTable` will be empty. If this is an existing combination, we'll get the RegisterID and the last instance of this ID.

Padding in VB.Net

A literal parameter is used to keep track of the Sales ID sequence.

General (Parameter)	
Name	paramLastSalesID
Description	
User Prompt	
Maintenance Unit	000 Parameters
Sort Order	0
Data Source	
Parameter Type	Literal Value
Default Value	1

Figure 6.45

C&CCC's Sales IDs follow an 11-digit pattern; this parameter value is left padded to fill to the 11 digits.

```
Dim strSalesID As String = String.Empty
Dim intLastSalesID As Integer =
ConvertHelper.ToInt32(BRApi.Dashboards.Parameters.GetLiteralParameterV
alue(si, False, "paramLastSalesID"))
Dim intLineItemNum As Integer = 0
If salesIDAndInstance.Rows.Count > 0 Then
    strSalesID = salesIDAndInstance.Rows(0)("RegisterID")
    intLineItemNum = salesIDAndInstance.Rows(0)("RegisterIDInstance") +
1
Else
    Dim intNewSalesID as Integer = (intLastSalesID + 1)
    strSalesID = "N" & intNewSalesID.ToString.PadLeft(10, "0")
    intLineItemNum = 0
    BRApi.Dashboards.Parameters.SetLiteralParameterValue(si, False,
"paramLastSalesID", intNewSalesID)
End If
```

This code section performs the following steps:

1. Create a String and an integer to hold the SalesID and LineItem information.

2. Get the last known new SalesID number from the parameter.

3. If the DataTable has a value, this means the "Entity-Product-City" combination exists. Get that RegisterID information and then increment the RegisterIDInstance by one to create the new record.

4. If the combination is not present, increment the last known number, and generate an 11-digit code.

5. Update the parameter with the new SalesID.

Creating the DataTable from Table View Row

Since the BULK Upload Method is used, we need to add rows to the empty DataTable with values from the Table View.

Calculated values, and the values that are present in the Table View, are added to the DataTable.

```
Dim regDR As datarow = insertDT.NewRow
Dim soldDate As Date = tblViewRow.Item(codeDict("ActiveDate")).Value
Dim decCustomerType As Decimal =
tblViewRow.Item(codeDict("NCode1")).Value
```

C&CCC calculates *Expected Payment Date* using the Sold Date and Customer Type. Capture those data values from the Table View.

For the columns that are present in the Table View, we are either going to read them from the Table View row or calculate them.

```
For Each regDC As DataColumn In insertDT.Columns
   If codeDict.ContainsKey(regDC.ColumnName) ' these are the columns
that are present in the Table View
      ' calculated columns
      If regDC.ColumnName.XFEqualsIgnoreCase("RegisterID") Then
         regDR("RegisterID") = strSalesID
      Else If
regDC.ColumnName.XFEqualsIgnoreCase("RegisterIDInstance") Then
         regDR("RegisterIDInstance") = intLineItemNum
      Else If regDC.ColumnName.XFEqualsIgnoreCase("IdleDate") Then
         If decCustomerType = 3 Then 'coffee shop
            regDR("IdleDate") = soldDate.AddMonths(2)
         ElseIf decCustomerType = 2 Then ' hotel
            regDR("IdleDate") = soldDate.AddDays(15)
         ElseIf decCustomerType = 1 Then ' restaurant
            regDR("IdleDate") = soldDate.AddMonths(1)
         End If
```

The code performs the following operations:

1. Loop through the columns present in the DataTable (all the columns in XFW_TLP_Register).

2. Check if the column is present in the Table View; check whether these are calculated. If they are calculated, then calculate the value and assign it.

Register Columns Present in Table View

If the Register columns are present in the Table View, we need to make sure that they have a value in the Table View. (NULL values cannot be inserted to the Register.)

```
      Else   ' These columns are the ones that are coming from
spreadsheet
         If
String.IsNullOrEmpty(tblViewRow.Item(codeDict(regDC.ColumnName)).Value
)
            If regDC.DataType.Equals(GetType(Int32)) Then
               regDR(regDC.ColumnName) = 0
            Else If regDC.DataType.Equals(GetType(Decimal)) Then
               regDR(regDC.ColumnName) = 0
            Else If regDC.DataType.Equals(GetType(DateTime)) Then
               regDR(regDC.ColumnName) =
Convert.ToDateTime("1/1/2000")
            Else If regDC.DataType.Equals(GetType(String)) Then
               regDR(regDC.ColumnName) = String.Empty
            End If
         Else
            regDR(regDC.ColumnName) =
tblViewRow.Item(codeDict(regDC.ColumnName)).Value
         End If
      End If
```

The code performs the following:

1. If the column is not a calculated column, and is present in the Table View, check whether the value from the Spreadsheet is an empty string.

2. If this is an empty string, check the data Type of the current column and assign a default value based on the data Type. Assign variable Type initial values as appropriate, e.g., the date field gets a default value of 1/1/2000, the string field gets a blank value, and so forth.

3. If the value from the Table View is not empty, assign that value to the current cell.

Register Columns Not Present in Table View

Columns that are not present in Table View get the default value.

Since WFProfileName, WFTimeName, and WFScenarioName columns are not added with the same name in the Table View (they are called as ProfileName, TimeName, ScenarioName in Table View), they are treated as if they are not present.

```
Else ' these are the columns that are not present in the table view
    If regDC.ColumnName.XFEqualsIgnoreCase("WFProfileName") Then
        regDR("WFProfileName") = strProfileName
    Else If regDC.ColumnName.XFEqualsIgnoreCase("WFScenarioName")
Then
        regDR("WFScenarioName") = strScenarioName
    Else If regDC.ColumnName.XFEqualsIgnoreCase("WFTimeName") Then
        regDR("WFTimeName") = strTimeName
    Else
        If regDC.DataType.Equals(GetType(Int32)) Then
            regDR(regDC.ColumnName) = 0
        Else If regDC.DataType.Equals(GetType(Decimal)) Then
            regDR(regDC.ColumnName) = 0
        Else If regDC.DataType.Equals(GetType(DateTime)) Then
            regDR(regDC.ColumnName) = Convert.ToDateTime("1/1/2000")
        Else If regDC.DataType.Equals(GetType(String)) Then
            regDR(regDC.ColumnName) = String.Empty
        End If
    End If
End If
Next
insertDT.Rows.Add(regDR)
```

The code performs the following:

1. Assign the Profile Name using the Entity value.
2. Assign Scenario and Time from the current Workflow.
3. For the columns that are not present in the Table View, they get the default values based on their data Types.
4. After the end of the column loop, add the new row to the DataTable.

This DataTable is saved once for better efficiency in the main code.

Performing the Actions

All the operations that were performed on the Table View are updated/deleted/inserted all at once for better efficiency.

```
If updateStmt.Length > 0 Then
    BRApi.Database.ExecuteActionQuery(dbConn,
updateStmt.ToString, True, True)
End If

If deleteStmt.Length > 0 Then
    BRApi.Database.ExecuteActionQuery(dbConn,
deleteStmt.ToString, True, True)
End If

If insertDT.Rows.Count > 0 Then
```

```
            BRApi.Database.SaveCustomDataTable(si, "App",
"XFW_TLP_Register", insertDT, True)
         End If
      End Using

   End If

   didSaveWork = True
Return didSaveWork
```

UPDATE and DELETE functions populate the SQL statements for the specific actions. Check whether the StringBuilder is empty or not by looking at its length. If there are SQL statements, we are executing them against the Register.

The INSERT function populates a DataTable with the new records. Check whether there are any new records by looking at the Row count. If there are new rows, save the DataTable to the Register.

C&CCC's Users are all (hopefully, given the not inconsiderable effort to make them so) happy with the new solution where they can use something near as damnit to Excel for performing their Volume Sales Planning.

Supplemental Data Analysis Without Wreaking Havoc on Stage

When a company's supplemental data is in flux (imagine frequently changing Sales Representatives), it requires a data re-load to bring in the frequently changing supplemental data. In cases like these, it is recommended *not* to use Stage attributes for supplemental data analysis.

The same situation can arise when trying to analyze transactional details like invoice numbers, invoice dates, etc., by performing a drill back to Stage. In this case, the first instinct is to load those records into Stage, and by doing so, make Stage act like a data warehouse where millions of records are loaded just for analysis purposes (this is the approach explored in the chapter *Planning Without Limits*).

When this data is loaded to the Cube, those millions of records are summarized to hundreds of thousands or less since transactional details like invoice numbers and invoice dates have no place in the Cube. The loading process and summarization of the records to Cube level in Stage can be time-consuming, almost certainly so when large datasets are considered.

Why Not Stage and Stage Attributes?

The supplemental data load to Stage approach discussed in the previous chapter assumes a simple and clean dataset.

In both scenarios described above, a more sophisticated approach that operates outside OneStream is required. On-Cube supplemental data is not loaded to Stage. Those extra data elements are retained at the source and summarized outside OneStream before loading to a Cube.

NB – This design presupposes a relational data source; file-based data would need to be imported into a custom table.

Product	Geography	Account	City	Sales Rep	Amount
10_010	Pennsylvania	Sales	Philadelphia		120.000
10_020	Pennsylvania	Sales	Philadelphia		93.000
10_020	South_Carolina	Sales	Charleston	Celvin Kattookaran	678.000
10_020	South_Carolina	Sales	Columbia	Celvin Kattookaran	125.000

Product	Geography	Account	Amount
10_010	Pennsylvania	Sales	120.000
10_020	Pennsylvania	Sales	93.000
10_020	South_Carolina	Sales	803.000

Figure 6.46

Once summarized, the data is loaded to OneStream. As shown in the example below, South Carolina's City and Sales Rep fields are dropped as part of the summarization process.

If OneStream no longer stores City and Sales Rep, how can it report on those elements of data?

The answer is **Connector Rules**. These rules allow the creation of custom multi-level drill backs for analysis. In the example above, one drill can provide Sales Rep and City information. A separate one could show the same Sales Rep and City fields as well as Sales Order Number and Sales Line Item details.

Connector Rules

Connector Rules are Business Rules that can reach a source and pull data from it. Drill backs to the external system using a Connector Rule can also be performed through them.

This section's use case examines the details of when a Connector Rule is used in a data source, during the load, and a drill back process.

> **Note:** The example given below uses an external database, and so, instead of a connection string, the external database name (found in the Application configuration) is used along with the `isNamedConnection` Boolean set to `True`.

How Does It Work?

Connector Rules used in conjunction with data sources are an alternative way to load data into OneStream.

A Connector Rule uses action Types to support the following functionality.

1. `GetFieldList` – returns the available columns in a rule for data source mapping.

2. `GetData` – queries the source (flat file, tables, REST API, anything that can be queried) and returns the data for the data source to load.

3. `GetDrillBackTypes` – returns all the different Types of drill backs defined in the rule to the User. (You can define multiple drills.)

4. `GetDrillBack` – returns the drill back data using the drill Type defined in the rule.

Fields in a Data Source

Creating a data source and assigning a Connector Rule shows all of the fields that the Connector Rule supports.

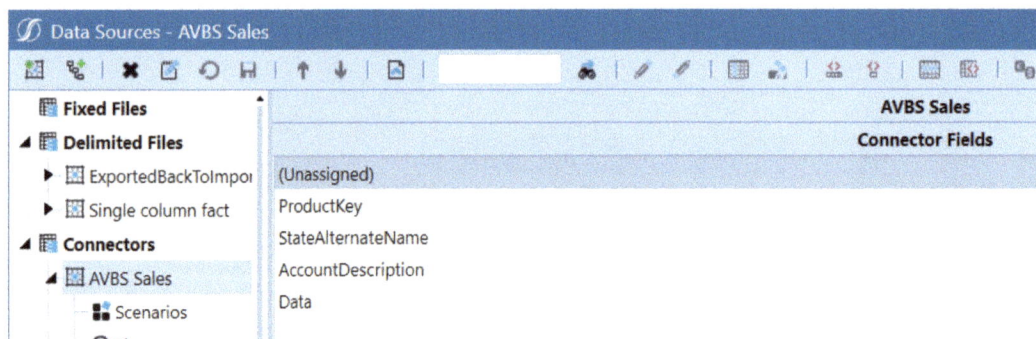

Figure 6.47

An Action Type populates this list in the Connector Rule, and it is called GetFieldList.

```
Case Is = ConnectorActionTypes.GetFieldList

    'Get the list of field names in the source table by selecting one
row
    Dim strSQL As String = "SELECT Top 1 " & Me.GetSQLColumns(si,
globals, api, args)
    Return api.Parser.GetFieldNameListForSQLQuery(si,
DbProviderType.SqlServer, "AVBS Warehouse", True, strSQL, False)
```

GetFieldList needs a list of strings to return the names of columns in the Connector Rule.

```
Private Function GetSQLColumns(ByVal si As SessionInfo, ByVal globals
As BRGlobals, ByVal api As Transformer, ByVal args As ConnectorArgs)
As String
    Try
        'Get the SQL string for the valid fields in the fact table
        Dim sql As New Text.StringBuilder
        sql.Appendline("a.ProductKey, c.StateAlternateName,
b.AccountDescription, Sum(Amount) As Data")
        sql.Appendline("FROM FactProductSales a")
        sql.Appendline("LEFT OUTER JOIN DimAccount b On a.AccountKey =
b.AccountKey")
        sql.Appendline("LEFT OUTER JOIN DimGeography c ON
a.GeographyKey=c.GeographyKey")
        sql.Appendline("GROUP BY a.ProductKey, c.StateAlternateName,
b.AccountDescription")

        Return sql.ToString

    Catch ex As Exception
        Throw ErrorHandler.LogWrite(si, New XFException(si, ex))
    End Try
End Function
```

This approach uses the GetFileNameListForSQLQuery Method to create the list of columns.

This code section performs the following steps:

1. As the data is summarized and loaded to OneStream, select a single row from the Datawarehouse Fact table.

2. Join the other Dimension tables (`DimAccount`, and `DimGeography`) to get more Dimension details.

3. Data summarization (`SUM(Amount)`) is done by grouping Product, State, and Account information.

4. Return the generated SQL for the parser to generate a list of columns.

Load Process

```
Case Is = ConnectorActionTypes.GetData
    Dim strSQL As String = "SELECT " & Me.GetSQLColumns(si, globals, api, args)
    api.Parser.ProcessSQLQuery(si, DbProviderType.SqlServer, "AVBS Warehouse", True, strSQL, False, api.ProcessInfo)
```

The same function is used to generate the column lists to generate the SQL data; all rows are selected.

`ProcessSQLQuery` is used to process and get the data from the source. If this was a flat-file load, you could use `ProcessTextFile`.

Drill Back Options

When a Planner navigates to the source data from a drilldown, and clicks on Drill Back, `GetDrillBackTypes` is responsible for presenting the possible drill back Types.

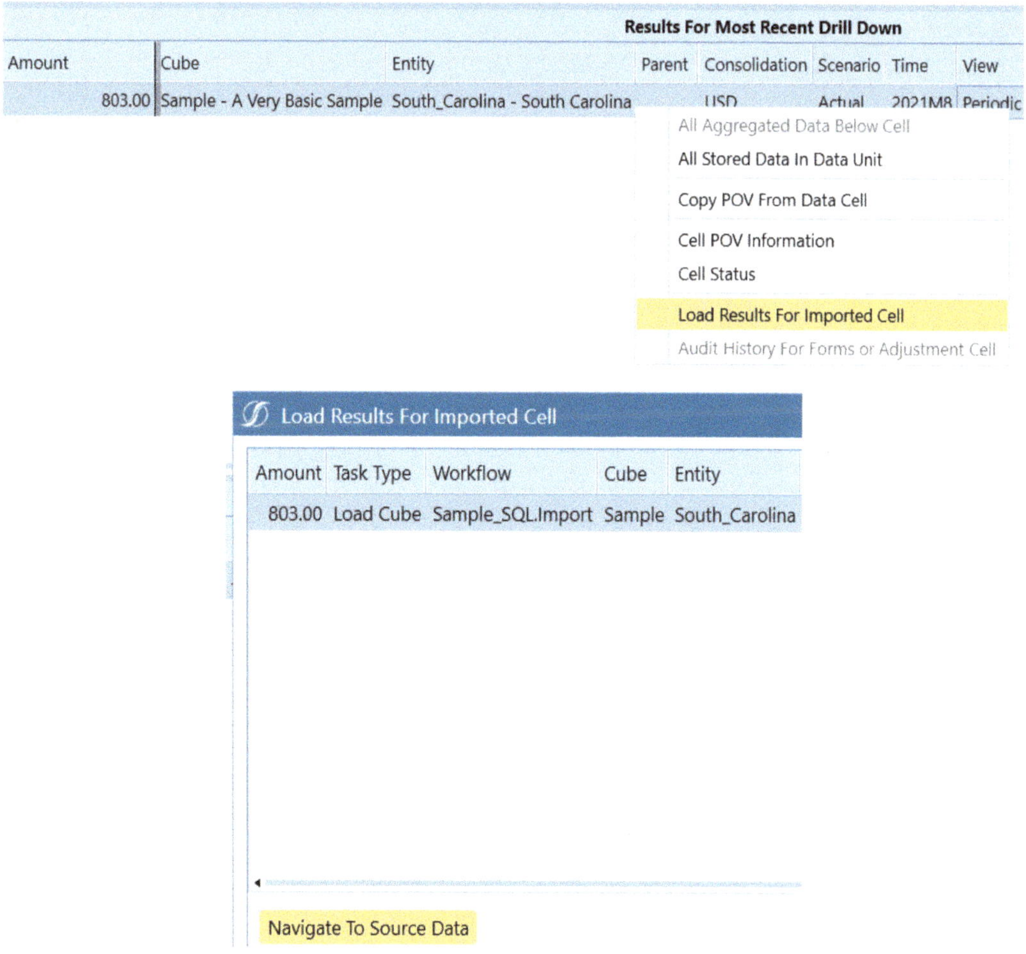

Figure 6.48

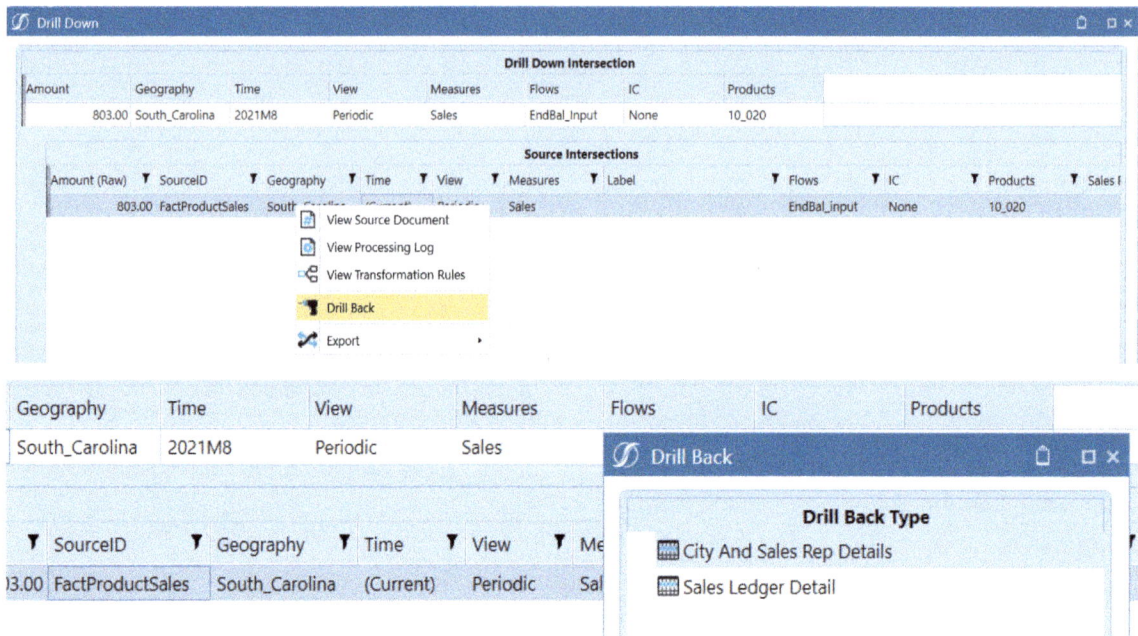

Figure 6.49

The drill back options could be based on a User or group.

```
Case Is = ConnectorActionTypes.GetDrillBackTypes
   'Return the list of Drill Types (Options) to present to the end
user
   Return Me.GetDrillBackTypeList(si, globals, api, args)
```

This function presents the drill back Types.

```
Private Function GetDrillBackTypeList(ByVal si As SessionInfo, ByVal
globals As BRGlobals, ByVal api As Transformer, ByVal args As
ConnectorArgs) As List(Of DrillBackTypeInfo)
   Try
      'Create the SQL Statement
      Dim drillTypes As New List(Of DrillBackTypeInfo)
      If
args.DrillCode.XFEqualsIgnoreCase(StageConstants.TransformationGeneral
.DrillCodeDefaultValue) Then
         drillTypes.Add(New
DrillBackTypeInfo(ConnectorDrillBackDisplayTypes.DataGrid, New
NameAndDesc("City And Sales Rep Details","City and Sales Rep
Detail")))
         drillTypes.Add(New
DrillBackTypeInfo(ConnectorDrillBackDisplayTypes.DataGrid, New
NameAndDesc("Sales Ledger Detail","Sales Ledger Detail")))
      Else If args.DrillCode.XFEqualsIgnoreCase("City And Sales Rep
Details") Then
         drillTypes.Add(New
DrillBackTypeInfo(ConnectorDrillBackDisplayTypes.DataGrid, New
NameAndDesc("Sales Ledger Detail","Sales Ledger Detail")))
      End If

      Return drillTypes
   Catch ex As Exception
      Throw ErrorHandler.LogWrite(si, New XFException(si, ex))
   End Try
End Function
```

286

Creating a New Drill Back Type

C&CCC's Users would like to see the Sales Representative information and the Sales Ledger details as two separate Reports when they perform the drill back.

They would also like to reach the Ledger details from the Sales Representative Report, too.

Your author likes to call the last drill Type a multi-hop drill as you are now performing a drill back from a drill back (drill within a drill, I sound like a movie director now 😊).

Sales Representative details and Sales Ledger details will get a default drill code. These are the Reports that are going to show when the User performs the first drill back click.

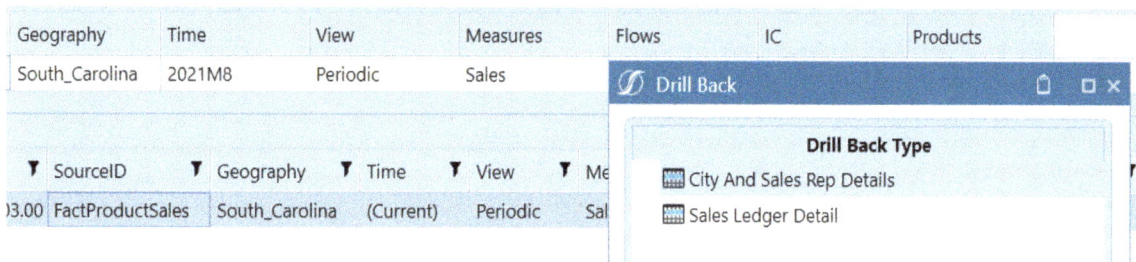

Figure 6.50

The above private function adds two DataGrid based drill back Types for the User. `DrillBackTypeInfo`'s name is shown to the User, which is why both name and description are repeated.

Now, for the drill from City and Sales Rep details (multi-hop); we are going to show the Sales Ledger detail again.

> **Note:** More detailed multiple drill backs could be added here as well.

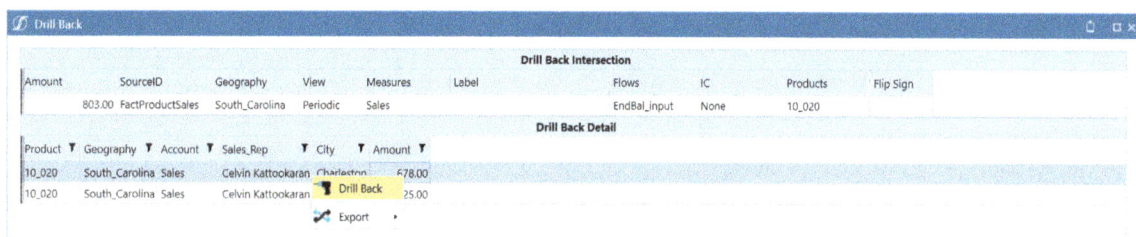

Figure 6.51

Drill Back

The action-Type `GetDrillBack` uses the `DrillBackTypeInfo` to present the information to the User.

```
Case Is = ConnectorDrillBackDisplayTypes.DataGrid

    Dim drillBackInfo As New DrillBackResultInfo

    If
args.DrillBackType.NameAndDescription.Name.XFEqualsIgnoreCase("City
And Sales Rep Details") Then
        Dim strDrillBackSQL As String =
GetDrillBackSQL_CityRepDetails(si, globals, api, args)
```

```
        drillBackInfo.DisplayType =
ConnectorDrillBackDisplayTypes.DataGrid
        drillBackInfo.DataTable =
api.Parser.GetXFDataTableForSQLQuery(si, DbProviderType.sqlserver,
connString, isNamedConnection, strDrillBackSQL, False, args.PageSize,
args.PageNumber)
        Return drillBackInfo

    Else If
args.DrillBackType.NameAndDescription.Name.XFEqualsIgnoreCase("Sales
Ledger Detail") Then
        Dim strDrillBackSQL As String = ""
        If args.DrillCode.XFEqualsIgnoreCase("City And Sales Rep
Details") Then
            strDrillBackSQL = GetDrillBackSQL_FilteredFullDetail(si,
globals, api, args, args.SourceRowDataTable.Rows(0))
        Else
            strDrillBackSQL = GetDrillBackSQL_FullDetail(si, globals,
api, args)
        End If
        drillBackInfo.DisplayType =
ConnectorDrillBackDisplayTypes.DataGrid
        drillBackInfo.DataTable =
api.Parser.GetXFDataTableForSQLQuery(si, DbProviderType.sqlserver,
connString, isNamedConnection, strDrillBackSQL, False, args.PageSize,
args.PageNumber)
        Return drillBackInfo

    Else
        Return Nothing
    End If
```

This code section performs the following steps:

1. We are checking whether the drill back display Type is a `DataGrid`. This check is required because multiple drill back Types (a file, a web URL, a text message, and more) are possible.

2. A new `DrillBackResultInfo` is created for processing.

3. Check that the name of the drill back Type matches the sales representative details.

4. A function to return the required SQL is called.

5. A `DataTable` is generated from the given SQL, and the Display Type is set as a `DataGrid`.

How to Pass Cube Members to External Tables

The function to get Sales Representative and City details use Entity, Account, and Product information from the Cube to get the results from the external Fact table.

The following helper functions are used from the existing Thing Planning Connector Rule.

1. `GetActiveDimensions`

2. `GetDataSource`

3. `GetDimensionCriteria`

```
Dim sql As New Text.StringBuilder
'Get the values for the source row that we are drilling back to
Dim dataSource As ParserLayoutInfo = Me.GetDataSource(si, args)
Dim sourceValues As Dictionary(Of String, Object) =
api.Parser.GetFieldValuesForSourceDataRow(si, args.RowID)
Dim activeDims As Dictionary(Of String, String) =
Me.GetActiveDimensions(si)
```

This code section performs the following steps:

1. A StringBuilder is created to capture the required SQL.

2. Data Source information is captured using the three helper functions.

3. Get the source values from the row the drill back was initiated using GetFieldValuesForSourceDataRow. This will produce a Dictionary with the connector column names and the value of that column from the drill back row.

4. All the active Dimensions from the Cube are captured using the helper function.

```
If (Not sourceValues Is Nothing) And (sourceValues.Count > 0) Then
    sql.Appendline("SELECT a.ProductKey As Product,
c.StateAlternateName As Geography, ")
    sql.Appendline("b.AccountDescription As Account, f.FirstName + ' '
+ f.LastName as 'Sales Rep', c.City, Sum(Amount) as Amount,")
    sql.Appendline("'City And Sales Rep Details' As " &
StageConstants.TransformationGeneral.DrillCodeFieldName)
    sql.Appendline("FROM FactProductSales a")
    sql.Appendline("LEFT OUTER JOIN DimAccount b On a.AccountKey =
b.AccountKey")
    sql.Appendline("LEFT OUTER JOIN DimGeography c ON
a.GeographyKey=c.GeographyKey")
    sql.Appendline("LEFT OUTER JOIN DimProduct d ON
a.ProductKey=d.ProductKey")
    sql.Appendline("LEFT OUTER JOIN DimSalesRep e ON a.SalesRepKey =
e.SalesRepKey")
    sql.Appendline("LEFT OUTER JOIN DimEmployee f ON e.EmployeeKey =
f.EmployeeKey")

    sql.AppendLine("WHERE 1 = 1")
```

This code section performs the following steps:

1. We are checking whether we have information on the current drill back row.

2. SQL is generated to get the Sales Representative and City information by joining multiple tables.

You might notice that an extra column with DrillCodeFieldName is added to the SQL. This is used to aid the multi-hop drill and is hidden from the drill back Report that gets presented to the User.

Since multiple IF conditions drive the WHERE clause, we are using an old technique of equating 1=1 (which is always true) to ensure that the SQL will execute without having a WHERE clause.

```
If activeDims.ContainsKey(StageConstants.MasterDimensionNames.Entity)
Then
    sql.AppendLine("And (c.")
    sql.AppendLine(Me.GetDimensionCriteria(si, args,
StageConstants.MasterDimensionNames.Entity, sourceValues, dataSource))
    sql.AppendLine(") ")
End If

If activeDims.ContainsKey(StageConstants.MasterDimensionNames.Account)
Then
    sql.AppendLine("And (b.")
    sql.AppendLine(Me.GetDimensionCriteria(si, args,
StageConstants.MasterDimensionNames.Account, sourceValues,
dataSource))
    sql.AppendLine(") ")
End If

If activeDims.ContainsKey(StageConstants.MasterDimensionNames.UD1)
Then
```

Chapter 6

```
    sql.AppendLine("And (d.")
    sql.AppendLine(Me.GetDimensionCriteria(si, args,
StageConstants.MasterDimensionNames.UD1, sourceValues, dataSource))
    sql.AppendLine(") ")
End If

sql.AppendLine("Group by a.ProductKey, c.StateAlternateName,
b.AccountDescription, f.FirstName, f.LastName, c.City")
```

If Account, Entity, and UD1 are active Dimensions of the current Cube, a WHERE clause is generated from each one of them using the Connector field and the value, e.g., if the User chose to perform a drill back from E#South_Carolina:U1#10_020:A#Sales, this will generate the SQL given below.

```
SELECT a.ProductKey As Product, c.StateAlternateName As Geography,
b.AccountDescription As Account, f.FirstName + ' ' + f.LastName as
'Sales Rep', c.City, Sum(Amount) as Amount,
'City And Sales Rep Details' As DrillTypeCode
FROM FactProductSales a
LEFT OUTER JOIN DimAccount b On a.AccountKey = b.AccountKey
LEFT OUTER JOIN DimGeography c ON a.GeographyKey=c.GeographyKey
LEFT OUTER JOIN DimProduct d ON a.ProductKey=d.ProductKey
LEFT OUTER JOIN DimSalesRep e ON a.SalesRepKey = e.SalesRepKey
LEFT OUTER JOIN DimEmployee f ON e.EmployeeKey = f.EmployeeKey
WHERE 1 = 1
And (c.
StateAlternateName = 'South_Carolina'
)
And (b.
AccountDescription = 'Sales'
)
And (d.
ProductKey = '10_020'
)
Group by a.ProductKey, c.StateAlternateName, b.AccountDescription,
f.FirstName, f.LastName, c.City
```

StateAlternateName, AccountDescription, and ProductKey are pulled from the data source fields.

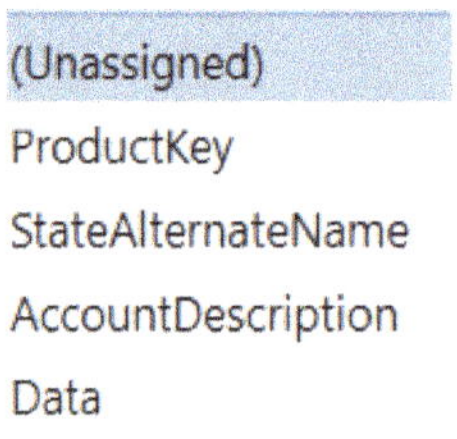

(Unassigned)

ProductKey

StateAlternateName

AccountDescription

Data

Figure 6.52

Here is what is reported back to the User after a successful drill back.

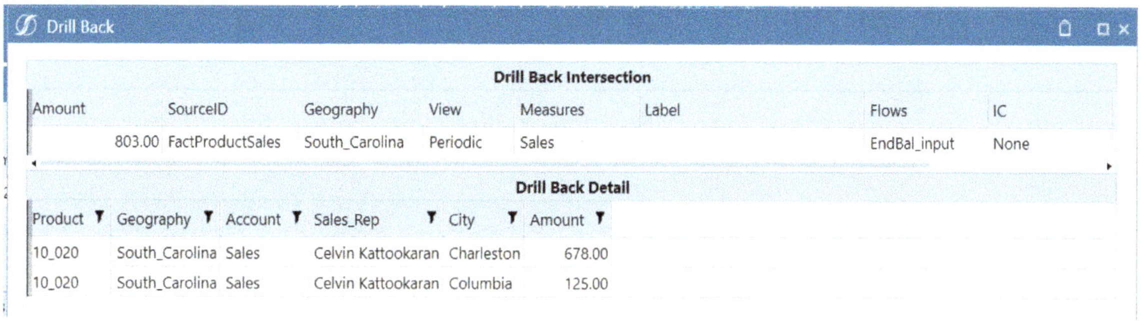

Figure 6.53

How to Pass Information from a Drill Back to Another Drill Back Report

As discussed in the previous section a DrillTypeCode is present (but hidden) in the drill back detail.

```
Else If
args.DrillBackType.NameAndDescription.Name.XFEqualsIgnoreCase("Sales
Ledger Detail") Then
    Dim strDrillBackSQL As String = ""
    If args.DrillCode.XFEqualsIgnoreCase("City And Sales Rep Details")
Then
        strDrillBackSQL = GetDrillBackSQL_FilteredFullDetail(si,
globals, api, args, args.SourceRowDataTable.Rows(0))
    Else
        strDrillBackSQL = GetDrillBackSQL_FullDetail(si, globals, api,
args)
    End If
```

For the Sales Ledger detail, the code checks whether the drill code is City and Sales Rep details (this means it is a multi-hop drill back). A different SQL code is used to provide the filtered results.

Pass the first row (since that is the row where the multi-hop drill originated) of the source DataTable. If the drill code is not City and Sales Rep details, show the full Sales Ledger details.

```
If (Not sourceValues Is Nothing) And (sourceValues.Count > 0) Then
    sql.Appendline("SELECT a.SalesOrderNumber, a.SalesOrderLineNumber,
a.ProductKey As Product, c.StateAlternateName As Geography, ")
    sql.Appendline("b.AccountDescription As Account, f.FirstName + ' '
+ f.LastName as 'Sales Rep', c.City, Amount,")
    sql.Appendline("'City And Sales Rep Details' As " &
StageConstants.TransformationGeneral.DrillCodeFieldName)
    sql.Appendline("FROM FactProductSales a")
    sql.Appendline("LEFT OUTER JOIN DimAccount b On a.AccountKey =
b.AccountKey")
    sql.Appendline("LEFT OUTER JOIN DimGeography c ON
a.GeographyKey=c.GeographyKey")
    sql.Appendline("LEFT OUTER JOIN DimProduct d ON
a.ProductKey=d.ProductKey")
    sql.Appendline("LEFT OUTER JOIN DimSalesRep e ON a.SalesRepKey =
e.SalesRepKey")
    sql.Appendline("LEFT OUTER JOIN DimEmployee f ON e.EmployeeKey =
f.EmployeeKey")

    sql.AppendLine("WHERE 1 = 1")

    If drillRow.Items.Count > 0 Then
        sql.Appendline("AND f.FirstName + ' ' + f.LastName = '" &
drillRow.Item("Sales_Rep") & "'")
        sql.Appendline("AND c.City = '" & drillRow.Item("City") & "'")
    End If
```

```
    If
activeDims.ContainsKey(StageConstants.MasterDimensionNames.Entity)
Then
        sql.Appendline("And (c.")
        sql.Appendline(Me.GetDimensionCriteria(si, args,
StageConstants.MasterDimensionNames.Entity, sourceValues, dataSource))
        sql.Appendline(") ")
    End If
```

The code to get Sales Ledger details is similar to the City and Sales Rep detail, except that it adds the Sales Representative and City details to pull the Sales Ledger details of the specific Representative and City.

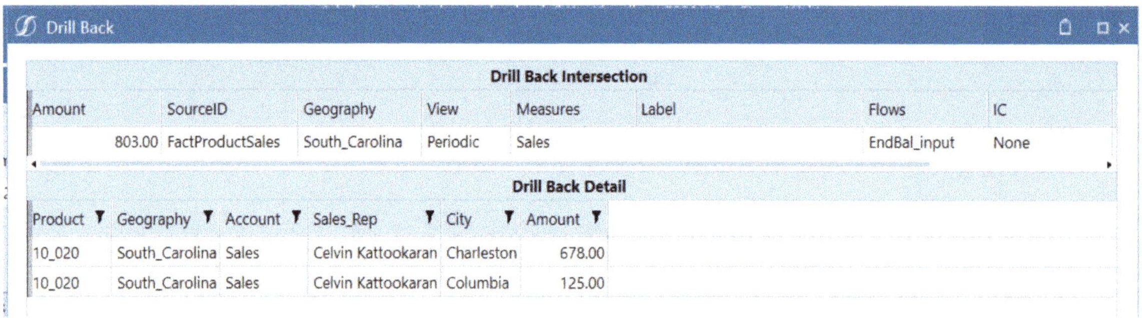

Figure 6.54

If a User performs a drill back from Charleston, the following Report will be displayed.

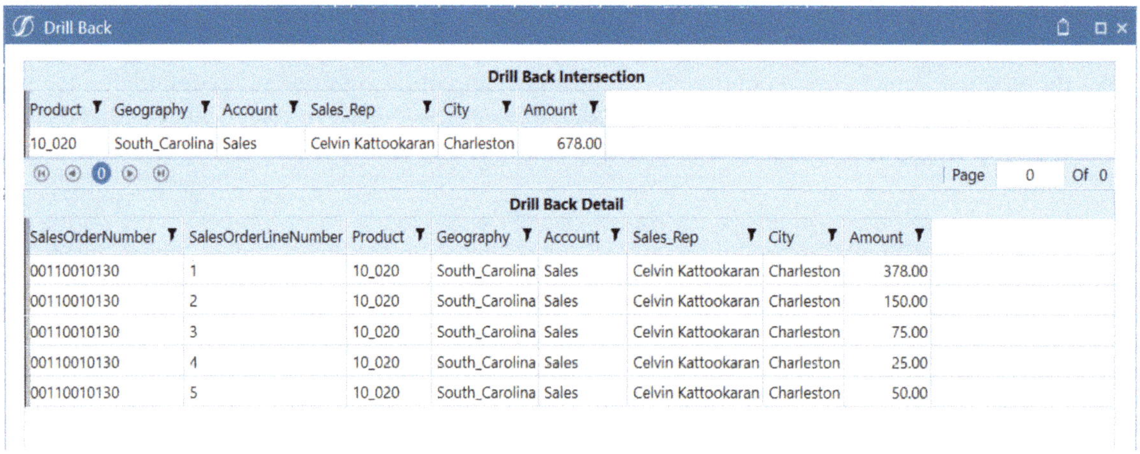

Figure 6.55

Et voilà, there we have it; drilling back to source supplemental details does not ever require bringing them into OneStream. If the data does not need to be loaded to the Cube, why load it? This approach excludes unnecessary details from OneStream itself while giving Planners the ability to view the data in a drill back.

Analyzing Specialty Data

The theme of this chapter was how to analyze supplemental data by merging the security information from the Cube and providing Excel-like features to Register. Your authors have seen implementations where Consultants were reluctant to provide an analysis option to Specialty data for the lack of security on relational tables (and Dashboard Components). Data without analysis is data poorly understood; without understanding, that data is useless. With analysis, data becomes information; information informs and drives and directs the Planning process.

Across all the chapters in this book, we have dealt with and referred to numbers; numbers that talk to us, and to you, and to the Users of our OneStream applications. This chapter takes analysis a step further by bringing in unrelated data or sending OneStream data to external systems for further consumption. Even though some of the topics discussed are advanced in nature, they explore and explain the underlying flexibility of OneStream as a platform. Your authors hope that you, as a User/Implementor, can relate to the close-to-real-world examples and understand:

1. The business need we were trying to solve.

2. How it was solved.

3. Why it was done in the way it was done.

4. When we should do it.

5. Why OneStream's flexibility, functionality, and Extensibility makes it the best product in the Performance Management space.

If we succeeded in helping you to understand the Why, How and When of Planning in OneStream, we have fulfilled this book's reason for being.

Afterword

"The cure for boredom is curiosity. There is no cure for curiosity." – Dorothy Parker

This book is the result of a long and arduous process on the part of your authors and hopefully a not-quite-as-painful learning experience for you, Gentle Reader.

From febrile anticipation to use case design, through exhaustive testing and retesting to (we hope) inspired writing, this book has been an exercise in curiosity. We asked ourselves: what will the OneStream Planning Practitioner care about, what is obvious and simple but not widely used, what is almost universal practice but really ought not to be, what missed opportunities are there because techniques are too hard or too obscure? We then tried to formulate the topics that addressed those questions, cogently write about them, and – with luck – imparted some of our knowledge to you.

This describes what we did, but not why. The OneStream product is a platform with few limits. Its open nature permits innovative and powerful solutions to Planning problems but equally exposes the Practitioner to poor design and implementation. We feel – we know – that the surest way to avoid a bad application is to understand *why* a feature or a function or a Method or a Component does what it does, and only then know how to best use it.

Our philosophy during the writing of this book was, and is, to inculcate that same level of curiosity and excitement around the discovery process. "How do I do it?" addresses only an immediate need and does not and cannot anticipate or address solving the next problem. "Why does it work that way?" answers not only that pressing question, but also provides the foundational knowledge for independent discovery and problem resolution.

Curiosity as methodology is hard work; it is the only way to understand and master a product as vast and as powerful as OneStream. We hope you join us in this spirit of curiosity so that we may all design, implement, and own the very best OneStream applications.

Index

Index

OneStream Foundation Handbook

The Definitive Reference to Design, Configure and Support Your OneStream Platform.

OneStream is a modern, unified platform that is revolutionizing Corporate Performance Management. This proven alternative to fragmented legacy applications is designed to simplify processes for the most sophisticated, global enterprises. Hundreds of the world's leading companies are turning to OneStream to help with reporting and understanding financial data.

In this practical guide, The Architect Factory team at OneStream Software explains each part of an implementation, and the design of solutions. Readers will learn the core guiding principles for implementing OneStream from the company's top team of experts. Beyond offering a training guide, the focus of this book is on the 'why' of design and building an application.

- Manage your Implementation with the OneStream methodology
- Understand Design and Build concepts
- Build solutions for the Consolidation of financial data, and develop Planning models
- Create Data Integration solutions that will feed your models
- Develop Workflows to guide and manage your End-Users
- Advance your solutions with Rules and Security
- Take advantage of detailed Data Reporting using tools such as Analytic Blend, Advanced Excel reporting, and Dashboarding
- Tune Performance, and optimize your application

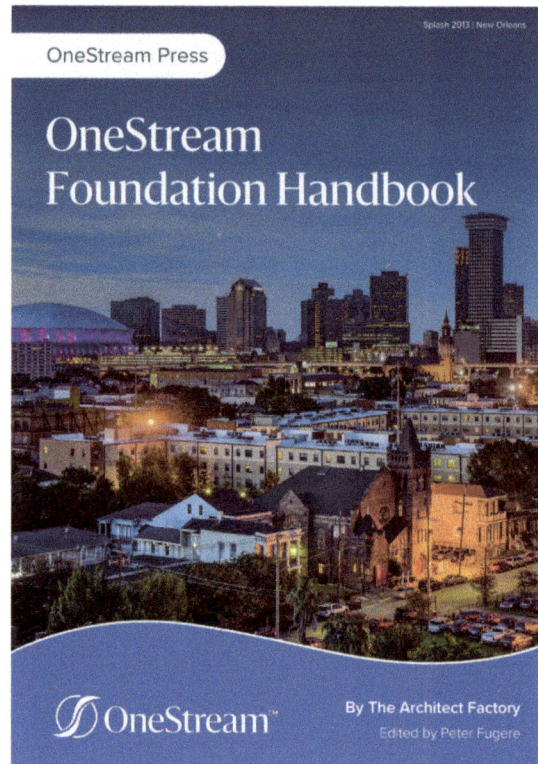

OneStreamPress.com

www.ingramcontent.com/pod-product-compliance
Lightning Source LLC
Chambersburg PA
CBHW041622220326
41598CB00046BA/7431